Best Wishes,

#34

Go Dores!

Bury #4

BUZZER BEATERS

and

MEMORIAL MAGIC

Jim -

Your daughter could do better...

MERCER UNIVERSITY PRESS

Endowed by

TOM WATSON BROWN
and
THE WATSON-BROWN FOUNDATION, INC.

BUZZER BEATERS

and

MEMORIAL MAGIC

A Memoir of the Vanderbilt Commodores

1987–89

Barry Goheen

MERCER UNIVERSITY PRESS
Macon, Georgia
1979–2019
40 Years of Publishing Excellence

MUP/ H976

© 2019 by Barry Goheen
Published by Mercer University Press
1501 Mercer University Drive
Macon, Georgia 31207

9 8 7 6 5 4 3 2 1

Printed and bound in the United States.

This book is set in Adobe Garamond Pro.

ISBN   978-0-88146-714-7
Cataloging-in-Publication Data is available from the Library of Congress

For Margie, Aldyn, and Katherine

CONTENTS

"It may be said that our lives are our supreme fiction."

—Robert Penn Warren,
Vanderbilt University
Class of 1925

FOREWORD

Buster Olney

Barry Goheen was a superhero, and like all superheroes, he owns a special power. Superman is faster than a speeding bullet, and armed with X-ray vision. Batman has his utility belt and other cool stuff. The Flash was, well, really fast. Aquaman communicates with sea creatures.

Barry Goheen? He had a gift for making shots in the waning seconds of basketball games, particularly from long distances. In four seasons at Vanderbilt, he compiled a list of big moments that seems impossible, even in retrospect. The clock would tick down, and he would transform...a bucket against Tennessee, a last-minute shot against Florida, vs. Penn. He hit a game-winning shot from near half court to beat a ranked Louisville team. Time and time and time again.

There was a Clark Kent side to Barry, I know, because we attended Vanderbilt at the same time and shared a class that he probably doesn't remember, about Latin American history, and he sat a few rows behind me. He didn't really stand out in a crowd, unlike teammate Will Perdue, who was a 7-footer with a size 21 7-A ½ feet, or power forward Frank Kornet, whose son Luke plays in the NBA. Barry wasn't the best player in the conference, or the best player on the team; he was unassuming, until somebody needed to score when it mattered the most. As Vanderbilt coach C.M. Newton said, it was downright spooky how often Barry succeeded in the most pressure-filled moments.

In March of 1988, my senior year, Vanderbilt reached the NCAA tournament and was behind Pitt in the last seconds. I was watching the game in the living room of the small house I rented on Acklen Avenue, just off campus, and with the Commodores trailing by four in the last minute, Barry drilled a three-pointer. After a Vanderbilt foul and a couple of Pitt free throws, VU was down three points with just seconds remaining. In my mind's eye, I can still see Barry getting the ball on the left side of the court, where he seemed most comfortable, as a left-handed shooter. From about 22 feet away or so, he rose with the ball in hand, and I remember being absolutely sure he was going to make it. Because he always made it.

And when he made it, tying the score at the buzzer and forcing an overtime that Vanderbilt would win to advance to the Sweet 16, I screamed loudly and raced out onto the porch, and heard other screams down the court, as well. Later, I went to Memorial Gym to play pickup basketball and saw others try to recreate Barry's game-tying shot, a sight which I turned into a column for the Nashville Banner, early in a writing career.

Since then, I've covered a lot of players in a lot of sports, great stars like Tony Gwynn and Cal Ripken, Mariano Rivera and Derek Jeter, Roger Clemens and Madison Bumgarner, Albert Pujols and Mike Trout. With the benefit of that experience, and seeing how even the best players struggle under pressure, I've come to believe that Barry excelled in those spots because he somehow emotionally walled himself from all of the outside stimuli—the shouts of 15,000 standing fans, the TV announcers barking analysis and critique at floor level, the pep band—and just focused on the task at hand. For him, it somehow became just as simple as playing the same game he had as a kid, making the same plays, over and over. The context became irrelevant, somehow.

Jeter played this way, for sure, and so did Rivera. Aaron Rodgers of the Packers, seemingly playing catch with friends in the last seconds of games, over and over. Michael Jordan, of course, because he, above all others, just *knew* he would find a way to win. The bigger the game, the bigger the moment, the better Bumgarner is.

Somewhere in Barry Goheen, he has that similar strand in his DNA, that special power that made his time at Vanderbilt unforgettable, and unmatchable.

DRAMATIS PERSONAE

1987–88, 1988–89

3—Derrick Wilcox, G, 5'11", Louisville, KY

4—Barry Booker, G, 6'4", Franklin, TN

12—Barry Goheen, G, 6'4", Calvert City, KY

13—Scott Draud, G, 6'2", Crestview Hills, KY

21—Chip Rupp, F, 6'7", Lexington, KY (1987–88)

24—James Amsler, F, 6'5", Spring, TX

31—Steve Grant, F, 6'5", Marietta, GA

32—Will Perdue, C, 7'0", Merritt Island, FL (1987–88)

32—Todd Milholland, F, 6'10", Waverly, TN (1988–89)

34—Frank Kornet, F, 6'9", Lexington, KY

35—Morgan Wheat, G-F, 6'5", Des Moines, IA (1988–89)

40—Charles Mayes, F, 6'7", Nashville, TN

42—Alberto Ballestra, C, 6'10", Bologna, Italy (1988–89)

52—Eric Reid, F, 6'8", Macon, GA

55—Fred Benjamin, C, 6'11", Manhattan, NY

Head Coach—C.M. Newton

Assistant Head Coach—John Bostick

Assistant Coaches—Ed Martin, Mark Elliott, Mike Petrone

PROLOGUE

FOUR SECONDS

00:04

Things look bleak on this March Sunday afternoon in Lincoln, Nebraska. With four seconds remaining in this second-round game in the 1988 NCAA Tournament, my team, the Vanderbilt Commodores, trails our opponent, the Pittsburgh Panthers, 70-67. For 39 minutes and 56 seconds, we've gone toe-to-toe with the Panthers, the #2 seed in the Midwest Region and the regular season champions of the Big East Conference, the best conference in college basketball in the mid-to-late 1980s. Our team, meanwhile, finished in a tie for fourth in the 10-team Southeastern Conference and were the seventh seed in the Midwest Region. Our 18-10 regular season record had been rewarded with just the third bid to the NCAA tournament in the program's history, and its first at-large bid.

The game was tied at halftime, and we had led by as many as four points with under seven minutes remaining, but Pitt scored eight straight points to lead by four with two minutes left, 65-61. The score was 67-63 when I hit a three-point shot with five seconds remaining to cut Pitt's lead to one, 67-66. Now, Pitt's All-American center, Charles Smith, has just drained two free throws to extend Pitt's lead to three, 69-66; worse, our own All-American center, Will Perdue, fouled out of the game when he was forced to foul Smith to stop the clock at 00:04 after Smith received the inbounds pass. Will, our team's only senior, wasn't just our best player; he was the SEC Player of the Year, soon to be named the SEC Athlete of the Year, and a few months from being drafted by the Chicago Bulls and beginning a long and successful NBA career. At this moment, however, Will was watching the rest of the game along with the sold-out crowd of 14,453 at the Devaney Center on the campus of the University of Nebraska. Absent something special occurring in the last four seconds, Will's Vanderbilt career—and our season—would come to an end.

Will may have been our only senior, but we had an experienced team. Three juniors—Barry Booker, Frank Kornet, and I—started alongside Will. Book and I had started the last two years, and I had also started some as a freshman in 1985–86. Frank also started some games that season before injuries temporarily derailed his career, especially in our sophomore season of 1986–87, but he bounced back in 1987–88 with a strong season and had starred in our first-round win over Utah State 48 hours earlier. Sophomore Eric Reid filled out the starting lineup, and two other experienced sophs, Scott Draud and Derrick Wilcox, backed up Book and me at guard while two freshmen forwards, Charles Mayes and Steve Grant, added depth to the frontline. With Will out of the game, the quintet on the floor for the final four seconds is Kornet, Booker, Reid, Draud, and me. When Smith's second free throw drops through the net, Reid picks up the ball, steps behind the baseline, and prepares to inbound the ball. One Panther slightly guards Book, who's on the right side of the court—he's right-handed, so that's his strong side—while I fan toward the left side, which is my strong side because I'm a southpaw. No one is even attempting to guard me in the backcourt, so Eric sensibly opts to inbound the ball to me. The clock will start when I touch the ball, which means those last four ticks could be "the most important four seconds of [my] career."

00:03

We need to make a three-point shot to keep our season alive and force overtime. The three-point shot had been introduced into college basketball only the previous season, and many college coaches derided the shot as a gimmick and refused to use it. Fortunately, our head coach, C.M. Newton, was not of those coaches. Coach Newton, one of the most respected figures in college basketball, had, entering the Pitt game, nearly 500 victories coaching for Transylvania University, the University of Alabama, and Vanderbilt over 30 seasons, and he had enthusiastically embraced the three-point shot beginning with its inception in fall 1986. In 1987–88, while other teams were still figuring out how, or even whether, to deploy this new offensive weapon, we led the SEC in three-point attempts, makes (exactly 200; no other SEC team made even 150), and percentage (43%; only one other SEC team made 40%).

Coaches' disdain for the three-point shot wasn't limited to how to execute it on offense; there was also the problem of *defending* the shot, and Pitt apparently had not figured that out yet. Reid inbounded the ball to me, and no Pitt player was near me or attempting to slow my advance. So, Eric was able to make an inbounds pass that traveled at least 20 feet in the air, meaning that the game clock didn't budge off 00:04 (tenths of seconds didn't display on the game clock in 1988) until I was already close to the half-court line. And by the time the clock showed 00:03, I had already crossed half court, dribbling at full speed.

00:02

On each team's bench is a coach who eventually will be inducted into the Naismith Memorial Basketball Hall of Fame. Our member, of course, is Coach Newton, enshrined in 2000. Pitt has a future Hall of Famer as well—29-year-old John Calipari, inducted in 2015. Fortunately for us, in 1988 Coach Cal is only an assistant coach; in a matter of months, he will accept the head coaching position at the University of Massachusetts and begin his successful head coaching career, culminating in an NCAA title in 2012 with the Kentucky Wildcats—C.M. Newton's alma mater. But for now, he's limited to the things that assistants do, which is to make suggestions to the head coach, who is the ultimate decision-maker. So, in the timeout that preceded Perdue's fifth foul and Smith's free throws, Calipari suggested that, if Smith made both free throws to give Pitt a three-point lead, Pitt foul whichever Commodore got the ball, preventing a three-point shot and putting us at the free-throw line. But Cal's boss, head coach Paul Evans, overruled that suggestion and, moreover, didn't call a timeout (Pitt had three remaining; we had none) after Smith's free throws to set his defense. Thus, Pitt is a little out of sorts as I cross the half-court line, dribbling down the left side of the court as another second ticks off the clock.

00:01

In 87 seasons of men's basketball prior to 1987–88, Vanderbilt had been to the NCAA Tournament two times (1965 and 1974) and had won the grand total of one game. That lackluster NCAA record, however, was misleading. Vandy was a national power in the 1960s through the mid-1970s under the leadership of Coach Roy Skinner. Indeed, in the 1960s, Vanderbilt was often ranked in the end-of-season polls yet had nothing to show for it in terms of an NCAA bid or even the consolation prize of a bid to the National Invitational Tournament (NIT) because, for nearly all of Coach Skinner's tenure, which ended in 1976, only the regular season conference champion was entitled to play in the NCAA Tournament, and, in the SEC, that was almost always the University of Kentucky. That meant that every conference was a "one-bid league" until 1975, when the tournament expanded to 32 teams, with gradual expansion over the next decade until the tourney fielded 64 teams, which was the field's size in 1988. Thus, such top-flight (and ranked) Commodore squads as 1965–66 (final ranking: #8), 1966–67 (#14), and 1967–68 (#13) had to stay home after the regular season ended, even though, in the twenty-first century, those rankings would have been good for high seeds in the NCAA brackets.

Our appearance in the '88 tourney was the program's first in this new era of tourney expansion, and it started a solid run, continuing to the present day, of fairly consistent NCAA appearances for the program:

	NCAA appearances	NCAA wins
87 seasons through 1986–87	2	1
1987–88 through 2018–19	13	9

Our victory over Utah State in Friday's first round was the program's second NCAA victory ever and first since 1965. If we could win the Pitt game, we would double the program's all-time NCAA tourney victory total in a span of 48 hours. Could we be the first Vandy team to win two games in a single NCAA Tournament?

It doesn't look likely as, after the fourth dribble, I am forced to pull up with the clock ticking from 00:02 to 00:01. I have no choice but to stop dribbling and launch a shot from about 22 or 23 feet away, a step or so behind the three-point line. The crowd holds its collective breath.

00:00

This is the time for Vanderbilt basketball to make its mark. In my four-year Vandy career, we would play nearly every blueblood men's hoops program in the country. Already we had played North Carolina, Duke, Indiana, Notre Dame, and Kentucky, and we would play a few of those teams again in my senior season; still to come are Kansas, Michigan, Ohio State, Texas, and Louisville. And we would win our fair share of those games: In my first three seasons at Vandy, we had notched several memorable wins over nationally ranked teams and great programs; we won several close games, including a few at the buzzer and a couple in spectacular fashion; and we beat several favored teams on our home floor, Memorial Gym, leading fans and writers to use the phrase "Memorial Gym Magic" or the shorter and more alliterative term "Memorial Magic."

This, then, is not just the story of the Vanderbilt Commodores of the late 1980s; it's the story of college basketball in the late 80s—of three-pointers and upsets, of great teams and All-Americans, of iconic coaches and unbelievable finishes.

Would Pitt be one such ending? The ball is still in the air and on its downward trajectory as the clock turns to all zeroes and the buzzer sounds. Already, it had been a good season: we had beaten the #1 team in the country (after having beaten the eventual national champion in 1986–87), then won that first NCAA tourney game on Friday. We will consider the season a success even if this shot doesn't fall.

But what if the shot goes in? And if it does, what if we are able to triumph over Pitt in overtime even without Will on the floor? That would mean the first "Sweet Sixteen" for Vanderbilt in the 64-team NCAA era. Better still, what if a victory served as a springboard for an equally memorable senior season of 1988–89, full of yet more thrilling wins, gut-wrenching losses, and possibly an SEC title? Could one shot mean that much?

Well, that would be a heck of a story . . .

PART ONE

PERDUNKS AND THE BOMB SQUAD:
THE 1987–88 SEASON

1

GREAT EXPECTATIONS

I

"I'm on my way, I'm making it"
—Peter Gabriel, "Big Time" ('86–'87)

In fall 1986, head coach C.M. Newton and associate head coach John Bostick were beginning their sixth season at the head of the Vanderbilt program after teaming at the University of Alabama in the 1970s to lead that school to what had been unprecedented success before Coach Newton left in 1980. Additionally, Ed Martin was beginning his second season as the other lead assistant, and those three men formed the most experienced trio in the SEC. Coach Bostick had been with Coach Newton since C.M. took the Alabama job in 1969 while Coach Martin had won over 500 games at multiple schools, most notably as the head coach of Nashville's Tennessee State University.

Coach Newton had guided the Commodores to the program's first-ever NIT appearance in 1983, but the Commodores had posted losing records the next three seasons, the last of which was my freshman season, 1985–86. But 1986–87 would represent the beginning of a turnaround for Vanderbilt basketball. As sophomores in 1986–87, Barry Booker and I stepped into permanent starting roles at the guard positions.

The center position would be manned by Will Perdue, a fourth-year, 7-foot junior from Merritt Island, Florida, who had played sparingly as a freshman in 1983–84 and had redshirted in 1984–85. Will had backed up starting center Brett Burrow in 1985–86 and would be the starting center even though he had played only 181 minutes in the entire 1985–86 season. Several forwards returned, and Coach Newton had brought in a strong recruiting class—a forward from Macon, Georgia, named Eric Reid, and two guards from Kentucky, Scott Draud (Newport) and Derrick Wilcox (Louisville). And, significantly, college basketball introduced the three-point line in fall 1986.

The first month of the 1986–87 season was a dream ride. We began the season in Hawaii in the second playing of what is now known as the Maui Classic, a Thanksgiving-weekend tournament featuring eight teams in which the teams play games for three consecutive days beginning the Friday after Thanksgiving. We swept the three games and claimed the championship trophy by beating Virginia Commonwealth, Missouri, and New Mexico. In a coming-out party, Perdue dominated all three games, scoring 56 total points and being named the tournament's MVP. Ten days later we upset Indiana, 79-75, a great win because the Hoosiers would go on to win the NCAA title the following spring. Just before Christmas, we defeated the Ivy League's Pennsylvania Quakers 71-70 at the historic Palestra in Philadelphia behind Will's great game (29 points) and my buzzer-beating 17-footer. We then won our own Music City Invitational holiday tournament by beating Kansas State and its star, All-American and 1988 Olympian Mitch Richmond, in the final, which was victory number 1000 for the Vanderbilt basketball program.

We peaked in the next game, a road win at LSU in our first SEC tilt, which sent us to Christmas break with a 9-1 record and victories over a slew of strong opponents. Someone, however, spiked our eggnog with Kryptonite, because the downward spiral began right after Christmas with two heartbreaking losses in the Sugar Bowl Tournament in New Orleans, a four-team affair that was held in conjunction with the football bowl game—one in double-overtime to South Carolina (then in the old Metro Conference) and another the next night to Houston when the Cougars' 7'1" center hit an 18-footer at the buzzer over Will's outstretched arm to beat us, 73-72. The final blow in a season-turning trifecta occurred when we returned home to face Tennessee, but without Coach Newton, who was hospitalized just after the New Year; without him we were completely out of sorts, falling behind 21-4 and losing 81-72.

Those three games undermined the confidence we had developed in the first month of the season, and we were never the same. There were a couple of games where we played like the team that had beaten Indiana, K-State, and Missouri. We thumped #10 Auburn 91-75 behind Draud's 23 points off the bench; we completed a sweep of LSU when Perdue hit a last-second turnaround jumper to turn a one-point loss into a one-point win; and in a non-conference game in February at Memorial, we beat Sweet Sixteen-bound Notre Dame 60-56. But in late February, we hit the wall with five straight losses, leveling our record at 14-14. We salvaged the final two games of the regular season with a quality victory over Sweet Sixteen-bound and #18-ranked Florida 84-76; Perdue (22), Booker (17), and I (25) combined for 64 points. We then beat Mississippi State to close the regular season at 16-14 but hit another low when we pulled a no-show against Tennessee in the SEC Tournament in Atlanta, losing badly, 74-57, ending the season—we thought—with a 16-15 record.

Fortunately, the NIT saw past the late-season swoon and invited us to that tournament. We edged Jacksonville 74-72 in the opening round, then spanked Florida State 109-92 in the second round, scoring 61 points in the second half alone. Perdue, Booker, and I scored 22 each, and Booker's 11 assists remain the most by any Vandy player in a postseason game. In the quarterfinals, we hosted Southern

Mississippi, with the victor to advance to the semifinals in New York City and Madison Square Garden. We played a miserable first half and trailed by 21 early in the second half before launching an amazing comeback, almost—but not quite—catching the Golden Eagles. Southern Miss held on to win it, 95-88, and went on to claim the NIT title the following week. Perdue, Booker, and I scored 73 of our 88 points—Will had a career-high 34 points (the most ever by a Vanderbilt player in a postseason game) and pulled down 14 rebounds.

We ended the season with a record of 18-16. That record seems pedestrian, but we played the country's seventh-toughest schedule as measured by *USA Today* and performed well against it: 19 of our 30 regular season games were against teams that played in the NCAA tourney, and our record was a respectable 9-10 in those games. We notched five wins over four Sweet Sixteen (or better) teams—Indiana, LSU (twice), Florida, and Notre Dame. And we beat four other NCAA tourney teams—Auburn, Missouri, Kansas State, and Penn. Plus, our five-win improvement from our 13-15 record in 1985–86 was the best in the SEC.

II

"These are the days to hold on to 'cause we won't although we'll want to"
—*Billy Joel, "This Is the Time" ('86–'87)*

We began plotting an improved season in 1987–88 as soon as our 1986–87 season ended. We took a trip overseas to represent the United States at the Jones Cup, an annual international basketball competition run by the International Amateur Basketball Federation (FIBA) and held on the island of Taiwan at Taipei. We finished 7-1 and brought home the silver medal in the Olympic-style competition (i.e., teams were divided into pools with the top two from each pool making the quarterfinal, single-elimination round), and Perdue and Booker played particularly well. All told, the trip served as a useful tune-up for the 1987–88 season.

Nevertheless, it seemed to me that the Vanderbilt men's basketball program was always rebuilding, and having to do it from near the bottom of the SEC. The 1983–84 team finished 14-15 and graduated its best player, 1984 Olympian and long-time NBA player Jeff Turner. The 1984–85 team finished last in the SEC and lost *its* best player, then-all-time leading scorer Phil Cox. And the 1985–86 team, which was my freshman year, went 7-11 in the SEC and lost its three leading scorers; in fact, I was the leading returning scorer for the 1986–87 team, having averaged 8.1 points a game as a freshman. While the 1986–87 team showed improvement, we posted the same 7-11 SEC record as the 1985–86 team.

But 1987–88 would be different. There would be no rebuilding, and the future was now. "This will be the best Vandy team I've had since I've been here," Coach Newton revealed early in the season in a conversation with Kentucky coach Eddie

Sutton. The '87–'88 team returned the three leading scorers from the previous season—Perdue (17.4 points per game), Booker (11.9), and me (12.3), along with Draud (7.3), who had been our fifth-leading scorer. Booker, Draud, and I were guards, as was Wilcox, meaning that we were well set in the backcourt. And, of course, we had the best center in the league in Perdue.

The forward spots were wide open, though. Four departures from the '86–'87 team were forwards—Bobby Westbrooks, Steve Reece, Glen Clem, and Randy Neff (who also doubled as the backup center), but there was plenty of talent available in the frontcourt anyway. Fellow junior Frank Kornet was recovering from off-season knee surgery and hopefully could return to the fine form he showed early in our freshman year. Sophomore Eric Reid would see increased minutes and had played well late in his freshman season. Chip Rupp, a redshirt sophomore, would also compete. And Coach Newton's two primary signees were forwards—hometown product Charles Mayes, a 6'7" forward and a great shooter whose range extended beyond the three-point line, as he would display in a couple of memorable wins; and Steve Grant, a 6'7" leaper and hardnosed defender who hailed from the Atlanta area.

So, as we reassembled on campus in late August, we fully expected to compete at a high level. Almost immediately upon arriving back to school, we began our preseason conditioning program under the management of strength and conditioning coach Brad Bates, a terrific guy who later served as the athletic director at Miami (Ohio) and Boston College, leading up to the magic date of October 15, which was the first day that all teams could officially begin formal practices to prepare for the season. (In 2013, the NCAA changed the rule and now allows teams to begin practicing on the first weekend of October.)

Coach Newton oversaw our practices, but Coach Bostick really ran them day-to-day. Our practices were efficient; it was unusual to be on the court for more than two hours. Coach Bostick also worked with the frontcourt players, as did Coach Martin when he wasn't on the road recruiting. The guards, meanwhile, would be coached by Mark Elliott, who replaced Al Walter when Al left to take the head-coaching job at Brescia College in Owensboro, Kentucky. "Coach E" had a strong Vanderbilt pedigree—he was a point guard there in the late '70s and had graduated in 1980, so he knew the program well. He also played baseball at Vandy; in fact, Mark helped lead the baseball Commodores to the 1980 SEC championship and then played a couple of seasons in the New York Mets organization, where his minor-league teammates included Daryl Strawberry and current Oakland A's general manager Billy Beane (of *Moneyball* fame). Mark returned to the Vanderbilt basketball program after a stint as the head coach of Nashville's Montgomery Bell Academy. There, he had coached one of our new recruits, Charles Mayes, through high school.

III

"I think about my grandpa, my neighbors and my name"
—*John Mellencamp, "Rain on the Scarecrow"* ('85–'86)

Following my favorite sports team, the St. Louis Cardinals, who made it to the World Series, relieved the drudgery of everyday practices. I grew up in Marshall County, in the far western part of Kentucky. The county is only about 180 miles from St. Louis, which explains my long-held devotion to St. Louis Cardinals baseball.

The Marshall County seat is Benton, a town best known for the annual "Big Singing," an event dating back to 1884 in which singers from all over the country (and world) gather to sinn hymns from *The Southern Harmony and Musical Companion*, the original American hymnal that appeared in the 1830s (only to be usurped in most places by *The Sacred Harp*, published about 10 years later). I'm from Calvert City, a town in the northern part of the county that was incorporated in 1871 and whose population was perhaps 2,000 to 2,500 in the 1970s and '80s; it's a little over 3,000 today. Calvert City is situated along the Tennessee River and is close to the Kentucky Dam, Kentucky Lake, and Lake Barkley areas, which draw thousands of vacationers every summer.

Calvert City High School was one of several high schools in Marshall County until, over roughly two decades, they all became one. CCHS was consolidated with others into North Marshall High School in the mid-'50s; both my parents graduated from North in 1961. North and the two other remaining high schools, Benton High and South Marshall High (which gave Vanderbilt one of its greats, Bobby Warren, in the late '60s), were consolidated into a single school, Marshall County High School, in 1974. I graduated from MCHS in 1985 and headed down the road about 120 miles to Nashville and Vanderbilt University.

Basketball may have been my ticket to Vanderbilt, but baseball has always been my favorite sport. My grandfather, Tye Goheen, was a longtime minor league pitcher from the 1920s into the 1940s and was (and is) something of a legend in that part of Kentucky. Our family loved hearing his tales of pitching against the likes of Dizzy Dean, a St. Louis Cardinals great, in off-season barnstorming affairs.

Until the late 1950s, St. Louis was the westernmost city in the major leagues, and the southernmost city until the '60s, when Atlanta and Houston obtained major league franchises, and the '80s were a great time to be a Cardinals fan. The team won the World Series in 1982 behind Bruce Sutter, Keith Hernandez, and Ozzie Smith. They returned in 1985 in the fall of my freshman year; I remember our head team manager, Todd Berry, greeting me as we came off the floor from a practice in late October with the news that Jack Clark's ninth-inning home run had clinched the pennant for the Cards and put the team back in the World Series. The Cards lost/were robbed of the Series that year (damn you, Don Denkinger!) but were back again in 1987. Alas, the Cards lost a seven-game series to the Minnesota Twins.

Little did I expect that by the time the Cards next appeared in a World Series (2004), I would have graduated law school, moved to Atlanta, gotten married, and had two daughters. But my Cardinals obsession was well known by my teammates and coaches. In 2009, Perdue parlayed a relationship with the Cardinals' video co-ordinator into a visit into the Cards' locker room and dugout where he and I watched batting practice prior to a Cardinals-Braves game in Atlanta.

I would continue to be entwined, often fortuitously, with the Cardinals over the years. One of my most treasured compliments appeared in a column by the legendary Fred Russell of the *Nashville Banner* during my senior season: "Some Memorial Gym observers liken Barry's extraordinary agility to the nimbleness of St. Louis Cardinals shortstop Ozzie Smith." That seemed like a stretch to me, but who was I to argue with the great Fred Russell, one of the greatest sportswriters of all time and who had just been elected, the previous year, to the National Sportscasters and Sportswriters Hall of Fame? Two decades later, when *Sports Illustrated* dropped a note on me and other NCAA tournament "heroes" in its annual "Where Are They Now?" issue, the cover subject was none other than Stan Musial, the greatest Cardinal of them all. And even the Musial name had its own eerie coincidence—one of the graduates in the Vanderbilt class of 1988 was Laura Musial, Stan the Man's granddaughter.

On the hardwood, competition was spirited for the starting positions and playing time, especially at the forward positions. The freshmen, Chuck Mayes and Steve Grant, were impressive, though in different ways—Chuck was an excellent long-range shooter, while Steve was a jumping-jack rebounder with a good touch around the basket and at the free-throw line. Clearly, they would be contributors. Eric Reid continued to improve while Frank Kornet was still working his way back from knee surgery. As we played intrasquad games and public scrimmages throughout November, it was clear that the forward position would have just as much depth as the guard position.

Unfortunately, that frontcourt depth left one person out. Chip Rupp, at the time my closest friend on the team, left the program.

Anyone even remotely familiar with basketball in Kentucky knows the Rupp name. Chip's grandfather, Adolph Rupp, single-handedly made basketball the passion-bordering-on-religion in Kentucky that has gripped the state since he became UK's coach in 1930. Chip was very close to his grandfather; he often spoke warmly of the pair's trip to Atlanta in 1977 to watch the Final Four—the last his grandfather would see (Adolph Rupp died that December). Chip was a star at Lexington's Henry

Clay High School and appeared, as did I, in the State Tournament in our junior year (1984), which was held in Lexington in the venue that bears his grandfather's name—Rupp Arena.

In summer 1984, Chip and I met and became fast friends on an all-star team of rising seniors in Kentucky that toured Europe for a few weeks. That tour was organized by Eddie Ford, a college teammate of my father's at Murray State in the '60s, and whose son, Travis (who accompanied his dad on the tour and was a rising eighth-grader, as best I can recall) would later play on UK's '93 Final Four team and currently is the head coach at St. Louis University where he led his team to the 2019 NCAA Tournament. Chip and I hit it off. We reconnected the following summer as teammates (along with Kornet and others) for the Kentucky-Indiana all-star games. We roomed together our freshman year at Vandy, which naturally fostered a close friendship.

In some ways, Chip was dealt a bad hand at Vandy. He red-shirted our freshman year of 1985–86, and then had to undergo surgery as practice started the next year, setting him back significantly. He eventually caught up, though, and played particularly well in the Music City Invitational. He played only sparingly the rest of the season, however, totaling only 91 minutes for the entire season. But he played more and better in the Jones Cup tourney in Taipei over the summer, and, with the mass departures at forward, Chip's hopes were high for more playing time in '87–'88.

Mayes, though, brought a new dimension to the team—a forward who had three-point shooting ability. As we prepared for our final preseason game, an exhibition against the USSR national team, it appeared that Coach Newton intended to make Mayes the first substitute in at forward. That didn't sit well with Chip. "If Mayes goes in before I do," he told me before the USSR game, "I'm quitting." I didn't believe it, and in the game, Mayes, in fact, did enter before Chip, though Chip did play a few minutes. After the game (which we lost), I went to dinner with my parents and returned to my dorm room around 11 p.m. or so. When I opened the door, I stepped on a CD Chip had borrowed from me a couple of weeks before and obviously was now returning by slipping it under my door. No note accompanied it, and at that moment I knew he had made good on his threat to leave. His room was close to mine and I knocked numerous times on several different occasions that night to no avail.

Coach Newton gave the players a couple of days off after the game, and I went home to Kentucky to relax before getting down to business the following week for our first real game. Coach Newton called me at my parents' home over the weekend. I told him all I knew, which wasn't much—the threat of leaving if Mayes entered the game first, etc. The coach professed to be surprised, but I don't think he should have been. For his part, I think Chip believed C.M. had recruited him at least in part as a defensive measure intended to keep Chip from signing with, for example, LSU and Dale Brown—who in the early and mid-'80s had become Public Enemy No. 1 in the Bluegrass State because of their rise to prominence in direct challenge to UK's stranglehold on SEC basketball—but then never really intended to play Chip much.

Regardless, I did talk to Chip over the weekend, but his decision had been made and there was no undoing it. "This has been a hard decision for me," he said to the press, "but it's not hasty." He transferred to West Virginia, which at the time was coached by Gale Catlett, who had been an assistant under Coach Rupp at UK for several years. Chip was no longer a Commodore, but a Mountaineer. We hadn't played a real game yet, but I already felt like we had one loss.

2

OPENING STATEMENTS

I

"This is a place where second best will never do"
—Bob Seger, "Shakedown" ('87)

Notwithstanding Chip's departure and the loss to the Russians in our last tune-up, we approached the beginning of the season with some optimism. That optimism wasn't shared by the national media, however. *Sports Illustrated*'s annual college basketball preview issue chose a "top 40" list of the teams it considered the best in the country, six of whom were destined to be on our dance card at some point in the season—Indiana (#2), Kentucky (#5), Pittsburgh (#8), North Carolina (#9), Florida (#10), and Kansas (#12). The other SEC teams in *SI*'s top 40 were Georgia (#21) and LSU (#34) while another of our non-conference opponents, Notre Dame (#29), also made the list.

Discussing the SEC, the magazine seemed to predict the finish as (1) Kentucky, (2) Florida, (3) Georgia, (4) LSU, (5) Auburn, (6) Vanderbilt, (7) Tennessee, (8) Alabama, (9) Ole Miss, and (10) Mississippi State. As things would turn out, that wasn't too far off. The magazine assessed the Commodores thusly: "Vanderbilt beat seven NCAA-bound teams last season with an inside-out game that's still intact. The all-Barry backcourt of Barry Booker and Barry Goheen scores long, while the 7-foot [Will] Perdue, who improved markedly last season, scores short. Vandy's game, though well suited to the three-point rule, suffers against the coast-to-coast quickness of the SEC." That was probably accurate based on our past performance.

Overall, the prognosticators didn't predict we would make the NCAA tourney given those apparent weaknesses and the general strength of the SEC. But the time for predictions was over; the time for proving it on the court was at hand. The team supplying our first test would be the Western Athletic Conference's University of Hawaii, something of a reversal of the 1986–87 season, which we had opened in Hawaii. The starting lineup, as it would be for the team's first 10 games, was Perdue at center, Kornet and Mayes at forward, and Booker and Goheen at guard. We jumped out to a 23-8 lead, but our energy quickly faded—as did our large lead. Hawaii cut the lead to five, 48-43, early in the second half. Happily, we had Will Perdue to bail us out, and he quickly proved that the previous season was no fluke.

II

"Don't be surprised to see me back in that bright part of town"
—Steve Winwood, "Back in the High Life Again" ('86–'87)

For those who asked in fall 1986, "Where did Will Perdue come from?" the smart-aleck (and truthful) answer was (and is) "Merritt Island, Florida." The actual answer is a bit more complicated.

I first visited Memorial Gym in late February 1984, on a Sunday afternoon. We made the two-hour drive from western Kentucky and arrived at least an hour before the scheduled tip-off, so we found our seats and waited for warm-ups and then the game. But first, the players on both teams came out for the pre-game shoot-around, which is an informal warm-up where players on the teams take whatever shots they want and get loose for maybe 15 or 20 minutes before returning to the locker room for a few words from the coach. Then they take the floor as a team for the formal warm-up period (i.e., the proverbial "layup line"). On this day, as we sat in our seats, a Vanderbilt player came to the floor to shoot around, the first player on either team to do so. He was tall and skinny. I checked my program to see who this guy was, and I learned that the player was a freshman named Will Perdue. Will later would say that "when I walked on campus" in fall 1983 "I was only 6'10", 195 pounds." (At some point, Will grew another two inches to top out at an even seven feet.)

Will grew up and went to high school in Merritt Island, Florida. He was 6'4" as a high school sophomore, then 6'6" a year later, and 6'10" by his senior year, when he averaged 30.1 points per game, set 10 school records, and was named to several high school All-American teams. Will recalled his decision to attend Vandy:

> I thought I needed to consider going to a place with a good solid education that would help me get a job when college [was] over. Coach Newton really connected with my parents, whom they liked over the other coaches. At that time basketball was the biggest sport there. They filled up Memorial Gym, which was loud and crazy. I [chose] the education and Vanderbilt and Coach Newton.

In other words, Will's decision-making process was a lot like that of his Vandy teammates: (1) he wanted a good education; (2) Coach Newton had a warm and winning personality that played well with both recruits and their parents; and (3) basketball was the most popular sport on campus. That was a potent combination, and Will chose Vandy over his home-state school Florida (whose coach, Norm Sloan, recalled climbing into and riding fire engines Will's father had in the family's garage in an unsuccessful effort to persuade Will to stay in the state), as well as Virginia, Georgia Tech, and Purdue.

Of course, I would learn those details much later, and I had no idea what lay ahead for Will when I watched him venture onto the Memorial Gym floor that day in February 1984—and I'm sure Will didn't either. But Will didn't play that day, which was typical that season; he played in only 17 games. He then encountered academic trouble and red-shirted in the 1984–85 season, and he used the down year not only to get his academics on course but also to improve his game and add some weight to that thin frame—about 25 pounds in fact.

Will improved his academics (changing his major to communication studies and finding a mentor in Professor Kassian Kovalcheck, who would similarly guide me through the same major and to whom Will and I remain close today), briefly considered but rejected the idea of transferring to another school, and was eligible to return to the team when Booker, Kornet, and I arrived on campus in fall 1985. My lasting memory of Will that fall, when I was a freshman, was his fondness for a gray T-shirt bearing the words, in large green capital letters, "IF IT WASN'T FOR BAS-KETBALL I'D QUIT SCHOOL." Happily, for us (and him), basketball was there. Coach Newton called him "Wilbur," and all of his teammates call him "Wilbur" to this day. As Will always noted with some amusement, his name isn't, and never has been Wilbur—in fact, his full name is William Edward Perdue. But "Wilbur" has been something of a term of endearment for more than 35 years, and there's no changing now!

By all accounts, the Will Perdue who returned to game action in 1985–86 was a vast improvement over the 1983–84 model. He still didn't play in every game—he played in 22 of our 28 games for a total of 181 minutes—but he was an effective backup to the incumbent center, senior Brett Burrow. And he showed enough potential to prompt some to wonder (then and later) why he didn't play more: in a December game he had a near double-double with 10 points and nine rebounds, and in a game at Auburn he went for 16 points and nine boards, both of which led the team.

When Burrow graduated in 1986, Will was the obvious choice to fill the center position. In spring 1986, Coach Newton issued something of an in-print challenge to Wilbur: "Will Perdue's development at center will be a key for us next year [1986–87]. We need him to play well on both ends of the floor and for longer periods of time." Will was determined not to waste the opportunity. He worked very hard in the off-season and pre-season to improve his conditioning and refine his post moves, working with coaches Bostick and Martin, both of whom had mentored some outstanding big men during their careers. "When Will came back for his junior year," Kornet recalled, "there was a tremendous change in his game. He had taken large strides in both his shooting game and his physical game." Steve Reece, Wilbur's closest friend on the team, predicted a breakout year. "I think Will Perdue is going to be a big help," Reece said. "He has improved and will surprise a lot of people inside."

Will did not disappoint. He flew out of the blocks by being named MVP of the season-opening Maui tourney and played at an extremely high level all season, averaging 17.4 points (shooting 60% from the field) and 8.7 rebounds while blocking 72 shots, finishing in the top five in the SEC in all four of those categories. He became particularly known for his forceful dunks, which a creative sportswriter nicknamed "Perdunks."

Coach Newton explained Wilbur's metamorphosis early that season: "The big difference is that he has gained strength and endurance. He has improved his skills, particularly defensively, and his techniques are all better." In addition to his Maui MVP, Will also made the All-Tournament teams for the Sugar Bowl Tournament and our own Music City Invitational Tournament, and he was named the SEC's "Most Improved Player" by several media outlets. In fact, LSU coach Dale Brown told Will at the SEC Media Days in fall 1987, "I've been coaching 31 years, and you're the most improved player I've seen." Brown probably spoke for many SEC coaches when he remarked that "I didn't know he was in the league for two years. Then he was slam-dunking on our heads."

The challenges for Will in 1987–88 were numerous. First, could he prove that 1986–87 was no fluke? Second, could he lead the team to the NCAA tournament, having led the team to the NIT quarterfinals the previous season? Third, and maybe most importantly, could he be a true leader and not just the team's best player? Will was the only senior on the team, and because of his redshirt year many of his best friends on the team had graduated. The Hawaii game was the first true test of his leadership.

Will supplied all the right answers to those questions against Hawaii. He was a rock inside, posting 29 points and 15 rebounds. In only one other game during the season would he exceed 29 points, and he would not surpass 15 rebounds. From that slender 48-43 margin early in the second half, we dialed up the intensity, especially on the defensive end, and forced several turnovers. A Perdunk highlighted an eight-point run that gave us a 56-43 lead, and the Rainbows never again got close. The final score of 91-62 was somewhat deceiving, but opening with a win is fine regardless of the score. Supporting Will were the impressive debuts of freshmen Steve Grant and Charles Mayes, who scored 12 and 11 points, respectively, while Frank Kornet (14) and Eric Reid (11) gave us five players in double figures.

The backcourt quartet played poorly against Hawaii, but we played more to our expected form three nights later in our second game, at home against Lehigh, a good team that would win its conference (the now-defunct East Coast Conference) before falling to Temple in the first round of the NCAAs. Lehigh was coached by Fran McCaffrey, who had become the head coach at Lehigh in 1985 at the tender age of 26 (the youngest Division I head coach in the country) and was led by Daren Queenan, who averaged a school-record 28.5 points a game that season—second in the nation to Bradley's Hershey Hawkins, who averaged an incredible 36.3 a game. But we started hot and never let up. Booker hit two treys in the first minute, setting the tone for a sensational performance. He hit all six of his three-point attempts (prompting Larry Woody of *The Tennessean* to dub him "the Long Ranger") and finished with a career-high 24 points on 9-for-10 shooting. I added 15 and six assists, and the contributions from Wilcox (10) and Draud (8) gave the backcourt 57 points.

Significantly, after hitting only three of 10 from beyond the arc against Hawaii, we nailed 14 for 24 from three-point range against Lehigh, prompting Coach Newton to remark, "We shot it about as good tonight as a team can shoot it." Perdue scored 20 (hitting all eight of his shots from the field), Mayes added 15, and we hit the century mark for the only time that season with a 102-91 victory. "We neutralized Perdue pretty well," Lehigh coach McCaffrey (currently the head coach at Iowa) said after the game. "He's the best big man we'll face all season. Our game plan was to get beat by somebody else. We did, by Goheen and Booker."

II

"Sleight of hand and twist of fate"
—*U2, "With or Without You"* ('87)

Winning the first two games of the season was satisfying, but the highlight of the opening weekend occurred off the court and had nothing to do with basketball. I saw my first U2 concert.

U2 had exploded in spring 1987 with the release of *The Joshua Tree*, which made the foursome from Dublin, Ireland, the most popular rock band in the world—a title the band has enjoyed for most of the last 30-plus years. The chance to see the band live for the first time was one of those things where everything had to work out, and it did.

I may have been the only person in Calvert City, Kentucky, who followed U2 from nearly the beginning, which for that band was the early '80s. In fact, a 1986 article, written after my freshman year and with spelling that demonstrated that U2 had yet to become worldwide stars, described me as "a rock music aficionado" and observed that "Goheen is plugged into U-2 [*sic*] and the Eagles and John Cougar

Mellencamp." (Which was true: I saw Mellencamp in concert the fall of my fresh-man year ('85), then Perdue and I saw him in concert in '88 with one of our Com-munication Studies professors.)

"U-2" may not have been a household name just yet in 1986, but by summer 1987 everyone knew who Bono, the Edge, Adam Clayton, and Larry Mullen Jr were. Yet, incredibly, when the group's lengthy U.S. tour schedule was released in fall 1987, Nashville—Music City, U.S.A.—wasn't on it. Then, just before Thanksgiv-ing, rumors began to circulate that the band would add a Nashville-area date, espe-cially given the one-week gap between the November 26 show at LSU's Assembly Center and the December 3 show at the Orange Bowl in Miami. And that's exactly what happened—it was announced that U2 would play the Murphy Center on the campus of Middle Tennessee State University in Murfreesboro (about 30 miles south of Nashville) on Saturday, November 28. Tickets did not go on sale until the previ-ous Saturday, November 21.

And, of course, U2 did not disappoint. The show began with "Where the Streets Have No Name," the opening track from *The Joshua Tree* and an enduring classic, and the next three hours were pure joy. Lead singer Bono brought Wynonna Judd to the stage for one song; he also playfully introduced "I Still Haven't Found What I'm Looking For" as "an old Hank Williams song." Unquestionably, it was worth the effort!

No teammates attended the '87 U2 show with me, but the U2 circle was closed in summer 2017 when Perdue, Charlie Dahlem, and I (and our spouses/significant others) saw the band in Louisville on the 30th anniversary tour of—wait for it—*The Joshua Tree*, playing the entire album in sequence. Full circle indeed!

So, the Cardinals went to the World Series in October and I saw U2 in concert in November. Maybe those were good omens that the rest of the season held good things in store.

3

CAROLINA IN MY MIND

The Hawaii and Lehigh games were nice warm-ups, but two real tests loomed: North Carolina at home and Indiana on the road. We figured that both games would provide an accurate measuring stick for us. UNC was the #1 ranked team in the country, and Indiana was the defending national champion. In effect, the North Carolina game, with a return game at Chapel Hill in 1988–89, would replace Duke as a tough ACC non-conference game on our schedule. We had played the Blue Devils each of my first two seasons.

I

"It was long ago, seems like yesterday"
—*The Smithereens, "Blood and Roses"* ('86)

We played Duke twice during my time at Vandy. The first time was in the fall of my freshman year in my first official game at Memorial Gym. That Duke team, which came into the game ranked #3 in the nation, was the first of Mike Krzyzewski's Duke teams to go to the Final Four, so the aura of "Coach K"—12 Final Fours and five NCAA titles later—hadn't quite taken hold yet, but he and the program were well on their way. Even then, as Coach K and Duke were clearly building a program that, 35 years later, is one of the two or three best in the country, there were whispers that Coach K, then the head coach at Army, had applied for the Vanderbilt job in the late 1970s but was rejected, thus feeding the suspicion that Vandy had let someone who, by 1985, was a hot young coach, get away. But that's not what happened, according to Coach K himself: "After the fourth year [at Army], I interviewed at Vanderbilt University, but I pulled my name out. I just wasn't ready." Though Coach K had been a finalist for the position, he withdrew from consideration and the job went to Richard Schmidt, then an assistant to Terry Holland at Virginia. After the next season, his fifth at Army, Coach K interviewed at both Iowa State and Duke, and he took the Duke job in March 1980.

After a tough first couple of seasons, Coach K struck paydirt with the recruiting class who were seniors on the 1985–86 team that we would play. The seniors on that team—Johnny Dawkins, Mark Alarie, Jay Bilas, and David Henderson—"changed the course of Duke basketball and my career," Coach K said. Dawkins, in particular, was incredible—amazingly quick with a deadly outside shot—and he was the 1986 Naismith Player of the Year and remains Duke's all-time leading scorer; Bilas—a good player himself and now a fine basketball color analyst (not to mention a fellow member of the bar)—calls Dawkins "the most important player in the history of Duke basketball."

So it was that my debut in Memorial would be against the Blue Devils, one of the three or four best teams we played in my four years, and when I entered the game as a substitute Coach Newton assigned me to guard Dawkins "the most important player in the history of Duke basketball." Welcome to big-time college basketball! Still, this game was one of the most important of my career, as well as Kornet's. Frank drew the start, in only his third college game, which he called "a very special moment." I would soon join him in the starting lineup because, in a scrum under the basket, Alarie swung an elbow that hit our starting guard, Jeff Gary, squarely in his cheekbone, shattering it. It was a tough break for Jeff, a fifth-year senior who had waited his turn behind Phil Cox for a few years, and now would be on the shelf for a couple of months, but it was an unexpected opportunity for me in only my third college game. And, notwithstanding the defensive challenges Duke's guards presented, I played well, scoring 12 points (my first-ever double-figure game as a Commodore), and the team played well, too; we just didn't have the talent to stay with Duke for a full 40 minutes. Despite our best efforts, the Blue Devils prevailed, 84-74, one of their 37 victories that year before bowing to Louisville in the NCAA championship game.

Because of Gary's injury, I started the next 12 games and had some strong performances—seven-of-eight shooting in a win against Austin Peay; a team-leading 12 points in a win at Princeton; and 33 total points in the two games of the Music City Invitational, earning all-tournament honors in the process. I returned to substitute duty when Gary returned from his injury, but I played well enough to earn a spot on the SEC All-Freshman team, and I led the team in both field goal (54.2%) and free throw (84.6%) shooting. The Duke game was a catalyst for a strong freshman season.

In December 1986, early in my sophomore season, we made our only trip to Duke. I was privileged to play in some wonderful, historic basketball venues during my four years at Vanderbilt, and perhaps the most historic of them all, at least outside of Madison Square Garden, is Cameron Indoor Stadium on Duke's campus. Christened as Duke Indoor Stadium, the arena hosted its first game on January 6, 1940, and changed its name to Cameron Indoor Stadium in 1972 in honor of Eddie Cameron, the school's basketball coach when the venue opened. Cameron in 1986 didn't quite have the aura and mystique that it does today, numerous Final Fours and NCAA titles later, along with the near-legendary status Coach K has attained. But it still was, and is, a unique basketball environment.

When we visited Cameron, we were coming off the season-opening championship in Maui and were 4-0. While Cameron was undeniably a great place to play, it was not an ideal choice for a young team's first road game of the season. We fell behind early, and the game fell apart from there. With around 10 minutes remaining, Duke's lead ballooned to 30 points. Coach Newton called timeout. "We're not this bad," he said calmly in the huddle. That observation seemed to light a fire, and we made a comeback to make the final margin less embarrassing. We almost did more than that: we scored almost every time down, and the Blue Devils—especially Billy King, a longtime NBA general manager who was a lousy free-throw shooter—kept missing free throws. But Duke held on, winning 78-66.

We would not play Duke again, as Coach Newton essentially replaced the Devils on the non-conference schedule with their rivals, the North Carolina Tar Heels, for a home-and-home series in my junior and senior seasons. But the mystique of Cameron and the two games against Duke remain a fond memory.

II

"There's a battle ahead...don't let them win"
—Crowded House, "Don't Dream It's Over" ('87)

In 1987, the University of North Carolina had been fielding a basketball team for more than 75 years. Beginning with the school's first championship, the 1957 title under Frank McGuire, UNC had been one of the premier programs in college basketball.

We played three truly great teams in 1987–88: North Carolina, Kentucky, and Pittsburgh. The Tar Heels had the best coach of the three, the legendary Dean Smith, who would retire 10 years later in fall 1997 as the all-time leader in coaching victories at the Division I men's level. Coach Smith was friendly with Coach Newton; in fact, Coach Smith had spoken at our team banquet the previous spring. They had much in common: both were true gentlemen and ambassadors for college basketball; both had played college basketball at blue-blood programs (C.M. at Kentucky, Smith at Kansas) though neither was a star; both won NCAA titles as collegians (C.M.'s Kentucky team in 1951, Smith's Kansas team in 1952). Coach Smith had helmed the Carolina program since 1961. He had guided the Tar Heels to several Final Fours and, as of fall 1987, one memorable national championship (1982 in the Superdome in New Orleans), and in 1987 the program was one of the most respected in the country.

The Heels started Jeff Lebo, J.R. Reid, Scott Williams, Renzino Smith, and Kevin Madden—an imposing mix of brawn, athleticism, and shooting prowess. They had a decent bench as well: Pete Chilcutt, King Rice, Rick Fox, and Steve

Bucknall provided quality depth just about on a par with Kentucky's. They were the #1 team in the country for a reason.

Of the Tar Heels, J.R. Reid garnered most of our attention. He was a bruising 6'9" power forward who had been an All-American the previous year as a freshman. Kornet accurately summarized Reid before the game: "I'll be facing some awfully good forwards in the SEC this season, but I don't expect any of them to be better than Reid. He's probably as good as I'll play." He was right; in the SEC, only Kentucky's Winston Bennett was in Reid's league as a true power forward. And Frank must have done some research on Reid: he somehow found out that J.R.'s given first name was "Herman," and we reminded Mr. Reid of that fact at various points during the game, much to his irritation.

Nevertheless, even though it was only December, it already had been an unfortunate and even tragic season for the Tar Heels. Reid and Bucknall had gotten into a fight with an N.C. State student in a Raleigh night club, which resulted in their suspension for the season's first game. Coach Smith had health problems in the form of persistent nosebleeds; on occasion he sat in the stands while assistant coaches Bill Guthridge and Roy Williams (the UNC head coach since 2003, winning three NCAA titles) ran practice. And, most tragically, on October 15, the first day of practice, Scott Williams' parents died in a murder/suicide incident.

Still, as always seemed to happen, Carolina found a way. We were trying to beat the country's top-ranked team, but the Heels had already done that; in the season's first game—without the suspended Reid and Bucknall—they beat top-ranked Syracuse 96-93 on a neutral court in Springfield, Massachusetts. That win moved the Heels to the #1 ranking, and they won their next three games to carry a 4-0 record into Memorial.

Coach Smith rightly focused on Will Perdue. "He's an All-American," Smith said; "they've also got two outstanding guards in Goheen and Booker." He expected the game "to be a good road test for us." That turned out to be an accurate prediction. The UNC game was the first visit to Memorial by a top-ranked team since the eventual national champion Kentucky Wildcats had visited in 1978.

III

"Welcome to the big time, you're bound to be a star"
—Richard Marx, "Don't Mean Nothing" ('87)

We wasted no time getting the crowd into the game because we came out hot: Mayes hit a three on each of our first two possessions, which turned out to be a great omen for us, and a Perdunk off a great Mayes feed made it 8-4. A Booker three on the next possession made it 11-4, and another Perdunk off a fine Reid pass made it 13-4.

Could it be that easy? Of course not—Carolina scored the next eight points to close the gap to one, and the game was nip and tuck from that point on.

Almost every player on our team, as well as the coaches, would agree that the Carolina game was the worst officiated game of our careers. Every game has calls that don't go your way; some bad calls even have catastrophic consequences (as we would learn the next season). And stretches of games have strongly one-sided officiating. But rarely is an entire game so badly officiated that one must question the officials' integrity and impartiality, and the UNC game was that rare and unfortunate example. As with most non-conference games, referees from the visiting team's conference officiated the game, meaning that we had three ACC officials. And they were terrible. UNC was in the bonus with 10 minutes left in the first half, as we had been whistled for seven team fouls; at that point, the Heels had been called for only one team foul. We had an incredible 13 turnovers in the first half—and not all were legitimate.

Then, with about four minutes left in the half, Dean Smith summoned Coach Newton to the North Carolina bench to complain about comments supposedly being made by Vandy fans directed at the Heels' assistants. That struck me as silly and an exercise in gamesmanship; it's hard to believe Smith and his team hadn't heard a lot worse during their annual visits to Duke, N.C. State, Maryland, and the other ACC campuses. These Smith tactics—trying anything to obtain, or maintain, even slightest (largely psychological) edge over an opponent, no matter how insignificant—even had a name: "Deanisms." But Coach Newton asked the fans to tone down the alleged harassment anyway, and we fought through the lousy officiating and gamesmanship to stay even with the Heels. We held a slim 35-34 lead at halftime.

We started the second half sluggishly, yielding the first four points to fall behind by three. But Perdue scored four straight points off great entry passes from Mayes to get us going. After a couple of minutes of back-and-forth, I scored five straight, and a Perdue free throw gave us a four-point lead at 48-44. Then Carolina scored seven straight, capping that run by drawing Perdue's fourth foul, to lead 51-48. Before Coach Newton could get Will out of the game, he scored to cut the lead to one, then, in a huge defensive play, drew a charge on Scott Williams on the other end—which was Williams' fourth foul. Both stars went to the bench with four fouls with 12:29 left. We then went over three minutes without scoring, but the Heels scored only two points themselves during that stretch, and thus led by only three when Coach Newton called timeout just inside the 10-minute mark. A Kornet tip-in out of that timeout cut the lead to one and stopped the bleeding, but only temporarily—after the teams traded baskets, Carolina scored five straight to push its lead to six, 60-54, with 7:31 left. In a huge play, Kornet went over J.R. Reid to claim an offensive rebound, which Mayes cashed in with his third trey of the game. It was 60-57, Heels, with seven minutes left. Reid atoned with a putback of his own on the other end to make it 62-57 with 6:45 left. Coach Newton called timeout and put Perdue back in with the four fouls.

The Heels led 64-59 when Will made a nifty left-handed hook in the lane and drew the foul on Reid. His free throw completed the three-point play and cut the Heels' lead to two. With five minutes to go, another Mayes three gave us back the lead, 65-64. When Perdue made another running lefty shot in the lane, we had scored eight straight points and led by three. J.R. Reid's two free throws cut the lead to one at the three-minute mark. Mayes then nailed his fifth trey of the game to extend our lead to 70-66. A J.R. Reid miss on the other end and Booker's rebound gave us the ball and a four-point lead as the clock neared the two-minute mark.

Then came the only thing close to a 50/50 call that went our way all night. We worked the shot clock down, and I had the ball with a few seconds left. I spun with the dribble and stopped at the free-throw line with Smith guarding me. I leaned around him with the intention of taking the shot when I saw Eric Reid cut toward the basket from my strong (left) side; I saw that his man, J.R. Reid, was watching me and had lost sight of Eric. I went into the air intending to shoot but, seeing the cutting Eric out of the corner of my eye, I fired the ball to him, and he caught it in step as he landed on the block. Scott Williams, who was guarding Will on the other block, rushed over to help and stepped in to take the possible charge. Eric bounced off Williams as he took the shot—he was practically behind the backboard when the ball left his hand. The whistle blew as the shot fell through the net. Block or charge? Happily, the officials got this one right: block on Williams (his fifth foul, thus disqualifying him from the game), basket good.

I had never seen Coach Newton so demonstrative; the play, which happened on the end of the floor where our bench was located, prompted an explosion of coaches and players from their chairs. Coach Newton led the cheers with a mighty punch in the air. Eric made the free throw—those were his only three points of the game—and we led 73-66 with two minutes to play. We were on a 14-2 run.

Lebo, who would have more favorable experiences in Memorial Gym a few years later as an assistant under Eddie Fogler and then more unfavorable experiences as the Auburn head coach in the 2000s, promptly answered with a three to make it 73-69. We still led by three, 78-75 when we threw away the inbounds pass with :02 left, giving Carolina a chance to tie with a three-pointer.

At this point, we benefited from one of the dumbest rules in the history of basketball. Carolina inbounded the ball along the sideline and ran a play that broke Lebo open across the court, in the corner. The long pass went to him there, behind the three-point line, and he went for the shot. But Booker recovered in time to get to Lebo and deliver a hard foul on the shot, which fell way short of the basket. Thus, Lebo was given…two free throws. That's right—in the first few years of the three-point shot era, a foul on a player in the act of shooting a three-pointer only gave the shooter two free throws, not three. That rule made no sense whatsoever, and it was sensibly changed a couple of years later to provide three free throws to a player who was fouled while shooting a three-pointer. "I don't agree with the rule," Coach Newton said. "I think a foul on a three-point shot should be a three-shot foul, but the rule's the rule and that's the way we're going to play it." And we had learned our lesson the previous season by not fouling with a three-point lead against South Carolina: a 25-footer at the buzzer tied the game, and we eventually lost in overtime. We were determined not let that happen again.

So, the two-free throw rule in 1987–88 meant that Lebo could not tie the game at the line; with only two free throws, he would have to make the first and intentionally miss the second, then hope for a tip-in by a teammate to tie the game. But Lebo, an 85% free throw shooter, missed the first one. He then inexplicably made the second, giving us the ball out of bounds with a two-point lead. We threw it the length of the floor to Perdue, who flung it into the air as the clock finally ran out. We won, 78-76.

Perdue and Mayes were the heroes—Wilbur had 23 points, 10 boards, and three blocks; as Kornet recalled, this game "put Vanderbilt and Will Perdue on the map," and North Carolina Coach Smith opined that "Perdue was just too much for us inside." Wilbur's stellar game earned him Player of the Week honors in *Sports Illustrated*. Meanwhile, Charles—who had once attended Coach Smith's summer basketball camp—had 16 on those five huge treys and one free throw, and he added four assists. I contributed 13 points and added seven rebounds and four assists. We offset the turnovers with 10 steals and hit eight of 16 three-point attempts; the Heels hit 10 threes of their own. All in all, it was a good, solid college basketball game. "I thought the level of play was outstanding," Coach Newton said later. "The intensity was terrific." Plus, the home crowd did not disappoint, as Coach Newton observed: "The magic of this game is the crowd. This is what it's all about."

We didn't think we had played all that well, yet we still managed to beat the top-ranked team. In addition to the turnovers, we hit only 12 of our 21 free-throw attempts. "We didn't play that great a game against North Carolina and we still found a way to win," I commented later. "That's cause for confidence when you don't play your best game and still beat the #1 team." And then there was the officiating, which still rankled after the game. Looking ahead to our visit the next season to Chapel Hill, Coach Newton, in his most diplomatically undiplomatic tone, said, "I don't think we'll get the same treatment from SEC officials that North Carolina got here, but that's all I've got to say about the officiating." But that was saying a lot.

Nevertheless, it was a great win. "It's a big, big win for our program, no question," Coach Newton observed. Dean Smith downplayed the loss, asserting that "we're not the No. 1 team in the country, not even the No. 10 team." Coach Newton stated things a little more accurately: "I don't know who the No. 1 team in the nation is, but North Carolina is one of the top teams in the nation. To beat a team like North Carolina is very meaningful."

Indeed, Coach Smith's poor-mouthing didn't diminish our accomplishment of beating the #2 and #1 teams in consecutive seasons. And the UNC win was the first of four consecutive games over the next 20 seasons where Vandy would beat the then-current top-ranked team at Memorial—Kentucky in 1993, eventual national champion Florida in 2007, and Tennessee in 2008. A loss to top-ranked Kentucky in Memorial in February 2012 broke that streak, but the Commodores memorably avenged that defeat a month later by knocking off the 'Cats in the finals of the SEC tournament to claim the school's second SEC title.

Moreover, the perception of Memorial Gym as a difficult place to play grew after the Carolina win. And there would be more big wins over the next two seasons.

4

HOOSIERS

There wasn't much time to celebrate the North Carolina win. In less than 72 hours, we would be playing the Indiana Hoosiers, the defending national champions, in their gym—exactly 52 weeks to the day since we had beaten them in Memorial.

I

"Now I'm sittin' on pins and needles"
—Talking Heads, "Wild Wild Life" ('86)

Our two games against Indiana, in December 1986 and December 1987, were played when interest in the IU program, and their coach, Bob Knight, was at an all-time high. They had one of the country's best head coaches and, for the 1986 game, one of its best players, senior Steve Alford. Knight arrived in Bloomington from Army in 1971, and in the ensuing 15 years led IU to several Big 10 championships and two NCAA titles, in 1976 and 1981. Knight, with the assistance of C.M. Newton, then coached the U.S. Olympic team to a convincing gold medal at the 1984 Games in Los Angeles.

Prior to the 1985–86 season, Knight accepted the offer of a young writer named John Feinstein and allowed almost unfettered access to the program from October 1985 to March 1986 for the purpose of a book that would detail the coach and his program. The result was *A Season on the Brink*, which was released just before Thanksgiving in 1986 and a couple of weeks before our game. The book quickly became one of the best-selling sports books of all time, and it spent an incredible 16 weeks at #1 on the *New York Times* bestseller list in 1987.

At about the same time that *A Season on the Brink* was released, the film *Hoosiers* appeared in theaters. The movie was based on tiny Milan High's improbable run to the Indiana State High School championship in 1954. The back-to-back releases of *Hoosiers* and *A Season on the Brink* created a new brand of Hoosier Hysteria in fall 1986, just in time for the team's visit to Memorial on December 9, 1986.

The '86–'87 Hoosiers welcomed back most of their starters, including star Alford and top inside players Daryl Thomas and Ricky Callaway. And with the addition of two junior-college transfers, Keith Smart and Dean Garrett, Indiana came to

Nashville ranked #2 in the nation. Unquestionably, the key was trying to contain Alford, who was the best shooter in college hoops in 1986 and one of the best I ever played against.

Alford averaged over 37 points a game as a high school senior in 1983, and went for 57 in the state tournament semifinals, ultimately winning the state's Mr. Basketball award. He averaged 15.5 points a game in his freshman season as the Hoosiers made a surprise NCAA tournament run, beating Michael Jordan and top-ranked North Carolina in the round of 16, and then averaged 10.3 points a game, on 64.4% shooting from the field, as the youngest player on the '84 Olympic gold medalists. In the "season on the brink" of 1985–86, Alford averaged 22.5 a game and shot 55.6% from the field—an incredible percentage for a mostly long-range shooter, and one that would be unheard of today. He and Knight made for a compelling coach-and-player duo, just as they made for compelling reading in *A Season on the Brink*.

Bob Knight and C.M. Newton, despite their diametrically opposing personalities and temperaments, were very good friends, and Knight called C.M. "a great basketball coach." Knight's '76 champs are, at this writing, the last unbeaten Division I men's champion, running the table for a 32-0 record, and their toughest game in the tournament was against the Newton-coached Alabama Crimson Tide, which, as C.M. recalled, "was the only [team] I coached that I thought was good enough to win the national championship." A controversial block-charge call late in the game went the Hoosiers' way, and IU won 74-69 on its way to the NCAA title.

In spring 1986, in anticipation of our game in the fall, Coach Knight was the featured speaker at our end-of-season awards banquet at the request of C.M., whom Knight always called "Charles"—his actual first name. And now Knight, who said on the day of the game that there "isn't anybody I root harder for than Vanderbilt" because "I like the way they run their program here"—would do his friend a big favor by bringing his team to Nashville for a game that we hoped would be a breakthrough victory for us.

The student body had some fun in welcoming the Hoosiers and their star player. The previous year, Alford had posed for a calendar and, in doing so, had unwittingly violated an NCAA rule. That infraction resulted in a one-game suspension. Now, the Vanderbilt student newspaper, the *Hustler*, published a "Stevie" calendar that included such to-dos as "Thursday: comb hair" and "Friday: admire yourself."

As for the game itself, we caught a break because Callaway was injured with a sprained knee and did not play. The Hoosiers' starters were Alford, Thomas, Smart, Garrett, and Joe Hillman. We started Perdue, Booker, Steve Reece, Glen Clem, and me. Like Indiana, we were without a starting forward, as Bobby Westbrooks was recuperating from surgery for a cracked right elbow. Defensively, the plan was to keep a taller player on the 6'2" Alford, primarily the 6'6" Clem, who did a fine job.

We controlled the opening tip, and Booker nailed a three on our first possession—something he would do frequently over the next three seasons, especially in big games. IU committed three early turnovers, but Perdue committed two fouls in the first five minutes, forcing him to the bench. We also committed several turnovers—six in the first 11 minutes—and IU converted the sixth into a field goal to take a 23-18 lead with nine minutes to play in the half. Steve Reece had kept us in the game with many of those 18 points, but Coach Newton was forced to put Will back in the game with those two fouls. I scored my first two a minute later to cut the lead to three; a deuce by Steve off a nice feed from Will, my putback of my own miss, and a fast break two by Will made it eight straight points and a 26-23 lead. Alford promptly tied it with a three, the first of 10 straight points for the Hoosiers, capped by a Smart three, to give them a 33-26 lead. Will answered with a tap-in of his own miss, but another Alford three made it 36-28 with two minutes to go in the half. Glen and I scored two each, but Thomas scored to give IU a 38-32 halftime lead, and when Alford opened the second half with a conventional three-point play, the Hoosiers had their biggest lead, 41-32. We needed to right the ship quickly if we didn't want the game to get away from us.

As readers of *A Season on the Brink* discovered, Bob Knight was not at all enamored of Steve Alford's defense, and his criticism of it reached occasionally comic heights in the book. Some of that was bluster seemingly designed to highlight a perceived area of the player's game that needed some work because he was such a great player on offense, but the truth was that Alford really wasn't that good a defensive player, so with him guarding me in the second half, I took full advantage to enjoy the single greatest scoring half of my four years at Vandy. I beat Alford off the drive and drew the foul from Garrett, who tried to help. The free throws cut the lead to seven. A minute later, Alford was slow-trailing me through the lane, and I hit a quick turnaround to make it 43-38.

A couple of minutes later, Booker's first bucket since his opening three made it 47-42. After a Garrett free throw, Kornet's basket off a Perdue assist made it 48-44, Hoosiers. I was fouled by Smart on a fast break and made one of two free throws to cut the lead to three, then pulled up off a fast break for a 12-footer to cut the lead to one with 15 minutes to go. After another IU miss, Booker hit a 12-footer along the baseline to give us our first lead in over 10 minutes. Alford's layup gave IU the lead back, but I answered with my only three-pointer of the game to put us up two. Alford promptly replied with a three—his fourth of the game—and a Thomas jumper put IU back up by three. We benefited from a questionable call on the other end when, with the shot clock running down, I was trapped on the baseline and jumped to pass; the Hoosiers were called for a foul, and the officials ruled that, in fact, I was in the act of shooting, thus entitling me to two free throws (which I made to trim the deficit to one). But another conventional three-point play by Alford gave him 24 points and the Hoosiers a four-point lead with just under 12 minutes remaining.

A Reece jumper made it 58-56, then Will blocked an Alford attempt on the other end, and a minute later Will's three-point play off an inbounds play put us back in front, 59-58. A Booker trey gave us eight straight points and a 62-58 lead. Two Thomas free throws cut it to two, but I answered with a 12-foot banker over Alford. Thomas's putback and two Smart free throws tied the game at 64. A Kornet free throw gave us a one-point edge, and a key exchange occurred a minute later: Thomas blew a wide-open layup on one end, and Kornet beat him back to the other end to score off a great lob pass to make it 67-64. IU called timeout with 7:08 left.

Out of the timeout, Alford hit a 12-foot leaner in the lane to cut our lead to 67-66. A Booker jumper made it 69-66. Alford then made a rare mistake, driving to his weak (left-handed) side and losing control of the dribble; trying to avoid the traveling violation, he flipped the ball back toward Hillman at the top of the key, but I got a hand on it and tipped it toward the half-court line. I won the footrace against the diving Hillman and was left alone to make what may or may not have been a dunk (Kornet always called it a "squeaker"). That deuce made it 71-66 with five minutes to play. Two free throws by Thomas cut the lead to three; Clem pushed it back to four with a free throw, and a Reece jumper in the lane made it 74-68 with three minutes to go. Alford hit two free throws, his final points of the game, to cut the lead to four, and a Thomas free throw after his steal made it 74-71. Smart fouled me at the 2:23 mark and fouled out in the process. I made both ends of the one-and-one for a 76-71 lead. Hillman answered with two free throws; we led by three with two minutes remaining.

On our next possession, I was called for a questionable charge, but Perdue came up with a great block off a Hillman drive to keep the lead at three inside 90 seconds to play. I redeemed myself by hitting both ends of the one-and-one to return the lead to five with a minute to play. Thomas quickly scored to make it 78-75. With 20 seconds left, Book was fouled; he hit the all-important front end of the one-and-one to make it a two-possession game. Alford missed a 15-footer with 12 seconds left; we recovered and ran out the clock to notch a huge win, 79-75.

Alford netted 28 points to lead all scorers, but he scored only four in the last 12 minutes. Thomas added 21, but he missed six of his 13 free-throw attempts. Smart previewed the skills that would be on display to the college basketball world the following March with 13 points before fouling out. I scored 26 points, 20 in the second half; it would be my career-high game until late in my senior season. I added six rebounds and a couple of steals, resulting in the ultimate Coach Newton public compliment: "Goheen just played magnificently." Perdue had 15 points, nine rebounds, and a team-high five assists, while Booker—who was great down the stretch—added 13 points and four boards. That was 54 points and 19 rebounds by a junior and two sophomores. "We couldn't slow down Will Perdue and Goheen," the Hoosiers' Todd Meier assessed it years later. As Kornet recalled, "you could really see that the future of the team was coming together in that game." Senior Steve Reece had one of his best games with 12 points, seven rebounds, and several strong defensive plays.

The joy in the locker room was unrestrained. To say it was a breakthrough win for the program would be an understatement: Vanderbilt had not beaten a ranked team of any sort for nearly four years, since January 1983, and had not beaten a top-5 team since a win over #4 LSU in January 1980. And the program's last victory over a top-3 team had been 17 years previous, a win over #2 Kentucky in January 1970. As always, the Memorial Gym faithful were critical to the outcome, as Coach Newton acknowledged: "That's our great home court advantage; the crowd wouldn't let us get tired."

We received some national publicity as well. *Sports Illustrated* published this snarky item on the game: "the home team shocked the Hoosiers 79-75 as guard BARRY (GO IN) GOHEEN scored 26 points and swingman GLEN CLEM—or was it Clem Glen? Alford never did figure it out—held the Indy star to a single basket over the final 11:54."

Coach Knight was diplomatic after the game. "I know they've built toward something like this," he said. "I hate to see it be us, but I'm very happy for Vanderbilt," he said. "The team that deserved to win it won it, and they did it because they made some plays and hung in there." He was apparently less restrained in the locker room, blistering Alford and Smart after Book and I combined for an incredible 30 second-half points: "That has got to be the worst defensive play by two Indiana guards that I have ever seen!" As Smart remembered, Knight kept up the harangue on the flight back to Bloomington.

Post-game, we received a surprise visitor in the locker room: Bob Knight, who congratulated us on what he knew was a huge win for the program. He had not engaged in any histrionics during the game—no tirades, no technicals, no tossing of chairs, etc.—which told me that he probably could control his emotions when he made a concerted effort to do so. And his locker room visit was, I thought, a classy gesture, no doubt prompted by his immense respect for Coach Newton. By the time I realized he was in the locker room, Will and I were the only players left, and I was impressed as he congratulated us ("You fellows did a good job") and wished us luck the rest of the season. We did the same, and the wonderful evening finally ended.

IU didn't need much luck the rest of the way. We would be the only team outside the Big 10 to beat the Hoosiers, and the only unranked team to do so. They would lose only three more games that season—to then-#1 Iowa in January, and consecutive losses at Purdue (#6) and Illinois (#14) late in the regular season. They capped their run to the NCAA title with a memorable 74-73 victory over Syracuse in the Superdome in New Orleans, won on Keith Smart's 18-foot baseline jumper with a second to go. Bob Knight would win the first-ever Naismith Coach of the Year Award in spring 1987.

The win over Indiana would be the first of three consecutive seasons in which we played the eventual NCAA champion, and the second of four consecutive seasons that we played a team that appeared in the NCAA championship game. (We played, and lost to, NCAA runner-up Duke in '85–'86.) And, in a unique double play, the Vanderbilt Lady Commodores also beat the eventual national champions that season, upsetting the Tennessee Lady Volunteers 77-76 in February 1987—the first time in NCAA history that a school defeated both the men's and women's national champions in the same season.

II

"Where does all time go?"
—John Mellencamp, "Check It Out" ('87–'88)

By fall 1987, the Hoosiers had lost their All-American, Alford, as well as solid inside player Daryl Thomas, but had many other quality players returning, including Ricky Callaway, Keith Smart, and Dean Garrett. They also welcomed an impressive freshman class led by Jay Edwards. One thing would be certain—we wouldn't sneak up on Indiana this time, especially after the win over North Carolina.

The relationship between Coaches Newton and Knight remained strong enough that Coach Knight felt that he could flash his sense of humor to welcome us to Bloomington. When we arrived at the gym to practice the night before the game, Coach Knight was waiting for us and wearing a god-awful sweater in the color of pale orange—no doubt tweaking Coach Newton and us by referencing the colors of the University of Tennessee (whose coach, Don DeVoe, had been a college teammate of Knight's at Ohio State and then an assistant under him at Army in the '60s).

Part of what had made *A Season on the Brink* so riveting was the near-constant drama that surrounded the program. And we encountered some preceding the IU rematch. The same night that we beat North Carolina, Indiana lost an overtime thriller to Kentucky, aided by a missed one-and-one and a turnover late in overtime by Smart. The game was the latest in a series of subpar performances for the NCAA hero. As Knight wrote later, the NCAA-winning basket "detracted greatly from Smart's approach and work ethic his senior year." So, Knight benched Smart for our game. Whether he would play at all was unclear; he was not going to be in the starting lineup.

As Coach Newton was fond of saying, a team must "fight through the distractions," and the benching of the opponent's star player certainly qualified as a distraction. You prepare for a team under the assumption that the opponent's players are healthy and available to play. You must adjust on the fly when, for whatever reason, there is a significant change in the opponent's roster. Having said that, you want to take advantage of a star's absence, and we had a great opportunity to do that against Indiana. One thing was certain—Coach Knight was no BS'er and was not one who would announce a benching and then put the player in a couple of minutes into the game; that's not much of a punishment. If Smart really was going to be benched, he would be down for much of the game, perhaps all of it.

Assembly Hall is one of the great college basketball venues. Then, as now, Indiana would sell out almost every game, and we played before a full house of 17,028. Unfortunately, we seemed a little awed by the surroundings, and played very poorly in the first half against the Smart-less Hoosiers, falling behind by as many as 16 points before rallying to close the deficit to five, 37-32, at the half. Smart sat out the entire first half and finally entered the game to a rousing ovation from the Assembly Hall faithful with about 10 minutes to go and the Hoosiers still clinging to a small lead. A Jay Edwards trey gave the Hoosiers a 58-53 lead with just under eight minutes to play. But the Hoosiers' offense then went cold, and we took advantage. At the 4:48 mark, my two free throws gave us our first (and, as it turned out, only) lead of the night at 59-58. Both teams traded fruitless possessions for the next couple of minutes until Smart hit a jumper that put the Hoosiers up one just inside the three-minute mark. Their defense was too tough, and our offense was not up to the task. We scored only two points after my free throws; the Hoosiers prevailed 63-61, and we sustained our first loss of the season.

Perdue greatly improved his NBA draft stock that night: he made 12 of his 17 field goal attempts and led all players with 27 points and 11 rebounds. But the rest of the team combined for only 11 field goals in 33 attempts, and no one else hit double figures; I was next in line with only nine points—quite a comedown from the 26 the year before against the Hoosiers, and I missed six of my nine field goal attempts. We also didn't help our cause by missing eight of our 18 free-throw attempts and committing 18 turnovers. Callaway, who had been injured and did not play in the '86 game in Nashville, led IU with 19 points, while Garrett added 12 points, 10 boards, and four blocks. Smart took just two shots but made them both, including the crucial go-ahead jumper late.

Still, we had acquitted ourselves admirably in our first road game of the season; we had gone toe-to-toe with the defending national champions at their place and lost only by a field goal. The loss was disappointing, but not crushing. As he had after the game in Nashville, Coach Knight paid a visit to our locker room after the game. He complimented us on our play and wished us luck for the remainder of the season. Then he said something I'll never forget: "I'm not sure the better team won the game." I thought that was the craziest thing I'd ever heard. They were the defending national champs with three titles in the previous 12 seasons; we hadn't won anything as a program during that span. Incredibly, as events would ultimately prove, Coach Knight was exactly right.

After the drama and tension of the North Carolina and Indiana games, we had a 10-day break to focus on final fall exams before the winter holidays. Coming out of that, the non-conference schedule was rather anticlimactic; these were tune-ups for the SEC schedule. First up was Ohio University, and after ending the first half tied at 39, we broke loose for 54 points in the second half and cruised to a 93-77 victory.

Two nights later, we beat Morehead State, from the Ohio Valley Conference, 81-73. With the Eagles surrounding Wilbur all night, Will was held to eight points (attempting only five shots from the field), one of only two games all season where he was held under double figures. But the guards picked up the slack, paced by Draud's 18, Booker's 14, and my 12. The team's shooting statistics were truly bizarre: we attempted 60 field goals and made exactly 30, with perfect division between twos and threes: 15 two-point field goals and 15 three-point field goals. We were 15-for-32 from three-point range and 15-for-28 from inside the arc, and those stats drew an odd rebuke from *Sports Illustrated* a couple of weeks later: "Does anyone think this three-point business has gone a little too far? In its 81-73 victory over Morehead State on December 21, Vanderbilt attempted more treys than deuces, 32 to 28. The Commodores made 15 of the former and 15 of the latter." That opening question was intended to be rhetorical, but it shouldn't have been: it would have been terrible coaching to have five good shooters, most of whom were left open for most of the game, not attempt the treys.

We had weathered both final exams and the early part of our schedule in fine fashion. Unfortunately, things were about to take a severe downturn as 1988 began.

5

MERRY CHRISTMAS, UNHAPPY NEW YEAR

I
"Holidays must end as you know"
—*10,000 Maniacs, "Verdi Cries"* ('87)

The Morehead game led into the holiday break. Coach Newton gave the players a three-day vacation to go home to their families for Christmas. Typically, we would return either on Christmas night or the following afternoon to begin preparations for our holiday tournament, the Music City Invitational Tournament. A distinguishing feature of the tourney (and playing off its title) was that a country music star served as honorary chairman of the tourney. The chairmen were well known in the country music community: in 1985, the chairman was Richard Sterban, the great bass singer of the Oak Ridge Boys (who were big Vandy basketball fans), and in 1986 it was Larry Gatlin and the Gatlin Brothers, who were one of country music's most successful acts in the '80s. For the 1987 edition, the honorary chairman was Steve Wariner.

Our opponent in the opening round was East Carolina. We showed no rust from the layoff and jumped on them early, rolling to a 99-63 victory. We nailed 13 three-pointers, and Charles Mayes led a balanced attack with 17 points. The win matched us against Cornell for the MCIT title.

᷽

We played at least one Ivy League team each year, and C.M. always scheduled one of that league's top teams. We played two of the Ivies in 1985–86, Penn and Princeton—at the time, the ruling class of that league. We beat Penn at home and then braved both the holiday exam period and snowstorms in Philadelphia (the airport we flew into) to take on Princeton, winning an ugly game 49-44 in the first game I ever led the team in scoring (with an extremely modest 12 points). One of the top reserves on that Princeton team was John Thompson III, the longtime Georgetown coach who coached his team to the 2007 Final Four.

Penn came to Nashville in 1985, so we paid a visit to Philly in December 1986 for a return matchup. The game fell, again, during the exam period, and just after we had beaten Indiana at Memorial. The game was played in the historic Palestra. Penn was a good team that would make the NCAAs that year as the Ivy League champion. In a hard-fought game, Perdue, who scored 29 points (19 in the second half), put us ahead 63-61 with five minutes to play. But the Quakers spurted again to lead 68-65 just inside the two-minute mark. Perdue scored again and was fouled, but he missed the tying free throw. Penn, however, traveled upon grabbing the rebound. With the new possession, I hit a 17-footer from the corner to give us a 69-68 lead with 32 seconds to play. Penn's two free throws gave the Quakers a 70-69 lead with 20 seconds remaining. As usual, Coach Newton didn't call timeout, and logically wanted us to get the ball to Perdue. It seemed that all five Penn players were surrounding Will, however, and we kept passing the ball around the perimeter as the seconds melted away. Finally, with just a couple of seconds to play, I had the ball around the top of the key and had no choice but to make something happen, which I did, taking a dribble inside the key, launching a 17-footer, and watching it swish through the net as time expired, my first real "buzzer beater" and giving us a 71-70 win. A game-winning shot in a venue as historic as The Palestra was, and remains, a great thrill.

A little over a year after the Penn game, our opponent in the MCIT final was Cornell, which, like the Quakers the year before, would go on to win the Ivy League title—in the Big Red's case, making its first appearance in the NCAA tournament since 1954. Against Cornell for the MCIT title, we led 66-43 midway through the second half, but they rallied to slice the lead to six with just over six minutes left. But the Big Red had no answer for Perdue, who, as he had done against Penn the previous year, feasted on a relatively undersized Ivy League team and scored a season-high 31 points, adding 12 boards, in a 95-79 win. Not surprisingly, Will was named the tournament's most valuable player, and he was joined on the five-man all-tourney team by Mayes and me, as Chuck and I each totaled 30 points in the two games, Chuck scoring 13 points and pulling down nine rebounds in the final, while I contributed 17 and four. The memento given each MCIT all-tourney player was unique: keeping with the Music City theme, the player received a framed gold record with the year and the participants, a much better and more original award than a trophy.

My favorite memory of the Cornell, however, game didn't involve the game itself. For the only time in my four years, Mike Petrone led the walk-through for the opponent. The players affectionately referred to Coach Petrone as "Petro," with or without the "Coach," and we still do; it's a term of endearment. His official title was "volunteer assistant coach," which is an amorphous title seemed to mean all-around factotum for the other coaches. But Petro brought valuable experience and character to the program. He had been the head coach at Father Ryan High School, which at the time was across the street from Vanderbilt, and averaged about 20 wins a year there. He continued to teach at Ryan even after becoming a volunteer assistant under Coach Newton and worked part-time as a counselor for the Metropolitan Nashville Sheriff's Department (he taught criminal justice at Ryan). So, in effect, Petro was working three jobs.

Petro also played a valuable role as a conduit between the players and the "non-volunteer" coaches. Players felt they could confide in Petro on subjects they might not feel comfortable talking to Coach Newton or Coach Bostick about—personal issues, academic issues, or anything else that was bothering them. We would seek advice from Petro on how and whether to disclose a sensitive issue to Coach Newton, and we knew that Petro would have our backs. That made him an invaluable member of the Vanderbilt basketball family.

Rarely would those significant contributions translate into meaningful responsibility for game preparation. Generally, Coach Bostick would oversee the scouting and preparation for the opponent. Coach Elliott would also lead the preparation at other times, and occasionally Coach Martin would take the lead. The responsible coach would put together the scouting report on the opponent, detailing the strengths, weaknesses, and tendencies of the opponent's starters and key reserves, as well as the team itself. Then that coach would lead the walk-through as part of our preparation.

Well, Petro had that responsibility for Cornell, likely due to the games on consecutive nights immediately following Christmas. And, in truth, while Cornell was a decent team, there was little chance we were going to lose to the Big Red. The one thing I'll never forget about the walk-through was Petro describing a Cornell player, whose name I clearly remember over 30 years later—Wolfgang Florin. Equally memorable was Petro's introduction of Mr. Florin and this zinger based on Petro's assessment of Wolfgang's game: "Wolfgang Florin—his name says a lot about the way he plays." I think that was intended to be a compliment to Florin's hard-nosed style of play, but it made no sense to me. I had to stifle a chuckle, and then I looked at Coach Bostick, who was standing next to Petro, and we both nearly lost it right there. I'm still not sure how Wolfgang Florin's name was connected, or said "a lot about," the way he played, but I guess Petro's scouting report worked: Florin, an all-Ivy player, scored only seven points in the game, and Petro would go 1-0 as Scout Czar for 1987–88.

II

"Let's play wild like wildcats do"
—Robert Plant, "Tall Cool One" ('88)

With the MCIT behind us, all but one of our remaining regular season games would be against SEC opponents. The Southeastern Conference was formed in 1932 with 13 charter members for basketball: Alabama, Auburn, Florida, Georgia, Georgia

Tech, Kentucky, LSU, Mississippi, Mississippi State, Sewanee, Tennessee, Tulane, and Vanderbilt. Over the years, Tech, Sewanee, and Tulane left the conference, leaving ten schools, which made up the conference's membership in the 1980s (and until the early 1990s, when Arkansas and South Carolina joined, and 2012, when the additions of Missouri and Texas A&M made the SEC a 14-member conference).

In the ten-team SEC of the late 1980s, each team would play a "double round robin," meaning each team would play the other nine teams twice each, once at home and once on the road, for a total of 18 conference games. With such a heavy conference schedule, the coming of the new year almost always meant that conference play was underway. And our first conference game for the '87–'88 season would be something of a showcase.

The omnipresence of ESPN, Fox, and other sports networks in the twenty-first century makes it easy to forget that the late 1980s were the Dark Ages by comparison. There was only one ESPN channel, and the network had been on the air for less than a decade in 1988. Thus, it was a big deal to have one of the team's games televised on ESPN. So it was that our first SEC game was to be aired by ESPN on December 31, 1987—a New Year's Eve party in Rupp Arena against the Kentucky Wildcats, ranked #2 in the country. The Wildcats would be our third top-10 opponent in our first nine games, following North Carolina and Indiana.

On December 31, 1987, Rupp Arena was exactly 11 years and one month old, having opened on November 30, 1976. The man for whom it was named, Adolph Rupp, died in December 1977. That season, the program he had built would win the school's fifth national title in April 1978 in St. Louis. Now, in 1987, Eddie Sutton, in his third year at the helm in Lexington, had assembled a deep and talented team that clearly had the potential to add title number 6 to the school's resume. The 'Cats had the best backcourt we played against that season—senior Ed Davender and a sophomore from Owensboro, Kentucky, named Rex Chapman. They had the best power forward in the SEC, fifth-year senior Winston Bennett, who had missed the previous season with a knee injury. They had an underrated center in Rob Lock, and the rest of the team was full of talented supporting players—Cedric Jenkins, Richard Madison, and highly-touted freshmen Eric Manuel and LeRon Ellis.

But we were good too, and we came to play. We matched them point for point, and then some. Unfortunately, Perdue was in foul trouble the entire game, eventually fouling out and playing only 28 minutes. But we stayed with the Wildcats all the way, jumping out to a quick 7-2 lead, and Wilcox's long three-pointer just before the buzzer gave us a 39-33 lead at the break.

We kept the pressure on in the second half, using the three-point shot as a weapon and hitting nine of our 18 attempts for the game. Booker was particularly brilliant, hitting six of his 10 attempts, and his three with just inside eight minutes to play gave us a 65-56 lead. But then the Wildcats, led by Chapman, exploded for 11 straight, including a damaging, lightning-quick sequence where first Booker and then I turned the ball over against their press, which the 'Cats quickly converted into baskets. By the 4:23 mark, they had taken a one-point lead. We still hung tough—a Reid basket tied it at 67 and my deuce tied it at 69, but Chapman scored again to put the 'Cats up to stay. I made one of two free throws at the 1:20 mark to close our deficit to two at 74-72, but Davender and Chapman combined for four free throws to put it out of reach. The final score was 81-74.

It was a disappointing loss for sure. Perdue, Booker, and I each scored 18 points, and Booker and I combined for 11 assists. But Will's foul trouble hurt us on the boards: he had only five rebounds, and we were outrebounded 40-30. And his counterpart at center, Lock, matched Will's 18 points with 18 of his own while also pulling down 10 boards, while Bennett, who played all 40 minutes, scored 10 and snagged a remarkable 17 rebounds. The backcourt of Davender and Chapman combined for 45 points (Davender 24, Chapman 21), and after a terrible first half Chapman had a great last 10 minutes. And, as always seemed to happen in Rupp Arena, the home team dominated the free-throw line: UK shot 26, making 19, while we shot only 10 (Perdue and I took them all). In any event, we wouldn't have to wait too long for the rematch. UK was to come to "our place" before the end of January, and a lot could happen in those four weeks. And did.

III

"Sometimes you kick, sometimes you get kicked"
—INXS, "Kick" ('87–'88)

We had nearly a full week after the UK game to prepare for our next game, which was against LSU. From that point forward, we would settle into a routine for the remainder of the regular season—game on Wednesday, game on Saturday, game on Wednesday, etc. Our one day off would be Sunday, followed by a hard practice on Monday, a lighter practice on Tuesday to prepare for the Wednesday opponent, a tougher practice on Thursday, and again a lighter practice on Friday to prepare for the Saturday opponent. Typically, for road games, those Tuesday and Friday practices would be on the opponent's home floor.

In 1987–88, LSU head coach Dale Brown likely was at the peak of his renown. Brown, a native of North Dakota, had come to LSU in 1972 after several years as an assistant coach at Utah State and Washington State. He took over the moribund LSU program and, by the late 1970s, had turned it into a winner. In fact, by the time he retired in the mid-1990s, he had the second longest consecutive tenure at an SEC school, behind only Kentucky's Adolph Rupp. He even appeared on the cover of *Sports Illustrated* in November 1985—a rarity for a college basketball coach.

That 1985–86 season turned into something special for Brown and the Tigers. In March 1986, he coached the seemingly short-handed Tigers to a tremendous upset over Kentucky in the regional final in Atlanta and thus made the Final Four as a #11 seed—the lowest-seeded team ever to make the Final Four to that point. Then, in 1987, with 13 losses going into the NCAA tournament and being seeded 10th in the Midwest Regional, the Tigers beat second-seeded Temple and third-seeded De-Paul, making it all the way to the regional final and coming within one second of consecutive, improbable Final Four runs until Indiana's Ricky Callaway tipped in the game-winning basket at the buzzer, sending the Hoosiers to New Orleans and the eventual NCAA title.

The Tigers' exploits in 1986 and 1987 confirmed my ultimate opinion of Brown—he was at his best when his team was the underdog, or at least when he could tell his players that they were the underdogs. When great things were expected, as they were a couple of years later with phenomenal talents like Shaquille O'Neal, Chris Jackson, and Stanley Roberts, he and the team didn't rise to the occasion. That LSU outfit won zero SEC titles and a total of one NCAA tournament game in Shaq's three years in Baton Rouge, which is hard to fathom.

But in January 1988, Brown could tell his players that they were fighting long odds against Vanderbilt—the Tigers were only 4-4 and had lost four of their previous five contests. And, always looking for a cause on which to base further motivation, by an incredible coincidence Brown was given two against us that season, the first of which occurred two days before our first contest, scheduled for January 7.

Two days before the game, a pickup game had taken place at the First Church of the Nazarene in Pasadena, California, one of thousands of pickup games that surely took place that day, as every day. But this one was different—a 40-year-old participant by the name of Pete Maravich had played, collapsed on the court, and died of an abnormal heart defect.

Pistol Pete was the greatest Tiger of them all, and probably the greatest player the SEC has ever seen. His records were as hard to comprehend then as they are today: in his senior season of 1969–70, he averaged over 44 points per game in an era with no shot clock and no three-point line. He won the Naismith Trophy as the College Player of the Year. His death was a shock to the basketball world, but particularly to the LSU basketball family, and it supplied extra motivation for a "win one for Pete" mantra from Brown. In fact, the LSU players wore black bands on the shoulder straps of their jerseys as a tribute to The Pistol.

Regardless of the reasons or motivation, we came out incredibly flat and played what would be our worst game of the season and unquestionably our worst game at Memorial in my four years. We seemed to be playing in slow motion all night, which was reflected by the football-like halftime score of 24-16, Tigers. And things did not improve in the second half; the ugly final score was 51-39. That's right, 39 points— exactly half of what would be our SEC-leading season average of 78.7. It was the only time in my four years at Vanderbilt that we were booed by the Memorial Gym crowd. I was the only player in double figures, scoring 16 points—over 40% of the team's offense. I was a modest 6 for 11 from the field, but the rest of the team was a dreadful 10 for 39. As Coach Newton would say, it was a total team breakdown—which is another way of saying that it was an embarrassment. Most importantly, in our first SEC home game, we had failed to protect the home court, which put us in a hole right off the bat, with two road games coming up.

The first of those road games was in Knoxville at the University of Tennessee. This would be our first game in UT's new facility, Thompson-Boling Arena. I had really liked the old gym, the Stokely Center, which seated somewhere between 12,000–13,000. But UT apparently was in some sort of contest with the University of Kentucky and felt compelled to build a bigger and better facility than Rupp Arena. While Thompson-Boling has a slighter larger capacity, UT overlooked the fact that Rupp is almost always full, while Thompson-Boling would not be full nearly that often (except, of course, when UK comes to town).

In any event, our struggles continued against UT, though we showed a little more spark than we had displayed against LSU. Will submitted a strong 22-point, 11-rebound performance, hitting 10 of his 12 shots from the field. But we again misfired from long range, hitting only two of 10 three-point attempts (making us 4 for 18 in the last two games), while UT outrebounded us 53-40; the final score was 80-72, Vols.

After a promising 7-1 start, our season threatened to unravel, just as had happened the previous season when we began 9-1, only to go 7-13 for the rest of the regular season. An 0-3 start in SEC play had everyone down—coaches, players, fans. If we couldn't reverse things quickly, the season would be lost.

6

TURNAROUND

I

"You're fighting with lost confidence, all expectations gone"
—Swing Out Sister, "Breakout" ('87)

We trudged into Oxford, Mississippi, on January 12 for our game the next night with Ole Miss without much confidence or swagger. People had begun to write us off as the "same old Vanderbilt," meaning a team that played hard and did things the right way, but simply couldn't compete at a high level in the SEC. Coach Newton's pregame talk took more of a bemused tone than one of anger or frustration. "I am so convinced that we can compete in this league," he said. It was just a matter of reclaiming our confidence. With an 0-for-3 start to the SEC, we had to find that confidence against the Rebels, who had blown us out in Oxford in '87.

Ole Miss was led by star guard Roderick Barnes, who was a great success story. He averaged only 1.1 points a game as a freshman, but he started every game in his last three seasons and, by the time he was a senior in 1987–88, he was one of the league's best guards. Plus, he knew (and knows) a lot about basketball, as he later proved in returning to his alma mater to coach the Rebels to 27 victories and the Sweet Sixteen in 2001, winning Naismith Coach of the Year honors in the process. The Rebels also had a fine center in Sean Murphy, whom C.M. had recruited for Vandy. But a small problem intervened—Sean's father, Ed, was named head coach at Ole Miss in 1986. He somehow persuaded his son to join him the next year.

Searching for the right combination of players, Coach Newton juggled the starting lineup again, this time more drastically. As Book was pressing (3 for 21 from the field, total of nine points in the last two games), the coach inserted Derrick Wilcox into the starting lineup. Then, at forward, he kept Eric Reid in the lineup but inserted Steve Grant as the other starter in place of Kornet. In truth, we didn't play much better against Ole Miss than we had played against UT, but Ole Miss wasn't as talented as the Vols. The game was close all the way; we were tied 29-29 at the half and Ole Miss forged and maintained a slight lead in the second half. The Rebels' lead was 55-50 inside two-and-a-half minutes when Booker hit a three to cut our deficit to two. But Barnes answered with a basket, the final two of his game-high 25 points, to push the lead back to four with about 90 seconds remaining. A Perdue layup cut the Ole Miss lead back to two at 57-55 with 56 seconds left. We called timeout.

Coming out of the timeout, Ole Miss's inbounds passer, Sean Murphy, had trouble inbounding the ball within the required five seconds after receiving the ball from the official. The rules at the time (1) prohibited coaches from calling timeout (unlike today, where either players or coaches can signal for time); (2) required the inbounds passer to call timeout, if he wished to do so, within four seconds, not five (unlike today); and (3) required that the ball reach the hands of a player inbounds within five seconds, as opposed to merely requiring the ball to leave the inbounds passer's hands within five seconds, as is the current rule. All those things, and a quick count by the official, combined to produce a five-second call against Ole Miss, turning the ball back over to us with under a minute to play. That call was probably the most favorable call we had all year—in film study the next day, we watched this sequence multiple times and counted the seconds along with the referee, and we never even made it to four seconds, let alone five, before the official signaled the turnover. "I thought it was a quick whistle," Perdue said after the game, "but we'll take it." Ole Miss coach Murphy agreed: "Other coaches in the league…timed that five-seconds on film and no one has come up with more than 4.2 seconds. I mean, even a third-grader can count to five." In other words, we had been given a huge break.

Still, we needed to capitalize on the break because we were still behind by two. Given the deficit, Coach Newton used a three-guard alignment with Booker, Draud, and me. With about 35 seconds left, Draud launched a three; it missed. Booker claimed the long rebound and kicked it to me; as an Ole Miss player left Book and rushed to guard me, I sent the ball right back to Book, who now was standing behind the three-point line with just under 30 seconds to play and had an open shot that would give us the lead and, hopefully, a season-changing victory. Book and I had known each other for 40 months at that moment, though it seemed much longer than that, such was our familiarity and friendship with one another.

I made my official visit to Vanderbilt in September 1984, the fall of my senior year in high school. As with nearly all fall visits for basketball recruits, the weekend was planned around a Vanderbilt home football game, and included visits with Coach Newton and his staff, events with the current Vandy hoopsters, and other assorted on-campus parties and gatherings. This was a big recruiting weekend for Coach Newton and his staff; I was one of five high school seniors visiting the campus. Another was Mark Griffin, a great guy who played at Union City in northwest Tennessee, not that far from where I played in Marshall County, Kentucky. Mark, a 6'8"

forward with excellent three-point shooting range, opted for the University of Tennessee. Another recruit was Marty Hensley, a center from Indiana who was clearly a project; he ultimately went to North Carolina, where he played sparingly. Another recruit, point guard Gerald Harris from Chattanooga, wound up at Middle Tennessee State University. The fourth recruit I met that weekend was Barry Booker.

Barry and I didn't see a whole lot of each other that weekend; we didn't get a chance to speak much at the various events, which were crowded, and his player host and my player host took us to different parties on campus. I found out that weekend that he had an older sister, Karen, who was a star player for the Lady Commodores. Certainly, I saw more than enough to realize that he had a splendid personality and great character. I assumed he could play a little ball too or he wouldn't have been there. I'll never forget our brief shared elevator ride in the hotel on Sunday morning as the weekend events were about to conclude. One of us said to the other, "So, what do you think?" The reply: "I think this is the place for me." "Yeah, me too." So, Book and I essentially committed to Vanderbilt—and to each other—that Sunday morning in Nashville.

Only later did I learn the amazing details about Book's family. His father co-owned a gas station in downtown Franklin. And Karen was only one Barry's siblings; he was the youngest of the 12. As Barry once quipped, "I'm glad they didn't stop with 11 kids." So am I, and so are all Vanderbilt fans! All 12 Booker children graduated from college, and many of them earned graduate degrees (including Barry, who holds an MBA from Vanderbilt's Owen Business School). Barry's parents and siblings made sure that Coach Newton had his priorities straight for the family's youngest child when the coach made a home visit to recruit Barry. "When I visited their home, about seven or eight of his brothers and sisters were in the room, too," Coach Newton recalled. "Their questions were excellent. Not about playing time or if I could make him a guard. [Mr. Booker] asked me, 'How are you going to prepare him for life?'" Pretty well, as it turned out.

Barry was the best athlete on our team. In high school at Franklin's Battle Ground Academy, he lettered in baseball and track in addition to basketball. On the diamond, he stole 31 bases and went 5-1 as a pitcher, and our mutual love of baseball is one of our many shared interests. Barry's athleticism and upbeat personality mask the fact that he may be the most competitive person I've ever met. "I'm a competitive person," Book said in 1988. "I always play to win." Whether it was pool, ping-pong, spades, poker, dice (as Draud recalled, "he would like to shoot dice, and he would take everybody's money"), you name it—he was competitive and stellar at everything he attempted.

Nevertheless, Barry had to make a difficult transition on the hardwood when he came to Vanderbilt—he had to learn how to play point guard, which had not been his position in high school. In fact, at BGA he had played inside, often with his back to the basket. The transition to point guard took a lot of time and hard work.

In our freshman year of 1985–86, Barry apprenticed under senior Darrell Dulaney while I backed up the senior 2-guard, Jeff Gary, but injuries to the incumbents meant that we started games as freshmen—12 for me and two for Book.

Book and I became full-time starters the next season, which coincided with the introduction of the three-point line. And Book was phenomenal from behind the arc; "You really felt like the ball was going to go in each time he shot it," I once observed. Book himself said, "I feel like I ought to hit half of my wide open jump shots," and that's exactly what he did in '86–'87—he hit 85 of 170 three-point attempts for an even 50%, a single-season mark for Vanderbilt bested only by Billy McCaffrey's 51.2% mark in '92–'93. And Book's career three-point shooting percentage of 46% remains the best in Vandy's history—an incredible achievement given the quality of three-point shooters that have come through the program since the three-point line was introduced in 1986.

In fact, Book's three-point shooting prowess was one reason I took, and made, so many game-winning shots. If your opponent needs a three to win or tie, who should you focus on defending first? The 50% three-point shooter, of course. I didn't really shoot that many threes; I was more of a slasher and driver ("I played forward my last two years [in high school]," I commented the previous year, "and I liked to drive, spin, head fake, and shoot. It wasn't until I got here [VU] that I worked on extending my shooting range."), but a couple of dramatic, memorable treys have left the impression that I was a three-point marksman. But that really was Book's forte. In fact, I attempted 282 treys in the three years we played when the rule was in effect; Book shot nearly twice as many, 535.

That is not to say that Book didn't take or make big shots. He directly had a hand in some of our most memorable wins in our four years—Tennessee ('86), Louisville ('88), and Georgia ('89) were examples of Book's clutch play late in games that facilitated the ultimate victory. So, when we desperately needed a big shot in chilly Oxford with 30 seconds to play and trailing by two, without hesitation I passed the ball back to Barry.

ঌ

Book went up for the three-pointer and, in one of the biggest shots of his career (and one of the biggest by anyone in our shared four years in Nashville), he nailed it to put us ahead by one, 58-57. We held Ole Miss scoreless on the other end, and Book added two free throws after an Ole Miss foul to give us a three-point lead, and that was how it ended: 60-57, Commodores, and we finally got into the win column in SEC play at 1-3.

Coach Newton's decision to bring Book off the bench took some pressure off Barry, and he responded with 13 points, tying Draud for team-high honors. The game was hardly a thing of beauty, and our 60 points in the win was by far our lowest output in a victory all season. Still, there should be no such thing as an ugly win, and now the schedule was about to turn in our favor, and we needed to build on the Ole Miss momentum.

II

"It's gonna take patience and time...to do it right"
—George Harrison, "Got My Mind Set on You" ('87–'88)

The first opponent in a seven-of-nine home game stretch was Alabama, a team we had not beaten in my first two years at Vandy. The Crimson Tide's coach, Wimp Sanderson, had been an assistant under Coach Newton during C.M.'s 12 years in Tuscaloosa and had been an assistant for most of the '60s before C.M. arrived as the head coach. Wimp got the head job when C.M. resigned in 1980, and he had maintained the high quality of the program his predecessor had established, reaching a peak the previous season of '86–'87 with an outright SEC championship and SEC tourney title. That team was loaded: seniors Mark Gottfried, Jim Farmer, and Terry Coner, and, especially, junior Derrick McKey were terrific players. Unfortunately for Wimp, all four were gone by fall 1987—most distressingly McKey, who was forced to forego his senior season when he signed with an agent in spring 1987. So '87–'88 was a rebuilding year for the Tide, and it would be the only season of the Sanderson-coached Alabama teams that would fail to make either the NIT or NCAA tournaments. The only returning starter from the championship team was the excellent junior forward, Michael Ansley.

Alabama came into the game winless in three SEC games—but then again, that was our record heading into Ole Miss, so no team could be taken lightly. Happily, we began to show some signs that the December version of the team had not gone on permanent vacation. We led 32-24 at the half, gradually stretched the lead in the second half, and cruised to a 76-60 victory. Encouragingly, the offense began to show signs of life: we shot a blistering 58% from the field and 86% from the line (missing only four of 29 free-throw attempts). The Tide made a determined effort to pack their defense around Perdue, a wise strategy given our recent struggles from the perimeter. As a result, Will attempted only four shots from the field, a season low. But he made all four, and he hit seven of eight foul shots for a team-high 15 points, leading the team with nine rebounds as well. I added 14 points, while Booker and Draud scored 12 each as we broke out of our long-range shooting slump by hitting seven of our 12 three-point attempts. Alabama Coach Sanderson was sufficiently impressed with our performance and declared, "They're a threat to win this league"—quite an endorsement for a team with a 2-3 league record.

The Alabama win was nice, but we considered the next opponent to be a greater test: Georgia. Like 'Bama, the Bulldogs had swept us the previous season; unlike

'Bama, neither game was that close (in fact, the margins of our past three games were 31, 23, and 16 points, all Georgia routs), and they had many of their best players back, including their two stars, guard Willie Anderson and center Alec Kessler. Anderson was 6'7" but seemed to have a wingspan much longer than that. The coach of the Dawgs, Hugh Durham, who took over the program in 1978, would coach the Dawgs for 17 seasons, 10 of which resulted in a trip to a postseason tourney—five NCAAs and five NITs. In 1988, UGA was only five years removed from an improbable run to the 1983 Final Four.

The Dawgs' visit to Memorial in '88 would be a reversal of recent fortune for the teams. In fact, after about five minutes, we turned the game into a complete blowout: ahead 9-8, we reeled off 19 straight points to take a 28-8 lead and built it to an incredible 27 points, 42-15, late in the first half. We led by 19 at the half, 46-27, and coasted to a 92-77 victory.

It was important for us to deliver a message to the Dawgs after the three straight blowouts we had suffered at their hands. "I felt like we owed them a little something," said Booker. Perdue, who had a great game with 22 points, 15 rebounds, and three blocked shots, agreed: "The fact that they had beat[en] us the last three times was a definite factor for us. We veteran players had never had much luck against Georgia, and we wanted to make sure we got this one." I backed up Wilbur with 18 points. In an eight-day stretch starting in Oxford, we had evened our SEC record at 3-3, and had improved our overall record to 10-4.

With three wins in a row, we took our newfound confidence on the road to Auburn. The Tigers had been coached since 1978–79 by Sonny Smith, who built Auburn into a formidable program in the '80s. They had three great players spread throughout the decade, each of whom had a long and productive NBA career: Charles Barkley in the early '80s, Chuck Person in mid-'80s, and Chris Morris in the late '80s. The three were never on the same Auburn team, but Barkley and Person overlapped for a couple of years, as did Person and Morris. Person was a senior in my freshman season of 1985–86, and he put on the greatest shooting display I have ever seen: in our final home game of the season, he scored 40 points without the benefit of a three-point line, and he would have scored at least 50 if there had been one. Book and I, watching from the bench, swore that his heel was touching the out-of-bounds line on a couple of those jumpers. That was probably the best Auburn team of the decade—the Tigers advanced to the Elite Eight before losing to eventual national champion Louisville in the regional final. The Tigers returned to the NCAAs the next year and again lost to the eventual national champion (Indiana).

The 1987–88 edition of the Tigers had great potential as well when the season began. Morris and 6'7" center Jeff Moore, both sophomores on the '86 Elite Eight team, were now seniors and all-SEC players. And completing a three-headed monster was Mike Jones, a talented junior forward who averaged over 20 points a game. But the Tigers were hit with a double whammy over the holidays—Jones was declared academically ineligible on December 28, and Moore broke his finger two days later and would be out for a few weeks.

The Tigers, however, rallied in the absence of the two stars. A little over a week after we lost to Kentucky at Rupp Arena, the shorthanded Tigers went into Rupp and stole a 53-52 win over the top-ranked Wildcats. Plus, Auburn had been the only team to date to post a conference win over Florida. But this game would prove the quality of our depth. The five starters combined for only 39 points, and only one was in double figures—barely (Perdue, with 10). In fact, Will scored 10 of our first 12 points on Moore's replacement, true freshman Matt Geiger, and did not score again because the Tigers began to surround him every time he touched the ball. That strategy worked, and we held a tenuous 29-28 lead at the half.

The problem with putting two or three players on Will was that someone would be left with open shots. With five effective long-range shooters on the team, chances were strong that at least one of them would take advantage of the open looks. And that person in this game was Charles Mayes, who came off the bench to have his best game of the season—20 points, driven by 6-of-11 shooting from beyond the arc on mostly open looks while Chris Morris was (overly) preoccupied with Perdue. At one point in the second half, Chuck scored 17 of our 22 points, 15 on treys, the last of which put us up 68-61 inside the five-minute mark. We held on to the lead down the stretch and came away with a big 75-71 win, pushing our record over .500 in the conference at 4-3.

After each game, win or lose, the players and coaches would join hands in the locker room for a prayer, to be spoken by someone of Coach Newton's choosing. After the Auburn win, he chose me. Normally, I would never mention a game or upcoming opponent—such matters are trivial in the larger scheme of things that might be happening in the world at any given moment—but this time I couldn't resist looking ahead to the next game, and, hey, it couldn't hurt to ask for a little help or divine intervention, could it? I closed the prayer with "Lord, help us to beat Kentucky!"

7

REDEMPTION

The rematch with Kentucky was the first of three in a row at home, and a great opportunity to prove that we were for real. Coach Newton was on edge—at our day-of-game shootaround, he came roaring into the locker room seething at a column in *The Tennessean*, which detailed Coach Newton's record against his alma mater while at Vandy—and it was an oh-fer, 13 straight losses since he took over at Vandy in 1981. Incredibly, I had been an eyewitness to Vanderbilt's last hardwood victory over Kentucky.

I

"The circus comes to town"
—*Def Leppard, "Animal" ('87–'88)*

It's hard—impossible, frankly—for a Kentuckian to describe to a non-Kentuckian the incredible hold that basketball has on the state. One former UK coach, Tubby Smith, said that "basketball is a way of life in Kentucky—a religion, really." Tubby's predecessor, Rick Pitino, observed that Kentuckians "eat, sleep, and drink the game of basketball." Yet another former UK coach, Joe B. Hall (unlike Pitino and Smith, a native Kentuckian), astutely described the grass-roots phenomenon of basketball in Kentucky:

> What you have to understand about Kentucky basketball is that it started in the high schools in the rural communities. The schools were so small they couldn't field football teams, but they could support a basketball team.... Going to the games was a social function in these towns, and basketball became a way of life. So there was a love of the game at the high school level and it carried over to the university.

It seems that everything in the state revolves around basketball, and not necessarily University of Kentucky basketball—though that is certainly at the top of most people's minds much of the time. The University of Louisville and UK have combined for 27 Final Four appearances (UK 17, U of L 10) and 11 championships (UK eight, U of L three). Smaller colleges in the state (Murray State, Western Kentucky, and others) have rabid fan bases as well. And then there are the high school ranks, where the fans are just as passionate about their local teams as they are about the college teams.

The definitive text on this phenomenon, at least through the mid-'70s, is *Basketball: The Dream Game in Kentucky* by Dave Kindred, the renowned sportswriter, who was a sports reporter at the *Louisville Courier-Journal* in the mid-'70s. In his book, Kindred thoroughly explained basketball in Kentucky from high school to the pros (meaning the Kentucky Colonels, the state's ABA team during that league's decade-long challenge to the NBA from 1967 to 1976, though, critically for the Kentuckian's obsession with hoops, the state has never had an NBA team), emphasizing the state's college basketball successes and personalities with a clarity that is about as close as anyone can come to explaining the passion of basketball in the state of Kentucky.

UK fans are knowledgeable and travel well, a trait that annually is displayed at the SEC tournament, when UK fans seemingly fill three-quarters of the venue, whether it is Atlanta, New Orleans, Nashville, or, as was the case in the early 1980s, Birmingham, which was where the tournament was held the first few years after it was revived in 1979, including 1981. A friend's father somehow got tickets to the tournament, and he chaperoned three or four of us eighth-graders in Birmingham for a few days in March 1981. Naturally, we were rooting for the 'Cats, who were ranked in the top 10 in the country and led by 7'1" star Sam Bowie.

In a 10-team league, the tournament was structured so that the bottom four teams played on Thursday, with the two Thursday winners joining the top six in an eight-team, single-elimination tournament beginning on Friday. UK was in the top six, so it would play on Friday. Its opponent that day? Vanderbilt, which had beaten Mississippi State in the opening round on Thursday. I picked up on some of the internal drama at the time and learned more a few years later when I got to Vandy, but apparently fans and players were divided over the Commodores' coach, Richard Schmidt. Two of Vandy's all-time greats, both seniors, were playing their final games—Charles Davis and Mike Rhodes, formerly known as "Town and Country" when they each were averaging 18 to 20 points a game. But now they were both riding the bench, to the dismay (if not fury) of Vandy fans. So Vandy would play the top-10-ranked Wildcats with two of the school's all-time leading scorers playing limited minutes. Amazingly, it worked: in a shocking upset, the Commodores prevailed, 60-55, over the same Kentucky team that, just a couple of weeks earlier, had humiliated them in Rupp Arena, 80-48.

The UK victory would be the last win for Richard Schmidt at Vanderbilt. In the semifinals, Ole Miss thumped the 'Dores, 71-51, and went on to win its first (and, until 2013, only) SEC tourney title the next day behind point guard Sean Tuohy, whose family would later be immortalized in the book and film *The Blind Side*. Schmidt was fired and the athletic director, Roy Kramer, needed a big-name coach—and one with a spotless reputation—to come in and clean up the program (not unlike UK would need on a larger scale in 1989, in a bitter irony), and he lured C.M. Newton out of a one-year sabbatical from coaching (C.M. had worked at the SEC offices in Birmingham) to return to the SEC coaching wars.

Coach Newton had gone 0-for-13 against his alma mater in his first six-and-a-half years in Nashville, and he obviously didn't like to be reminded of it. In fact, I received similar treatment from the local newspaper back in the western Kentucky area; the paper wrote an article previewing the game with an emphasis on the large number of tickets my parents would request of the wonderful Lucy Jones and the Vandy ticket office, but the writer felt compelled to add a bar in the middle of the article, in large print: "Winless in 5 tries: The Commodores are 0-5 against Kentucky since Barry Goheen has been in a Vanderbilt uniform." Ouch! That line made it seem like I was the reason we had lost those five games.

In any event, that win in Birmingham in March 1981 with the naïve, left-handed eighth-grader in the stands remained the last Vandy win over UK. Now, seven years later as a junior at Vanderbilt, I wanted badly to end the drought.

II

"I want a shot at redemption"
—Paul Simon, "You Can Call Me Al" ('87)

The Wildcats had been somewhat inconsistent since our New Year's Eve game. They were 6-2 in the conference, and, surprisingly, both losses had been at Rupp Arena, to Auburn (53-52) and Florida (58-56). Still, Memorial was electric, as it always was (and is) with Kentucky in town. The atmosphere for this game had an even greater electricity; we had won four in a row and were starting to regain some of the national attention we had first attained in the win over North Carolina and near-miss at Indiana. We felt confident. We had almost beaten them in Lexington ("We should be 1-0 against them this year," I said before the game), so there was no reason we couldn't close the deal this time.

UK jumped to a quick 11-5 lead as we missed three of our first four three-point attempts, but Draud's entry into the game changed that; Scott nailed a trey to give us our first lead, and he hit another after a great hustle play by Grant to put us up 17-13, capping a 12-2 run, and his third trey of the half put us up five, 24-19. With 4:54 left in the half, we led 28-27. After a Wildcat basket put UK ahead 29-28, my conventional three-point play put us up two. Rex Chapman answered with a three to make it 32-31 UK, but our fast break off that trey broke Perdue open for a layup, which he made as he was fouled by Sean Sutton. Will missed the free throw, but Mayes rebounded. Booker then nailed a three to make it a five-point possession, and the gym practically exploded. We led 36-32, and when Book knocked down his third trey of the game on the next possession, our lead was seven. Perdue had two fouls, so Coach Newton wisely returned Will to the bench at the 2:40 mark for the remainder of the half. After two Rob Lock free throws, Mayes drained a three to make it 42-34. Two Chapman free throws and an Ed Davender jumper made it 42-38.

Just before the half came one of the biggest plays of the game. UK, holding for the final shot, gave the ball to Chapman for the last shot. He drove around me and elevated in the lane about eight feet from the basket. He crashed into Reid after the ball left his hand and was called for the charge, his critical third foul. Reid then sank both ends of the one-and-one to give us a six-point margin at the half, 44-38. The five-point trip and the last play of the half were enormous momentum-changers. Still, we had led by the same six-point margin at the half in Lexington and had been unable to finish off the 'Cats. We would need a complete final 20 minutes to win the game.

We opened the second half with my layup off a nice pass from Will for a 46-38 lead. UK scored four in a row to trim the lead to four, and Lock's dunk off an offensive rebound made it 46-44. Then came another huge call: double-teaming Mayes 30 feet from the basket, Chapman reached in and was called for his fourth foul, sending him to the bench with over 16 minutes remaining. A Perdunk off a great Wilcox feed extended the lead to four, but Wilcox and Grant picked up their fourth fouls on UK's next possession. After UK scored off the inbounds play, Mayes hit a three to make it 51-46. Unfortunately, Davender drew Booker's fourth foul with 15:05 remaining; as Draud and I, both Kentuckians, would be the backcourt for most of the remainder of the game, and we knew they would be emotional and memorable, one way or the other.

We led 52-46 after a Reid free throw, and in another key sequence in the ensuing possession, UK missed five shots from inside five feet before Perdue finally claimed the rebound, and Draud drained a three to give us our biggest lead, 55-46. But UK was a Top-10 team for a reason, and the 'Cats promptly scored six straight points to trim our lead to three. Draud's two free throws made it 57-52, and my three off Draud's assist returned the lead to eight. After a UK deuce, Draud's most difficult three of the night—contested by Davender and with his momentum carrying him to his right—made it 63-54. But UK responded again: Davender's two free throws and Eric Manuel's jumper made it 63-58 with 8:56 to play. Again, we had an answer: Two spectacular steals by Booker, back in the game with four fouls, kept the lead at five, and after the second one he hit a three to make it 66-58. UK called timeout at the 7:52 mark. The circumstances were eerily like the first game, when we had led by nine, 65-56, with 7:52 remaining, and we had not been able to close the deal. Could we do it this time?

Chapman, who finally returned to the game with four fouls, missed a jumper out of the timeout, and my layup off a Perdue feed gave us our biggest lead of the game at 10. Lock answered with a field goal, but my two free throws at the 4:49

mark made it 70-60. A free throw by Bennett, and one each by Perdue and me, pushed the lead to 72-61 with 3:40 left.

Chapman quickly scored on the other end, but after a near-turnover off their press, Draud hit his sixth trey, a real backbreaker that gave us a 75-63 lead with just over three minutes to play. We could smell victory now. UK came up empty on the next couple of trips, and Draud's two free throws extended the lead to 14 with two minutes left. When Derrick Miller shot an air ball on UK's next possession, the countdown to victory was on. We worked the shot clock down, and I spun on Davender, who reached around me and tried for the steal; when he failed, I turned to face the basket and found myself wide open from 17 feet. I made bigger shots in my career, but none sweeter: I nailed the jumper, and our bench exploded; Coach Newton gave a fist-pump reminiscent of his reaction to the Reid three-point play late in the North Carolina game, and the crowd went bonkers. All that was left was running out the clock. Perdue closed it with a monstrous, reverse dunk ("That one was for the fans," Wilbur said) to end it, 83-66. The crowd rushed the floor to celebrate the first Vanderbilt victory over UK at Memorial Gym since 1979.

Of all the memorable wins I experienced in four years at Vandy, I was never as happy after a game as this one. The UK win was necessary to give us credibility within the conference; then, as now, a victory over Kentucky functions as some sort of statement, as an announcement that the team must be taken seriously within the SEC. I said exactly that after the game: "This is a win that can put us on the map." And that is precisely what it did. While the 17-point final margin was deceptive (it was our biggest margin of the game), the win was no fluke. Unlike the wins over Indiana and North Carolina, we never trailed in the second half; in fact, we never trailed for the final 23 minutes. It was a decisive victory. "I think it turns another corner for our program," Coach Newton said after the game. In other words, "I could just say this was another day at the office, but it wasn't."

Then, of course, there was the fact that four of the top nine players on the team were native Kentuckians, and we all basked in the emotional high of the victory. One of them, Draud, was spectacular—he scored 22 points, hitting six of his nine three-point attempts, prompting Eddie Sutton to observe, "That Draud was running a fever." It was Scott's best game in our two years of playing together. Perdue and I each contributed 17 points and four assists, while Booker scored 14, giving that quartet 70 of the team's 83 points. Also, this was the game where our three-point shooting really made a difference. We hit an amazing 13 of 20 shots from behind the arc—65%—including an incredible 10 of our last 13 (77%). Kentucky shot only four treys, making one; thus, we outscored the 'Cats 39-3 from behind the arc. "I have never seen anything like it," a startled Chapman said. "If they saw daylight, they put it up. And, if they put it up, it went in." Coach Sutton observed after the game, "Tonight was a great example of what the three-point shot can do and how it's changed basketball at the collegiate level. The three-point goal has really changed the game."

The victory moved our record to 12-4. "This stamps us as a contender for the [SEC] title," I said after the game. "It's time the NCAA tournament people started noticing us." Eddie Sutton agreed: "Vanderbilt is a good basketball team and they have proved that this season. They will be a team in the NCAA tournament, one of the teams out of our league." Perhaps, but for now, beating Kentucky was sufficient.

8

THE BOMB SQUAD

Our white-hot performance behind the three-point line against Kentucky drew attention to the team's three-point shooting ability. Beginning with the Alabama game, we had shot a sizzling 33-63 (52.4%) from behind the arc (7-12 Alabama, 4-12 Georgia, 9-19 Auburn, 13-20 Kentucky) over the next four games. All 63 treys were taken by the quintet of Booker, Goheen, Draud, Wilcox, and Mayes. At some point during our winning streak, someone—apparently Vandy play-by-play man Charlie McAlexander—dubbed that fivesome "the Bomb Squad." The Bomb Squad gave the team an additional identity beyond our esteemed center, and it also illustrated one of C.M. Newton's greatest coaching achievements.

I

"Just take a deep breath and work your way up"
—Mick Jagger, "Let's Work" ('87)

In the early to mid-1980s, Coach Newton was the chairman of the NCAA's Rules Committee. As he would recall, his leadership would result in three significant developments introduced into college basketball—the shot clock (originally set at 45 seconds), the coaches' box, and the three-point shot. While the shot clock was a necessary development, the introduction of the three-point shot in 1986 arguably is the most significant rule change in the history of college basketball.

In addition to his involvement in the NCAA's Rules Committee, Coach Newton's experiences assisting Bob Knight in the 1984 Olympics and coaching in other international competitions (where the three-point line had long been used) eventually put Vanderbilt near the head of the class when the three-point line became operative in NCAA Division I play. Early in the 1987–88 season, when our team's three-point shooting prowess was just beginning to draw attention nationally, Coach Newton said, "As a member of the NCAA rules committee, I was privy to some of the research that had been done on the three-point shot in experimental use. Plus, I had had experience with the shot as a coach in a lot of international-rules games." Armed with that knowledge and experience, Coach Newton and his staff began immediate preparation for this brave new world. "As soon as the rule was passed," he said, "our coaching staff began to prepare for it. I even went to some friends in the pros for ideas. I knew what was coming."

Did Coach Newton recruit players in the mid-80s knowing that the three-point shot was coming? Draud thought so. "I think he had some vision that the shot was coming to the collegiate game," he said, "and he started to design his recruiting efforts based on that." Whether by design, luck, or some combination of both (which is my theory), Coach Newton had assembled a terrific cast of shooters—two sophomores and two freshmen—by the time the three-point line became effective in fall 1986.

̃̃

Bomb Squad Trivia Question No. 1: Who made the first three-point shot in Vanderbilt history after the three-point rule became effective in 1986? The answer is Scott Draud, against Virginia Commonwealth in the first game of the Maui tournament in fall 1986. That was entirely fitting because, as Will Perdue once said, "Draud might have been the best pure shooter I've ever seen"—heady praise from the man who played in the NBA with such lethal marksmen as John Paxson, Steve Kerr, and, of course, Michael Jordan.

Three-fifths of the Bomb Squad (Goheen, Draud, Wilcox) hailed from Kentucky—in Scott's case, the town of Newport, just across the Ohio River from Cincinnati. Not only was he a great basketball player, but he was also an accomplished tennis player; Scott, in fact, was a three-time All-Stater in tennis and was named a high school All-American in tennis in 1986. We all laughed during Scott's freshman year when Coach Al Walter, a tennis enthusiast, kept challenging Scott to a tennis match, but Scott kept politely declining. But Al was persistent, and Scott finally relented. The result was predictable—a double-bagel rout by Draud, 6-0, 6-0. But basketball is what got Scott to Vanderbilt. He led all Kentucky high schoolers in scoring in both his junior (30.4) and senior (35.3) seasons, and once scored 69 points in one game. He brought a needed offensive explosiveness to West End.

When Scott got on a roll, as he did against Kentucky, we just wanted to free him up as much as we could and ride his hot hand. His scoring could be prolific as a substitute—22 points in only 24 minutes against the Wildcats—and he was the ultimate zone-buster. He also had the greatest range of our group of shooters; Scott had, as I said, "incredibly long range. It wasn't just an inch or two beyond the three-point line. He could go out to 25 feet or so, which is very important when you have Will Perdue under the basket. You wanted to stretch the defense if you could, and it helps to have shooters with range." We upset a ranked Auburn team in '87 when Scott, in another of his outbursts, exploded for 25 points off the bench. No deficit seemed too large once Scott started hitting treys.

Scott was a gym rat, as he explained: "Dad is a school superintendent and we always had access to a gym. I would shoot a couple of hours every day (even during basketball season after practice). There were days when shaking hands was a chore because my arm was so tired." That work paid off handsomely—Scott was simply an outstanding shooter made for the three-point era.

Coach Newton embraced the three-point shot more than any other coach in the country with the possible exception of Providence's Rick Pitino, but by no means did he give the players a blank check to fire three-pointers whenever we wanted. In fact, C.M. laid down some very specific rules to govern our three-point strategy. One was that the standard 17- or 18-footer was essentially abolished. C.M. explained his philosophy on this point: "It makes no sense to shoot from 17 feet for two points when you can shoot for three from 19'9". Let's either take the ball and penetrate or take a step back and shoot for three." Thus, Coach Newton stressed that we should "eliminate the mid-range shot." In fact, 19'9" seemed "a little too easy," as I opined during that first three-point season of 1986–87. I predicted that the NCAA would move the three-point line either out to the international distance of 20'6" or a little more. My prediction ultimately proved true, but not for two decades: the three-point distance was changed to 20'9"—slightly longer than the international distance—prior to the 2008–09 season.

We followed Coach Newton's "eliminate the mid-range shot" directive to the letter; other than a semi-desperate situation where the shot clock or game clock was about to expire, we almost never attempted shots beyond 15–16 feet unless we were behind the three-point line. And we knew exactly where the line was, too—I can't remember a single instance where a would-be trey was ruled a two-pointer because the shooter's foot was on, not behind, the three-point line. We practiced that foot-work all the time and made sure that each time we attempted a trey we had both feet firmly behind the line. "He wanted to take advantage of the three-point line and take good shots," Booker recalled of Coach Newton's mandate on this point; "he would say the worst shot on the court was your foot on the inside of the three-point line, where you aren't getting credit for making this long-distance shot."

The second rule was that we would never come down and fire a three-pointer without first pressing the ball inside, with the knowledge and confidence that the big men would return the ball to us after the defense naturally collapsed toward the ball. "Coach Newton would say, 'we never want to come down, dribble the ball up, and take a three-point shot," Booker explained. "We want all of our three-point shots to come from inside out. Passing the ball into the post and kicking it out, or dribble penetration and kicking it out.'"

Before the 1986–87 season even started, Coach Newton explained the significance of that strategy and Perdue's role in it: "I believe the best way to have success with the three-point play is to go inside out: A big guy like Will who is an excellent passer and sees the court so well can help us do just that." Our big men were excellent at running the floor; that was a definite strength of both Perdue ("He runs the court very well, something you like and want in a big player," said Coach Newton) and Kornet. If guards just come down and fire a trey without trying to pass the ball to one of the bigs, those guys might not run quite as hard the next time, or the time after that, and so on. Then the "fast break" isn't really "fast" at all, and the three-point attack is much less effective.

It also helped that Perdue and Kornet were exceptionally smart, alert players when they received the ball in the post. They almost always made the right decision when working around the basket. If they were only single-teamed, they would maneuver for a good shot, but if they were double-teamed, they always found the open shooter outside the three-point line—which explains why, three decades later, Perdue remains Vandy's most accurate field-goal shooter (60.6%) and Kornet is sixth (53.4%). Within those parameters, though, the coaches gave the green light to the three-point shooters. "You have to free your shooters," Coach Newton reasoned. "You can't have indecision. You can't have them glancing over at the bench before and after each shot. They have to be given the green light."

≈

Bomb Squad Trivia Question No. 2: Which of the five Bomb Squad members led the team in three-point field goal percentage in the 1987–88 season? The answer is Derrick Wilcox, who connected on 18 of 39 three-point attempts for a strong 46.2% clip. As I commented, Derrick "would take the three-point shot if it was presented to him, as opposed to trying to find it. I think he was a very underrated shooter. He was a very good shooter."

Derrick was the only born-and-raised point guard on the team. He played high school ball at Louisville's Pleasure Ridge Park High School, where he started for three years and led PRP to a runner-up finish in the Kentucky Sweet Sixteen as a senior. Derrick excelled in that high-pressure environment, prefiguring some clutch performances at Vanderbilt; he was selected to the All-State Tournament team and was runner-up in the balloting for the tournament's Most Valuable Player award.

Derrick was a great floor general. As Perdue remarked, Derrick "took the time to know where the post players wanted the ball." Draud concurred: "Derrick was a really good point guard, exceptionally quick, and he would always find the open man. He would get you the ball in good scoring opportunities." Plus, as Draud observed, Derrick could be a one-man press-breaker: "You never had to worry about being pressed, because he could beat it himself."

Derrick played somewhat sparingly as a freshman in 1986–87, but he had some key moments, most notably notching 10 points in a road win at Mississippi State and scoring seven points and grabbing four rebounds in the last-second win over Penn. He improved his shooting between his freshman and sophomore seasons and became a fine all-around guard—which he would really display in 1988–89. Derrick had the fewest three-point attempts of the Bomb Squad, but, as his high percentage indicates, he made sure they counted. In fact, of the best three-point shooting seasons in Vandy history measured by percentage (minimum 30 attempts), Derrick is the only player with two seasons in the top 10—the seventh best in 1989–90 (46.7%) and eighth best in 1987–88 (46.2%). And he had a knack for making big plays, whether on offense or defense; some memorable wins in '88 and in '89 were made possible by clutch play from Derrick.

ॐ

George Washington is known as the father of his country. James Madison is considered the father of the Constitution. And Ed Steitz is known as the father of the three-point shot.

Steitz was the secretary-editor of the NCAA Rules Committee in the mid-1980s, a position he took after a long career as basketball coach and athletic director at Springfield College in Massachusetts—the same school where James Naismith invented the game in 1891. Steitz sent questionnaires to every coach in the college game, from Division I to NAIA, junior colleges, and all points in between, and with data in hand, he persuaded the 12-person Rules Committee, whose chairman was C.M. Newton, to adopt the three-point shot. Apparently, Steitz was persuasive: as the secretary of the Rules Committee, he didn't even have a vote, but he convinced Coach Newton and 11 others to go along with the plan. And Coach Newton was not an easy sell. He later revealed that he had been against the three-point shot originally. In fact, after some three-point dramatics in 1988 brought some national attention to the program, Coach Newton seemed to revel in recalling his initial opposition to the rule, going so far as to say that he "adamantly opposed the three-pointer," adding that "I think I might've even cursed him a time or two."

At that point, I think C.M. began to proest too much; I believe he saw the irony in how we had thrillingly benefited from the three-point shot when he had expressed reservations about it a couple of years earlier, but if he really had been "adamantly opposed" to the rule, I doubt that he would have let Ed Steitz (or anyone else) change his mind. But, whatever the strength of his reservations or opposition had been, it's to C.M.'s everlasting credit that he quickly adapted to the new rule rather than complain about it like many other coaches did. And when Coach Newton issued a public apology to Steitz in March 1988 ("I'd like to take this occasion to not only apologize, but to thank him for pushing it through"), I have no doubt it was sincere.

After the three-point shot was introduced into college basketball in 1986, most coaches immediately started complaining about it. In a 1986–87 preseason poll, the National Association of Basketball Coaches voted 65%-35% against the rule change, and some notable coaches were particularly critical. For example, Lou Carnasecca of St. John's called it "a Mickey Mouse rule." Villanova coach Rollie Massimino urged a letter-writing and phone-calling campaign to have the three-pointer erased from the rulebook; in fact, as Rick Pitino recalled, coaches like Carnasecca, Massimino, and Georgetown's John Thompson "would [not] even *attempt* a three" when the rule first became effective. A national publication derided the rule by saying that the teams that would benefit most would be "pencil-necked jump shooters." But at the end of that season, a vote of that same NABC body revealed that 80% of its members favored the rule. As Coach Newton said in his *mea culpa* to Mr. Steitz in 1988: "Ed kept saying it'll add a lot to the game. Ed, you were right. It's been good for the game." Besides, what's the use of protesting the rule by refusing to shoot three-pointers? That just punishes your team. As C.M. remarked during all thus hubbub, "the three-point rule is in effect and it's up to us to learn to make the most of it. That's been our plan from the start."

Indeed, the "good for the game" part includes the excitement generated by late-game threes, stirring comebacks, and deadly shooters who get on a roll from behind the arc. As Draud remarked, "I think fans really like the shot. It makes the defense work more on the perimeter and adds a little more strategy." Steitz believed that a team should make between 36-38% of its three-point attempts. He would have embraced the 1987–88 Commodores, as each Bomb Squad member hit at least 42% of his three-point attempts, led by Wilcox's 46.2%. Booker and I each hit 43.3%, Draud hit 42.6%, and Mayes hit 42.4%. Incredibly, more than 30 seasons after the three-point shot became effective, the four players who were in the program when the shot was introduced in the fall 1986 are still in the top 10 for three-point shooting accuracy, led by top-ranked Booker with a remarkable 46% and third-place Draud at 43.8%. Wilcox is eighth at 42.1%, and I am tenth at 41.8%. For that matter, after 30-plus years of the three-point era, those first three seasons—1986–87 (42.9%), 1987–88 (43.1%), and 1988–89 (41.4%), remain the three highest percentages for a Vanderbilt team from behind the arc. Ed Steitz, who died in 1990, would have been proud of the Bomb Squad.

❧

Bomb Squad Trivia Question No. 3: Which member of the Bomb Squad was the only freshman to start in his first game in C.M. Newton's eight years at Vanderbilt? The answer is Charles Mayes, a homegrown product of Nashville's Montgomery Bell Academy. What made Charles valuable in the new era of the three-point shot was his size and position—a 6'7" forward entering college in 1987 wasn't really expected to shoot and make 20-footers, but Charles did, and that gave us a real edge over the teams that felt that they could match up with the guards and still be able to contain Perdue in the post. As Booker observed, Charles was the one player "you had to guard, which made us better inside and helped other people get shots." Charles's two best games in 1987–88 were two of our biggest wins—the North Carolina triumph in which he hit five threes and the road win at Auburn when he nailed six. And he wasn't just a smart player; he was just plain smart. He came to Vanderbilt planning to become a doctor, and that's what he did, earning him the nickname "the Swishin' Physician" and graduating from the Vanderbilt Medical School, as his father had.

Bomb Squad fever reached its peak (or its nadir, depending on one's point of view) when the five of us filmed a video promoting our exploits. We were taken to Nashville's Air National Guard airbase, donned flight suits, and, about 18 months after *Top Gun*, filmed a video to the tune of "Danger Zone" that was shown on Coach Newton's weekly television show. Meanwhile, Bomb Squad T-shirts began to appear. The most popular one featured cartoon likenesses of the five members crammed into a rickety airplane and dropping "bombs"—actually basketballs—on a cartoon likeness of Will Perdue. And Will's appearance on that shirt underscored the final significant piece of The Bomb Squad's success—our effective inside game. Will led that group in 1987–88, and Frank Kornet effectively filled that role the next year; both were outstanding passers from the post position. As C.M. preached, an effective three-point shooting attack must originate with a strong inside game. For my final three years at Vanderbilt, we had both, which didn't guarantee victory, but did present enough balance that teams could not focus on stopping one without exposing themselves to the other.

All told, "that Bomb Squad stuff…was kind of fun," Coach Newton recalled. And it was. It created a reputation for Vanderbilt as a haven for great shooters that has been maintained for the past 30-plus years.

II

"One man to the left, one man to the right, one man in the middle"
—Foreigner, "Inside Information" ('87–'88)

The Kentucky win was great, but the 'Cats were not leading the SEC as the conference season neared its halfway point. The leader was Florida, bringing a 6-1 conference record and a #14 national ranking to Memorial just three days after we had conquered Kentucky. The Gators were a very good team, led by one of the SEC's best players, Vernon Maxwell. He could be counted on for at least 20 points nearly every night, and he had a solid all-around game, evidenced by his long and productive NBA career. The Gators also had the league's assist leader, Ronnie Montgomery, and one of the league's best three-point shooters in forward Pat Lawrence. Their inside game was led by power forward Livingston Chatman and center Dwayne Schintzius, both of whom were in the league's top 10 in rebounding.

Florida was clearly a team on the rise. In 1986–87, Florida finished second in the SEC and advanced to the NCAA tournament for the first time in school history. And they made the most of the opportunity, beating North Carolina State and Purdue to advance to the Sweet Sixteen before bowing to national runner-up Syracuse.

With five consecutive wins, we were playing well, too, so all signs pointed toward a tight, close game. But it didn't happen. Florida led early, 11-10, but Draud sparked a run with a pair of treys, part of an eight-point spurt that gave us an 18-11 lead. After that, the rout was on and Florida never really threatened. We led by 16 at the half, 41-25, and coasted in the second half to a 92-65 romp that was the Gators' worst loss in 217 games.

The Florida game was perhaps our best all-around team effort of the year. Perdue had 19 points on 8-of-12 shooting and 15 rebounds; Booker had 16 points on 4-of-9 three-point shooting. Kornet had six rebounds; Wilcox and I had four assists each. And the two freshmen were sensational: Mayes scored 11 points, while Steve Grant, in the best game of his first two years, scored 13 and pulled down five rebounds. As a team, we hit all 23 of our free throws—a team and SEC record that still stands for most free throws made in a game without a miss. (That was our second free-throw shooting record in three seasons; in a 1986 win against Mississippi State, we set an NCAA record (twice matched) by hitting an amazing 35 of 36 free-throw attempts, the best team percentage ever with a minimum of 35 free throws made.) "I just don't know if we could play any better," Coach Newton said after the game.

Other than the fact of the blowout itself, the most memorable part of the game involved Florida-native Perdue, who brought an extra intensity to this, his last home game against his home-state school. That intensity manifested itself late in the first half in an increasingly chippy exchange with Schintzius. According to Will, "Dwayne's talking a little trash. He said something to Eric Reid on our team, and I just said, 'If you are going to talk to somebody, talk to me.'"

Schintzius didn't get the message. Right after that, Will took an entry pass, drove around Schintzius, who would become something of a bête noire for us in the next couple of seasons, and reverse-dunked in front of the Florida bench. Running back down the floor, an animated Will was yapping at Schintzius while motioning toward him with both hands in the manner of "let's get it on, Dwayne." As Will recalled, after that dunk Schintius "was still talking. That's when that whole thing started to get heated. Nothing happened physically." Indeed, cooler heads ultimately prevailed, but we had a merry time ripping into Will for it after the game (and the days, weeks, months, and years beyond), as he conceded in 2012, "My friends and ex-teammates give me a hard time about that." Schintzius did score 23 points, but Will destroyed him on the boards, 15-3, which was nearly our entire rebounding margin for the game (44-31). Perdue fired off this missive after the game: "Schintzius has told people he's the best center in the nation. There are a few doubts in my mind."

The decisive back-to-back wins over ranked teams Kentucky and Florida had Vandy fans and scribes waxing nostalgic over the last time a Commodore team had beaten ranked opponents in consecutive games. The games most often referenced were consecutive wins in Memorial over #5 North Carolina (89-76), #8 Davidson (81-79), and top-10 Duke (76-75 on a buzzer-beater) in December 1967—wins that shot the Commodores to a #3 national ranking and had been called "the greatest three-game stretch in Vanderbilt history." That North Carolina win had occurred just under 20 years to the day from our victory over the top-ranked Heels in December 1987, and it had been the program's last victory over North Carolina before our December triumph.

The national media began to take notice of our six-game winning streak. The result was that we appeared in the top 20 for the first time in the season, and the first time for the program since 1979. We had appeared in *USA Today*'s Top 25 rankings earlier in the season after the win over Carolina (and stayed there until the disastrous week of LSU-UT losses in January); we also had appeared in *USA Today*'s top 25 for several weeks in the 1986–87 season following the win over Indiana. But that poll didn't have the cache that it does now; the "official" ranking was the Associated Press Top-20 poll. Now, in early February 1988, we shot from unranked all the way to #15 in the AP poll. In the *USA Today*/CNN Top 25 poll, we went from unranked to #16.

It's hard to describe the excitement we had generated in the Vanderbilt community, especially on the Vanderbilt campus. Students lined up in the cold January weather to claim tickets; every remaining home game was sold out. Will wasn't exaggerating when he called it a "phenomenon": "At night, during the week of those games going to the library or walking across campus, I'd see students waiting in line at the student center to get their tickets the next morning at 8 a.m. for the games," he recalled. "It was like a phenomenon. It was the hot ticket in town, but only for the people in Nashville. There were [only] so many student tickets available. The students and other athletes around campus kept telling us how exciting the games were." Booker said almost the same thing, using the same key word as Will. "Vanderbilt basketball was the biggest show in town. The environment in Memorial Gym was phenomenal in those days. No way it will be like that again. It is impossible to explain to the people who were not there for it."

There were a couple of reasons for this excitement. First, Vanderbilt simply had not performed at such a high level for many years, so the "newness" of achieving notoriety by beating ranked teams—and true college basketball bluebloods—like North Carolina and Kentucky was a factor in creating the excitement on campus. Second, as Booker noted, was that there were no professional sports in Nashville at that time. The NFL Titans and NHL Predators would not make Nashville a "major league city" until the mid-'90s, so Nashville focused on college basketball. Coach Newton effectively used that fact in recruiting, emphasizing that Vanderbilt basketball was the biggest sporting event in the city over the winter. That pitch was enticing for someone who played, as I did, in a town where basketball was the major activity and a community rallying point.

To be clear, being the "biggest show in town" doesn't mean "only show in town" because there was some great basketball being played in Nashville in 1987–88. Across town at Tennessee State, senior Anthony Mason, one of Coach Martin's final recruits at TSU, averaged an even 28 points a game, third in the nation, and enjoyed a successful NBA career, most notably with the Knicks. Meanwhile, Coach Don Meyer was in the midst of an incredible run at David Lipscomb College, having won the NAIA title in 1986 and posting some incredible victory totals—35 in that championship year of '86, then 27, 33, 38, 41(!), 35, 31, 34, 29, 30, 33, and 30 through 1996–97.

All in all, it was an electrifying time to be playing basketball for Vanderbilt. There was a close relationship between the players and the students who came to the games. And Book was exactly right—it's impossible to describe the atmosphere with any accuracy to those who weren't there, and it will never happen again (unless, of course, Vanderbilt goes another decade and a half without an NCAA appearance).

Our first opponent as a ranked team was Mississippi State, which came to Memorial on February 2, the day after Coach Newton celebrated his 58th birthday, with a 3-5 conference record. The Bulldogs relied heavily on four freshmen, and clearly were the least talented of the opponents we met on this three-game homestand. The Bulldogs were coached by Richard Williams, who took the route to major-college head coach that isn't seen much any longer: he coached at two junior high schools, two high schools, and a junior college—all in Mississippi—before joining State, his alma mater, as an assistant in 1984. He took over as head coach in 1986, so this was his second season as the Bulldogs' head coach. Coach Newton never seemed to warm to him, and Williams and Dale Brown feuded for several years. But Williams eventually would win in Starkville.

Not in 1987–88, though. State was a last-place team and we were on a roll. We began the game firing on all cylinders, and it looked like another blowout was at hand: we led 25-12 with 7:30 left in the first half, and 36-30 at intermission. We came out hot in the second half and pushed the lead to 13, 45-32, in the first three minutes. We won by 16, 82-66, for our seventh win in a row.

Perdue was in the middle of a terrific run of basketball, and he was the key to the State win. He hit eight of his 11 field goal attempts and all seven of his free-throw attempts for 23 points while carding 11 rebounds and four blocks, all game highs. Mayes again was splendid off the bench with 13 points, while Reid posted a solid 10-point, six-rebound effort, and the good work of the front line of Eric, Will, and the rest limited State to just one offensive rebound for the entire game.

The State win gave us seven consecutive SEC victories, the most by a Vanderbilt team in many years. Our 7-3 record was tied with Kentucky for second in the league, just behind 7-2 Florida. The 0-3 start seemed like a long time ago.

9

MAINTAINING MOMENTUM

"I won't apologize for the things I've done and said"
—Lou Gramm, *"Midnight Blue"* ('87)

Following the three home wins over Kentucky, Florida, and Mississippi State, we would put our seven-game winning streak on the line at LSU. The Assembly Center, renamed the Pete Maravich Assembly Center in 1988, was nicknamed the "Deaf Dome," but in truth it really wasn't all that loud though it was a difficult place to play. We had stolen a win there the previous season when we were flying high before Christmas 1986, but the Tigers traditionally had done a good job of protecting their home court. And they knew we were anxious for a rematch after the 51-39 embarrassment in Nashville.

I

"I won't apologize for the things I've done and said"
—Lou Gramm, *"Midnight Blue"* ('87)

Winning streaks don't happen very often—particularly seven-game winning streaks in the SEC where your team has shot from the bottom of the league standings to near the top. And you want to maintain your same routines even though the line between "routine" and "superstition" is blurry. "When it comes to being superstitious," one journalist wrote during the season, "Goheen may rank at the top of the list." The most tangible evidence of the "don't mess with the streak" mentality was that I declined to get a haircut until we lost. (Those were the days!)

So it was that every time I touched the ball in the game, the LSU students decided to have a little fun. With the Saturday afternoon game being televised as the SEC game of the week, my friend Emma, who worked at the Vanderbilt Salon and cut my and many of my teammates' hair, watched in horror as the LSU students chanted "Cut your hair!" every time I touched the ball. I was not singled out; every time Draud—another Emma customer, who sported permed curly blond hair—touched the ball, the chant changed to "Perm your hair!" That stuff never really bothered Scott or me, but the cold facts are that I went 3-for-10 from the field and he missed all seven of his shots from the field.

Chants aside, the reason we lost the game was poor defense, just as our offense had taken a vacation in the first game against the Tigers. LSU rang up 94 points, the most we would yield in any game that season. The Tigers led 44-33 at the half and cruised to a 94-79 victory, snapping our seven-game winning streak. Further hampering our chances was that we had to play most of the game without Booker, who sustained a hip pointer early in the game and played only six minutes. Compounding that problem was the fact that the game was the most tightly whistled of the season— 56 fouls were called, 31 on us, not counting the technical foul Coach Newton picked up for complaining about the officiating. LSU shot 52 free throws in the game, nearly double the 28 we shot. All three frontcourt starters (Perdue, Kornet, Reid) fouled out, and three other players (Wilcox, Draud, Mayes) ended the game with four fouls.

Perdue continued his strong play with 29 points and seven rebounds, but Book's absence hurt our three-point attack—we hit only two of our 12 three-point attempts, our worst effort in terms of percentage all season. Still, there wasn't the same level of disappointment after the second LSU game as there had been following the first game. LSU played well the second time, and we had to play most of the game without Book. Plus, we were coming back to Memorial for two games, where we had begun to feel unbeatable.

The first of those games was against Tennessee. We had lost four in a row to the Vols in the past two years, so the pressure was on to break that modest streak, just as we had broken the longer Kentucky losing streak two weeks earlier. We had not beaten UT at Memorial since January 15, 1986, in a game for the ages.

II

"I wonder to myself, 'Could life ever be sane again?'"
—*The Smiths, "Panic" ('86)*

When I came to Vandy, I didn't know much about the University of Tennessee and its basketball program. Having grown up in Kentucky, I naturally disliked UT because it was a consistent rival to the Wildcats, and the Vols had an uncanny ability to beat even the best UK teams in Knoxville—they won 12 of the 13 games there during Joe B. Hall's tenure in Lexington. (I managed to take a shot at both schools after helping us beat UT in Stokely in '86: "That's why I came to Vanderbilt, so I could beat Tennessee at Stokely.") I knew that Don DeVoe, who came to Knoxville in the late '70s, had done a fine job of keeping the Vols in the upper echelon of the SEC. His first seven UT teams went to postseason tournaments, the first five to the NCAAs and the next two went to the NIT. The '85–'86 season was his eighth in Knoxville.

My first taste of Vandy-UT as a player was in January 1986 at Memorial. We were shorthanded; one senior starting guard, Jeff Gary, had been out for over a month, and putting me in the starting lineup, the other starting guard, Darrell Dulaney, went down very early in the game with an ankle injury, not to return; that injury earned my fellow freshman Booker a battlefield promotion to floor general just a couple of minutes into the game. UT, meanwhile, had a much-touted freshman class headlined by hometowner Doug Roth, a highly recruited 6'10" center from Knoxville, and the aforementioned Mark Griffin. Less touted was an athletic forward from Fort Walton Beach, Florida, named Dyron Nix, but in the pregame walk-through for this first game against UT, Coach Bostick presciently noted that Nix had all the tools to be a fine player and it was only a matter of time before he broke out. And, led by their All-SEC guard, Tony White, the Vols had some talent.

With Dulaney and Gary injured, Booker and I played most of the game—the first time we shared the backcourt for a full game. We got off to a good start and took an early 10-3 lead, but the Vols spurted ahead toward the end of the half. Then a Booker steal and layup tied the game late in the half, and a couple of minutes later my 16-footer at the halftime buzzer gave us a three-point lead at the break, 28-25. We came out hot in the second half and stretched the lead to eight, 37-29. But we went stone cold and the Vols heated up, outscoring us 30-14, capped by White's driving layup with under a minute to play to give the Vols a 59-51 lead. With no three-point line in effect, the game seemed over.

On our next possession we had the ball out of bounds under our basket with 51 seconds to play. I inbounded the ball to Steve Reece on the block, and Steve hit a half-hook over Roth and drew the foul on Doug with 48 seconds to go. Steve missed the free throw, but Booker came all the way from the fourth lane to tip in the miss—it's a play that couldn't even be made today because only three lanes are occupied for free throws—and the four-point trip made it 59-55. With 32 seconds left, White was called for traveling, giving us another possession. I hit an off-balance 10-footer in the lane to trim the lead to two with 25 seconds left. We immediately fouled Anthony Richardson, who missed the front end of the one-and-one. Bobby Westbrooks rebounded and started dribbling down the floor, but he turned it over. The Vols got the ball back with 18 seconds left, and we were forced to foul White, a 90% free-throw shooter.

Incredibly, White also missed the front end of the one-and-one, and we rebounded. I wound up with the ball and the play was "Winner"—a simple 1-4 set where I would take the ball at the top of the key and try to make a play while the other four players were spaced along the baseline, one in each corner and one on each block. We would run this play often in my four years, and the idea was that if I could create a good shot, I would take it, but if I drew a double-team, I would pass to the open player.

I moved on the Vols' 2-guard, Fred Jenkins, faked spinning around him but kept moving left, and shot an open 15-footer from the left side of the court, free-throw line extended, with about eight seconds left…and bricked it. The ball was tipped around underneath as I followed the miss, drifting toward the baseline. Miraculously, the ball was batted right to where I was standing, about eight feet from the basket. I caught the ball and immediately shot it as Dyron Nix—who indeed had broken out with an excellent game off the bench—lunged for the block. I got the shot off before he could get there, and because he was late, he hit my shooting hand, committing the foul. The shot, meanwhile, hit nothing but net; the game was tied at 59 with four seconds left, and Memorial Gym erupted in the loudest cheer I had heard in my then-short Commodore career.

After UT called a timeout, I made the free throw to give us a 60-59 lead. Having to go the length of the floor in four seconds, the Vols ran a great play that somehow broke White wide open on the baseline in front of UT's bench for an 18-footer and the chance to steal the victory back, but he missed the buzzer-beater, and the game was over: Vandy 60, UT 59. We had rallied from eight points down to score nine straight points in 50 seconds, without the benefit of a three-point line and with a turnover. I was never part of a greater comeback than the UT rally, and I had what easily was the best game of my freshman year, leading the team in all three major offensive categories with 16 points, eight rebounds, and six assists—one of only two times I did that in my four years.

We streamed into the locker room, ecstatic and a little bit in shock at what had just transpired. We celebrated there for a few minutes, and then something incredible happened: we were called back to the floor by the fans. I had never heard of such a thing—a curtain call for basketball players! Well, Memorial Gym seems like a stage, so why not? This was the moment I realized that Vanderbilt fans were special. "We came back to give the fans a hand," I said after the game. "We were down by eight points with less than a minute to play and they didn't leave. They are the best fans in the country. If they weren't, there wouldn't have been more than 2,000 left at that point, and they would've all been for Tennessee." Coach Newton concurred: "That crowd up there tonight and this place is the reason I got back into coaching. The crowd—my goodness! They just wouldn't allow us to lose." And it was true: the gym at the end was as loud as at any time in the game. It was an incredible win and it was a great moment to share with the fans.

When we returned to the locker room after the curtain call, it was handshakes and hugs all around. Coach Al Walter told me, as he shook my hand, "You'll never be forgotten." At that moment, I realized that beating Tennessee was something special. And I also realized that Memorial Gym and the fans were special too. I knew after the game that it was my "greatest athletic accomplishment." That probably was true in January 1986, but I would be revising that judgment a couple of times in the ensuing three seasons.

III

"Can't help but think of yesterday"
—*George Michael, "Faith"* ('87–'88)

We and the Vols both finished out of the postseason in '86—UT was 12-16 and we were 13-15. The next year, we made it to the NIT quarterfinals while UT again missed the postseason with a 14-15 record. The Vols' 1987–88 season got off to a shaky start: a newly-hired assistant coach was arrested in a drug bust, and Nix, now the team's best player, was involved in a fairly serious car accident and spent a night in intensive care. Then B. Ray Thompson, whose name would grace the Vols' new arena that was about to open, died on October 22, 1987, before the Vols were able to play a game there.

But UT played well once the games began. The Vols routed Marquette to christen Thompson-Boling, and after they beat us there in January, they were 9-1 overall and 2-0 in the SEC while we were 7-4, 0-3. At that exact moment, though, the two teams' fortunes went into reverse. We rallied to pull out the win at Ole Miss, starting a seven-game winning streak. UT, meanwhile, led LSU by seven with just over two minutes to play and saw the Tigers score the last eight points of the game to steal a 52-51 win. The Vols were then blown out by Kentucky and Illinois to fall to 9-4. Things only got worse for the Vols from there. They were routed at home, 76-56, by Florida—UT's worst home loss in 26 years. Then Elvin Brown, the team's third-leading scorer, was arrested for shoplifting and dismissed from the team. By the time they came to Memorial, they were 12-8 overall and 5-5 in the conference.

Just as the game in Knoxville reflected the two teams' confidence levels in January, the game in Nashville reflected their confidence levels in February. It was never close, reminiscent of the Georgia rout. "No one could have beaten Vandy that night," one SEC coach commented. "Tennessee didn't know they were running into a buzzsaw." This was one of the best games Book and I combined to play all season, and we were both hot out of the gate. Shots were falling that made an opponent say early on, "I don't think this is our night." A couple of minutes in, I was driving toward the hoop and was nearly forced out of bounds on some good defense, but I threw the ball up from about 12 feet anyway; it went in. A minute or so later, I went up for a contested 15-footer only to have the Vols player go right up with me. I simply hung in the air a little longer and launched the shot just before my feet hit the ground—it went in, prompting ESPN's Tim Brando to utter a line that was never used before (or after) on one of my jumpers: "Look at the hang time!"

Off the bench, Wilcox hit a three and Draud made an incredible layup as he was sailing out of bounds. Wilcox made a great steal out of our zone and, as he was heading out of bounds, flicked the ball to Mayes; Chuck led the fast break and fed Perdue for a thunderous dunk that created the loudest roar of the evening...until a louder one erupted a couple of minutes later when Will and Derrick executed a perfect pick-and-roll that resulted in a beautiful lob feed from Derrick for a one-handed Perdunk. As Brando remarked, "The Howitzers are loaded, folks!" The last tie was 7-7 just over two minutes in; about four minutes later it was 22-9, and we were just getting warmed up. With five minutes to go in the half, were up by 23, 38-15. The peak came near the end of the half when Kornet went up for a likely dunk only to be hammered by a Vols player, sending the ball flying out of his hands, straight up in the air; of course, it fell right through the basket. That extended the lead to 25, and we were comfortably ahead by 19 at the half, 47-28. UT could not dent the lead in the second half. We maintained a 21-point lead, 70-49, inside 10 minutes, and later, after a mini-run by UT, Book and I combined for 11 straight points and an 81-57 lead with 3:43 remaining. The final score was 90-62.

"Barry Goheen was the key to the game early," Tennessee Coach DeVoe remarked. "I thought it was Goheen who masterfully brought the ball up the floor and did the things to get his team going." While such a sentiment from an opposing coach is always nice to hear, the fact is that this was probably the best game all four guards collectively played all year. In Coach Newton's words, "You have to hand it to our guards. They played really well." Booker, wearing padding to protect the hip he had injured at LSU, scored 16 points; I had 13 points and five assists; Wilcox had seven points and seven assists; Draud had four points and two rebounds. Perdue and Kornet combined to go 14-for-16 from the field and scored 35 points (22 for Will, 13 for Frank). We shot a scorching 63.5% from the field—our best of the season. It was a total team victory, and a sweet one, exemplifying DeVoe's compliment about Coach Newton: "C.M. hasn't got any high school All-Americans on that team, but they sure play like they are."

The good times continued three nights later against Ole Miss, which came to town still seething over the quick whistle in the final minute in Oxford that enabled us to rally for our first SEC victory. That seemed like eons ago; we had won eight of nine games starting with that one and had vaulted into the national rankings while Ole Miss remained mired in the second division. "It's the only time in my two years in the conference that I thought we got a terrible call," mused Ole Miss coach Ed Murphy on the eve of the rematch. Happily, we made sure that we wouldn't need a questionable call to take the second game against Ole Miss.

I was typically a slow starter in games; rarely would I take the first shot or even attempt a shot for the first few minutes. But not in this second game against Ole Miss. With the Rebels packing the defense around Perdue to open the game, it was like target practice from behind the arc, and I took full advantage by hitting four treys in the first five minutes of the game. The team hit a remarkable 9-of-13 three-point attempts in the first half to build a lead of 46-33. We rolled to a 93-68 victory behind a balanced attack of Perdue's 17 points (capping a great week where he went 16-of-19 from the field in the two games), my 15, and three others in double figures.

We kept up the hot shooting—57% from the field—and with the rout, we pulled into second place in the SEC with a 9-4 record, a game behind 10-3 Kentucky, which had not lost since our game in Nashville, and a half-game ahead of Florida and LSU, who were 8-4.

With the win, we closed the book on a remarkable stretch of play—9-1 in a 10-game span that was bookended by both Ole Miss games. We went from last place and an afterthought in the SEC to a national ranking and challenging for the league title. We won all seven home games we played—each one, apart from Kentucky, in convincing, often dominating, fashion: margins of 16 (Alabama), 15 (Georgia), 17 (Kentucky), 27 (Florida), 16 (Mississippi State), 28 (Tennessee), and 25 (Ole Miss)—an average margin of over 20 points. "We played about as good as a team could play," Coach Newton said then (and later). "We were very solid defensively and we had good board work. We handled the basketball and shot it well. We did all the things you had to do to win."

Unfortunately, the party was about to come to an end. Most of our remaining games were on the road, and we would not win another game at Memorial Gym that season.

10

FIGHTING THE IRISH

I

"Be yourself no matter what they say"
—Sting, "Englishman in New York" ('87–'88)

We would now play five of our final six regular season games on the road. We didn't view that as a daunting task; we had won two of our first five SEC road games and had two near-misses against Top 10 teams in the close losses at Indiana and Kentucky. While we were confident that we could weather this road-heavy grind, that confidence was misplaced in the first game of this stretch, at Alabama. We had thrashed the Tide by 16 a month earlier in Memorial, but they had played much better since then, and they outplayed us for the 88-77 win. Alvin Lee, who had scored 21 off the bench for the Tide in Nashville, blistered us for 36 in Tuscaloosa. That same night, Tennessee upset Kentucky in Knoxville, dropping the 'Cats to 10-4 in the league. Our loss at Alabama cost us a chance to tie for the league lead, but we remained only a game back with four conference games remaining.

Three days later we arrived in Athens, Georgia, for the return game against the Bulldogs. To say the least, Vandy's recent history in Athens had been lackluster— 11 straight losses—and my only two trips there had been disasters: a 101-70 shellacking in '86 (the only game in my four years at Vandy where the opponent hit triple digits) and a 76-53 rout in '87. Blowouts in two prior trips to Athens by a combined 54 points, coupled with a loss to an SEC bottom-feeder in the previous game, did not bode well for us.

It was obvious from the opening tip that there would be no blowout by the Dawgs this time. In fact, early on, it looked the reverse might occur as we raced to a 12-point lead, suggesting that maybe we would hang a second rout on the Dawgs this season. That was wishful thinking, though, as we promptly went cold and committed several silly turnovers (we would commit a season-high 22 for the game), allowing Georgia not only to catch us but also to establish a seven-point lead at the half, 39-32, highlighted by a fast-break half-court alley-oop to Willie Anderson, who rose over Perdue for the dunk and the foul, bringing the typically sedate Georgia crowd to life. Georgia held on to the lead for much of the second half, but we regrouped and fought our way back. We were limiting Georgia to one-and-done on the defensive end, and we hit some big shots on the offensive end. My shot on the baseline with around three minutes to go edged us into the lead, and Bulldog star Anderson struggled on offense despite his spectacular first-half alley-oop. We played one of our best closing stretches of the season, making free throws, grabbing rebounds, and eventually putting the game away. We broke the Athens hex with a huge 77-71 victory.

Perdue led a balanced attack with 17 points and 10 boards, with Booker adding 16 and five while I chipped in with 13 points. Our MVP, however, was Eric Reid, a native Georgian who had played his high school ball at Macon's Central High School. As special as the Kentucky game was for the native Kentuckians and the Florida game was for Perdue, the Georgia game was special to Reid and Grant, and Eric was terrific: 5-for-6 from the field and 5-for-6 from the line for 15 points, at that time a career high, and he added seven rebounds to contribute to our 41-23 domination of Georgia on the boards. We learned after the game that Kentucky had lost again, meaning that we were tied for the SEC lead with the 'Cats, each team at 10-5, with three league games to play. And, at 17-6 overall, we began to think seriously about an NCAA bid. "This win gets you close to where you want to be," Coach Newton said after the game. But not quite all the way there.

৵

We returned home for the season's final home game, which would be the final home game of Will Perdue's career. I wouldn't experience, or appreciate, the full emotion of the "final home game" until the next season, but this was a special game for Will and the fans. First, Will had been at Vandy for five years, having had the redshirt year in 1984–85, so he had been around a year longer than most. Second, the fans were literally able to watch Will grow up as a player and a person; he was a non-factor as a freshman, absent as a redshirt the next year, and a capable backup the year after that before becoming an "overnight sensation" in fall 1986. He arrived on campus as a 17-year-old teenager; he would graduate in May as a surefire first-round NBA draft pick.

Finally, I think that fans easily could see how Will's improvement as a player paralleled the improving fortunes of the program. His redshirt year, the year before Booker, Kornet, and I arrived, was a last-place SEC finish for the Commodores; the program had gone from worst to, at the time of his last home game on February 24, 1988, first in under three years, while Will had gone from bench-warming near-transfer to superstar who, in a couple of months, would be named the SEC's Male Athlete of the Year for 1987–88.

The ceremonies before the game were relatively brief but emotional. The sold-out crowd gave Will an extended ovation. Then it was game time. The opponent was Auburn, whom we had defeated on the road in January. But the January and late-February versions of the Tigers featured one big difference—the latter had Jeff Moore, a 6'8" seemingly undersized left-handed center but a burly bruiser with a nice shooting touch. Whereas Chris Morris had felt compelled to take 23 shots, missing 15, in the first game because Moore was sidelined with a broken hand, the two seniors now formed an effective, experienced combination.

We started the game well enough; fittingly for his final home game, Will slammed home a Perdunk for the game's first points, and we twice led by as many as seven in the first half, 19-12 and 21-14. Steve Grant scored the last five points of the half to send us to the locker room with a 37-30 lead. The second half began just like the first with a Perdue basket, which gave us our largest lead at nine. But Auburn ran off 10 straight points, taking a 40-39 lead on Moore's layup. We went back and forth for the next several minutes, and Kornet's jumper with over 14 minutes to play put us back in front, 48-47. Unfortunately, that would be our last lead of the game. Moore was terrific, and after holding Morris in check for three straight halves—the entire first game in Auburn and limiting him to two in the first half in Nashville— he exploded for 16 in the second half. Auburn's lead reached double digits with around six minutes to play, and we could get no closer than six. The result was sweet revenge for the Tigers, who ruined Will's final game in Memorial with an 81-68 victory. It wasn't Will's fault—he scored 20 points, the eighth consecutive game he led us in scoring, and his 15 rebounds tied his season high. I added 16 points, but no one else reached double figures, and our second half was awful—we were out-scored 51-31 on our home floor.

"It was a very disappointing loss," Wilbur commented after the game, "because it was a special night for me." Nevertheless, he added, "we've still got a lot of games to play; we still plan on going to the NCAA Tournament." In addition to falling out of first place (Kentucky won its game to take over sole, and permanent, possession of the league lead), we lost our final home game—something I would remember the next year.

II

"Games turn into life"
—Victoria Williams, "Main Road" ('87)

A welcome, but challenging, break in the SEC schedule came in the form of a trip to South Bend, Indiana, and a game with Notre Dame. With the recent downturn in our play, we needed a win to solidify our NCAA hopes, and so did Notre Dame— both teams entered the game with a record of 17-7.

అ

It speaks highly of the esteem in which C.M. Newton was held by his coaching peers—and his ability to get along with just about everyone in the profession—that he was able to schedule home-and-home series with such high-profile coaches as Bob Knight, Dean Smith, and Denny Crum, each of whom was temperamentally different from C.M., and from each other, and each of those coaches agreed to come to Vanderbilt for the first game of the home-and-home. While each of those coaches was a personality in his own right, perhaps no coach in the game had the personality and panache of Notre Dame's Digger Phelps, who agreed to a home-and-home series with Coach Newton beginning with the 1986–87 season. Phelps had coached the Fighting Irish since 1971 and guided them to the 1978 Final Four.

We first played Notre Dame in February 1987 at Memorial. The Irish were led by David Rivers, who was the quickest guard I ever played against and was one of the special stories in college basketball. One of 14 children, Rivers was perhaps the first truly notable player produced by Bob Hurley's now-legendary hoops program at St. Anthony's High School in Jersey City, New Jersey, graduating in 1984 and joining Phelps's Notre Dame program. He was an immediate sensation; he ignited the program with his superlative point guard skills and his intelligence both on and off the court. In one game that season against UCLA, after a particularly heads-up play, NBC broadcaster Al McGuire famously remarked of Rivers, "He's an Einstein! He's a Michelangelo!"

After two excellent seasons, though, Rivers's career, not to mention his life, almost ended on August 24, 1986, when he was involved in a serious car accident in Elkhart, Indiana. A passenger in a Chevy van being driven by teammate Ken Barlow, Rivers was thrown 20 feet through the shattered windshield and came to rest 90 feet beyond the vehicle. Glass ripped a 15-inch gash into Rivers's abdomen. It took three hours of emergency surgery and several pints of blood to save his life. Playing basketball again seemed iffy, and playing the 1986–87 season seemed out of the question. Phelps urged Rivers to redshirt. Incredibly, Rivers made it back for the 1986–87 season opener, and at the 1987 Final Four Rivers would be deservedly honored by the U.S. Basketball Writers Association as the Most Courageous Athlete of 1987.

Phelps said Rivers "was my best player in my 20 years at Notre Dame." That's quite a compliment given the competition, which includes Adrian Dantley, Bill Laimbeer, John Paxson, John Shumate, and Kelly Tripucka, among many others. But it was deserved: Rivers was electrifying—lightning fast—in the open floor. He was only six feet tall, but he had very long arms to go with his quickness. He made his teammates better on both ends of the floor. He did, however, have an Achilles heel: he was not a particularly good outside shooter. If he got to the basket, good things would happen for the Irish, but Rivers was not especially potent 20 or more feet from the basket. In the ultimate testament to Rivers's penetration skills, earlier in the 1986–87 season, Indiana coach Bob Knight did the heretofore unthinkable and played a zone defense against the Irish for the entire game, a 67-62 IU victory in a game played a week before we beat the Hoosiers. That strategy likely wasn't lost on Coach Newton, and, for our tussle with the Irish in February 1987 at Memorial, we would adopt the IU strategy of limiting Rivers's penetration and forcing him to shoot jumpers.

The strategy worked, as Notre Dame's offense could not get untracked in the first half. Unfortunately, ours couldn't either, and the result was the ugliest half of basketball we and an opponent combined to play all season. The score was tied at 19 in the final seconds of the half when my deuce gave us the lead inside five seconds to play. Then came a key play: rather than let the clock run out, Notre Dame threw a lazy inbounds pass that an alert Scott Draud intercepted about 12 feet from the basket (bizarrely called a "reverse steal" on the telecast) and shot just ahead of the buzzer, draining it. Those four points in five seconds gave us a four-point halftime lead and a ton of positive energy heading into the locker room. The second half was more watchable than the first and just as tight. With Perdue in foul trouble (he would foul out), backup center Randy Neff stepped up to play the best game in his two-year Commodore career, scoring 11 points in only 14 minutes, while Draud came off the bench to score a team-high 14 points. Perdue and I scored 13 points apiece to go with Draud and Neff's combined 25 points off the bench, and we had just enough offense to squeak out a 60-56 victory—the margin provided by those four points in the final seconds of the first half.

We kept Rivers firmly in check—he missed 10 of 13 shots from the field and committed six turnovers to only three assists. And this was a quality win, too—just five days earlier, Notre Dame had beaten #1-ranked North Carolina. The Irish would go on to claim a Sweet Sixteen berth in March, led by Rivers, where North Carolina exacted revenge in the regional semi by beating the Irish behind freshman J.R. Reid's 31 points.

~

With both teams sporting 17-7 records, the February 27, 1988, game in South Bend was a big one. Coming into the game, Rivers already was Notre Dame's all-time leader in assists and steals, and he had the highest free-throw percentage as well. He also was the school's third all-time leading scorer behind Dantley and Austin Carr, and he was averaging 22.5 points per game on the season. We would need to pack our zone deep and force him to beat us from the outside.

We looked forward to the trip, and country star Larry Gatlin was part of our traveling party. I fondly remember our flight to South Bend in which Larry schooled Charles Mayes and me in the finer points of bourre (or booray), a card game not unlike spades, which was the favored game of many of the players on trips (the primary participants being Booker, Mayes, Wilcox, Kornet, and me). Adding to our enthusiasm was the fact that this was our final ESPN game of the season, a Saturday night affair worked by network's A-team of Tim Brando and Dick Vitale. The Joyce Convocation Center was sold out to its nearly 11,500 capacity. The gym had hosted some great games in its history, most memorably Notre Dame's win over UCLA in 1974 that snapped the Bruins' record 88-game winning streak. And the Irish were good there in 1987–88 too, bringing a home record of 12-2 into the game.

Of Vitale's two keys to the game for us, the first was that the "Bomb Squad must unload." He felt, sensibly, that the Irish must contain Perdue while also neutralizing our three-point attack. The Irish did, in fact, accomplish both objectives.

From the outset, we showed a balance that would typify our scoring all night as Perdue, then I, then Reid, and then Kornet scored our first four baskets, and after another Reid basket, a fifth player, Grant, scored to tie the game at 12, while a Perdue basket gave us a 14-12 lead with 11:56 left in the half. Baskets by Wilcox and Draud off the bench kept the pace, giving us points by seven different players in the first 12 minutes. Then Kornet and I caught fire, combining to score nine straight points: he hit a basket, then I drained a three-pointer off a controlled fast break, followed by a spin move and layup off a great outlet pass from Perdue, followed by a Kornet 15-footer. Suddenly it was 27-18. Joe Fredrick, Notre Dame's best player on this night, broke the run with a jumper, but Kornet scored again with a spectacular 10-foot fadeaway off one foot that Booker and I later dubbed, somewhat unimaginatively, "Air Kornet." Wilcox ended our first-half scoring with another spectacular play—an underhanded scoop shot in the lane around Rivers. We led by eight, 38-30, at halftime.

The second half did not start well for us. Rivers's jumper and Kevin Ellery's free throws after Perdue's third foul made it 38-34, but a Perdunk-putback off my miss stopped the Irish momentum. After an Irish basket, back-to-back buckets by Kornet and Perdue returned the lead to eight. Opportunity knocked for the Irish, however, at the 15:51 mark when Perdue was called for a highly questionable fourth foul. Gary Voce's two free throws cut the lead to 47-42, and we would need to maintain the lead for at least 10 minutes while Will was on the bench. Happily, we were able to weather his absence. I hit a 12-foot jumper in the lane; Kornet bagged a 17-footer; Grant hit an eight-footer off the glass; I drove from the baseline into the lane for an eight-foot banker. The lead was 55-46 with 11 minutes to play. Seconds later, Draud and Wilcox fashioned another highlight-reel play on a two-on-one fast break off a Draud steal, with Scott feeding Derrick with a beautiful behind-the-back pass for the layup. A Kornet free throw stretched the lead to 10 with nine minutes to go. After a couple of empty trips on both ends, Reid hit a short jumper on the baseline, and Draud followed with a 10-footer in the lane for a 62-48 lead.

After an Irish timeout, Rivers hit a jumper, then hit one free throw following a turnover, and two more following another turnover. The lead was nine, and Will returned to the game; we had added four points to our lead in his absence. Wilbur contributed immediately with a great pass to me for a layup to return the lead to double digits, and off an out-of-bounds play I scored another layup off a Booker feed to make it 66-53 inside three minutes, and the countdown to victory was on. Four Wilcox free throws sandwiched around an Irish deuce made it 70-55, and Derrick would hit four more free throws in the last two minutes as we closed it out, 75-66.

Kornet scored 17 points, his best performance for the season to date, in a team-high 36 minutes. Early in the season, Coach Newton had called Frank "the key to the team," and he was making C.M. look prophetic. His improved health had produced improved play as the season progressed; he led the team with nine rebounds at LSU, and in the next few games (UT, Ole Miss, Alabama, Georgia), scored a total of 40 points, making him a potent fourth option (or better) on offense. And he had been excited about the Notre Dame game; he had chosen Vandy over neighboring Purdue and felt that he was ready for a big game. As it turned out, he was right, and this game made it clear that Frank Kornet was back, and two years of injuries and frustration were a thing of the past.

❧

I first saw Frank Kornet play in January 1985 at the Louisville Invitational Tournament, a prestigious mid-season tournament that, at the time, featured 16 high schools in Kentucky, eight of the best from the Louisville area and eight top schools from elsewhere in the state. His team (Lexington Catholic) and mine (Marshall County) were two of the non-Louisville schools in the '85 event, and in the first round our teams anchored each end of a doubleheader. Frank encountered foul trouble in that game, but I was impressed with what I saw; clearly, he was a talented player. He averaged 18.2 points and 10.3 rebounds a game that season, shooting 64% from the field and leading Catholic to the state tournament.

Frank chose Vanderbilt over several schools, most notably Purdue. He was recruited hard by Purdue head coach Gene Keady's staff, particularly a young assistant on that staff named Kevin Stallings. As Frank recalled, "My dad actually graduated from Purdue, so I was a Boilermakers' fan growing up. I would tell everyone to put Vanderbilt and Purdue in a hat and pick [and] either one would have been a great decision." (Stallings did eventually nab a Kornet, though, signing Frank's son Luke in 2013, and Luke had a fine Commodore career in his own right, graduating in 2017.) Frank and I formally met and had our first experience as teammates in summer 1985 as members of the Kentucky squad in the Kentucky-Indiana All-Star games, the nation's oldest interstate all-star games (dating back to 1940, with one game played in each state over consecutive weekends) and a goal of every basketball-playing Kentucky (and Indiana) youngster. We hit it off during the two weeks of practice and games, then reconvened in Nashville with another freshman, Barry Booker, in fall 1985, to help the 'Dores escape the SEC cellar.

All three of us played well and made immediate contributions, and Frank was terrific in the pre-SEC schedule, starting 10 games and turning in some great games. He scored 10 points and pulled down six rebounds against eventual NCAA runner-up Duke; he led the team with 20 points in a victory over Penn; and he paced the team with 15 points and eight boards in a win over Baylor. But soon thereafter, he sustained an ankle injury and missed two games. He was still a little gimpy when he returned—"it was difficult to come back," he said later—and would not get back into the starting lineup for the rest of the season.

Our sophomore year of 1986–87 was immensely frustrating for Frank. He started well, scoring 12 points and grabbing eight rebounds in the championship game victory over New Mexico in the Maui Classic, and followed that up with 11 and six in our next game, against UT-Chattanooga. But a week later, in the first practice after our big win over Indiana, Frank injured his knee. An X-ray "showed nothing," but Frank was hurting badly. As he recalled, "I was hurt and wanted to redshirt"—his injury had occurred early enough in the season that he could have had immediate surgery and pushed the reset button on his sophomore season in 1987–88—"but Coach Newton said he really needed me that year." So, Frank soldiered on, but rarely played and was always in pain—he played in only 27 games and scored only 59 points the entire year. After the season, Frank had an MRI "that showed I had a hole in my patella tendon. So, after the season I had knee surgery." As he said later, "My sophomore year was a total waste," and he went so far as to say that "I was thinking about giving up basketball." Frank was hurt, and so were we by his absence; there's no doubt we would have made the NCAA Tournament in 1987 with a healthy Frank Kornet on board.

Frank was still recuperating from the surgery during fall 1987 and our preseason practices, but he was clearly on the mend and took a lot of pressure off Perdue, often filling in at center when Wilbur needed a break or was in foul trouble. The Notre Dame game was something of a coming-out party for a pain-free Frank Kornet; he would make significant contributions for the remainder of the season, then take a leading role along with Booker and me in our senior season of 1988–89, prompting Tennessee coach Don DeVoe to remark, "No one in the conference the last four years has made more progress than Frank Kornet."

࿔

Frank had a great game against Notre Dame, but the win was an all-around team effort. I backed Frank up with 16 points; he and I each hit 7-for-11 from the field. Wilcox had his best game of the season—in fact, he was perfect by hitting all three of his field goal attempts and all eight of his free throws to finish with 14. Perdue added 10 with a team-high seven boards, while Reid made all four of his field goal attempts and scored nine. Playing all 40 minutes, Rivers scored 18 and had eight assists, but he was only 7-for-18 from the field. Fredrick led the Irish with 19 but did not do much in the last 10 minutes.

All in all, it was probably our most complete game of the year—we had only eight turnovers (a season best prior to the postseason) and hit a sizzling 58.8% from the field. The win over Notre Dame proved two things. One is that we could defeat a quality opponent without a big game from Perdue. Will was characteristically generous in praising his teammates after the game, consistent with the team-first attitude he displayed all season long: "I've been getting so much attention this season that a lot of people don't realize how good the rest of our team is. I'm glad to see Frank and Barry and some of the other guys finally get some credit. They've deserved it all along." Knowing that we were entering the final stretch of games we would play with the big guy, the rest of the team, which would return intact for the next season, could—and would, often—refer back to the Notre Dame game as an example of how we could take down a tough, NCAA-caliber opponent, on the road no less, with Will absent for long stretches of time.

The second significant thing the Notre Dame game proved is that we didn't have to hit three-pointers to be effective. It's well known that, as of the end of the 2018–19 season, Vandy is one of just three teams (the others being Princeton and UNLV) to make a three-pointer in every game since the rule became effective in fall 1986, but in terms of makes and attempts, the Notre Dame game in '88 is the closest a Vandy team has come in more than 30 seasons from being blanked from behind the three-point line. Other than my trey in the first half, we attempted only one other triple in the entire game (a Draud miss in the second half). There have been a couple of other games over the years where a Vandy team made only one three (including the next season, as well as a game at Florida in 1996 when Drew Maddux hit the Dores' first and only three in the waning seconds of a Florida blowout in Gainesville), but never, to my knowledge, has a Vandy team attempted anything close to the two attempts we had against Notre Dame.

Of course, "the streak" was only about 60 games strong by the time of the '88 Notre Dame game (it's now over 1,000), so the fact that we hit only one trey didn't make much of an impression on me other than a passing thought of "that's interesting." As always, getting a big win was more important than hitting a bunch of (or any) three-pointers.

The Notre Dame win pushed our record to 18-7 and, we thought, put us into the NCAA field. *The Tennessean* agreed: the next day's headline blared, "Vandy Romps; NCAA Hopes Now Soaring." Digger Phelps agreed: "Don't be surprised to see them in the final eight," he opined. "This was no fluke tonight." Maybe it wasn't, but wins were about to become an endangered species for us.

11

MARCH BADNESS

I

"Everybody knows it's coming apart"
—*Leonard Cohen, "Everybody Knows"* ('88)

A couple of days after the Notre Dame victory, the calendar turned to March, and we entered the last week of the regular season. It would be a brutal week: a road game at Florida on Wednesday followed by a road game at Mississippi State on Saturday. Worse, the week would be the last one before spring break, which meant that midterm exams were on tap. We somehow had to take midterms while being out of town some or all of every day of the week except Monday leading up to the dismissal of classes on Friday.

To say the least, Florida was thirsting for revenge after the humiliation in Nashville. At the team meal, Coach Newton announced that Will had been named to the five-man All-SEC First Team and that I had been named to the Third Team. That was about the only thing that went right in Gainesville.

I always thought that Gator fans were the most abusive in the league. Now, for the '88 visit, the students and their elders fixed their attention on home-state thorn Will Perdue. Not surprisingly, they hadn't forgotten Will's "bring it on" gestures to Dwayne Schintzius in the game in Nashville, and they were lying in wait, beginning with the player introductions. When Will was introduced, the entire student section stood, and each student made the same gesture toward Will. Things went downhill from there. The game was not quite the blowout we had inflicted on Florida in Nashville, but, like that game, this one wasn't close. Florida roared to a 38-27 lead at the half and stretched the margin to as many as 26 points in the second half. "I thought up there [in Nashville] we got ahead of them and they almost quit," Booker said. "Tonight, I thought it was just about the other way around." The 81-65 final score would be our worst margin of defeat all year. Kornet, Wilcox, and I, the three leading scorers in the Notre Dame game, had combined for 47 points in that game; we were held to 13 (Frank seven, me six, Derrick zero) by Florida.

Schintzius scored a career-high 28 points on 13-for-18 shooting, supported by Vernon Maxwell's 24 points, which moved him into second place on the SEC career scoring list, behind only the untouchable Pete Maravich. Dwayne also claimed a game-high 10 rebounds and kept up his trash talk to Will: "I was talking junk to him, trying to get him mad. I was saying 'Come on man, you got to play.'" To the delight of the home fans, Perdue was held to 11 points and nine rebounds. The lesson, as always: don't trash-talk the other team when you still have to visit their place!

❧

As bad as that game was, the 24 hours beginning Thursday morning, upon our return to Nashville, were even worse. Several players had missed midterm exams because of the Florida trip; I had missed three, and another one was already scheduled for Thursday. Because we had to head back on the road on Friday afternoon, that meant I had to take four midterms in a little over 24 hours. I never believed that classroom and academic commitments were an excuse for poor play—a good player should be able to free his mind from all outside influences once the game starts—but the players were tested in every conceivable way this first week in March.

Overall, I always held my Vanderbilt professors in very high regard. It's a tight-knit academic community, and many of the professors were season-ticket holders or, at least, followed what the basketball and other athletic teams were doing during their seasons. And the excitement we had created on campus during the 1987–88 season wasn't limited to students; several professors would congratulate us and, on occasion, talk about a recent game. As a result, most professors were accommodating and understanding when the basketball schedule forced us to miss class or, more importantly, an exam. Coach Newton enjoyed enormous respect within the faculty, and Coach Bostick regularly checked in with faculty members on each player's progress in each class, which conveyed the seriousness with which the coaching staff took the team's academics. Thanks to that goodwill, I had little trouble scheduling my makeup exams.

But there are always exceptions—those professors who apparently believe that academics and athletics are wholly incompatible, and if ever the two should come into conflict, not only should academics come first (not unreasonable), but those who participate in varsity athletics should be penalized for doing so (wholly unreasonable). How else to explain the professor who taught a class that one of my teammates took and who announced on the first day of class that there would be four exams, all given equal weight, and that the lowest would be dropped for purposes of the final grade. We were on a road trip right before the first exam, and the player didn't do very well as a result. After a decent second exam, the player missed the third exam entirely—because we were playing in the NCAA tournament!—and the professor refused to allow the player to take a makeup exam, gave the player a zero, and told him that he could just use that one as the "drop" exam anyway—never mind that the player had planned to use the first, road trip-affected exam as the drop. Here we were, bringing incredible goodwill (not to mention money) to the university by participating in the highest-profile tournament college sports has to offer, and one of our team members is penalized for missing an exam that the professor would not allow the player to make up when we returned!

Coaches Newton and Bostick became actively involved in the matter and appealed the professor's refusal of a make-up exam all the way to the dean of the College of Arts & Science, to no avail, and likely to Chancellor Joe B. Wyatt, who proved what everyone on campus knew anyway—he cared little for athletics and knew even less. (I recall seeing Chancellor Wyatt visiting our locker room exactly one time after a game in my four years, and that was in my freshman year after the incredible comeback win over Tennessee.) Anyway, the upshot was that the player had to nail the fourth exam even to pass. Thankfully, he did.

Fortunately, I didn't have that professor and enjoyed strong relationships with most of mine, particularly the professors in my major of communication studies such as Kassian Kovalcheck, Ann Pettus, and the then-chair of that department, Randall Fisher. The same would be true during my three years at Vanderbilt Law School, which in the early '90s was filled with great professors and more than a few rabid basketball fans, including Jon Bruce, David Partlett, Tom McCoy, and especially the late Don Hall, not to mention the professor who enjoyed a successful tenure as the chancellor of the university—Nick Zeppos.

Anyway, we survived our midterm exams and prepared for the final regular season game, at Mississippi State. Playing at Mississippi State isn't much better than playing at Ole Miss. In fact, the combined attendance for our two games in Mississippi in 1988 was 9,125 (4,306 in Starkville)—which would have qualified as the worst crowd at Memorial Gym in my four years. But maybe the low turnout was a good thing, because this was our most frustrating game of the year.

We flew out of the gate by scoring the first nine points of the game, and it looked like we would have little trouble with the last-place Bulldogs. Kornet's basket five minutes in gave us an 11-point lead at 15-4. At about this point, Coach Newton made the usual wholesale substitutions of the four top reserves (Wilcox, Draud, Mayes, Grant), leaving Perdue as the only starter on the floor. That was the catalyst for the most incredible run by an opponent of the entire season. State started pressing, and we had trouble getting the ball over half court, let alone getting a decent shot at the basket. The Bulldogs rang up 13 steals in the game—the most by an opponent all season. They embarked on an incredible 25-2 run, and the only substitution Coach Newton made during that run was...taking out Perdue! That hardly stopped the bleeding, and by the time the starters returned to the floor, the State lead was double digits, and it would remain there most of the rest of the game. The Bulldogs led 40-31 at halftime, shot a sizzling 56.1% from the field—highest by an opponent all year—and coasted to a 73-68 victory, a highly misleading final score that reflected a bunch of garbage points we scored in the last couple of minutes.

It was of little solace to me that I had scored a season-best 22 points, the first time I had hit for at least 20 all season. Perdue, with 21, was the only other player in double figures. I was irritated at the dogmatic substitution pattern that the coaching staff refused to break, even when it was obvious that the game was getting away from us. I've never seen a team go from double digits ahead to double digits behind quicker than happened in this game. Afterward, I commented that we "made some substitutions and after that didn't maintain intensity." That not-so-subtle comment led to the obvious question of whether the substitutions killed our momentum. I refused to comment, which, of course, *was* a comment—and an unfavorable one at that.

In light of the State blitzkrieg, the media began questioning "Newton's puzzling substitutions" and criticizing the "pre-conceived substitution pattern." Of course, C.M. had been using the same "pattern" for several weeks, which was his defense: "nobody criticized it back when we were winning." Maybe not, but we clearly were in a slump and perhaps it was time to shake things up as we entered the postseason.

We ended the regular season with a conference record of 10-8, which reflected an odd symmetry: we lost our first three conference games, including our only home game; and we lost our last three conference games, including our only home game. For the 12 games in between, we went 10-2 and were the best team in the league during that stretch. The 10-8 record was the first winning SEC record for a Vanderbilt team since 1978–79. But we entered the SEC tournament in a severe slump.

II

"Never give up, never slow down, never grow old, never ever die young"
—*James Taylor, "Never Die Young"* ('87–'88)

For us, the 1988 SEC tournament could be summed up thusly: "The hits just keep on comin'." The tourney would be hosted by LSU, so naturally our opponent would be LSU, the only team in the league we hadn't beaten—and on its home court! And if that weren't enough, yet another tragedy struck the LSU family a couple of days before the game—this one much more immediate than the Maravich passing in January.

The '88 Tigers were just two seasons removed from the most improbable (at least as measured by seeding) run to the Final Four of any team in the 64-team era until 2006. The 1985–86 squad was good, but not great, during the regular season, finishing in fifth place in the SEC. The Tigers snuck into the NCAA tournament as an 11-seed and were promptly handed an incredible gift: the first two games would be held on their home floor, a ridiculous rule (especially for such a poor seed) that the NCAA wisely discontinued a couple of years later. The Tigers capitalized on the home court advantage by beating sixth-seeded Purdue in double overtime and then edging third-seeded Memphis State.

The situation was essentially reversed for the regionals in Atlanta as LSU had to play the hometown (and second-seeded) Georgia Tech Yellow Jackets in the Omni. Incredibly, the Tigers won that one, 70-64, setting up a regional final with Kentucky, which to that point had won 21 of 22 games against SEC opponents that season, including all three over LSU. But the Tigers shocked the 'Cats, 59-57, to earn a trip to the Final Four in Dallas. They led Louisville by eight at the half in the national semifinal but ran out of gas in the second half and eventually lost, 88-77. The keys to that improbable run were Don Redden and Ricky Blanton. Redden, a senior and the team's captain, was a decent player, averaging about 13 points a game during the regular season, but he caught fire in the tournament, averaging over 21 points in the Tigers' five games and scoring 27 in the win over Tech. He was named MVP of the Southeast Regional and garnered part of *Sports Illustrated*'s Final Four cover.

Meanwhile, the post player for this unexpected Final Four run was Blanton, a sophomore reserve who had been averaging only 14 minutes a game. But due to injuries, defections, and other problems, Dale Brown was without a center, and he moved Blanton into the post for the NCAAs—possibly the best move of his long coaching career. Blanton held his own against such stars as William Bedford (Memphis State), John Salley (Georgia Tech), and Kenny Walker (Kentucky), and he scored the clinching basket against UK off a feed from Redden. The Tigers' run to the '86 Final Four was one of those things that makes the NCAA tournament so special; the next time a team seeded as low as 11 would make the Final Four was George Mason in 2006.

On March 8, 1988, three days before we were to play LSU in the SEC tournament, Don Redden died. A couple of days later it was revealed that the cause of death was heart disease; in other words, apparently it was just one of those things—no crime, no drugs, nothing other than a heart condition that no one saw coming. And that was the sobering part; Redden was the first player I had played against who had died, and only two years after our teams had played each other. If it could happen to Redden at such a young age, couldn't it happen to anyone?

Well, if I was asking questions like that, you can imagine how shaken Dale Brown, Ricky Blanton, and the rest of the LSU coaches and players were. Brown recalled Redden's death as "the biggest shock I've ever had" and "the biggest blow I ever suffered." Redden's funeral was held on Thursday afternoon, 24 hours before our game. Brown gave the eulogy; Blanton, who was dating Redden's sister (a member of the LSU women's hoops team) was a pallbearer. With the game to be played in the Deaf Dome, the stage was set for the most emotional opponent I ever faced.

Blanton clearly was emotionally exhausted. But the adrenalin of sports pushes people to ignore fatigue and emotional pain, and perhaps even use them as additional motivation. And Blanton was, most assuredly, emotional; he was normally a bit of a chatterbox anyway on the court, but he was wildly emotional in this game, yelling at us, the refs, and anyone who did anything that stood in the way of victory. He would play all 40 minutes and score 30 points in an epic performance. For his part, Brown, no doubt just as drained and emotional as his star player, let his emotions get the best of him a couple of times. In fact, he committed what I think is the ultimate sin by a coach in the heat of battle—yelling at an opposing player. In the first half, Perdue took a charge from Jose Vargas that Brown thought was a flop, and as the players walked back to our end for Will's free throws, Brown unleashed a profanity-laced tirade toward Will on what he thought was Will's faking the charge. But either intimidated by the crowd, sympathetic to the Tigers' situation, or both, the refs let it go. We were on our own.

Against this backdrop, as one writer later said, "nobody could've beaten the emotionally charged Tigers" in this game. But we played better than in our previous two losses against the Tigers. The game was competitive at the half (LSU led, 42-35), but a few minutes into the second half, I tried to chase down Bernard Woodside on a breakaway, and as he went for the layup he accidentally elbowed me in the nose (somehow the foul was on me). I was dazed and bloodied and didn't return to the game. The Tigers eventually prevailed, 87-80. After the game, in an emotional scene, Blanton led a group of Tigers into the stands and presented the game ball to Redden's parents. Brown later wrote that the game was "[t]he greatest victory [he had] ever been associated with." Still playing on an emotional high, LSU gave Kentucky a real scare the next day before bowing, 86-80.

At the end of the slightly surreal week, our record stood at 18-10, having lost three games in a row, four of our last five, and five of our last seven—not exactly the strong statement we had wanted to make to the selection committee in our effort to snag that elusive NCAA bid. But it was out of our hands now.

III

"It's even worse than it appears, but it's alright"
—Grateful Dead, "Touch of Grey" ('87)

After the loss to LSU on Friday afternoon, no one was in the mood to hang around Baton Rouge. We returned to Nashville on Saturday to sweat out the NCAA selections, which were to be announced on Sunday evening.

The first NCAA selection show was aired in 1980 on a six-month-old network called ESPN. CBS took over the NCAA selection show in 1982, and ever since, "Selection Sunday" has taken on a life of its own—a standalone show where the 68 teams selected to play in the NCAA tournament are announced, broken into four regionals, the all-important "brackets." Even in 1988, the announcement of the NCAA teams "slam-dunk[ed] all regular-season college basketball programs."

Over the past three decades, the NCAA basketball tournament has contributed new words and phrases to the American sports vocabulary ("Selection Sunday" being one of them), as well as new meanings to old words. Thus, in the days and weeks leading up to Selection Sunday, "bracketologists" hold forth on which teams are "on the bubble," meaning teams that are borderline candidates to be chosen for "The Dance," i.e., the NCAA tournament. In 1988, the NCAA tourney was in a run of "phenomenal growth," which had boosted the popularity of college basketball. But terms like "bracketology" and "on the bubble" hadn't yet saturated the basketball landscape. I can't speak for the other players, but I had little idea what our NCAA chances were, whether we were "a lock," on the bubble, or anything else. Coach Newton didn't project much confidence to us after the LSU loss in the SEC tournament; he said he didn't know whether we would be invited; we would have to wait and see. My guess, though, is that he was cautiously optimistic, as we all were.

In addition to Kentucky, Florida and Auburn were considered safely in the tournament field. That left us and LSU. We had the better record, but Dale Brown had the reasonable argument that his team had beaten ours three times. In fact, politicking for a bid in a television interview prior to the announcement of the selections, Brown said exactly that—"we beat Vanderbilt three times." That was a sign that we had elevated the program—LSU's primary argument for entry into the NCAAs was beating Vanderbilt three times. Things had changed!

To say the least, I was nervous leading up to the selection show—more nervous than I was before any game. And the selection would turn out to be an agonizing, nerve-wracking process. CBS began by unveiling the East Region matchups. LSU didn't have to wait too long—the Bayou Bengals were in the first quartet of games announced, an 8/9 game against Georgetown opposite the top seed, Temple, which would play another of our '87–'88 opponents, Lehigh. Two more season opponents wound up in that region—Indiana (4 seed) and Notre Dame (10 seed). No more SEC teams were placed in the East. The West Regional featured three more teams we had played during the regular season—Cornell (a 16 seed matched against top-seeded Arizona), North Carolina (2 seed), and Florida (6 seed). That left two regions, and certain SEC entrants Kentucky and Auburn, and hopefully us. UK and Auburn were placed in the Southeast Region, Auburn in an 8/9 game against Bradley with top-ranked Oklahoma awaiting the winner, and UK the #2 seed.

With 48 teams announced, only 16 remained—the Midwest Regional. The top half of the bracket was revealed—Purdue and Farleigh Dickinson (seeds 1 and 16),

Baylor and Memphis State (8/9), DePaul and Wichita State (4/13), and Kansas State and LaSalle (5/12). Still no Vanderbilt, and only eight teams remained. The bottom half of the bracket, constituting the final eight teams in the field and with games to be played in Lincoln, Nebraska, was revealed. North Carolina State (3 seed) would play Murray State (14), and Kansas (6) would play Xavier (11). Four teams left. Finally, we saw "Vanderbilt" appear as the seventh seed, matched up against 10 seed Utah State. Out of 32 opening-round pairings, we were the 31st announced; the 32nd was second-seeded Pittsburgh against the 15 seed, Eastern Michigan. As it turned out, that was the first of several dramatic moments in our 1988 NCAA experience.

Whew! There was a combination of joy and relief all around. In truth, as that seventh seed indicated, we weren't really on the bubble after all—nor should we have been, in retrospect. Based purely on the seed, the Selection Committee thought we were somewhere between the 25th and 28th best team in the country. Nevertheless, given our recent struggles, Coach Newton had to defend the inevitable "Does Vandy belong?" questions, and he left no doubt where he stood on that issue. "This team has earned the chance to play for a national championship," he said. "I think the selection committee took into consideration our season as a whole, not just the last few games. And based on our overall season, I felt we deserved to be in the tournament."

I agreed. The poor play in late February and early March obscured the overall profile of 10 wins in one of the nation's toughest conferences, as well as high-quality nonconference wins over North Carolina and Notre Dame. That's probably why, a few years ago, the NCAA officially eliminated "last 10 games" as a criterion for selection to the tournament—quality wins in December should stand equally with quality wins in February. Still, with a lackluster oh-fer in March, there inevitably were some doubters—and maybe we even doubted ourselves a bit. I observed that this was "our chance to show people we belong. We also want to prove something to ourselves."

12

QUICHE: BREAKFAST OF CHAMPIONS

I

"Two kinds of people in this world—winners, losers"
—Lindsey Buckingham, "Go Insane" ('84)

While my junior year in college had turned into a memorable one, complete with a trip to the NCAA tournament, my junior year of high school, the 1983–84 season, was incredible too. It was one of those magical seasons that deserves a book of its own; certainly, everyone in Marshall County, Kentucky, would buy it. The girls' basketball team, coached by my cousin Howard Beth (who won nearly 800 games in 30 years as head coach), went undefeated and won the state title with, incredibly, two Kentucky Miss Basketballs on the roster: Carol Parker ('84 winner) and Mary Taylor ('87 winner, future player and longtime head coach at Western Kentucky).

On the boys' side, we had lost four of the top six players from my sophomore season, and had a new coach, Allan Hatcher, an intense 31-year-old who came to western Kentucky from his native West Virginia after coaching one of the country's top high school seniors in 1982–83, Wake Forest signee Mark Cline. Allan promised that "[w]e are really going to get after people. We are going to do a lot of pressing and try to get the ball up and down the court in a hurry." He was right, and the result was an exciting brand of basketball as I teamed with four seniors—guards Danny Butler and Cary Allen, forward Tim Miller and center Jerry Powell—and had a remarkable season.

I had averaged 12.2 points a game as a sophomore and still wasn't sure whether I had the talent to play at the next level. But the racehorse-style basketball we employed really suited my game and brought out my potential. In the third game of the year, I scored 37 points in a win over district rival Calloway County, and I scored at least 20 in most of our games. Still, breaking in a new coach and his system resulted in a slow start in terms of wins and losses. We were 4-2 heading into the annual Christmas tournament hosted by Paducah Tilghman. We won the first two games to meet Tilghman, which happened to be the top-ranked team in the entire state at that time and would be for most of the season, in the final. The Blue Tornado won that one, 72-65, to drop us to 6-3.

Our very next game was our regularly scheduled visit to Tilghman a week later in the same gym, and we felt we were ready this time. Tilghman, alma mater of Vandy's legendary coach Roy Skinner, is in the heart of Paducah, which is the only thing resembling a "city" in the far western part of Kentucky. Its county, McCracken, adjoins Marshall County, which made Tilghman my high school's primary rival in all sports, but especially in basketball. Tilghman was the state's top-ranked team for good reason—it was an immensely talented squad, led by two first-team all-staters, Sam Arterburn and Terry Shumpert. The 6'6" Arterburn, a signee of the University of Tennessee, was an athletic leaper who controlled the Tornado's inside game. Shumpert was a splendid point guard who could do everything in the backcourt—shoot, handle the ball, and generally lead the team. He too could have played basketball at the next level, but he was even better at another sport—baseball, where he starred at the University of Kentucky on his way to a 14-year major league career (1990–2003) with seven teams, most notably the Royals and especially the Rockies, for whom he hit .347 in 1999. (The Tilghman hoops team was good, and so was the baseball team—one of Shumpert's diamond teammates was another long-time major leaguer, Steve Finley.)

Shumpert and I had posted relatively modest point totals the week before—I scored 19 and he scored 12, perhaps attributable to the fact that the championship game was the second game we played that day. This time around, though, he and I engaged in a real shoot-out. I won the battle, outscoring Terry 37 to 36, but he won the all-important war, leading Tilghman to a 75-66 win to drop our record to 6-4. In the locker room after the loss, Coach Hatcher reminded us that Tilghman still had to come to our gym, "and they'll be hanging from the rafters" for that one.

From that point, we started to gel and gain confidence. A couple of weeks later we participated in the craziest tournament imaginable, the "Superman Classic" in Massac County, Illinois, just across the Ohio River from Paducah and whose county seat is Metropolis—the home of Superman. Befitting the tourney's name, five teams played a round-robin schedule over five nights, meaning each team played four games in five nights with only one night off, and two of those teams would play four nights in a row because their off night would be either the first night or the fifth one; naturally, we were one of those two teams, drawing night one as our night off, so we had to play four games in four nights. Somehow, we won the tournament, beating four teams from three different states, including the defending AAA champions from Missouri and, in the fourth game, host Massac County (which had beaten us on the same floor in the season's first game) for the title.

From there, we were determined not to lose again. I missed a key road game a week later at district rival Mayfield with the flu, and Cary Allen, our second-leading scorer, was also under the weather and barely played at all; Jerry Powell picked up the slack with 32 points and we won by a point. I missed the next night's game too, but Jerry came through again with 22 points and 14 rebounds to lead us to another win.

Finally, on February 11, Tilghman made its trip to Marshall County and our home floor, the Reed Conder Gymnasium. The gym is something special; it opened in 1980 and, somewhere along the line, has picked up the nickname "Little Rupp Arena." In 2004, *USA Today*, weighing more than 2,600 responses, selected Conder as one of the 10 best places in the country to watch high school basketball. For the past 20 years or so, the gym has been the site of Hoopfest, a December event that brings in top high school teams from around the nation, such as Oak Hill Academy, to play against other high-profile programs. Such notables as Carmelo Anthony (who took his ACT at the gym to become eligible to play for Syracuse), Kevin Durant, Derrick Rose, and Rajan Rondo have graced Hoopfest over the years. That 2004 *USA Today* piece mentioned four "memorable moments" that had taken place at Conder over its first 25 seasons (one of which was Anthony's ACT). This Tilghman game, played on February 11, 1984, made that list as well, and for good reason.

Our gym was, as Coach Hatcher had predicted, packed to the rafters—5,500 at least—for this third game of the season against Tilghman, and supposedly some people were even turned away at the door. That game was everything it was supposed to be, and in a thriller, we won it, 75-74, for our 14th straight victory. Shumpert was hampered by foul trouble and fouled out with 6:43 remaining, having scored only 10 points; I scored 36 points, including 23 in the second half and 14 in the fourth quarter. It was an incredible game and victory, and it didn't seem like we could top it.

II

"Believe it or not there's life after high school"
—Daryl Hall & John Oates, "Adult Education" ('84)

We kept on winning, closing the regular season with 18 straight victories and a 24-4 record. Two steps remained for a trip to the State Tournament—the district tournament (there are 64 districts in Kentucky) and the regional tournament (16 regions, with the winner and runner-up from the four district tournaments in each region advancing to the eight-team regional). We blew through the district tourney, which was held on our home floor, winning the title against Calloway County, 92-57, behind my 42 points in the final; our winning streak was at 20 heading into the regional tourney. An opening round blowout in the first game brought us to the regional semifinals, where we would face Tilghman for the fourth and final time, with the entire season for both teams on the line.

The game was played on Friday as the first game of the semifinal doubleheader at Murray State's on-campus arena, which seated around 6,000. Our game would begin at 6 PM, so we arrived at the arena around 4:30, 90 minutes before tipoff. When we walked in to the gym, we saw something incredible: at least 80% of the gym already was filled with Marshall County fans, who were just sitting there, 90 minutes before tipoff, in utter, eerie silence—like the final scene in Hitchcock's *The Birds*—and the tension in the building already was palpable. Our school's colors were bright orange (in fact, when I first visited Vanderbilt's campus a month later and was wearing orange somewhere in my wardrobe, more than one person—players and coaches alike—remarked, not entirely jokingly, "You'll have to lose that orange," a reference to Tennessee), so it was like walking into a burst of sunshine in an indoor gym. Once the fans noticed us, however, they began cheering us wildly. It was one of the most incredible basketball-related experiences of my life that didn't take place during a game.

Both schools displayed the usual banners and rah-rah items around the gym, but the one that caught my eye was a 10-foot long sign the Tilghman supporters unfurled across the railing in their cheering section: "BARRY GOHEEN EATS QUICHE." I had absolutely no idea what that meant at that time, but later I learned that in 1982 a writer named Bruce Feirstein hit the best-seller lists with a book titled *Real Men Don't Eat Quiche*. The author posited, in language that was in vogue in 1982: "We've become a nation of wimps. Pansies. Quiche eaters." I guess that banner somehow was supposed to get under my skin, but happily I didn't really know what quiche was in 1984, so the sign was more of a head-scratcher than anything.

If this had been a college game and there had been such a network as ESPN Classic in 1984, this fourth and final Tilghman game would have been rerun the next day and for days thereafter, because it immediately attained "instant classic" status, one that, immediately afterwards, was predicted to "go down as one of the greatest for years to come," a game that "left all witnesses limp," and was "one of the finest...ever seen." Many termed it "the greatest game I've ever seen" or "the game of the century," and I'm sure, 35 years later, it's still in the discussion of the greatest high school basketball games in the history of Kentucky's First Region.

The game was a nail-biter all the way. Tilghman led by two after one quarter and by one at the half, and neither team was able to forge any meaningful lead. The third quarter was tight as well, and we led by one going into the fourth quarter, the final eight minutes of the game. Unfortunately, Tilghman took charge in the fourth and used a 14-3 run to build a 64-56 lead with 3:23 to play. With no three-point line or shot clock in effect, things looked bleak. I hit two free throws to cut the deficit to six, and a Tilghman turnover resulted in two Jerry Powell free throws to trim Tilghman's lead to four with 2:50 left. Then Tilghman began to milk the clock, forcing us to foul with 90 seconds to go. Two free throws pushed the Tornado's lead to six, but we scored 10 seconds later, then forced the Tornado into a bad shot with a minute remaining, which we converted into a field goal with 53 seconds left to cut the Tornado lead to two. Shumpert, however, scored out of the Tornado's delay game, and Tilghman's lead was 68-64 with 30 seconds left. My jumper with 17 seconds left cut the lead back to two, and we were forced to foul Shumpert, an 80% free-throw shooter, who could have iced the game with two free throws. But he missed the front end of the one-and-one, giving us a final chance with seconds to play. Tilghman blocked Tim Miller's shot attempt under the basket, but the loose ball came to me, and my putback narrowly beat the buzzer to force a three-minute overtime period. The electricity and tension in the gym were practically off the charts by now.

We claimed the tip and ran nearly two minutes off the clock before I drew a foul. I hit both ends of the one-and-one to put us ahead 70-68. We fouled on the other end, but Tilghman made only one of the two free throws, and we had the ball and a one-point lead, which I extended to three when I was fouled and hit both ends of the one-and-one with 42 seconds left. But Shumpert drove the baseline, hit a layup, and drew a foul. His three-point play tied the game at 72. I then made the dumbest play I would ever make late in a game: we could have held for the final shot, but, with around 30 seconds left, I thought I saw an opening on the baseline and drove to the basket, barreling into a Tilghman player; I was called for the charge, turning the ball back to the Tornado, which could hold for the final shot. After running a little clock, the Tornado called timeout with 11 seconds left to set up the final play. Out of the timeout, Shumpert prepared to inbound the ball on the sideline at half-court. The 6'6" Arterburn was being face-guarded by the 6'1" Miller; all Shumpert had to do was lob the inbounds pass to his tall teammate. But he decided to throw a bounce pass instead; though face-guarding Arterburn, Tim saw the ball out of the corner of his eye, shot the gap and stole the pass, racing to the wide-open basket on our end. Arterburn nearly caught him, and as Tim laid the ball off the glass, Arterburn batted it away—an obvious goaltend, which was properly called with around five seconds left, giving us a two-point lead. Tilghman still had a few seconds left, but Shumpert, racing downcourt and looking for Arterburn under the basket, threw it over his head out of bounds. Ball game! We had prevailed in one of the all-time thrillers, 74-72.

Notwithstanding the silly charge in overtime, I had perhaps my greatest game ever, high school or college: 13-for-17 from the field and 12-for-13 from the line for 38 points. Shumpert scored 28 points in his final high school basketball game, but he had a tough last three-and-a-half minutes—the missed free throw to facilitate overtime, the two turnovers late in overtime. It was just an amazing game.

It was an awesome win, but it did not put us in the Sweet Sixteen. We had to come back 24 hours later for the regional championship—against Calloway County, the same team we had beaten by 35 points for the district title a week earlier. But this game was totally different—we led only by six, 39-33, after three quarters. We still led 42-37 with five minutes to play, but Calloway scored six straight points in the next 75 seconds to claim the lead. We hit one of two free throws to tie it at 43 with three minutes to play. The Lakers then attempted to hold the ball for the final shot, but their center, Jamey Johnson—whose father had been a college teammate of my father's at Murray State—was called for traveling with about 90 seconds to play. Now we could hold for the last shot, and we ran the clock down to about 15 seconds; Cary Allen missed a jumper, but I rebounded and was fouled on the put-back attempt. I made one of the two free throws to put us ahead by one, and we survived two missed free throws by Calloway to claim an ugly but heart-stopping 44-43 win to put us in the state tournament at Rupp Arena in Lexington.

I don't think I have ever heard a louder crowd than the eruption in Racer Arena when the clock showed all zeroes and we had clinched a trip to Lexington. When the All-Tournament team was announced, I literally couldn't hear the PA announcer because of the noise—I think I ran out three different times to accept All-Tourney honors under the assumption that my name must have been called at some point. The whole experience was pure ecstasy for players and fans alike.

We not only got the last laugh against Tilghman on the court, but our students got the last laugh on the Great Quiche Controversy. A couple of weeks later, the students bought some billboard space on a well-traveled thoroughfare in Paducah and posted this sign:

HEY TILGHMAN—"QUICHE"…
THE BREAKFAST OF CHAMPIONS
MCHS.

Now THAT is sweet revenge!

III
"Fate—up against your will"
—Echo & the Bunnymen, "The Killing Moon" ('84)

"The Kentucky State High School Basketball Tournament is a social phenomenon that only a slightly basketball-crazy sociologist could explain." As with trying to describe the importance of Kentucky basketball to a non-Kentuckian, explaining the Kentucky State High School Basketball Tournament to the uninitiated—even a hoops fan—is a challenge. One author put it as well as anyone when he described the "Kentucky state basketball tournament" as

> a contest unlike almost any other in the country. Here, there are no divisions—no 6A, 5A, and so on. In Lexington's Rupp Arena, home of the University of Kentucky Wildcats, where the tournament takes place, big schools face small schools and country boys from coal-mining hamlets take on inner-city kids from Louisville. It isn't about pitting same against same, or making sure kids take home trophies. Kentucky doesn't care so much about fairness. What people want here is excitement, to see who's

best, plain and simple. And what they like about its format is its purity, its mathematical simplicity. Sixteen teams, playing for one title, over four days in March.

Louisville Ballard's Allan Houston, later a star at Tennessee and in the NBA, also was spot-on in describing the tournament: "It seemed like the lights were much brighter. It seemed like you were just on this huge stage and the whole world was watching." Suffice it to say that practically every young Kentucky boy or girl, at some point, dreams about playing in what has always been called the "Sweet Sixteen"—the term used for this event long before the NCAA tournament co-opted that term. Talent and other circumstances will extinguish that dream for most, but it remains a centerpiece of Kentucky culture.

The tournament is bracketed through a blind draw of the 16 regions—so great is the interest that the draw itself is televised—before the regional champions are crowned. In '84, the First Region was paired with the Tenth; after the regional champions were determined, the teams would be Marshall County against Bourbon County—a great name for a Kentucky county if ever there was one.

The way the draw shook out, we felt that we could make it to the finals if we could win that first game. And it would be our third consecutive nail-biting thriller. The Colonels led 17-14 after the first quarter, but we caught them in the second and tied it at 33 at halftime. We then forged a 51-48 lead at the end of three quarters and led 60-56 with just over three minutes remaining. But the Colonels scored on a putback, stole the ball in the backcourt, and converted that turnover into the tying basket. We then turned it over again on a charging call, but the Colonels missed a couple of shots underneath, and we rebounded with 1:20 to play. As in the regional final, we held for the last shot; as in that game, I was fouled inside 10 seconds to play. Unlike that game, however, I missed the front end of the one-and-one, and now the Colonels could win it. We fouled their best player, Jeff Royce, with four seconds left, but he too missed the front end of the one-and-one, so it was on to overtime with the scored tied at 60.

Bourbon County scored first in overtime, but I tied it with 1:39 left. With just over a minute to play, Royce hit an improbable hanging bank shot from 10 feet to give the Colonels the lead. And we would not score again—a missed shot and a turnover doomed us, and a Colonels free throw late put it away given the absence of a three-point line. The final score was 65-62. Our 23-game winning streak and our truly magical season were over.

IV

"My childhood memories slowly swirled past like the wind through the trees"
—*Pretenders, "My City Was Gone"* ('84)

The silver lining was that I dramatically improved my college stock in our one-and-done appearance in the State Tournament—I was on fire in the first half, scoring 21 of our 33 points, though the foul problems of our other wingman, Cary Allen, meant that I saw fewer opportunities in the second half. I finished with 27 points on 12-of-16 shooting from the field, making the all-tournament team, and experienced a significant increase in recruiting interest. Coach Hatcher said, "I would say the number of schools that are interested in him numbers in the 100s right now," though I think that was a slight exaggeration. I wound up as a Second Team All-State selection, the only junior on that 10-man team. The 10-man First Team included two juniors—Louisville Seneca's Tony Kimbro and Greenup County's Mike Scott, along with the Tilghman duo of Shumpert and Arterburn, but I edged Shumpert for the First Region Player of the Year honor. It was a great confidence builder for my senior season. Indeed, in the last five games of that season—the district final, the three Regional Tournament games, and the State Tournament game—I was playing in some other zone that even today, as I look back on it, seems hard to believe: 60-for-81 from the field (74%), 32-for-37 from the free-throw line (86.5%), and 152 total points (30.4 per game).

Still, that state tournament experience was a painful lesson, the third of three heart-stopping games that, taken together, proved, somewhat paradoxically, that (1) I could play with the best in the state and (2) I had a lot to learn about performing under pressure. Indeed, in all three games I made errors in the closing seconds that could have cost my team the game: the charge in overtime against Tilghman, the missed second free throw against Calloway County, and the missed one-and-one against Bourbon County. Those were learning experiences for me and, ultimately, allowed me to handle those situations much better as a high school senior and as a collegian at Vandy. And, now that I had helped the Commodores earn the program's first NCAA bid since 1974, I was determined to perform better in those pressure situations.

13

FRIDAY THE 18TH

I

"There comes a time when a boy must leave and a man has to enter"
—Rick Springfield, "Rock of Life" ('88)

So, four years after the dramatic March as a high school junior, it was a thrill to be one of the 64 teams playing for the NCAA championship as a college junior in 1988. As recent history had proven, anything could happen if you could just get into the tourney: 8-seed Villanova shocked everyone by winning the title in 1985, playing the so-called "perfect game" against heavily favored Georgetown in the final in Rupp Arena; 11-seed LSU made it to the Final Four in '86; and 6-seed Providence crashed to the Final Four in '87.

So, naturally, having gotten that elusive NCAA bid, we returned to the court on Monday and had a lousy practice—no energy, no enthusiasm, no sharpness. You might see that in late October, but it should never happen in March. It was hard to figure, really, and Coach Newton was more perplexed than angry. His meeting with the team after our lackluster practice took more of a fatherly tone. He noted that Tennessee, which hadn't been to a postseason tournament in a couple of years, surely was excited to have made the NIT with a 16-12 record. Coach Newton emphasized that we were one of only 64 teams with a chance to play for the national championship. Just relax and have fun, he advised.

That meeting demonstrated one of C.M. Newton's strengths as a coach: he had the ability to sense what motivational technique was best for the moment. Sometimes it might be yelling (and, make no mistake, he could yell with the best of them), but other times it might be a more persuasive, lighter touch. This was one of those "other times," and it did the trick. We had three more days of practice before our game on Friday afternoon, and we practiced with more crispness and purpose than we had displayed in the previous couple of weeks. We flew to Lincoln on Thursday afternoon. We had a quick practice to prepare for Utah State, and were ready to go on Friday.

❧

I've always thought that the best two days of the sports year, and certainly of the basketball season, are the first two full days of the NCAA tournament, Thursday and Friday. Each day has 16 games, four each at four different sites. There always seems to be something exciting going on somewhere—a buzzer-beater here, a potential upset there, a great individual performance somewhere else. I liked the idea of playing on Friday, the second day of the first round. By the start of Friday's games, 16 teams already had been sent packing to their off-season. I felt like that by Friday, the tournament was truly in full swing and not just getting started.

Our game with Utah State would be the second game of the four in Lincoln that day. The first matched the second seed in the Midwest, Pittsburgh, against 15th-seeded Eastern Michigan. We watched the first half before repairing to our locker room to prepare for our game. It was an entertaining game—EMU stayed right with Pitt for the first half, trailing only 52-49 at the half. But the Panthers proved too much for EMU in the second half, and pulled away to win by the NBA-like score of 108-90. Thus, when we took the floor, we knew that we would play Pitt on Sunday if we got past the Aggies.

We didn't know much about Utah State when we saw the brackets, but we engaged in a crash course on the Aggies between Sunday evening and Friday afternoon. The Aggies sported a 21-9 record and had gained the automatic berth into the NCAAs by winning the Pacific Coast Athletic Association (later named the Big West) conference tournament—an impressive achievement given that, at the time, the PCAA housed a traditional college basketball power, UNLV. Their coach, Rod Tueller, who was retiring at the end of the season, described his squad as "a very up-tempo team. We like to get the ball up and down the court and score some points." That sounded compatible with our strategy too, and Coach Tueller was right—his team averaged 83.6 points a game on 50% shooting from the field. So, the game didn't figure to be a defensive struggle, which was fine with me.

The two teams started veteran lineups. These days, you don't often see NCAA tourney games where no freshman is among the 10 starters, and nine of the starters are juniors or seniors, but that's what we and Utah State put on the floor to start the game. Kevin Nixon, a first team all-conference pick, was a senior and averaged 16 points a game. The other four starters were juniors: guard Reid Newey (14 per game) and forwards Dan Conway (16 per game and second team all-conference) and Gilbert Pete (more of a bruiser), with Greg Houskeeper (nine a game, 59% from the field) at center. And the Aggies also had a Draud-like sharpshooter off the bench, Jeff Anderson, who led the team with an impressive 45% mark from behind the three-point line. Those were the team's six primary players; in fact, only one other player (Jon Judkins) would leave the bench, and only for nine minutes. "We don't have a superstar approach," Coach Tueller said. "We have good balance between five or six players."

The Aggies had won five in a row coming into the tourney, which contrasted starkly with our three-game losing streak coming in. Will discounted how we had played coming into the tournament: "That's all in the past. That part of the season's over. The tournament is a whole new beginning." I felt like we had the advantage playing a team that had never seen us (other than on game film) before: "Because of our style of offense, it's to our advantage to play a team that hasn't seen us." I'm sure I had in mind our many impressive non-conference victories over a string of quality opponents in the past two seasons (Indiana, North Carolina, Missouri, Notre Dame twice, etc.), each of whom was better than Utah State. Nixon, though, thought otherwise: "The advantage is definitely with us. The momentum and rhythm of the game is in our favor because of the way we've been playing."

Both teams found that "rhythm" hard to find at the outset, however. The teams traded turnovers in the first minute, and we started sluggishly on the defensive end as Houskeeper drew fouls on Perdue and then Kornet. That demonstrated the Aggies' strategy—they intended to take the ball inside right at Perdue, hoping to get him in foul trouble. But Will, despite the early foul, would steer clear of serious foul trouble for most of the game. We led 10-6 five minutes in. Then, Wilcox and Draud provided great energy off the bench. First, Derrick scored on a nifty move, then Scott nailed the game's first two three-pointers on consecutive trips, and suddenly it was 18-8, and we stretched the lead to 24-10 at the 9:20 mark. Utah State found some rhythm from there, but we kept the Aggies at bay for the rest of the half, and went to the locker room with a 38-28 lead.

We felt a lot better in the locker room than we had felt in our prior three games, where we had trailed, often badly. In fact, we had shut out their best player, Nixon, in the first half. He quickly announced that the second half would be different by scoring his first bucket to open the half and, after a Reid basket, fed Conway for a deuce. I answered the Conway basket with a trey and a 43-32 lead. The teams continued to trade baskets for a few minutes, with Kornet's 15-footer and my layup off Booker's steal and assist keeping us with a comfortable 49-40 margin with 14:15 left and the first media timeout.

We maintained that margin for the next couple of minutes, but then the Aggies made their run, scoring five straight to close the gap to 51-45. A Perdue basket pushed the lead back to eight, but the Aggies wouldn't go away; they had a four-point trip on a free throw and an offensive rebound off the missed second free throw, which they converted into a three-pointer, and Conway's jumper at the 10-minute mark cut the lead to two, 53-51. Then, Anderson's second consecutive trey put the Aggies ahead for the first time since it was 2-0. The Aggies missed an opportunity to add to their lead (and their 9-0 run) when Conway missed two free throws.

The five starters (Perdue, Kornet, Reid, Booker, Goheen) had been in the game as Utah State took the lead. Now, with around 10 minutes remaining and the season hanging in the balance, Coach Newton made an unusual substitution, removing

Reid in favor of Draud, which gave us a three-guard lineup to go with Perdue and Kornet inside. That lineup, which stayed on the floor until the final minute, clicked; it was the key tactical move of the game.

After the substitution, Kornet gave us the lead back with a 15-footer, but Nixon quickly answered with a 15-footer to give the Aggies a one-point lead. Kornet's dunk off my spin-and-pass in the lane put us back on top. After a much-needed defensive stop, I drove the lane for a layup, made it and was fouled; the three-point play made it 60-56. Nixon's baseline jumper cut the lead to two, but Perdue quickly answered with his final two points of the game and a 62-58 lead. Nixon scored again, but Kornet's dunk off Perdue's great feed pushed the lead back to four. Houskeeper's basket made it 64-62, but we responded yet again: Booker hit his first three of the game for a five-point lead and then drew a big charge on Conway with 3:45 to go. My 16-footer extended the lead to 69-62 with just over three minutes left. After a Conway free throw, Booker hit another three to stretch our lead to nine. An Aggies basket made it 72-65 with 1:48 to go.

Then we—really, I—got sloppy. I turned it over on the ensuing inbounds pass, which Nixon, drawing Perdue's fourth foul, converted into a free throw to cut the lead to six. He missed the second free throw, though, and the Aggies inexplicably had no one covering the backcourt, leaving Draud for a wide-open layup off Perdue's rebound and outlet pass; our lead was 74-66. After an Aggies bucket, I made another silly pass and turnover, and Nixon converted that one into another free throw; the lead was 74-69. Wilcox, inserted into the game for Draud, missed a one-and-one with 40 seconds left, and a trey by the Aggies cut the lead to two, 74-72, with 31 seconds remaining. The Aggies fouled Wilcox again, but this time, under tremendous pressure to keep our season alive, Derrick nailed both ends of the one-and-one for a 76-72 lead with 29 seconds remaining. I rebounded the Aggies' missed trey, was fouled, and made both ends of the one-and-one for a six-point lead. An Aggies deuce made it 78-74 with 11 seconds left, and they called timeout. Out of the timeout, I broke free off the inbounds play, received the pass from Booker, and fed a wide-open Kornet for the game-clinching dunk. Nixon hit a three at the buzzer, but it only served to reduce the final margin to three: 80-77, Commodores.

Perdue and Kornet each had a double-double—20 points and 11 rebounds for Will, 20 and 10 for Frank. Reid added eight rebounds, and the 29 rebounds from our starting front line (not to mention six more from Charles Mayes off the bench) led to our 47-34 domination on the boards. Despite the two silly turnovers late in the game, I was pleased with my debut in the NCAA tournament: 14 points (which, I was informed after the game, put me over 1,000 for my career) on 5-for-6 shooting from the field and a career-high eight assists—still the most by a Vanderbilt player in an NCAA tournament game. I was especially proud of the second half—I was perfect from the field, hitting all four field goal attempts (including a three) and all three free-throw attempts for 12 points, which led the team for the half. Frank and

I had combined to go 14-for-22 from the field in our last win, at Notre Dame; we bettered that against Utah State by combining for a sizzling 15-for-19 from the field (79%), with Frank going 10-for-13 along with my 5-for-6.

Coach Newton described the win as "Commodore ball," and it was a team effort, as evidenced by the fact that we scored 32 field goals on 24 assists, an impressive ratio. In addition to Mayes's six rebounds, the reserves played well. Draud was great off the bench—his eight points weren't as splashy as the 22 he scored against Kentucky, but he performed very well down the stretch. In fact, his insertion into the lineup was one of Coach Newton's best in-game moves all season—with Frank and Will controlling the boards inside, Coach Newton figured that we could go smaller to match up better with the Aggies' outside game (they hoisted 22 treys but only made six). The quintet of Perdue, Kornet, Goheen, Booker, and Draud turned out to be the winning five on this day, which was Vanderbilt's first win in the NCAA tourney since 1965, and only the school's second NCAA victory ever.

It had been an emotional day already, helping Vandy notch its first NCAA win in 23 years. But the day wasn't over yet, and neither was the emotion.

II

"You're a chip off the old block; why does it come as such a shock that every road on which you walk your dad already did?"
—John Hiatt, "Your Dad Did" ('87)

Indiana, the defending national champion, fell in the first round to Richmond while we were beating Utah State. Nearly 25 years earlier, in 1964, Loyola-Chicago was the defending champion, having claimed the title in 1963 in something of a watershed moment for NCAA basketball (that was the year they played injunction-defying Mississippi State in Michigan). The Ramblers started four black players during the tournament, the first champion to start that many. The Ramblers returned to defend their title in 1964, and drew a small school from the far western part of Kentucky in the first round—the Murray State Racers, champions of the Ohio Valley Conference. The OVC traditionally had been dominated by Western Kentucky University, and one of its all-time greats—Clem Haskins, who in the mid-80s was the coach at Western and recruited me—was in his prime in the mid '60s. But the Racers took the crown in 1964 and made the school's first-ever NCAA appearance, exactly one year before Vanderbilt, led by Clyde Lee, made its first-ever NCAA appearance.

Racers versus Ramblers (Loyola)—it sounds like it should be a run-and-gun affair. And indeed, it was: the defending champs prevailed, 101-91, ending Murray's season. The Racers' sixth man was a third-year guard named Benny Goheen—my father. Dad acquitted himself well, scoring seven points on 3-for-5 shooting and making his only attempt at the charity stripe. So, he appeared in the NCAA tournament as a junior, just as I would 24 years later. He and my mother, high school sweethearts at North Marshall High School (class of '61), were then attending Murray State, about 20 miles from where each grew up in Marshall County (Dad in Briensburg, Mom in Calvert City). In high school, he was part of a title-winning team in 1959, the North Marshall Jets, then starred as a senior in a return trip for the Jets in 1961, then moved on to college hoops at Murray State. And the Racers' 1964 NCAA appearance—right there with Kentucky, Duke, UCLA, Louisville, and other basketball powers, wasn't even the greatest thing that happened to my parents in 1964: in August, they got married, then finished up at Murray in 1964–65. I came along in October 1966, and my brother was added in 1970.

I grew up as a big Murray State fan—how can you not root for your parents' alma mater? But the program had not been able to return to the NCAAs since 1969, despite some very good teams in the early '80s coached by my father's good friend (and former Racers great) Ron Greene. Ron coached the team into several NITs, most notably in 1980, when the Racers went to Tuscaloosa in the second round and upset Alabama—which turned out to be the last game C.M. Newton coached for the Tide—and then, with a trip to Madison Square Garden for the semifinals on the line, lost a heartbreaker at Illinois, 67-65. (We made the trip to Champaign-Urbana for that game.) Ron left for Indiana State in 1985, and his long-time assistant, Steve Newton (no relation to C.M.), became the head coach. Finally, the Racers put it all together in 1987–88 with a record of 23-9 and won the OVC tournament to advance to the NCAAs for the first time in 19 years. I was as excited for the Racers' NCAA bid as I was for our own bid.

I've always thought of the '88 NCAAs as one of the all-time coincidences. Murray and Vandy had not been to the tourney in 19 and 14 years, respectively. Yet, not only did both programs break those streaks in 1988, they wound up in the same regional—and, even eerier, in the same side of the same regional! I'm sure some statistician could calculate the odds of all that happening, but they seem remote to me. And yet there both teams were in Lincoln, Nebraska.

After our victory over Utah State, I temporarily traded all black-and-gold loyalties for the blue-and-gold of Murray State. Our team went back to the hotel, grabbed a bite, and returned to the arena for the night's doubleheader. Our team, as participants in the tourney, had good seats in the lower bowl of the arena, but I abandoned mine, with Coach Newton's blessing, and joined the Murray rooters in their section (which, naturally, included my parents), sporting my own blue-and-gold shaker. I intended to have fun. And, boy, did I!

Murray had two stars—really, one superstar and one star. The superstar was Jeff Martin, a silky-smooth 6'7" forward from Arkansas who was simply a great all-around player, especially on the offensive end; in 1987–88, he averaged an even 26 points a game, fifth-best in the nation. The star was Donald Mann, a 5'8" fireplug of a point guard from northwest Tennessee. Martin was the OVC Player of the Year, and Mann joined him on the all-conference team. The rest of the team consisted of role players, but they knew—and, more importantly, played—their roles very well.

North Carolina State, the Racers' opponent, was just five years removed from the amazing victory over Houston in The Pit in Albuquerque to win the '83 NCAA championship. In '88, it was still a power, as its #3 seed in the Region attested. And the Wolfpack's coach, Jim Valvano, still oozed charisma and one-liners. Not many people gave 14th-seeded Murray much of a chance; in fact, the Racers were a 250,000-to-1 shot to win the tournament.

The game was nip-and-tuck all the way. The Wolfpack took an eight-point lead in the first half, but Mann—with Martin on the bench with three first-half fouls—hit four straight three-pointers to pace Murray to a 41-36 lead at the half. As always seems to happen in the tourney, the crowd, other than those fans tucked into the higher seed's cheering section, got behind the Racers when it looked like a head-line-making upset was possible. Martin started the second half on fire, scoring nine of his team's first 12 points, and the Racers pushed the lead to 11 points. The Wolf-pack, however, slowly chipped away at the lead, and when Vinny Del Negro scored with 1:37 left, the Pack had trimmed the lead to two, 73-71. Missed Murray State free throws kept the Pack alive, but Murray rebounded one of them for a putback and a 75-71 lead. A Pack basket and two Racer free throws made it 77-73; then Charles Shackelford's basket trimmed the lead back to two. When Murray's Paul King hit only one of two free throws inside 10 seconds remaining, the Pack had a shot for the tie, but Del Negro's potential game-tying trey missed, and Murray claimed the 78-75 upset win, the biggest upset of the 1988 tourney.

Martin was brilliant—despite early foul trouble, led all scorers with 23 points. Mann had 16 points, eight assists, and six rebounds. It was a great win, and everyone in the Racer cheering section was thrilled—the school had just won its first-ever NCAA tournament game. (The second win would come 22 years later at the expense of Vanderbilt on a buzzer-beating shot in the opening round of the 2010 tourney.

అ

All in all, it was an incredible day. We won, and my parents' alma mater won too. It would take something special on Sunday to improve on Friday. Would we be up to the challenge?

14

PITT

I

"Gettin' ready for the big time"
—Aerosmith, "Rag Doll" ('87–'88)

In 1988, there was no doubt as to which conference was the most powerful and successful in college basketball—it was the Big East, which had done remarkably well for a conference that still was less than 10 years old. In the previous four NCAA tournaments, five schools from the conference had produced six of the 16 Final Four teams, including three in 1985 and two in 1987, with two champions (Georgetown in 1984 and Villanova in 1985) and two runners-up (Georgetown in 1985 and Syracuse, a last-second loser, in 1987). For all the challenging games that we had played during my first three seasons, we had not yet played a team from the Big East. But that would change in the second round of the 1988 NCAAs, as our opponent would be the Big East's regular season champion, the University of Pittsburgh Panthers.

"Pitt was probably the most talented team we ever played," I once remarked, "and that's saying a lot, because we played Kansas, Indiana, [and] Michigan over a three-year span—three straight teams that won national championships." The Panthers did not have the depth of North Carolina or Kentucky; they went only about seven deep, and that depth had been seriously compromised in early January when Rod Brookin, at the time the team's second-leading scorer, was ruled academically ineligible for the remainder of the season. But their starting five were immensely talented—"the most talented [starting five] I ever played against in college," I asserted years later.

Pitt's starting front line of Charles Smith, Jerome Lane, and Demetrius Gore was, undoubtedly, the best we faced all season. Smith, called "the signature recruit of the era" in Pitt's effort to revive its basketball program, was a 6'10" All-American senior who would make the Olympic team a few months later. In 1987–88, he was named Big East Player of the Year, First Team All-America by Scripps Howard, and Second Team All-America by the NABC. His 2,045 career points remain the school's record. He would be the third pick in June's NBA draft.

Meanwhile, Lane, a junior, had created quite a name for himself at forward. He hailed from Akron's St. Vincent-St. Mary's, the same school that would produce

LeBron James nearly 20 years later. Lane was being compared favorably to Charles Barkley, and for good reason: he had the same build—he was about 6'6" and took up a lot of space—and he was a rebounding machine. "No one in the country," Syracuse coach Jim Boeheim said, "I don't care how tall he is, can out-rebound Jerome Lane one-on-one." Lane would prove that in our game. Oh, and he was also strong—in a January game against Providence he made headlines, and endless Sportscenter highlight reels that continue to play to this day, by smashing a backboard into a thousand pieces following a ferocious dunk, leading to Bill Raftery's immortal line, "Send it in, Jerome!"; such exploits earned Lane a spot on two of Dick Vitale's creatively-named squads—the "All Dipsy Doo 'Dunkaroo'" team and the "All-Windex Glass Eaters" squad. He also turned in one of the great performances of the year in the last game of the regular season, a winner-take-all game at Syracuse for the conference title—29 points and 15 rebounds in an 85-84 Pitt victory that gave Pitt the school's first outright regular season Big East title. Like Smith, Lane was named to several All-America teams in 1987–88.

With that powerful duo, it would be easy to overlook Gore, but he was a strong player in his own right. He averaged 13 points a game and shot nearly 80% at the line. That trio combined for an incredible 77 points and 32 rebounds in Pitt's first-round win over Eastern Michigan; we would have our hands full trying to contain them.

The rest of Pitt's rotation consisted of four talented freshmen. They were "considered the country's best," and were rated by FOXsports.com as one of the top 25 recruiting classes of all time; it was even deemed "legendary" years later. Sean Miller, a Pittsburgh-area native, was the point guard and the Big East Freshman of the Year, as well as something of a ballhandling prodigy. I recall attending Joe B. Hall's Kentucky Wildcat Basketball Camp in the late '70s, and one day the campers were treated to a ballhandling display by Miller, who couldn't have been more than 10 or 11 years old at the time. (Miller even displayed his precocious skills for Johnny Carson on *The Tonight Show*.) Two other freshmen, Jason Matthews and Darelle Porter, were effective wing players, and a fourth freshman, Bobby Martin, a 6'10" center, provided frontcourt depth; he and Matthews would join Miller on the Big East's All-Freshman team.

Those top seven players would combine to play all but three of the 225 game minutes for the Panthers. Incredibly, all seven players—plus Brookin, who would return to the team the next season—would become members of the school's 1,000-point career scoring club. (Our team featured four such members—Perdue, Booker, Draud, and me.)

Pitt was coached by Paul Evans, a combative sort who was in his second season at the school. He had made his first splash as a head coach in the late '70s at Division II St. Lawrence. He then moved to the Naval Academy, where a late-blooming David Robinson carried that program to unprecedented heights, including a first-round

NCAA upset of LSU in 1985 and an Elite Eight appearance in 1986, beating Syracuse on its home floor along the way. Evans took the Pitt job in '86 and fired every coach on the staff except one—a young go-getter named John Calipari, a local product from the Pittsburgh suburb of Moon, who had joined the program in 1985. Evans then guided the Panthers, winners of only 15 games the year before, to 24 in '86–'87 and a share of the Big East title. But, seeded third in the West Regional, the Panthers lost to a lower-seeded team, sixth-seeded Oklahoma, in the second round.

Despite the outright Big East regular season title in 1987–88, it had been a trying season for Evans and his team. The Calipari-led recruiting of Martin—he verbally committed to Villanova, then changed his mind and signed with Pitt—led to some sniping between Evans and Villanova coach Rollie Massamino, which in turn led to near-fisticuffs between the two head coaches in a postgame on-court contretemps. Then there was a nasty recruiting battle with Notre Dame that resulted in hard feelings between Evans and Irish coach Digger Phelps. And there was an on-court brawl in the final seconds of a February victory over Georgetown, leading the officials to declare the game over with four seconds remaining to play. (Happily, our game would not be declared over with four seconds left.) And if that weren't enough, Evans and Calipari (now Evans's "lead assistant") took a nightmarish recruiting trip to Los Angeles, where they endured an earthquake and, on the flight home, the loss of an engine, forcing an emergency landing in Las Vegas.

Moreover, as would become obvious to all immediately after our game, most of Pitt's players neither liked nor respected Evans. That was especially true of Lane, who later claimed that when Evans took over in 1986, "he wanted me to transfer" and that Evans "was trying to force me out"; in fact, Evans threw Lane out of his very first practice in fall 1986. As Martin noted, at times "it got a little chippy between them."

Thus, as Calipari recalled of the '87–'88 season in an apparent understatement, "there was some turmoil that season, but the kids fought through it." Indeed, notwithstanding, or maybe because of, that "turmoil," Pitt thrived all year. The Panthers began the year in everyone's top 10, and UPI even ranked the Panthers as its preseason #1 team. They lived up to the hype, winning all nine games they played prior to Big East play, the last two of which were over SEC schools—an 87-51 blowout of Alabama and an 80-68 thrashing of Florida. The Florida victory vaulted the Panthers to #2 in the country; they lost only six games prior to the NCAA tournament, all to tourney-bound teams: Oklahoma, Georgetown, Seton Hall (twice), Syracuse, and, in the Big East tournament, Villanova. They were never ranked lower than #11 at any point in the season, and they entered the tourney with a #8 ranking. As Lane had said early in the season, "If we don't get to the final eight or the Final Four, then definitely something is wrong."

II

"The time to rise has been engaged…your finest hour"
—*R.E.M., "Finest Worksong"* ('87)

Pitt was a formidable opponent, but our game plan wasn't all that different from our plan for any opponent—play solid defense, rebound, and shoot it well on our end. Despite Pitt's strength, we were taller than Pitt at every position on the floor—our front line was 7'0", 6'9", and 6'8" compared to Pitt's 6'10", 6'6", and 6'6". One person who would need to step up for us, however, was Eric Reid. While contributing eight rebounds in the Utah State victory, Eric missed five of his six shots from the field, committed three turnovers, and was benched for the stretch run in favor of Scott Draud, leading to a rare in-print criticism from Coach Newton: "[We] can't keep playing four-on-five at both ends of the court. Eric has to start playing. If I were Paul Evans, I wouldn't even bother guarding him." Maybe Evans read that remark.

Predictably, Evans focused his attention on the center matchup between Perdue and Charles Smith. Evans worried about Wilbur getting Smith in foul trouble: "Charlie, it doesn't matter if Perdue scores his 25. What matters is that he doesn't score them from the foul line. You know we need you in the game." Yet, one had to wonder about the team's preparation and focus when Lane asked Evans if he was to take the ball out against our press. Evans replied: "Jerome, this team doesn't press." But exactly that sort of mental focus would factor in a key play in the second half and would test Evans' pregame observation that "[i]f we concentrate, we're fine. But with this group, you never know."

We knew it would take a very good game to beat the Panthers, but not a perfect one—we had played well against North Carolina and Kentucky in those victories, but certainly had not been flawless in either game. We figured that we had a deeper bench and a better all-around offensive attack, especially with Kornet's strong play late in the year representing a second inside force to go with Perdue. As long as we got off to a decent start and showed them that the wins over Carolina, Kentucky, Notre Dame, and Florida had not been flukes, we would be fine. Unfortunately, that's not what happened.

Pitt came out playing well, while we, as Coach Newton said, "were so tight it was unbelievable" at the outset. We weren't necessarily playing terribly, but we were ice cold; we missed seven of our first eight shots from the field. Pitt made only half of its first eight shots, but that's all it took for Pitt to grab a quick 10-3 lead in the first five minutes. Off the bench, Charles Mayes hit a three to help stem the tide, and Perdue and Lane traded baskets to keep the deficit at four. Baskets by Booker and Perdue answered Pitt scores to keep the Panthers' lead at 16-12 eight minutes into the game. But that spurt was only temporary: a 9-0 run stretched the Pitt lead to 13, 25-12 with about nine minutes to play in the first half. This was a real danger zone; in each of our big wins over the previous two seasons (Indiana, North Carolina, Kentucky), we had trailed at various points in the game, but never by double digits in any of them. We couldn't afford to trail a team as talented as Pitt by double digits going into the second half. It was imperative that we trim the 13-point deficit before halftime.

We did. Perdue's two free throws stopped Pitt's run, but during this stretch of the game, Pitt had a real chance to build on its lead, and it failed to do so. I twice missed—badly—driving layups, Reid shot an air ball from eight feet, and Perdue missed both ends of a two-shot trip to the free-throw line. But Pitt failed to convert any of those offensive missteps into points, and we finally found our rhythm in the last seven minutes of the half.

Reid trimmed the lead to single digits by converting both ends of the one-and-one. After two Miller free throws, Perdue's three-point play, drawing Smith's second foul, cut the lead to eight. I then stole an entry pass, took it the other way and missed an ill-advised one-on-three layup, but Booker was there for the putback, and suddenly the deficit was only six, 27-21. Then, another steal, this one by Reid, gave us a possession that Booker converted into a trey to slice the lead to three. Perdue drew a charge on Smith, his third foul, forcing him to the bench for the rest of the half. Book, who was all over the place, then claimed an offensive rebound off Reid's miss, which I cashed into an eight-footer in the lane to cut Pitt's lead to one.

Gore hit a jumper to end our run, but I hit two free throws to reduce Pitt's lead back to one, 29-28, at the 4:24 mark. After Lane and Perdue traded putbacks, Kornet's 15-footer gave us our first lead of the game, 32-31, with three minutes remaining in the first half. Lane hit one of two free throws to tie it, and Reid's jumper gave us a 34-32 lead with two minutes left. Neither team distinguished itself in the final two minutes of the half—we turned it over on three straight trips, while Lane charged on one possession and traveled on the next. Pitt had the last possession and, after a couple of misses, scored on a tip-in to send the teams to the locker room tied at 34.

That last Pitt possession, where the Panthers had several chances to score before finally converting, illustrated our biggest problem with them—rebounding. They dominated us on the boards in the first half, 25-12, and Lane, not surprisingly, was particularly difficult for us. Otherwise, there was nothing much to improve upon, and it was difficult to complain about being tied with the Big East champs with 20 minutes to play after trailing by 13 midway through the first half.

Meanwhile, things apparently were not calm in the Pitt locker room. As John Feinstein, who was in the Pitt locker room, later reported, Coach Evans had some choice words for his players during intermission: "It's always the same shit with you guys. You don't know how to put people away. Charlie, you pull up and shoot when everyone else is expecting you to pass. There's no one to rebound and we blow a possession. You can't do that at this level! This time, when you build the lead up, keep going inside and don't start rushing." But there would be no big lead for Pitt to build on in the second half.

Smith opened the second half by taking it right at Perdue—an aggressive move considering Smith had three fouls—and scored to give Pitt the lead. Booker answered with a three to put us up one. Two Martin free throws gave Pitt the lead back, but I scored off a steal and Reid scored off a fine Perdue pass to give us a three-point lead. Gore scored but charged while doing so, his third foul. A Smith dunk off a Lane feed put Pitt back up by one, and Perdue's dunk off his own miss swung the lead back to us. Smith answered with a jumper, and my missed jumper led to a Gore jumper and three-point Pitt lead, 46-43, at the first TV timeout five minutes into the half.

Perdue, Booker, and I went to the bench after the timeout, and Pitt once again missed an opportunity to establish a sizeable lead. We had three or four empty trips in a row, but Pitt couldn't convert any of them until a Gore layup, which gave Pitt a 48-43 lead but was costly for the Panthers because Gore was called for charging, his fourth foul, sending him to the bench with 12 minutes left. Mayes hit a huge three to cut Pitt's lead to two, and, back in the game after a quick breather, Perdue cleanly blocked Smith, leading to two Draud free throws to tie the game at 48. Scott followed his free throws with a trey on the next possession, giving us eight straight points and a 51-48 lead. Porter stopped the run with a baseline jumper, but a Reid layup off a great entry pass from Draud returned our lead to three with 9:25 left.

It was around this time that, as Feinstein later wrote, "It became a game where every possession seemed like life-and-death." He was right; the teams went at each other with great intensity. Smith drew Perdue's third foul out of the timeout, and his free throws cut our lead to one, and a few seconds later Porter put the Panthers back in the lead with an 18-footer. A Perdunk gave us the lead back at the eight-minute mark, but a Porter trey put Pitt up by a pair. A great Perdue pass to Reid for a layup tied the game at 57. After Smith took an ill-advised three, Book rebounded, and his stop-and-pop from 15 feet gave us the lead back, 59-57.

Pitt then made the game's silliest turnover. After Book's basket, Miller was holding the ball beyond the baseline, waiting for Lane to come and inbound it. Miller tossed the ball to Lane, who was still standing out of bounds, but Lane let it drop, meaning that Miller's toss became the inbounds pass, which landed out of bounds—a silly, unforced turnover. "We might look back in a game like this," CBS color man Billy Cunningham said, "and say, hey, a silly play like that could have cost them the ballgame." Pitt Coach Evans wisely called time so that Pitt could regain its composure, but out of the timeout I converted the turnover into two points with a baseline jumper. We now led 61-57, our largest lead of the game, and when Martin fouled on the other end, things looked great for us. In fact, since we had found our rhythm at the nine-minute mark of the first half, we had outscored the Panthers 49-32.

Gore re-entered the game for Pitt, meaning that both teams would enter the stretch run with their starters on the floor. And, unfortunately, we picked that moment to go ice cold again, going nearly five minutes without scoring. Book missed a three, but Reid rebounded, giving us a fresh 45-second shot clock. Smith then committed his fourth foul on Perdue, giving us another 45 seconds, which we milked down to the end before I missed a runner in the lane. Pitt rushed down the floor and Smith scored to cut our lead to two with four minutes to play. We again exercised patience on the offensive end, and Smith blocked my driving layup attempt; Book recovered the ball but turned it over. At the 2:30 mark, Porter hit a three to give Pitt the lead by one, 62-61. After a Perdue miss, Porter scored again, this time a long two-pointer that gave Pitt a 7-0 run and a 64-61 lead with two minutes to play. We called time.

Out of the timeout, Eric Reid hit one of the biggest shots of his career, a 14-footer in the lane that ended our dry spell and cut Pitt's lead to one, 64-63; maybe Coach Evans had read Coach Newton's in-print "advice" not to guard Eric, and Eric made him pay. Ninety seconds remained. Now it was Pitt's turn to be patient, nursing that one-point lead, and the next minute would be incredibly frustrating for us. With about a minute to go, Gore took a 17-footer. He missed, but Lane grabbed the rebound—his 19th of the game—and was fouled by Kornet. It was only our fourth team foul of the half, so Pitt was not yet in the bonus. Pitt inbounded the ball and again worked the shot clock down, feeding Smith on the block. Smith went up for the shot and drew the fourth foul on Perdue. Seventeen seconds remained, and we called timeout. Sensing that we might need a three-pointer, Coach Newton substituted Draud into the game for Reid.

Smith made the first free throw for a 65-63 Pitt lead. He missed the second, and Will grabbed the rebound; Lane, however, knocked the ball from Will's hands and into Smith's, and in desperation I fouled Smith with 13 seconds left, our sixth team foul, meaning that Pitt still was not in the bonus. We called another timeout. Pitt successfully inbounded the ball to Jason Matthews, and I immediately fouled him. Finally, Pitt was in the bonus. Coolly, the freshman Matthews sank both ends of the one-and-one to give Pitt a 67-63 lead with 12 seconds remaining. Pitt applied some modest man-to-man pressure in the backcourt. Draud took the inbounds pass and quickly headed straight down the middle of the floor, as I fanned out behind the three-point arc on the left side of the floor. Scott got to about 20 feet, drew a double team from my man (Porter), and flicked the ball to me in the corner for the shot. I hit the three to close the deficit to 67-66. We called our final timeout. Five seconds remained.

Much has been written and discussed from the Pitt side about exactly what was or wasn't said in the Pitt huddle during this timeout and how the Panthers played the final five seconds of regulation, but this first late-game three-pointer is hardly ever mentioned. In fact, Pitt made its first critical late-game error here. There was absolutely no reason for Porter to leave me open behind the arc and double up on Draud as Scott approached the top of the key. Preventing a driving layup—Porter's apparent intention by doubling Scott—might have been nice, but a deuce would only have cut Pitt's lead to two; preventing a three was much more important because my three, which cut the Pitt lead to one, meant that we would have a chance to tie even if Pitt made two more free throws. This first late-game three was as poorly defended, and maybe more so, than the next one, and it put us within striking distance.

We were forced to press on the inbounds play coming out of the timeout, but Pitt lobbed it over our press to Smith, who was immediately fouled by Perdue, Will's fifth, putting him out of the game. Coach Newton greeted Will as he left the game, seemingly trying to console him, as it appeared that his Vandy career might be over. As Sean Miller recalled, the entire crowd "gave Perdue a standing ovation when he fouled out." Wilbur may have been out of the game, but at least he had fouled quickly, as only one second had ticked off the clock before the foul. Four seconds remained, and Reid returned to the game to replace Will.

Smith had missed his last free-throw attempt, the shot where Lane tipped the ball out of Will's hands, but that had been his only miss in six attempts. And he was equal to the challenge again, nailing both ends of the one-and-one to give Pitt a 69-66 lead. You had to give the Panthers credit for making four straight pressure free throws in the final seconds; they didn't make it easy on us. Pitt had three timeouts left but opted not to use one after either of Smith's made free throws.

In 1988, unlike today, the game clock did not show tenths of seconds inside the final minute. So, the game clock merely showed 00:04, which meant that there could be anywhere from 00:04.9 to 00:04.0 seconds left. Either way, there wasn't much time to travel the length of the floor, and Smith's two free throws meant that we had to hit a three-pointer to extend the game and, therefore, our season. With three guards in the game, Coach Newton termed the play "our 'home run' play. Any of the three guards can take the shot." There wasn't much time to run a true "play"— we just needed to inbound the ball to one of the three guards and hope he could make a play either by creating a shot himself or drawing a double-team and dishing to one of the other two, as Scott had done a few seconds before.

The ball was inbounded to me simply because the inbounds passer, Reid, happened to pass it to me instead of Booker or Draud. "The play wasn't designed for me," I said afterward. "I just happened to get the ball." Even though Pitt had applied token pressure after Matthews' free throws at 00:12, this time no Panther stayed on Pitt's end of the floor to contest the inbounds pass or apply any pressure at all; they all retreated to our side of the court. Thus, when Reid inbounded the ball to me, I was already running toward our end of the floor and caught the ball in step, like a running back or wide receiver catching a short pass with his momentum already leading him upfield. I caught the ball right in front of Pitt's coaches—about 25 feet worth of prime hardwood real estate covered without even a nanosecond ticking off the clock. And, after catching the pass, I turned to start dribbling toward our end, and to my astonishment, as I said after the game, I saw "nothing but 30 feet of open court. I couldn't believe it. They were all bunched up past half-court." Porter was on our side of the floor, the closest Pitt player to me.

I simply dribbled as fast as I could, continuing down the left side of the court, with Porter still not too close. By the time I reached the center line, he was still about 10 feet off me. I feigned toward the center of the floor, which was enough to throw him slightly off-balance, and I kept going down the left side. After the fourth dribble, at 00:02, I stopped about 22 or 23 feet from the basket; by now, Porter had closed, and Smith, an intelligent player who could see what was happening, rushed over to help—but a bit too late. I pulled up to go for the shot, but for a split second the ball slipped in my hands, it wasn't a head fake, because there was no time for that, just a slight slippage. But the unintentional hesitation turned out to be fortuitous because Matthews glided past me, while Smith was still coming toward me. In other words, I had an opening to launch the shot, which I did with the clock showing 00:01. It cleared Smith's outstretched arm by about six inches. While the shot was in midair, the clock turned to all zeroes and the buzzer sounded. But I didn't hear any of that; I remember nothing but total silence as I went up for the shot; it was like an out-of-body experience…until the shot found nothing but net, tying the game and sending it to overtime.

The crowd—14,453, a sell-out at Devaney—exploded at that moment. People naturally root for the underdog in these situations, but we, especially I, received extra support from the numerous Murray State fans in attendance—I had just been in the Racers' cheering section less than 48 hours earlier, and now they returned the favor, joining the many Vandy fans who had made the trip to Lincoln in leading the cheers. "Every year there are four or five games in the tournament that come down to shots at the buzzer," I recalled. "It's the greatest feeling in the world to hit one."

It was, for sure, a great shot (as late as 2007, it checked in at #8 on one expert's list of the "10 Greatest 3 Pointers in NCAA Tourney History") and a great feeling ("It's certainly a pleasant memory" was my recent understatement), but it wasn't a game-winner. There were still five minutes of overtime to play. Immediately after the game, people assumed we would win, through some combination of our flying high after the tying trey and Pitt being so devastated at not having closed us out in regulation that it couldn't sufficiently regroup in overtime. Even three decades letter, John Calipari said, "We have absolutely no shot in overtime. The whole team's frazzled." That's not how I felt, though. While I'm a firm believer in the principle that the team with the momentum going into overtime has a decided advantage (a maxim that would be proven at least twice the next season), that assumes that the teams are at equal strength; because Perdue had fouled out, we had to play a five-minute game against the Big East champions without our best player. If we couldn't maintain the momentum and win the game, the post-Perdue era at Vanderbilt would already have begun with four seconds left in regulation.

Replacing Draud, Mayes joined Kornet, Booker, Reid, and me to start the overtime. Pitt claimed the opening tip and thus had the chance to strike first in overtime. We returned to our zone defense. On this critical first possession, Smith had the ball on the baseline about 16 feet out, and Lane, who was floating in the middle looking for gaps in the zone, broke open under the basket and would have had an easy two if Smith had fed him. But Smith opted for a difficult jumper contested by Booker, and the ball bounced off the rim and over the backboard, giving us possession. On our end, we worked the ball down to Kornet on the block. Guarded by Smith, who had four fouls ("I knew Smith had four fouls, so I took it at him," Frank said after the game), Frank turned for a soft jump hook—it bounced in, giving us a 71-69 lead with four minutes left.

Pitt then tried to attack our zone by throwing behind it; from about 26 feet, Miller threw a lob pass to Smith, who had cut behind Kornet. But Frank was able to barely graze the ball with his fingertips, altering its path ever so slightly; as a result, Smith missed the dunk and, worse for the Panthers, hung on the rim, drawing a one-shot technical foul. I made the technical free throw for a 72-69 lead, and out of the inbounds play Booker faced up Miller and drilled a three for a 75-69 lead with 3:30 remaining.

But Pitt wouldn't be put away so easily. The Panthers finally got on the board on a Smith putback, and, after my missed shot, Gore knocked down a three to cut our lead to one, 75-74, with two minutes left. It was still anybody's game. With around 90 seconds to play, I drove into the lane and was clipped on the feet by Matthews, drawing the foul; I put up the shot and it went in, leading to a possible three-point play. But the official waved off the basket, ruling that the foul had occurred before the shot attempt. It was a close call, and probably the correct one, but now I had to make both ends of the one-and-one, which I did to make it 77-74. Still, it was now a one-possession game.

Pitt was patient on offense, and Gore attempted another three, which would have tied the game; he missed, and Reid rebounded with a minute to play. We milked the clock, maybe a little too well; we were a little out of sync and not in a position to get off a good shot when Booker, working to create a shot about 18 feet from the basket, was fouled by Miller with 00:22 remaining on the game clock and about five seconds left on the shot clock. After a Pitt timeout, Booker hit the critical first free throw to push the lead to four, making it a two-possession game. He missed the second free throw and Pitt rebounded. Now the roles were reversed from the final seconds of regulation; we were ahead by four and Pitt needed a three. Miller had an open look at one, certainly not any worse than the look I had for my first trey at the end of regulation, but he missed; Kornet blocked out Smith for the rebound, and Smith went over the back and was called for his fifth foul with 12 seconds to play.

Frank, however, missed the front end of the one-and-one, giving Pitt a ray of hope, but it was Lane who decided to launch the three—not the Panthers' first choice I'm sure. He missed, and after a bit of a scrum in the corner, the ball wound up in my hands, and I was fouled with the clock showing 00:02. With a four-point lead, it was over, and I clutched the ball and gestured toward our section of the arena as I moved toward the other end for the final free throws—I felt like running to the other end, but I thought that would be poor form, a premature celebration that would unnecessarily rub salt in Pitt's wounds; on the other hand, I was too excited to simply walk, so I unconsciously combined walking and running to the other end, which was…skipping. I took some good-natured heat from my teammates for that, and happily so. I couldn't contain my happiness as I stepped to the line, though—someone said something from our bench as I received the ball, and I looked over and laughed—a snippet that CBS included in its "One Shining Moment" montage after the tournament's final game two weeks later.

The free throws were academic, but I made them and closed out the game. We scored what remains one of the two or three biggest wins in Vanderbilt hoops history, beating Pitt 80-74.

For the first time in the history of the program, a Vanderbilt team had won two games in the NCAA tournament. Those two wins doubled the total number of NCAA victories in the program's history before 1988. The 72 hours we spent in Lincoln were 72 of the greatest hours of my life, and no doubt my teammates would say the same. When we departed for Lincoln on Thursday, 64 teams had a chance to win it all. When we returned to Nashville on Sunday evening, only 16 teams still had that chance. And we were one of them.

One of the 14,453 in attendance at the Devaney Center was an elderly, gray-haired gentleman who sat at the scorer's table throughout the game. I doubt that he had a rooting interest in the game, but he may have felt some satisfaction, and perhaps vindication, when he saw, in this second NCAA Tournament with the three-point line, a thrilling finish that resulted from three-point shots. That man was none other than Ed Steitz, the mastermind of the three-point line.

15

AFTERGLOW/AFTERSHOCK

I

"Do anything for my sweet sixteen"
—Billy Idol, "Sweet Sixteen" ('87)

It goes without saying that we were ecstatic in the locker room. The Sweet Sixteen! It took a while to sink in—heady stuff, at least for me. In fact, having followed the NCAA tournament as a passive, though interested, bystander for about 12 years prior to 1988, what struck me as a participant was how fast the field is reduced. It had always seemed to me like it took weeks and weeks to reduce the field in half, then in half again, then in half again. Not this time. It seemed like the field of 64 had been reduced to 16 in the blink of an eye. It was an incredible feeling.

The Pitt win was the biggest of the 1987–88 season. But it also was one of the biggest wins of the 1988–89 season. We played the entire overtime session with a lineup of Book and me at guard, Reid and Mayes at forward, and Kornet in the post—quite possibly the starting five for 1988–89. Even with the momentum going into overtime, it was quite a feat for that quintet to beat Pitt's star-packed lineup. Kornet, Book, and I—the three juniors and thus the ranking members of the team on the floor during overtime—took great pride in the Pitt win. Indeed, the three of us scored the team's final 17 points, beginning with my closing threes in regulation, and we traded big plays: I hit the threes to get the game into overtime; Frank scored the first basket in overtime and then tipped the lob pass to Smith that led to a turnover and technical foul; Book then hit the dagger of a three that put us up six, and he and I closed it out by making five of six free throws. In fact, the three of us had done the same thing down the stretch against Utah State, the only difference there being that Will was on the floor for the final minutes of that game. Frank, Book, and I scored 21 of the team's final 27 points to hold off the Aggies. Thus, the two wins in Lincoln gave us enormous confidence that we would be able to win the next season even though Wilbur would be in the NBA.

Against Pitt, Book (16) and I (22) led the team in scoring. While Perdue scored 15, Eric Reid, answering Coach Newton's pregame criticism, had a great game, including that clutch jumper inside the two-minute mark in regulation that cut Pitt's lead to one, with 12 points and four boards. We compensated for Pitt's 42-27 re-bounding advantage by not giving Pitt extra possessions via turnovers: in 45 minutes of play, we turned the ball over only six times—our season low and a remarkable figure considering we were playing the Big East champs in the crucible of the NCAA tournament. In fact, in the final 25 minutes—the entire second half and overtime period—we committed only a single turnover. Pitt, meanwhile, committed 15 turn-overs, including six each by Lane and Gore. All in all, it was a very good, hard-fought game.

෨

I knew I had done something special with the last-second threes, but I didn't appreciate just how big a deal it was when the game finally ended. The next 24 hours would be a head-spinning experience. To begin with, there was the post-game media session, which lasted about as long as the game. It was accurately described as "a marathon media session"; by the time I exited the session, showered, and re-entered the arena, Kansas and Murray State were midway through the second half of their game. I didn't realize until that moment how large the NCAA tournament had be-come; there were media from all over the country in Lincoln. I must have answered questions about the final four seconds of regulation about 20 times, and probably was not consistent in my answers. My best description of the shot was this one to Joe Biddle of the *Nashville Banner*: "I figured the best route to go was left, to my strong side. It wasn't totally uncontested, but it felt good when I shot it. I just hoped it was going in. I was a little off-balance, so I wasn't totally certain."

There wasn't just an explosion in the Devaney Center when the tying three found the net; I've heard many stories from then-students, watching in dorm rooms or common areas around the Vanderbilt campus, reporting that the campus itself suddenly exploded with cheers. It became one of those "where were you when..." things, as Booker recalled: "It was like the Kennedy assassination. Do you know where you were when Goheen made that shot to go into overtime?"

The original Commodore himself, Cornelius Vanderbilt, died in January 1877, nearly four years after he founded the school and several years before James Naismith invented the game of basketball. How would Commodore Vanderbilt have reacted to all this excitement? I don't know, but one of my all-time favorite pictures is the one of his statue in the middle of the campus, taken just after the Pitt game, showing the Commodore "wearing" a white T-shirt that says "GOHEEN 12." Of course, all of that was transpiring while we were still in Lincoln, so we found out about it later. After we watched the second game, we made our way to the airport to fly back to Nashville. We figured there might be a small group that would greet us and welcome the conquering heroes home. As the flight approached Nashville and we started our descent, the pilot had been informed, and announced to us, that there were quite a few people that had gathered at the airport. Gee, that's nice, I thought; there might be a few dozen hearty souls that made the late-night trip to the airport. It was after 11:00 on a Sunday evening. How many people could possibly come to the airport at that time?

Well, we found out when we got off the plane and walked into the terminal and one of the most incredible scenes I've ever experienced. It seemed like the entire city of Nashville was in the airport, and had shown up to greet us at the gate as we walked in. (Of course, in a post-9/11 world, this couldn't happen.) "Walking down the terminal," Kornet recalled, "it kept getting warmer and warmer and the noise kept getting louder and louder as we got closer to all the people." And it was *loud*. People were cheering, yelling, chanting—it was an outpouring of excitement and emotion unlike anything I'd ever seen. Television cameras were everywhere; the pep band had shown up and was playing the Vandy fight song, "Dynamite." "This is what basketball is all about," I shouted over the din.

To this day, I don't know how many people were in the airport that night. It certainly was in the thousands. Two contemporary reports estimated 2,000; another estimated 4,000. Booker estimated 4,000. My future mentor and close friend Judge Lew Conner was there: "Darnedest thing I ever saw. Can you believe this?" He wasn't alone. We shared Coach Newton's sentiment when he said, "I'm overwhelmed." I was a little more verbose: "It's incredible; I knew a few people would be out to see us, but to have this kind of a crowd this late is unbelievable. It's a credit to our fans, who are very special." During this circus, which truly was "March Madness," Barry Booker had, without question, the greatest line about the Sweet Sixteen, which he had the wit and composure to utter during the mob scene: "This is unbelievable. If I'd known all we needed to do was to get to the final 16 to get all this attention, we'd have done it years ago!"

By that point, three years into my Vandy career, I didn't really need any reminders that Vanderbilt fans were the best in college basketball. But that scene at the airport late on that Sunday evening in March 1988 was a vivid reminder of how special they are. What I said in the airport then has held up for over 30 years: "This is a once-in-a-lifetime thing for anybody." Considering my horrible summer of 1987, I had come a long way.

II

"Take back your basketball"
—Tom Petty & The Heartbreakers, "Jammin' Me" ('87)
[Erroneously transcribed lyric on cassette purchased in Taipei]

In summer 1987, we took advantage of Coach Newton's contacts and reputation to represent the United States in an international competition called the Jones Cup, an annual international basketball competition run by the International Amateur Basketball Federation (FIBA) and held on the island of Taiwan at Taipei. The tournament was named for R. William Jones, one of the two co-founders of FIBA and the first international person to be inducted into the Naismith Memorial Basketball Hall of Fame, but who will forever be known in U.S. basketball circles as the knucklehead who gave the U.S.S.R. team three chances to play the final seconds of the 1972 Olympic gold-medal basketball game against the U.S. team, and the third time was the charm for the Soviets. Coach Newton's extensive experience in international basketball (Bob Knight called C.M. "the leading college representative in America's international basketball"), particularly with FIBA, enabled the trip; he had taken the Commodores in the summer 1983 as well.

For the 1987 version of the Cup, teams representing such countries as China, Japan, Germany, and Australia participated. The event was structured somewhat like the Olympics, with the participating teams placed into one of two pools, out of each of which the top four teams advanced to the quarterfinal round, with the winner of three games from that point claiming the gold medal and the Cup.

The trip allowed the team and coaches to conduct organized practices in the middle of the summer and play meaningful games against top-flight competition in the off-season, none of which ordinarily would be allowed under NCAA rules. And, as Coach Newton constantly reminded us, we were representing the United States; so, even though we wore our normal Vanderbilt game uniforms, our team was announced as the "United States" and the programs and scoreboards reflected that as well. So, this trip was more than just a lark; it was a valuable opportunity to get a jump on our SEC competition, while representing our country at the same time.

For sure, the international experience helped team chemistry—you can't help but become a closer unit when you're competing for your country in an international competition. And goofy things helped too, like the banquet for the teams where each team was required to create and perform a song. Derrick Wilcox led our effort at concocting a rap song, and happily there was no You Tube then because any viral or other evidence of that performance could harm future careers. (Still, our rap was a lot better than the Australian team's off-key butchering of "Waltzing Matilda"!) And trips to Snake Alley for surprisingly great deals on "Rolex" watches were fun as well. Less fun were the cab rides and general traffic, which made New York City seem positively rural by comparison.

On the court, after a sluggish start in the competition, our team (which included the just-graduated seniors such as Steve Reece, Glen Clem, and others) played reasonably well, claiming the silver medal with a 7-1 record in the tournament. Booker was terrific, averaging 16 points and 4.6 assists a game, shooting 56% from the field and 94% from the line; he also tipped in a shot at the buzzer to give us a 64-62 win over Korea. He was named to the all-tournament team, as was Perdue, who maintained the momentum he had established both during his breakout junior season and on a post-season trip to Europe with an all-star squad picked from NIT participants.

In contrast to the performances of Book and Will, I played poorly. It's been something of a running joke among the team for the past 30 years that I wasn't too excited about the trip, and my lackluster play reflected my lack of enthusiasm for the whole endeavor. I had been laid low by mono in summer 1986, and I eventually hit a wall late in the '87 season; I still hadn't fully recovered by summer 1987 and wasn't at all excited about sacrificing rest and relaxation for weeks of practice and competition. I wound up questioning whether I needed to take a more permanent break from things—and I think the coaches were wondering that too. It took some soul-searching following the Taipei trip to get my mind back into basketball and have a solid season in 1987–88.

After the Pitt game, some writers noticed this 180-degree turnaround. The arrival at the Nashville airport in March 1988 capped a turnaround in my attitude and general mindset from eight months' previous, and I would not slip back into the Taipei funk again.

III

"It was a Sunday, what a black day"
—*Michael Jackson, "Smooth Criminal"* ('87–'88)

What Pitt was experiencing in March 1988 was much worse than my "Taipei funk" of 1987, as euphoria for Vanderbilt and its fans meant heartbreak and recrimination for the Pitt players and fans. In particular, the loss ruptured whatever fragile chemistry Pitt had been able to maintain during the season, and the loss brought public the complete disconnect between the players and Paul Evans, and the lack of respect that appeared to run both ways. John Feinstein was granted special postgame access to the Pitt locker room by Evans (which the NCAA no longer allows), just as he had been at halftime, for purposes of his book that would be called *A Season Inside*, and he did neither Evans nor the program any favors by reporting, and later writing, about those crushing, private locker-room moments immediately after the players returned to the locker room.

Feinstein wrote that Evans began to criticize Charles Smith for missing the open Jerome Lane in the critical first possession of overtime: "Jerome was wide open, Charlie." Lane echoed Evans, and the latter backed off. Still, even to broach the subject was inexcusable. Smith was at the time, and I think remains, the greatest player in Pitt hoops history, and he led the team with 21 points in his final game in a Pitt uniform. To even suggest that one questionable play by the team's best player is worth singling out after the game is ridiculous. What about the giveaway turnover when Lane and Miller screwed up a routine, undefended out-of-bounds play, which not only robbed Pitt of a possession but which we converted into a basket? I couldn't imagine, had my last-second three-pointer not fallen and we had lost, Coach Newton beginning his post-game remarks to the team by saying, "Will, if you had just held on to that last rebound...." But Feinstein's reporting of those private locker room moments surely hurt the team and the program; as Pitt's publicist recalled, "When Feinstein came out of the locker room, he proceeded to tell the reporters some of the stuff that had happened inside."

But the controversy that's really percolated in Pitt basketball circles for the last 30 years is what transpired in the final seconds of regulation after we called our final timeout following my three-pointer that cut the Pitt lead to 67-66 with five seconds remaining. The issue turns on whether the Pitt players were instructed to foul us if one of them was fouled (which Smith was) and hit both free throws (which Smith did) to give a Pitt a three-point lead. "An entire generation of disgruntled Pitt fans," said one such fan 25 years later, "is still pissed the Panthers didn't foul the Commodores' Barry Goheen with a three-point lead at the end of regulation."

Then and later, the Pitt players frequently used the words "chaos" and "confusion" to describe the huddle in the timeout after the first three-pointer. "Everybody was confused," Smith said immediately after the game. "No one knew what to do, that was the problem. No one said what to do. We could have called a timeout, or we could have mugged [Goheen]. Darelle [Porter] should have known to foul the man...but everybody was confused. Nobody knew what to do." Gore concurred: "No one ever said anything about fouling. We let the game get away on that play." Martin said the same thing 20 years later: "Barry freaking Goheen...I remember the timeout. I remember chaos in the timeout. There was nothing said to not let Goheen shoot the ball. That's for sure."

Porter, the player who bore most of the criticism because he supposedly failed to foul me, described the huddle like this: "In the huddle, both of them were being said, 'Foul! Don't foul!' I don't know what was said last. I remember him saying it, but I just missed the assignment. There was more than one person talking." Matthews said nearly the same thing: "There was a lot of noise in the huddle. A lot of coaches were talking. Some of them were saying foul, some of them weren't. He didn't know whether to foul or not." Gore and Miller were more succinct. Gore: "Nobody was told to foul." Miller: "We were never told."

As Lane remembered it, Assistant Coach Calipari was advocating for the foul, but Evans overruled him. "Oh, man, Paul Evans was so big-headed," Lane recalled. "Calipari told him to just foul them and send them to the line. We have the two best rebounders on the floor. He tells Calipari to shut the hell up and sit down." Two other Pitt assistant coaches, Norm Law and Mark Coleman, agreed that fouling was mentioned in the huddle, "but they weren't certain if the players fully understood the assignments." It's obvious that the players had *no* understanding of "their assignments," but those statements might have been the product of those coaches trying to be good foot soldiers and taking the bullet for their boss, Evans. As Miller summarized, the whole thing demonstrated a "lack of communication." Certainly, I had anticipated being fouled, as I said post-game: "I was surprised to get the shot that I did. I expected them to foul me."

What appears to have angered the Pitt players the most, beginning right after the game and continuing for the past 30 years, is not so much that Evans failed to tell them to foul, thus facilitating the tying three, but that Evans had the temerity to tell the media post-game that he unequivocally gave an order to foul, and the players didn't execute on that alleged order. Evans said after the game, "I told our guys to foul any of their guards in the backcourt." But, he said, "We couldn't catch up with him." Neither of those statements is credible.

First, Evans couldn't possibly have told anyone to foul one of us in the backcourt for the simple reason that no Pitt player remained on the Panthers' side of the court after Smith's second free throw. Every Pitt player retreated to our side of the court after the second free throw; no Panther was "in the backcourt," so it was surely inaccurate for Evans to say that he ordered a foul in the backcourt; I can't imagine all five players would have defied that order if it had been given.

Second, the "couldn't catch up with him" notion simply makes no sense. The first problem is that I wasn't being chased; I was driving *toward* the Panthers, not away from them, because they had retreated to our side of the court. So, no one needed to "catch up" with me. But beyond that is the sheer absurdity of a claim that Porter or Matthews couldn't chase me down if they were required to. They were faster than I was, and I would have been slowed because I was dribbling. So, even if they were in a position where they had to chase me down, I have no doubt that they would have.

Evans likely realized he had made a serious error by not ordering the foul and tried to correct his mistake, or at least deflect attention from it postgame, by promptly engaging in a bit of immediate revisionist history about the advice he had given and the actual position of the players on the floor in those final four seconds. But his deflection only compounded it—and he likely lost a measure of respect from his players that he would never regain. Miller, years later, put the whole thing in better perspective: "There are a lot of different ways to play that scenario. The point is that Barry Goheen had to make dramatic three-point baskets, both off the dribble.... [H]e did a great job."

☙

"Presentism" is defined as "an attitude toward the past dominated by present-day attitudes and experiences" and "the application of contemporary perspectives in explaining past events rather than placing these events in their historical context." In other words, it's easy, on the cusp of the third decade of the 21st century, to blame

Pitt for not fouling me and allowing me to shoot a tying three-point shot in an NCAA game played in 1988. With each passing year, the decision not to foul becomes that much more of a head-scratcher because, quite simply, almost every team holding a three-point lead late in the game will foul prior to the three-pointer being attempted in a last-second situation, which forces the opponent to (1) make the first free throw, (2) intentionally miss the second free throw, (3) rebound the intentionally-missed free throw, and (4) score a field goal that would tie the game.

In Pitt's defense, the 21st-century strategy on defending late-game three-point leads was nowhere close to being mature in 1988. Remember that '87–'88 was only the second season where all teams played with the three-point line in effect. Given the hostility with which many coaches greeted the introduction of the rule as an offensive weapon, it seems reasonable to assume that these coaches were similarly uninterested, at least at first, in devising strategies on how to defend the shot. Maybe Paul Evans was such a coach, and if he was, it would be hard to blame him given his terrific frontcourt of Smith, Lane, and Gore. One can understand why there would be confusion in the huddle during the fateful final timeout; it's likely that Pitt had never encountered that situation before.

If the situation had been reversed, and we were the team clinging to the three-point lead, we would have fouled Pitt. Why? Not necessarily because we had a better coach (though we did), but because we had encountered the same situation the previous season in the Sugar Bowl Tournament. Playing South Carolina, we blew a double-digit lead in the final three minutes and were forced into overtime. Still, we led by three in the extra period with seconds remaining. South Carolina, with the ball, called timeout and had to go the length of the floor. I'll never forget Steve Reece—future high school coach of Commodore great Drew Maddux and Kentucky star Ron Mercer—asking Coach Newton in the huddle whether we should foul the Gamecocks to put them on the free-throw line rather than allow a possible game-tying three-pointer. Coach Newton said no, let's play it out. You can guess what happened next—Terry Dozier hoisted a desperation 25-footer at the buzzer, and drained it. That sapped our confidence, and the Gamecocks won it in the second overtime period, 96-91. Thus, we played it in December 1986 exactly the way Pitt would play it in March 1988—we didn't foul and allowed a player to shoot a not-quite-contested, not-quite-uncontested three-pointer that found nothing but net. Like Pitt, we lost the game in the next period. The silver lining in that loss was that we learned not to assume that an opponent will miss a game-tying three-pointer, and a team leading by three in the final seconds probably should foul, give up two free throws, and not risk a tie.

So, unlike Pitt, we had been there; we had experienced late-game heartbreak by not fouling and would have known better had we been presented with the situation of a three-point lead with four seconds to play. In fact, we had employed the fouling strategy against North Carolina a few months before when we were leading by three, and it worked—we fouled Jeff Lebo, who missed the first free throw, made the second, and we won by two. So, we knew the proper strategy because we had learned the hard way, and Pitt would learn the hard way too—just on a more public and important stage, which made for a more painful lesson.

And dramatic, game-tying threes still occur. Exactly 20 years after the drama in Lincoln, John Calipari was again victimized by a game-tying, buzzer-beating three—this time as head coach of Memphis in the 2008 national championship game against Kansas. With a two-point lead and 10 seconds remaining, Derrick Rose hit only one of two free throws that left the Tigers with a three-point lead, then failed to foul the Jayhawks' Mario Chalmers, who hit a three at the buzzer to send the game into overtime, where Kansas won the title. One author wrote: "Within minutes, a friend emailed: 'Somewhere in America tonight, Barry Goheen smiled, and Paul Evans allowed himself a wry chuckle.'" I imagine that I did smile after the Chalmers shot—it's the kind of thrilling moment that makes the NCAA tournament so special. I doubt Paul Evans chuckled, however.

∾

One thing that has amazed me for the past 30 years is how much Pitt fans cared about what happened in Lincoln. Like most people, when I think of sports in Pittsburgh, I think of the NFL's Steelers. The city has never had an NBA team, and it didn't really support its ABA team. In other words, I never figured Pittsburgh to be much of a basketball town, so I assumed that the loss, while painful for the coaches and players, would sting a bit for the fans, but they would move on.

Wrong, wrong, wrong. The late '80s was something of a down period for the city's professional sports teams, so Pitt basketball found itself in the spotlight. As one person connected with the program explained,

> If you look back at that time in Pittsburgh sports, the Steelers were between the end of the Steel Curtain and the [Bill] Cowher era. The Penguins had just gotten Mario Lemieux. The Pirates were coming out of drug scandals and hadn't really picked up with [Barry] Bonds and [Bobby] Bonilla. Pitt basketball was nationally ranked. It kind of became the big sport in the city for that period.

So, with Pitt basketball being the "big sport" in the city in 1988, the loss was a shocker for the town. "You had the sense that the whole city of Pittsburgh was just in disarray," Sean Miller recalled.

The result was that I became part of a rogues' gallery of villains to Pittsburgh sports fans. As one longtime Panthers fan remembered, "It still kills me. The only play as crushing in my life was [the Atlanta Braves'] Sid Bream sliding into home to keep the Pirates out of the World Series [in 1992]." That's exactly what I was told by one of my good friends and long-time law partners, a Pittsburgh native, when I met him in 1996—I ranked with Francisco Cabrera, the person who hit the single that scored Bream to send the Braves to the Series in 1992, as those that have broken Pittsburghers' hearts on the field/court. Here's another one: "For a generation, there have been two things to say to stop any Pitt fan cold. The first is '48-14,' the score by which hated rival Penn State upset an undefeated and Number 1-ranked Pitt football team led by Dan Marino in 1981. The second is 'Barry Goheen.' Both have been said to me many times." As late as 2014, a blog on the 10 most disappointing moments in Pitt sports ranked the '88 NCAA game as #5.

Another reason the '88 game seems to linger with Pitt fans is that the program hit a rough patch for the next several years. If, for example, Evans had regrouped and led the team to a couple of Final Fours and more Big East titles, the loss to us probably would be recalled less as a stake in the heart of the program and more as a stepping stone or a learning experience, albeit a painful one, on the road to top-tier status in college basketball. But it didn't happen. Instead, as Martin recalled, "things did start to fall apart a little bit for the program." Another writer was more candid: "the Pitt program slid downhill for almost 15 years." Under Paul Evans, the Panthers never advanced past the second round of the NCAA tournament. Evans coached at Pitt for six more seasons, was fired after the 1993–94 season, and has not coached since. He's a real estate agent in Annapolis, Maryland, the town where he achieved his greatest coaching success with Navy and David Robinson. Some attribute his downfall to the immediate aftermath of our game—not that Pitt lost the game necessarily, but that Feinstein's post-game reporting of the locker room dissension brought "a lot of negativity" to the program, and Evans "got painted by a pretty heavy brush for that."

Pitt would rebound in the late 90s and 2000s behind Ben Howland and then Jamie Dixon, both of whom would win Naismith Coach of the Year honors at Pitt. A Pitt broadcaster compared the '88 team to these more recent Pitt teams in what may well be the last word on the '88 hoopsters.

> I think everyone would agree that was one of Pitt's most talented teams ever. They had everything—height, shooting, defense, All-Americans and a super freshman class. I'm not criticizing Paul Evans, but, if that team would have played with the same cohesiveness that the Ben Howland and Jamie Dixon teams have played with, I think they would have won the whole thing.

So, as I recently commented, "Maybe the statute of limitations is about to run out on the pain" for Pitt players and fans.

IV

"Money talks, it never lies"
—Bryan Ferry, "Kiss and Tell" ('87–'88)

The stories from the Vanderbilt side following the Pitt game are more light-hearted, if not downright whimsical, in comparison to the Pitt controversies. The most widely reported, and still the most enduring, anecdote is Coach Newton's apparently oracular statement to Perdue when Wilbur left the court after his fifth foul with four seconds left in regulation: "Your college career's not over." That was how Wilbur himself wrote it in a first-person column for the *Nashville Banner*.

Did Coach Newton predict to Perdue—with Wilbur fouled out and Pitt leading by one and free throws with only four seconds left—that we would win? I've always been a tad skeptical of that theory, but *Sports Illustrated* and *The Sporting News* quoted Coach Newton as telling Perdue, "Your basketball isn't over yet." And C.M. apparently qualified it even further in a subsequent postgame interview, saying that he told Will, "Your basketball may not be over," while another report quoted him as, "You may have more basketball left to play."

The more benign statement quoted in *SI* and *TSN* would be true. Wilbur's basketball wasn't nearly over, as his fine career in the NBA, complete with four championship rings (three with the Bulls, one with the Spurs), would prove. But I suppose that only two people haave ever known what was said, and it's always made for a good story. I'm just glad that I didn't learn any of that until after the game—if I had heard that "prediction," I would have bricked the shot for sure. And I'm glad we won the game so that we made Coach Newton look so wise and all-knowing—or, as one writer said, making Coach Newton look like "Nostradamus [on] Sunday."

And then there was the semi-kerfuffle over CBS's selection of our team's player of the game—Perdue. That one even merited a mention in *USA Today* in an item humorously titled "The polls must have closed early." The *Nashville Banner* felt compelled to call CBS for an explanation, and was informed that "such selections are made by the 'talent' involved and are not voted on by the media at large." I had to chuckle at this tempest in a teapot. The network would do something like donate $1,000 to the university's general scholarship fund in the name of the player of the game. The player himself certainly wouldn't receive any money and, as far as I can tell, wouldn't even receive a certificate or other memento of the selection. So, it was hard to get worked up over this one, as I'm sure that Dick Stockton and Billy Cunningham made the selection with a few seconds left in regulation under the not-unreasonable assumption that Pitt would win and they would immediately need to throw the broadcast to some other game in progress. Nevertheless, I must have subconsciously felt this so-called snub because the next season we were the SEC game of the week four times, and I was our team's player of the game every time (once a co-winner with Kornet). And, for those four games, I received exactly what Wilbur received for being the player of the game against Pitt—nada.

As the years pass, and the videotape and You Tube clips become ever grainier (just like our memories), the tying shot becomes a little longer, a little tougher, just a little more miraculous. That exaggeration was brilliantly foreseen by fellow Commodore Buster Olney just two days after the game, where he imagined a "weekend warrior" pickup game at Memorial where the tying shot was to be recreated, but the combatants argued over whether the shot was from 30 feet, 35 feet, or even 45 feet; that Smith, who was "a little more than 7 feet tall," was in my face; and other increased degrees of difficulty. Buster has looked positively clairvoyant, given certain accounts of the game that extend the shot to 25 feet and beyond. In fact, nearly 25 years to the day after the game, Sean Miller, by now the coach at Arizona (and doing a fine job there), recalled that "Barry Goheen made two 30-footers in a row."

There also were the reports on the amount of money the university was to receive for advancing to the Sweet Sixteen, which are humorous in retrospect. In 1988, each school making the NCAA tourney grossed roughly $230,700 for each round it remained in the tourney. Thus, by making the Sweet Sixteen we earned $461,500 for the school and guaranteed at least $692,200, given that we had advanced to the regional semifinal round. Those figures seem positively quaint these days, with the NCAA tourney contract measured in the billions of dollars and each school receiving multiples more than $230,700 for making the NCAA tourney. But it was a big deal for a private school like Vanderbilt to add money from athletics to the coffers of the university, so the media played up the financial angle in the aftermath of the Pitt game. Thus, the university earned another $230,700 when we made the Sweet Sixteen, or "approximately $10,000 a foot" for the distance of the game-tying trey, as one writer put it.

֍

If we ask why Pitt fans cared so much and took the loss so hard, the opposite question is also worth asking: why was it such a big deal for Vanderbilt fans to go to the Sweet Sixteen? That one is much easier to answer. John Bibb of *The Tennessean* explained it quite well the day after the game: "For years, this Commodore coterie has grown accustomed to near misses, moral victories, and 'wait 'til next year' promises. Not so, this morning." A fan at the airport mob scene put it less poetically but more to the point: "Vanderbilt fans don't get to do this very often, but when we do, we cherish it." I received several kudos not just from the Vanderbilt community but also from others, such as Kentucky coach Eddie Sutton, who sent me a nice congratulatory note (and whose Wildcats were the only other SEC team to make the Sweet Sixteen).

To say that the team became something of a cause célèbre locally would be an understatement. This was exciting stuff for everyone—players, students, fans. We didn't practice on the Monday following our return from Lincoln, and it was a beautiful spring day in Nashville—a great day to be a Commodore! There were two or three items in each of the local newspapers every day that week. The three local television stations ran pieces on the team or specific players. My favorite, or at least the one I remember most, involved a local station dispatching one of its reporters to campus to find me. The reporter (who was not in the station's sports department) had no idea where or who I was—a bizarre premise for a piece that had our intrepid reporter roaming the campus and accosting random students and even professors asking about me. The reporter eventually found me outside the Branscomb Quadrangle, where I had lived as a freshman and where, at that time, the athletes' training table was housed. The only thing I remember from the brief Q&A was her question about the university earning $250,000 by our advancing further in the tourney. I told her, "I've heard that, but I haven't seen any of that $250,000 yet." Her detective work accomplished, the reporter—probably not all that delighted with her assignment in the first place—returned to the station.

If ever there were a day not only to show up but to be on time for class, this was the day. Unfortunately, we had been out of town so much over the past three weeks that my class attendance had been lackluster. So, I had to salute the professor of my Western Civilization class—a "lecture" class that enrolled well over 100 students—who saw me waltz into the lecture hall after not having attended the class for a couple of weeks (or more) and fired off this zinger: "Welcome back, Mr. Goheen. I was beginning to think that you were taking the class on a correspondence basis." My friend Cheryl, who was sitting beside me, led the raucous laughter from the students, which I happily endured, then joined in myself. After a few seconds, the professor added, in the same even tone but with a wry smile, "But nice shot anyway, Mr. Goheen."

Even better than that was the greeting from Kassian Kovalcheck, the same professor who had guided Will through the Communication Studies major for the past three years, when I sauntered into his class on Tuesday. This was a smaller class of maybe 20–25 people, most of whom shared my major. On this day, Kass waited until everyone was seated and quiet before directing the day's first question to me:

KK: Goheen, how old are you?

BG: Twenty-one.

KK: Hmmm. Twenty-one. [Strokes beard during a perfect pregnant pause of about five seconds.] How does it feel to be 21 years old and know that your life is going to go straight downhill from this moment on?

That is one of the greatest lines I've ever heard, and no one laughed harder than I did. Sadly, Kass's joking prediction was going to come true a lot sooner than either of us expected.

16

MANNING UP

I

"I took a wrong turn on the astral plane"
—Warren Zevon, "Bad Karma" ('87)

Of course, there was a game to play on Friday evening, against the Kansas Jayhawks, yet another in the line of blue-blood college basketball programs we had played in the past couple of years (Kentucky, Duke, North Carolina, Indiana). They were just as lucky as we were to be playing in the sweet sixteen. They comfortably beat Xavier in the first round in Lincoln, 85-72. The most amazing thing about that game was Xavier's stupidity in the days leading up to it—when the brackets were announced on Sunday, the Cincinnati-based Musketeers, led by star guard Byron Larkin (brother of Hall of Fame shortstop Barry), whose 25.3 points-per-game average was ninth-best in the nation, publicly complained, not about their seeding or their opponent (a common gripe from someone every year), but about being sent to Lincoln, which they felt was a little too rural for their tastes. The most demeaning comment quote was "Lincoln is Siberia with a bunch of 7-Elevens." Not surprisingly, the Musketeers received a hostile welcome from the Nebraskans when they took the floor; they were booed incessantly all game long, and it seemed to unnerve them right from the opening tip. The game was a blowout—Kansas built a 19-point lead at the half, 48-29, and coasted to the victory.

The Jayhawks' second-round game against Murray State, though, was anything but comfortable. Like Pitt in our game, Kansas jumped out to a double-digit first-half lead, holding a commanding 25-13 lead about two-thirds of the way through the half. And, like Pitt, the Jayhawks let their opponent back into the game, as the Racers closed the deficit to five, 28-23, at the half. The Racers then claimed a two-point lead in the second half, 34-32. The game was nip-and-tuck the rest of the way, and Murray showed great mettle in staying with Kansas and eventually forging a three-point lead, 56-53, just inside the four-minute mark. Kansas scored the next four points to take a one-point lead, but Jeff Martin's two free throws with 51 seconds remaining gave the Racers a 58-57 lead. Danny Manning quickly answered from six feet to put the Jayhawks ahead, 59-58, with 38 seconds left. Murray held for the final shot. As so often seems to happen in these situations, the team works the clock down too far and is forced to take a shot that is less than ideal, and that's what happened to the Racers. It was obvious that one of Murray's two stars, Martin or Don Mann, would take the shot—they were the only two Racers in double figures—and, with the clock melting away to under five seconds, it was point guard Mann, who was 4-for-14 from the field for the game, who kept the ball on a drive into the lane. He was heavily defended by Scooter Barry, and Manning came over to seal off the little space Mann had created with his drive. His driving scoop shot rolled off the rim, and Manning rebounded with a second to go. His two free throws ended the scoring and Kansas escaped, 61-58. So, it would be Commodores versus Jayhawks in the Midwest Regional semifinals in Pontiac, Michigan.

⁊

We returned to the practice floor on Tuesday afternoon, anxious to get back to work and put all the attention behind us. Coach Newton was anxious too. Having allowed us to soak up the adulation on Monday, he put a stop to further media requests. It was time to prepare, and Coach Newton made sure we knew the stakes by writing this on the chalkboard in our locker room: "2 games away from Final Four."

Kansas, in some ways, represents the birthplace of college basketball. James Naismith, the Canadian who invented the game in Springfield, Massachusetts, in 1891, came to Kansas a few years later to teach and coach, which he did from 1899 to 1907. Naismith's protégé, Phog Allen, began coaching the Jayhawks in 1907 at the tender age of 22, and Allen transformed Kansas hoops into something special. He also coached, 30 years apart, two of the greatest coaches of all time: Kentucky's Adolph Rupp (KU class of 1923) and North Carolina's Dean Smith (KU class of 1952). By the time Allen retired, just after recruiting Wilt Chamberlain to Lawrence in the mid-1950s, he had notched 590 wins and turned Kansas into a basketball-crazed state.

Kansas entered the NCAAs with 11 losses, one more than us. Unlike us, the Jayhawks had been expected to be much better than that. Various preseason polls rated the Jayhawks anywhere from #1 (*Basketball Times*) or #2 (*The Sporting News*) to #20 (*Inside Sports*). Nevertheless, it's fair to say that the Jayhawks had underachieved going into the tourney. They lost two of three games in the Maui Classic to open the season, then lost a starting forward, Archie Marshall, for the season to a knee injury during a December 30 loss to St. John's. Another front-courter, 6'10" Marvin Branch, was lost for the season in January due to academics. After a home loss to Oklahoma on February 3, the Jayhawks' record was 12-8, and they were on a four-game losing streak. But they regrouped to win eight of their last 10 games to finish the regular season with a 20-10 record, placing third in the Big Eight Conference with a 9-5 mark. Then they were blown out by in-state rival Kansas State in the conference tournament, and came to Lincoln with a 21-11 record but not a lot of momentum. For what it was worth, we and the Jayhawks had one common opponent during the season: we both played at Notre Dame. The Jayhawks played at South Bend on January 23, a little over a month before we did, and they didn't fare as well—behind 29 points from David Rivers, the Irish prevailed, 80-76.

I naively thought that KU would be a better matchup for us than Murray State. Perdue would have had his way inside with the undersized Racers, but Murray was quick on the perimeter, and Martin was truly a great player—the kind of athletic, offensive-minded small forward that had given us trouble all year (Dyron Nix, Ricky Blanton, Rick Callaway, etc.). As for Kansas, Manning was a great player too, but the Jayhawks didn't seem to have a lot of athleticism around him; there was no way the Jayhawks were better than Pitt, but as it turned out they had infinitely better team chemistry than the bickering Panthers.

The Jayhawks were coached by the peripatetic Larry Brown, a North Carolina graduate who, though only 47 in 1988, already had coached in the ABA, NBA, and NCAA, leading UCLA to a title-game appearance in 1980, where they lost to the Darrell Griffith-led Louisville Cardinals. From Westwood, Brown went to the NBA's New Jersey Nets, resigning in 1983 to take the Kansas job after his college coach, Dean Smith, declined the offer to bolt North Carolina and return to his alma mater.

The Jayhawks were led on the court by Danny Manning, the best player in college basketball in 1987–88, his senior season. Manning played high school ball in Greensboro, North Carolina, where his team won the state title in his junior season of 1983. That summer, new KU coach Brown, filling out his coaching staff, hired one Ed Manning, at that time employed as the driver of an 18-wheeler, as an assistant coach. Ed, of course, was Danny's father, and had played for Brown in the old ABA. "I told Ed, 'You're not gonna lose your job if you don't get Danny,'" recalled Brown, "'but you'd be a pretty bad recruiter if we couldn't get your son.'" The whole Manning family relocated from Greensboro to Lawrence for Danny's senior year, and the University of North Carolina—Brown's alma mater and where Danny himself had said he most likely would have committed if not for his father's new job—was irate at what it termed Brown's questionable ethics (which, in fact, have been on display at every coaching stop Brown has made in his college career). Not surprisingly, Ed did in fact successfully recruit his son to KU beginning in fall 1984.

Manning's four years in Lawrence had been a success. He averaged 14.6 points a game as a freshman. As a sophomore, he led the Jayhawks to the 1986 Final Four by averaging 16.7 per game, though the Jayhawks lost to Duke in the national semifinal in Dallas. Manning upped his scoring significantly as a junior, averaging 23.9 points a game and shooting a school-record 61.7% from the field. He had saved his best for last, though, averaging just under 25 points a game as a senior as the Jayhawks navigated their up-and-down season.

We would meet Kansas in the Silverdome in Pontiac, Michigan, just outside Detroit. We would be playing the first game, almost with an undercard feeling given that we and KU were low seeds at 7 and 6. The main event, in game two, would feature #1-seeded Purdue and #4-seeded Kansas State. Still, over 31,000 fans were in attendance, and a strong contingent from Nashville made the trip.

Our game plan wasn't overly complicated. Manning had scored 24 and 25 points in his team's first two NCAA games, right on his season average of 24.8 a game. We needed to keep him right about there; if we did, we should have a good chance to win the game because that would mean the rest of the team would need to score about 50 points, which wasn't likely. We had scored exactly 80 in each of our first two games; we felt confident that we could score on Kansas.

The first minute set the tone for the entire game. We won the tip and thus had the first possession. We patiently worked the ball around, then fed the ball to Perdue on the block. Predictably, a couple of smaller Jayhawk defenders collapsed around Will, and I fanned out behind the arc, where Will found me with a perfect pass for the game's first shot. It felt good when it left my hand, looked good in the air…and rimmed in-and-out. It was going to be that kind of night for me. Kansas claimed the rebound, and barely a minute later Manning, to our surprise, attempted a trey of his own. Until that attempt, he had made exactly seven three-pointers all year. He drained this one, though. It was going to be that kind of night for him. (He would make one more during the game and would make no more the rest of the season.)

As in the Pitt game, we started cold from the field, missing 10 of our first 12 shots. Unlike Pitt, though, we would be unable to climb out of the early hole. Less than nine minutes into the game, KU led 19-4, and Manning was the reason. He was, clearly, the best player for one game that I ever played against. He did everything: he hit three-pointers and mid-range jump shots; he hit little soft hooks down low that were lightning-fast—it seemed like the ball was in his hands for less than a second after receiving the entry pass before it left his hands; he led fast breaks. In an incredible first half, he went 12-for-17 from the field and totaled 25 points—his season average in only twenty minutes. As Kornet said, "It seemed like everything he shot was going in. I kept saying, 'When's this man going to miss?'" Meanwhile, as a team, we scored only 29 points and the Jayhawks held a commanding lead at the break, 41-29.

We played a little better in the second half but couldn't do much to dent the Kansas lead. Booker had one of his best games, scoring a team-high 22 points on 6-for-13 shooting from beyond the arc. His shooting, combined with Manning's finally cooling off, enabled us to reduce the deficit to single digits a couple of times in the second half. But we could get no closer than nine, and Kansas cruised to a 77-64 victory.

Manning finished with 38 points—about half his team's total. The only other Jayhawk in double figures was Kevin Pritchard, who had a fine game with 11 points and five assists. Manning scored 13 points above his average—which also was the final margin of victory for his team. If we could have limited him to an average night, we would have been in it. "It was a case of a great player rising to the occasion," Coach Newton said. "We needed Manning to have a so-so night, and he didn't." I didn't think the rest of the team "played that great. But he carried them, and they followed his lead." Their defense was solid as well. Our 64 points were the fewest we had scored since the win at Ole Miss nearly three months earlier.

In his final college game, Perdue scored 16 points and led the team with eight rebounds, justifying Manning's praise that he was "[o]ne of the best centers in the country." He and Book were the only two players in double figures. Wilcox had a fine game off the bench with seven points, and no else scored more than four. Meanwhile, I never found the mark after that opening-possession miss. I had my worst game of the year—three points on 1-for-7 shooting from the field and 1-for-2 from the line. Pritchard did a good job defending me, and I couldn't get to the basket for open looks. I was able to penetrate the Jayhawks' zone in the second half from the top of the key, draw a couple of defenders to me, and dish back out to Book for a three-point attempt. My four assists tied Kornet for team honors. Still, scoring only three points was bitterly disappointing. I played in four NCAA tournament games. In the other three, I averaged 18 points a game. Bad games happen, but you don't want them to occur in the Sweet Sixteen. But that's the beauty of sports: hero one game, goat the next. Every game is "a new day," as Booker would say. A great game means very little when the ball tips for the next game, while a poor game brings the chance for redemption the next time out. Except that this time there would be no "next game," and that's what hurt the most.

Will tried to keep things light even though his Vanderbilt career had ended. On the bus ride back to the hotel, he took Coach Newton's traditional seat, which was the right front seat. The coach was often one of the first people on the bus, but his wife, Evelyn, rarely was ("timely but not necessarily on time," as Coach Newton put it), and many times Coach Newton would ask our trainer, the legendary Joe (Bird) Worden, "Is everybody here?" and often adding "Where in the hell is Evelyn?" On this occasion, Coach Newton walked right past his seat without realizing Will was in it. Then came Will's voice booming from the front: "Joe, is that everybody? Where in the hell is Evelyn?" Everyone cracked up, with Coach Newton laughing the loudest.

Behind Naismith Player of the Year Manning, Kansas would go on to win the NCAA title, winning its next three games over teams that had beaten the Jayhawks a total of five times earlier in the season. KU beat in-state rival and conference foe Kansas State (upset winner over Purdue) in the regional final to advance to the Final Four in Kansas City—practically home turf for the Jayhawks. In the national semifinal, they took down Duke—a team that had beaten the Jayhawks in Lawrence late in the season—to advance to the national championship game against another Big

Eight foe, Oklahoma, which had swept the teams' two regular season games. But Manning was just as phenomenal against the Sooners as he had been against us, scoring 31 points and grabbing 18 rebounds to lead the Jayhawks to the 83-79 victory and the NCAA crown. At 23-11, the Jayhawks were the first team with more than 10 losses to win the NCAA Tournament. Brown left KU to return to the NBA to coach the San Antonio Spurs; the Jayhawks were banned from postseason play in 1988–89 and placed on probation for recruiting violations during Brown's tenure.

II
"May good fortune be with you, may your guiding light be strong"
—Rod Stewart, "Forever Young" ('88)

Meanwhile, we would have to be satisfied with a Sweet Sixteen appearance and the knowledge that, at least, we had been knocked out of the tourney by the eventual national champion. There would be no throng at the airport awaiting our arrival back to Nashville this time. Nevertheless, we could look back with pride on what we had accomplished during the 1987–88 season. We had (1) beaten the team ranked #1 in the country at the time of the game; (2) won seven straight conference games; (3) brought a national ranking to the program for the first time in nearly a decade; (4) made the program's first NCAA appearance in 14 years; and (5) won two games in the NCAA tournament for the first time in school history. After the disappointment of the Kansas game subsided, we would be able to better appreciate these accomplishments. But, first, we would need to get back to academics: Petro told me that spring that, by the time we returned to Nashville after the Sweet Sixteen, we had been on the road for all or part of 24 of the previous 28 days, a difficult travel schedule that began with the Notre Dame trip at the end of February.

A few weeks later, we held our annual team banquet. Former Boston Celtics great John Havlicek was the guest speaker. Perdue, of course, was awarded the team's Most Valuable Player award chosen by the team. He averaged a double-double of 18.3 points and a league-leading 10.1 rebounds a game—the last time a Commodore player has averaged a double-double for an entire season. He also blocked 74 shots, then a team record, and shot a sensational 63.4% from the field, easily leading the SEC. He also dished out 81 assists, only eight shy of my team-leading 89. Deservedly, Wilbur was named the SEC's Player of the Year by all media outlets and capped a great year by being named the SEC's Athlete of the Year in late spring.

I was honored that my teammates elected me co-captain along with Will. I finished second to Wilbur in scoring at 12.4 per game, while Book was our other double-figure scorer with 10.9 per game. Mayes finished an excellent freshman season as the team's fourth-leading scorer at 7.1 points per game, while Draud was close behind at an even 7.0 per game. Those two were the stars of three of our biggest wins of the season—Kentucky (Draud), and Auburn and North Carolina (Mayes). Reid and Kornet, the starting forwards for most of the season, averaged 6.5 and 6.4 points per game, respectively, and supported Perdue on the boards by combining for 9.4 rebounds per game. Wilcox (5.1 points per game) and Grant (5.0 points per game) gave us nine players that averaged at least five points per game, an impressive demonstration of our depth. Derrick led the guards in shooting from the field (48.5%) and from behind the three-point line (46.2%), while Grant's 59.6% field-goal percentage was second only to Perdue, and his 84.5% mark from the free-throw line was the best among the primary nine players.

In addition to Perdue's slate of honors, there were other great individual accomplishments. Coach Newton was named SEC Coach of the Year by both Associated Press and UPI. Booker and I were named honorable mention All-America by Basketball Times, and I was selected Third Team All-SEC by AP and UPI. As a team, we led the SEC in scoring at 78.7 points per game, and our scoring margin of +5.9 trailed only Kentucky's +8.1. Shooting, of course, was a strength: we led the league in field goal percentage at 49.7% and paced the SEC in every three-point shooting category—makes (200), attempts (464), and percentage (43.1%).

The team performed well in the classroom, too. Balancing on-court success with in-class performance, both Booker and I were named to the Academic All-SEC team, and Perdue's graduation in May gave Coach Newton a perfect 18-for-18 record in graduating seniors in his seven years at Vanderbilt.

I stayed in Nashville in May to attend a "Maymester" course taught by Professor Kovalcheck, which allowed me to knock out a few hours to lighten the load for my senior year (the course: Rhetoric of Irish Nationalism). I also worked out some with Will, who stayed in town to prepare for the Olympic trials and the NBA draft, and with Wendy Schoeltens, one of the all-time greats produced by the Vandy women's program, and who had just finished her freshman year, helping lead the Lady 'Dores (along with senior Carolyn Peck, future NCAA title-winning coach for the Purdue Lady Boilermakers in 2000 and another Communication Studies major, like Will and me) to an NCAA bid.

We were thrilled when Wilbur was drafted by the up-and-coming Chicago Bulls with the 11th pick in the NBA draft. Twenty-five players were chosen in the first round. It is a testament to the strength of the SEC during the 1980s, and the challenging non-conference schedule that Coach Newton annually assembled, that of the other 24 picks, we had played against 11 of them (indicated in bold) at some point in the previous three seasons, including four of the first five selections and six of the first 10:

1. **Danny Manning—Kansas**
2. Rik Smits—Marist
3. **Charles Smith—Pittsburgh**
4. **Chris Morris—Auburn**
5. **Mitch Richmond—Kansas State**
6. Hersey Hawkins—Bradley
7. Tim Perry—Temple
8. **Rex Chapman—Kentucky**
9. Rony Seikaly—Syracuse
10. **Willie Anderson—Georgia**
11. *Will Perdue—Vanderbilt*
12. Harvey Grant—Oklahoma
13. **Jeff Grayer—Iowa State**
14. Dan Majerle—Central Michigan
15. Gary Grant—Michigan
16. **Derrick Chievous—Missouri**
17. Eric Leckner—Wyoming
18. Ricky Berry—San Jose State
19. Rod Strickland—DePaul
20. Kevin Edwards—DePaul
21. Mark Bryant—Seton Hall
22. **Randolph Keys—Southern Mississippi**
23. **Jerome Lane—Pittsburgh**
24. Brian Shaw—UC-Santa Barbara
25. **David Rivers—Notre Dame**

That four players from the SEC went in the first 11 picks speaks of the talent in the SEC in 1988. What's more, Florida's Vernon Maxwell was drafted late in the second round, and, like the other four, enjoyed a long and productive NBA career. The quintet of Perdue, Morris, Chapman, Anderson, and Maxwell combined to play 58 seasons and win six NBA titles. I doubt that many conferences have ever had a more successful NBA draft than the SEC did in 1988.

Will didn't make the Olympic team, which may have been a good thing given that the U.S. suffered its first legitimate loss in the Olympics during those Games. In another demonstration of how Coach Newton had elevated the program, we had played against six of the 12 '88 Olympians (Manning, Smith, Anderson, Grayer, Richmond, and North Carolina's J.R. Reid).

In early June, I returned home to Kentucky for a couple of months of rest and relaxation. There would be no overseas trip in summer 1988, but I looked forward to my senior season and the challenge it would bring—helping return the Commodores to the NCAA tournament.

Will Perdue, C.M. Newton, myself, and Barry Booker
at the 2011 Naismith Awards Invitational golf tournament, Atlanta, Georgia.

Reuniting with Chip Rupp, Final Four weekend 2017, Scottsdale, Arizona.

Will Perdue and me posing with the Naismith Trophy
at the 2017 Final Four, Glendale, Arizona.

Nailing a jumper over Jeff Lebo in our victory
over #1 ranked North Carolina, December 1987.

I slipped here but netted 26 points in our upset
of Steve Alford and #2 ranked Indiana, December 1986.

Matching up with Kentucky's Rex Chapman
in a 1987 game at Rupp Arena in Lexington.

A great friend and a great player—
trying to solve Barry Booker's defense in practice.

This time it's Chapman, with Ed Davender, guarding me
in our big win over Kentucky, January 1988.

Will Perdue was an outstanding passer from the post position,
which was a critical component of the Bomb Squad's success.

Pandemonium reigns after we completed a miracle comeback against Tennessee in January 1986, scoring nine straight points in the final 50 seconds without the three-point line and with a turnover, and I celebrate by leaping into the arms of center Brett Burrow.

Bedlam erupts at Racer Arena in Murray, Kentucky, when our team, the Marshall County Marshals, clinches a trip to the Kentucky State High School Tournament—the Sweet Sixteen—with a thrilling victory, March 1984.

I scored 27 points in the 1984 state tourney game
against Bourbon County, but it wasn't enough.

Louisville's LaBradford Smith and I seem to be distracted by action
elsewhere on the court in the game against the Cardinals, November 1988.

I enjoy a free ride off the court after sinking a half-court shot
to beat Louisville, November 1988.

Members of the 1988–89 team reunited twenty years later
to be honored by Vanderbilt in January 2009.

Country superstar Vince Gill chaired our 1988 Music City Invitational holiday tournament, and I participated in his annual charity golf tournament, The Vinnie, in 2017 at Golf Club of Tennessee.

We're down two to Georgia with five seconds to play and I've just dribbled out behind the three-point line with the intention of shooting a three for the win, glancing at a scoreboard clock to make sure I have enough time, January 1989.

Making a layup against Texas in Coach Newton's 500th victory;
48 hours later, the coach announced his resignation.

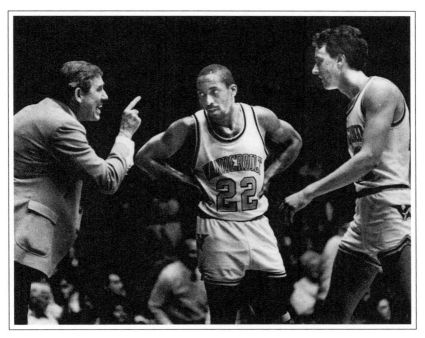

Coach Newton has some instructions for Darrell Dulaney and me
in this game from my freshman year of 1985–86.

Tri-MVPs, tri-captains: with Frank Kornet and Barry Booker
at our basketball awards banquet, April 1989.

Steve Reece, Frank Kornet, myself, and Will Perdue enjoy golf with Coach
Newton during his retirement weekend in 2000 in Lexington.

Graduation day, May 1989.

A strong Vanderbilt contingent of former players, coaches, and administrators made the trip to Tuscaloosa, Alabama, for the funeral and celebration of the life of C.M. Newton, June 2018.

PART TWO

WITHOUT A WILL, THERE'S STILL A WAY

THE 1988–89 SEASON

THE CHALLENGE

I

"The promise in the year of election"
—U2, "Desire" ('88)

I returned to campus in late August 1988 ready for my final season at Vanderbilt. The seasons seemed long and the school years unending, but overall it was amazing how quickly three years had passed. "I was talking to Barry Booker the other day," I remarked in a preseason interview, "and it's hard to believe that we're now seniors. It seemed like only yesterday that we were freshmen on a struggling basketball team, and now we feel like we're a team that can compete with anyone." I was determined to make my senior year memorable, but I had no idea exactly how memorable it would be.

The 1987–88 season had a definite arc to it, almost like a "W": we began with a high with the UNC win as part of a 7-1 start, then lost three in a row, then hit another peak with seven straight SEC wins (and 10 out of 12), hit a second low by losing four out of five prior to the NCAA tournament, and finished on a high (if Kansas were excluded) by making the Sweet Sixteen. The 1988–89 season, on the other hand, had no such structure at all. To be sure, there were both winning and losing streaks, but there also were weeks where thrilling highs were followed by crushing lows, and vice versa. And sometimes those events happened in the same game, perhaps even a few seconds apart. Victories were snatched out of the jaws of defeat, and defeats were snatched out of the jaws of victory. It was almost like the weather: if you didn't like it, wait a few minutes and things would change. It all added up to one of the most interesting and exciting seasons in Vandy history.

෴

We faced the substantial challenge of building on the success of 1987–88 without SEC Player of the Year Will Perdue, who had gone on to the NBA's Chicago Bulls. But Wilbur was the only one of the nine primary players we lost, so we felt that we could compensate for his absence based on the sheer number of key players returning. Still, it would have been foolish to believe that we could duplicate the prior season's success if the eight primary players did not significantly improve. "Everybody else has to work harder," I asserted in October as we began practice. "Even with Will gone, we feel like we can still have a good year, and we're all looking forward to it." Booker expressed an even greater degree of optimism: "I think we will do pretty well without Will. We can be at least as good as we were last season. We have the experience, we just have to make up the rebounding."

We weren't the only SEC team grappling with the loss of its best player. Several teams faced the same challenge: Auburn lost Jeff Morris and Chris Moore; Ole Miss lost Rod Barnes; Florida lost Vernon Maxwell, and Georgia lost Willie Anderson. Most significantly, Kentucky lost nearly every major contributor, including seniors Ed Davender, Winston Bennett, and Rob Lock, as well as sophomore Rex Chapman, who entered the NBA draft—and the losses were just beginning for the 'Cats.

With Perdue gone, four players sought to join the rotation with the eight primary returnees. One, center Fred Benjamin, had been on the 1987–88 team but had played only 39 minutes in 15 games. Three players new to the team rounded out the potential rotation. One was another center, Alberto Ballestra, a junior college transfer who would be entering his junior season. We also welcomed two true freshmen, Todd Milholland from nearby Waverly, Tennessee, and Morgan Wheat from Des Moines, Iowa. Todd was 6'10", which would suggest that he would play center, but his thin build and soft shooting touch made him more of a forward. Morgan had great athleticism and, at 6'5", could play the 2-guard or the small forward positions, thus giving us greater flexibility.

Adding to the challenge of returning to the NCAAs was the difficult schedule Coach Newton had lined up. In addition to the talent-packed Maui Classic, where we would open the season with a game against Michigan, our non-conference schedule featured (in this order): Louisville at home, at Alabama-Birmingham, at North Carolina, and at Kansas State—and that only took us through the first 10 days in December before we took a break for our SEC debut against Auburn. Even the games with the so-called "small conference" schools (today generally referred to as "mid-majors") were going to be challenging—home games with Murray State and Dartmouth would be difficult. Then, after the Christmas break, our likely opponent in the final of the Music City Invitational would be Stanford, the Pac-10 preseason favorite. The final non-conference game, dropped into the middle of the SEC schedule in late January, was a home game against another conference favorite, Texas of the Southwest Conference. That's a tough schedule; three of those opponents were in *Sports Illustrated*'s top six preseason teams (Louisville #3, Michigan #4, UNC #6), while three others made its top 40 (Ohio State #14, Stanford #21, Murray State #38). Coach Newton surely wasn't exaggerating when he said of the schedule, "I've never asked one of my teams to play a better one." Years later, Coach Newton recalled, "If you look back at the schedule we played back in '89, those guys played Michigan, Ohio State, Louisville, Stanford, and North Carolina at North Carolina.

That's how we scheduled back then, and it was a lot of fun to play the top teams." So, for 1988–89, one thing would be certain: if we didn't snag an NCAA bid in March, it wouldn't be because of a weak non-conference schedule.

II

"L.A. Lakers fast break makers, kings of the court shake and bake all takers"
—Red Hot Chili Peppers, "Magic Johnson" ('89)

There were a couple of events in the fall that enlivened an otherwise dreary and predictable preseason. One was the opportunity to observe the defending NBA champion Los Angeles Lakers practice at Memorial prior to an exhibition game in October. In June, the Lakers had become the first NBA team in nearly 20 years to win consecutive championships; they were at the top of the NBA heap, as these were the waning days of "Showtime." Kareem Abdul-Jabbar, Earvin "Magic" Johnson, James Worthy, A.C. Green, Byron Scott, and others were beginning their quest for a "three-peat," a term their coach, Pat Riley, had coined while they were still popping the champagne celebrating the "repeat." Like Coach Newton, Riley was a graduate of the University of Kentucky—he was a starter on the one-loss 1965–66 UK team that famously lost the NCAA final to Texas Western, which fielded an all-African-American starting five in what is probably the most overrated game in college hoops history. Coach Newton used the UK connection to get us into the gym to watch the practice because Riley generally closed most of the team's practices. There was no doubt who was in charge for the Lakers—it was Magic Johnson, except that no one called him "Magic." And they didn't call him "Earvin" either; everyone, from Riley on down through the players, called him "Buck," which, I learned later, was Johnson's preference. "Buck" directed the drills and generally kept the trains running on time in practice. Kareem, in the final year of his legendary career, generally kept to himself to one side of the floor, almost aloof from his teammates, though the Lakers would not "three-peat" in 1988–89, falling in the finals in a four-game sweep to the Detroit Pistons.

About three weeks later came the SEC media days, where the head coach and a couple of players from each SEC school converged on Atlanta to discuss the up-coming season with the regional media. Book and I represented our team, so we traveled with Coach Newton to Atlanta for the event, which resulted in my all-time favorite "travels with C.M." story. We arrived in Atlanta the evening before the event and made our way to a fine hotel on Peachtree Street; in fact, I never would have dreamed that almost eight years later to the day, I would begin practicing law in Atlanta in a building directly across the street from that hotel. We approached the front desk, and Coach Newton gave his name to the clerk. She confirmed that, yes, indeed, there was a reservation under the name "Newton, C.M." So far, so good. But then she said, matter-of-factly, "We don't have a room for you."

Well, now, that one threw Coach Newton for a major loop. Patiently, he once again confirmed that the hotel had a reservation under his name. And again, he was told that, the reservation notwithstanding, there was no room at the inn, at least for the moment. I'll never forget the clerk's name because C.M. made a point of looking at her name engraved on the small nameplate she wore before looking back at her: "Tell me…[looks at nameplate]…Nancy, how can it be that the hotel can have a reservation under my name but not have a room?"

Nancy's explanation was somewhat plausible. She explained something to the effect that a reservation guarantees the right to a room but not the room itself. Coach Newton was nonplussed, to say the least. Exactly this same scene would play out on the small screen about three years later in a classic episode of *Seinfeld* though it was set in a car-rental agency, not a hotel, where Jerry had reserved a rental car only to be told at the desk that a car wasn't available. Jerry's fictional reaction was just like C.M.'s real one in '88: "What good is a reservation if I don't have a room?"

Meanwhile, Book and I, who were there at the desk (and had no trouble getting our room), were doing our very best not to burst into laughter. Of course, C.M. eventually got his room, but the media day was boring compared to that comic scene.

In addition to presenting the league's head coaches and many of its top returning players to the regional media, the Media Day featured the preseason predictions for the teams and all-SEC players. The media's predicted order of finish for the teams had Georgia on top, with Florida and Tennessee close behind: (1) Georgia (483 points); (2) Florida (479); (3) Tennessee (454); (4) Vanderbilt (350); (5) Kentucky (281); (6) Ole Miss (251); (7) Alabama (233); (8) LSU (208); (9) Auburn (133); (10) Mississippi State (99). In fact, none of the 10 teams would finish in the slot predicted by the media, and several of the predictions were wildly incorrect. The prognosticators agreed, however, that the SEC would be "suddenly down," as *Sports Illustrated* put it. While most "experts" had Florida and Georgia as the top two teams, they also predicted a wide-open race for the title. And that prediction would be right on the money.

We completed the four-game public intrasquad scrimmage schedule on November 10 at Montgomery Bell Academy, alma mater of Charles Mayes (and, later, golf star—and Vanderbilt graduate—Brandt Snedeker). Soon after that game came the season's first curve ball: it was announced that Scott Draud would redshirt for the season. Apparently, Scott had floated the idea to Coach Newton the previous spring, and Coach Newton denied the request. Scott renewed the request in the fall, and Coach Newton remained skeptical at first, and for good reason: we needed to compensate for Perdue's 18 points a game, and losing a player of Scott's caliber—especially the ability to come off the bench and score points in bunches—would result in the loss of even more offense. In fact, in his first two seasons, Scott had led the team in scoring eight times—and we won all eight games, proof positive that a Draud outburst off the bench guaranteed a victory. And if he was worth three or four of those a year as that statistic would suggest, then losing that production could be the difference between making the NCAA tourney and being relegated to the NIT. Plus, Scott had played well in the intrasquad games—he had scored at least 20 in every game, and it was apparent that he was a much better all-around player, improving both his defense and his ballhandling.

Nevertheless, Coach Newton eventually relented and allowed Scott to redshirt, giving him two full seasons of eligibility remaining beginning in 1989–90, after Booker and I had graduated. Scott then would likely be able to start for his final two seasons of eligibility. "This will be beneficial to all in the long run," he explained. "I won't be cutting into their time now, and this enhances my chances to get more playing time in the future."

So, Scott would practice and travel with the team, but he wouldn't play in any games. His absence would create another hurdle for us in our quest for Vanderbilt's first-ever back-to-back NCAA appearances. He and Will had combined for 25 points a game in 1987–88; I knew that I had improved, as had Booker, Wilcox, Reid, and especially Kornet (finally playing without pain in his knee). But had we improved enough to replace the 25 points Will and Scott had averaged each game the previous season? We were about to find out, and the early returns would not be promising.

18

ALOHA, OY

I

"Even the Soviets are swinging away"
—Big Audio Dynamite, "The Bottom Line" ('85–'86)

As in prior seasons, our first "unofficial" game of the season, i.e., one where we played an actual opponent, would be an exhibition game against a national team, in this case the Soviet Union's national team. While the game wouldn't count on our official win-loss record, we treated it as a real game, especially given that the Soviets had beaten the U.S. team in the '88 Summer Olympics in Seoul, relegating the U.S. to the bronze medal while the Soviets claimed the gold. The roster for the touring team in fall 1988 was almost identical to the Olympic roster. We played well, though the Soviets nipped us, 74-71. Still, the close loss was enough to quell, at least temporarily, any fears that we would be unable to compete at a high level without Perdue. In fact, Eric Reid and Frank Kornet were our best players for the game and more than held their own against the towering Soviet front line—Reid scored 18 points, grabbed six rebounds, and dished our four assists; Kornet blocked three shots and snagged a team-high nine rebounds. All in all, it was enough to provide some optimism as we looked forward to the trip to Hawaii and the Maui Classic.

❧

The first Maui tournament was held in 1984. When we won the event in 1986, we triumphed over a decent field—we beat Missouri and New Mexico on the way to the title—but now, two years later, the tournament had taken the shape it still has today. In other words, the field is full of ranked teams and good players, and it represents a three-day gauntlet. The 1988 version demonstrated the strength of the field that has become the event's calling card: Oklahoma was, in many publications, the preseason #1, having lost the NCAA championship game to Kansas the previous April; UNLV was on the cusp of a mini-dynasty and would win the NCAA title in 1990; Memphis State and Ohio State were ranked in most preseason polls; and De-Paul was an annual NCAA tourney participant.

The other two teams were the Commodores and Michigan, and we drew the Wolverines in the opening round. Michigan was ranked #3 in most preseason polls, and it had one undeniable superstar: senior forward Glen Rice, who had averaged nearly 23 points a game in 1987–88, leading the Big 10 in scoring. We shared some similarities with the Wolverines, primarily that each team returned four starters, and the missing starter had been his league's player of the year the previous season—Perdue for us and Gary Grant for Michigan. And no one knew in November the similarities both teams would encounter with their coaches later in the season. Only one other double-figure scorer returned for Michigan—center Terry Mills—while the other three starters were guards Rumeal Robinson and Mike Griffin and forward Sean Higgins.

In these earlier versions of the Maui tournament, the three-day event began the day after Thanksgiving and concluded on Sunday. Because Vanderbilt—unlike most schools at the time—gave students the entire week of Thanksgiving off, we were able to fly to Hawaii over the weekend and enjoy the entire week without worrying about missing classes. And what's not to like about Maui? It's 80 to 85 degrees year-round and is a beautiful island. The two Maui tourneys I participated in were my first trips there, but I've returned multiple times. My wife and I honeymooned in Maui, and we spent Thanksgiving there in 2009 when Vandy played in the tournament. That year we saw all the Commodores' games in the same high school gym we had played in 21 years before. That high school gym, though, would host some major-league talent in '88, and Michigan was loaded—an extreme test to open a season.

I tired quickly of hearing the questions of how we could be competitive without Perdue. Presumably, Rice and company didn't have to answer questions ad nauseum about how they would fare without Grant, but we continued to be bombarded with questions about LAW (Life After Wilbur). I finally drew the line the day before the Michigan game: "I'm tired of hearing that Will Perdue was 75 percent of our offense," I complained. I'm not sure I ever heard that or who possibly would have made such an outlandish statement, but Booker said it a little more adeptly: "Other people around the country probably thought Will Perdue was our whole team—people like *Street and Smith* and *Sports Illustrated*. We don't pay that much attention to them."

Of course, the appropriate response would have been to go out and play a great game against the Wolverines, which would have silenced the doubters. Unfortunately, that's not what happened—not by a long shot. Reid and Grant joined Kornet, Booker, and me in the starting lineup, and we got off to a promising start, scoring 10 of the game's first 14 points. But things went decidedly and irreversibly downhill from there; Michigan outscored us 33-9 for the remainder of the first half, which may have been the worst basketball we played during my four years. The Wolverines missed five of their six three-point attempts and didn't shoot a free throw yet led by 18 at the half because we misfired on all five of our three-point attempts and shot only 32% (9-for-28) from the field—missing 15 of 17 shots during one particularly unsightly stretch. We found a little rhythm on offense in the second half, scoring 47 points, and at one point a Kornet trey cut Michigan's lead to single digits at 51-42. But the Wolverines finished the game on a 40-24 run, pulling away for a 91-66 thrashing.

I was impressed with Michigan, commenting after the game that the Wolverines "may be the best team I've ever played against. They're great both inside and on the perimeter and very quick in all phases of the game...When you combine that with the way we played, it wasn't close." Coach Newton was more concerned with "the way we played" part of that equation, and he didn't mince words in the locker room after the game. "The guard play was the worst I've seen since I've been here," he said, and that wasn't much of an exaggeration. Booker scored two points and missed all four of his three-point attempts, and Wilcox also scored only two. I scored 12 and hit a couple of threes, but I committed five turnovers—which, I'm sure, was a career high, and certainly was the most I committed in any game over my final two seasons. C.M. threatened to rescind Draud's redshirt status. It was no idle threat, but ultimately decided against it.

While I gave Michigan that glowing post-game review, little did I suspect that we were playing the next NCAA champions—meaning that we had played back-to-back games against NCAA champions, having closed 1987–88 with that season's champ (Kansas) and opened the 1988–89 season against that season's eventual titlist. Adding the win against Indiana in 1986–87, we played against the eventual national champion for three straight years.

~

Mike Griffin, a lanky 6'7" guard, covered me for most of the game. Early in the game, I had the ball around the top of the key and started dribbling to my left. Griffin thought he knew what was coming next, so he shouted to his teammates: "Watch his spin move!"

If I had one calling card on offense, it was a "spin move." An offensive player who has the ball on the dribble and wants to change direction, either because the defender has cut him off or because he simply wants to beat his defender by changing direction, can do one of three things if he wants to maintain the dribble. One is the behind-the-back dribble, i.e., change the dribble from one hand to the other with a single bounce of the ball behind the player's back to keep the ball away from the defender. A second option is the crossover dribble, meaning the player continues to face the defender with the dribble, and moves the ball from one hand to the other while maintaining the dribble. The problem with the crossover is that the player keeps the ball visible to the defender, and I was no Allen Iverson with the crossover; plus, with so many quick guards in the SEC (Vernon Maxwell, Tony White, Willie

Anderson, Ed Davender, etc.), it invited a turnover to crossover the dribble right in front of the defender.

The third option, and the one I chose, is what Brad Gaines, the fine Vanderbilt linebacker, called "that wheel move." Dribbling to my strong side (the left side), I would plant my right foot, keep the dribble in my left hand, and whirl around in the opposite direction in one motion. The disadvantage of the spin move is that the player must temporarily turn his back to the basket and the defense; the player must always maintain court awareness for the half-second or so that he's blind to the basket and defense.

I developed the move by accident in a junior high game, and from that point on, through high school and college, I used the spin move to create a scoring opportunity for myself or maybe just to separate myself from the person guarding me. And, whenever Coach Newton called "Winner," the one-on-one play for end-of-shot-clock or late-game situations, I invariably used it. It wasn't productive every time, but so few other players used it that it was hard to prepare for defensively. For that reason, it was my most potent offensive weapon.

II

"Round and round the ring I go"
—Paul McCartney, "Figure of Eight" ('89)

There weren't many effective spin moves against Michigan, not because Mike Griffin thought he could anticipate them, but because, at 6'7", Griffin was more difficult to work around. And we just played a poor game, plain and simple. The good news is that our next opponent was Honolulu-based Chaminade, which would practically be a guaranteed win. The bad news was that Chaminade was not a Division I school. It was an NAIA institution, and as such the win wouldn't count in the data that the NCAA Selection Committee would assess in March to determine our candidacy for an at-large bid. Still, better teams than ours had overlooked Chaminade in the past, with historic consequences.

It had been only six years since Chaminade had pulled what remains the greatest upset in the history of college basketball—a shocking 77-72 victory in December 1982 over the #1 team in the country, Virginia, which was led by the best player in the country, 7'4" three-time Naismith Player of the Year winner Ralph Sampson. The next year, Chaminade stunned a Louisville team a year after that, they beat the Cardinals again, and in their very next game they beat #3 SMU.

But the Silverswords program had fallen on hard times since those heady days, and they had been pummeled by Memphis State, 88-44, in the first round of the '88 tourney. We didn't deliver that sort of punishment, but we raced to an early 11-2 lead, extended the lead to 40-22 behind three straight Booker treys, and led 45-30 at the half. We stretched the lead to 30 at one point in the second half, and coasted to a 94-70 victory behind Kornet's 19 points and eight rebounds and Booker's 15 points.

After that breather, we took on another Big Ten team, Ohio State, in the final game of the tourney. The Buckeyes were a solid team, ranked #16 in the country and coached by the uber-intense Gary Williams, who at season's end would move to his alma mater, Maryland where he would win the 2002 NCAA title. Their on-court leader was guard Jay Burson, who was something of an Ohio State version of Steve Alford, meaning a homegrown hoops legend who was front-page news even in high school—in Burson's case, setting the state's career scoring record (broken a few years ago) with nearly 3,000 points. Burson was their unquestioned leader, having averaged 18.9 points a game in 1987–88. Led by Burson, the Buckeyes pressed us from the beginning, and we proved incapable of handling the pressure. We committed seven turnovers in the first six minutes and an incredible 15 in the first half alone. The Buckeyes zoomed to a 34-17 lead with 9:18 remaining in the first half and led comfortably, 57-41, at the break. Combined with the 54 points Michigan scored in the second half of that game, we had surrendered 111 points in our last 40 minutes against D-1 teams. Things didn't improve much in the second half. OSU extended the lead to as many as 33 points, 89-56, with just over seven minutes remaining. We closed the final margin to 15, 97-82, which was not indicative of the noncompetitive nature of the game. The Buckeyes shot an astounding 63% from the field for the game and forced 20 turnovers (including a remarkable 15 steals).

One bright spot for us was Eric Reid, who led all players with a career-high 25 points and claimed seven rebounds. Kornet's 19 proved that he was going to be a force all season—he scored 53 points in the three games. But, as a team, we were only 2-for-16 from behind the arc, and we missed all 12 of our attempts in the second half. It was an ugly conclusion to a lackluster three days of play.

The return home from the second Maui trip wasn't nearly as joyful as it had been two years before when we brought the championship trophy home with us. Clearly, we had plenty of work to do on both ends of the floor if we wanted even to approach, let alone match, our achievements of 1987–88. And there wouldn't be any opportunity to work out the kinks on an undermanned opponent—when we returned to Nashville, we would play our third ranked team in less than a week.

19

A HELL OF AN EXPLOSION

Disappointed and tired after three days of generally poor play in Maui, we went to the airport after the Ohio State game, flew through the night on Sunday and, with a layover on the West Coast, finally arrived back in Nashville on Monday afternoon. In a classic example of "no rest for the weary," we had just over 48 hours to prepare for our Memorial Gym opener—the University of Louisville, our third ranked opponent in a six-day span.

I

"A little voice inside my head said, 'Don't look back, you can never look back'"
—Don Henley, "The Boys of Summer" ('84–'85)

The University of Kentucky has been, and always will be, first in the hearts of most Kentuckians for basketball. Nevertheless, there was no question that U of L had, at least temporarily, eclipsed UK in success on the hardwood in the 1980s. UK went to exactly one Final Four in the decade, and even that one appearance was infamous: a 3-for-33 shooting nightmare in the second half of the national semifinal game against eventual champion Georgetown. Meanwhile, U of L had established itself as one of the top programs in the country. In the previous nine seasons coming into 1988–89, the Cardinals had been to four Final Fours (1980, 1982, 1983, 1986), winning it all in '80 and '86.

Coach Denny Crum had been at the school since 1972 and had led the Cardinals to six Final Fours. His success put UK in the awkward position of defending its historical decision not to play other in-state schools, including Louisville. So, the NCAA Selection Committee decided to play matchmaker. In 1982, in a 52-team field where four teams received first-round byes, Louisville was given a bye and would play the winner of the first-round game between UK and Middle Tennessee. But MTSU foiled that plot by stunning UK in that game, which was played at none other than Memorial Gym on Vandy's campus.

In 1983, the Selection Committee again placed the schools in the same regional, and this time they met with the highest stakes on the line—a trip to the Final Four. In the regional final, the Cardinals beat the Wildcats in overtime to advance to the Final Four in Albuquerque, where they played one of the most famous national semifinal games in history, losing to Houston's Phi Slamma Jamma squad. With some arm-twisting applied, or at least threatened, by the Kentucky legislature, as well as then-Kentucky governor John Y. Brown, a UK graduate, UK finally relented and, in fall 1983, began playing one game each season against U of L.

Coach Crum's teams generally had the same characteristics. It seemed that every player was between 6'4" and 6'9". The Cardinals usually played man-to-man defense and would switch on nearly all screens, so that the guards needed to be big and strong enough to cover frontcourt players, while the taller guys needed to be quick enough to cover backcourt players 20 or 25 feet from the basket. Offensively, Crum, a long-time assistant to UCLA Coach John Wooden, would run his mentor's high-post offense, where the big guards would often post up their smaller backcourt counterparts.

It was more than coincidental, however, that Louisville's run of Final Fours and NCAA titles under Denny Crum effectively ended in 1986, the last season before the three-point line was introduced. The Cardinals were slow to adapt to the changes in the game that the three-pointer brought, and as a result it was possible to outscore the Cardinals by making three-pointers, which (at least in the first couple of years of the three-point era) they were neither much interested in nor capable of making.

The 1988–89 Cardinals still had a ton of talent, though. Pervis Ellison was a long-armed 6'9" center who was named the Most Outstanding Player of the '86 Final Four as a freshman (the first freshman so honored since 1944), and whose laid-back demeanor inspired the nickname "Never Nervous Pervis." In the current college basketball environment, Ellison would have turned pro immediately after that spectacular performance as a freshman; instead, he stayed in school and was now a senior, having led the team in scoring at 17.6 a game in 1987–88. Perhaps the most talented of the Cardinals was guard LaBradford Smith, a muscular 6'4" sophomore who was drawing comparisons to Michael Jordan because of his athleticism, shooting ability, and impressive vertical leap. He was the Cardinals' second-leading returning scorer, having averaged 12.7 per game along with a team-leading 4.5 assists while shooting over 90% from the free-throw line. Another key returnee was Kenny Payne, who averaged 10.7 points a game in '87–'88. The Cardinals' most important reserve was Felton Spencer, a 7'1'" center from Louisville and a terrific guy—I had gotten to know Felton the previous summer when we roomed at a basketball camp. He had come late to the game of basketball, and was still learning some of the fundamentals, and his height put him a bit outside the mold of a typical Denny Crum player, but Felton was a force inside. The Cardinals' top newcomer was 6'5" guard-forward Evrick Sullivan. Two other Cardinals of note were Tony Kimbro and Keith Williams. I was acquainted with both dating back to high school.

II

"Glory days, they'll pass you by…in the wink of a young girl's eye"
—*Bruce Springsteen, "Glory Days"* ('84–'85)

Kimbro and Williams were teammates at Louisville's Seneca High School, the school best known for producing U of L and NBA great Westley Unseld. Heading into our senior year of high school in fall 1984, Seneca was the consensus #1 team in Kentucky, and they were ranked as high as the #3 high school team in the entire country. Kimbro, a smooth 6'8" forward, was considered the better of the two—"at least among the top two or three [seniors] in the country," according to one college recruiter—and had the more checkered background. He had attended multiple schools prior to landing at Seneca, and academics were always a challenge for him. Williams and I were similar—6'4", lefthanded, and cocky. And, unlike his more touted teammate, Williams was also solid in the Seneca classroom—a trait that would not follow him to college.

I first encountered this dynamic duo in the King of the Bluegrass Holiday Classic in December 1984. Held at Fairdale High in suburban Louisville, the KOTB was a 16-team affair of mostly Kentucky-based schools, with some top-rated high schools from outside the state completing the field. The emphasis was on great players rather than teams—the four non-Kentucky squads included a team from Laurel, Mississippi featuring U of L recruit Kenny Payne, and Philadelphia powerhouse Dobbins Tech, which featured future Loyola Marymount superstars Hank Gathers and Bo Kimble.

My team, the Marshall County Marshals, was matched up against Seneca in the last game of the first round. We surprised Seneca by leading by three after one quarter, but the Redskins blew us out in the second quarter with a 20-1 run and pulled out to a 14-point lead, which they stretched to 19 midway through the third period. But we slowly clawed our way back, cutting the lead to 10 by the end of the third and eventually to two in the final minute before succumbing by three, 78-75. Kimbro and Williams scored 18 each—equaling the 36 I scored on my own. I thought they were decent, but not appreciably better than some of the players I was facing in western Kentucky. And I was livid when Williams, commenting on my 13 free-throw attempts (he had eight), opined postgame that "the refs sort of protected him tonight."

That loss dumped us into the losers' bracket and, worse, required us to come back the next afternoon for our second game even though the Seneca game had ended after midnight. Our opponent was Apollo High from Owensboro, led by a spectacular junior named Rex Chapman; it would be our only meeting as highschoolers. In a nip-and-tuck game, I outscored Chapman 28-26, but Apollo prevailed, 68-65, meaning that we were two-and-done at the KOTB. Still, in two games,

I had scored 64 points in the span of about 15 hours against three of the state's top-ranked players, two of whom were guarding me most of the time. That gave me confidence that I could compete at a high level in the SEC.

A month later, we met Seneca again in the semifinals of the Louisville Invitational Tournament, the same event where I first witnessed the skills of future Vandy teammate Frank Kornet. Between the two Seneca meetings, we had scored a couple of big wins, including one over Louisville Male, a traditional power that has produced many great players, including Louisville's Darrell Griffith and Kentucky's Winston Bennett. In the LIT, we beat Louisville Western 67-50 and took down another Louisville-area school, Fern Creek (ironically, the alma mater of Richard Schmidt, Coach Newton's predecessor at Vanderbilt), 46-42, as I scored 28 of the team's 46 points.

Meanwhile, Seneca, whose only loss on the season to date had been to the Gathers/Kimble Dobbins Tech team in the KOTB final, survived Chapman and Apollo in the LIT quarters to meet us in the semis. The rematch was like the December meeting—we trailed by seven going into the fourth quarter, rallied and cut the lead (and had a chance to take the lead with around three minutes remaining), but ran out of steam to lose 68-58. This time, Kimbro made a believer out of me—playing with two sprained thumbs, he scored 30 points, pulled down 11 rebounds, and blocked seven shots, and generally showed why he was so highly touted. I had 20, while Williams scored only seven. Seneca won the title the next night by beating Pleasure Ridge Park and my future Vandy teammate Derrick Wilcox. Weeks later, Kimbro was named Kentucky's Mr. Basketball. I finished second, just ahead of Chapman, who would win the honor in '86. Williams finished fifth, and another future Vandy teammate, junior Scott Draud, finished seventh. Felton Spencer was ninth.

Kimbro, Williams, and I got better acquainted in summer 1985 as teammates on the Kentucky All-Star team who would play the Indiana All-Stars in the annual two-game series. Frank Kornet and Chip Rupp were also on that team. I never thought Kimbro cared much for the games, as his lackluster performance in both games reflected. Williams did, though, at least in the first game, and he and I formed an effective team in that game, in Rupp Arena; he scored 24, I scored 18, and we won. Both he and Kimbro mentally checked out of the second game, though, and in Indianapolis the Hoosier stars spanked us. I led the team in that one with 17. After those games ended, we embarked on our collegiate careers, with Kimbro and Williams staying in their hometown to play for U of L while I headed about 125 miles southeast to Nashville to join the Commodores.

III

"I'll give you something to write home about"
—Midnight Oil, "Gunbarrel Highway" ('88)

The two Seneca stars joined Ellison and Payne at U of L in fall 1985 as part of a highly touted recruiting class. Freshman Ellison led the Cardinals to the '86 title, but Louisville missed the NCAAs entirely in '87 with an 18-14 record, not far from our 18-16, NIT-quarterfinalist mark that same year. Without Kimbro, who sat out the year for academic reasons, but with highly-regarded freshman LaBradford Smith on board, the '87–'88 Cardinals rebounded with 24 victories. Like us, the Cardinals reached the Sweet Sixteen and were eliminated by a title-game finalist from the Big Eight—in their case, national runner-up Oklahoma.

We and the Cardinals came into the game with vastly different degrees of rest— but both hungry for a victory. Louisville had played only one game and lost it, an 85-83 upset loss to Xavier in the preseason NIT. That game had been played 12 days before our game. In contrast, we would be playing our fourth game in six days, and tip-off would be less than 72 hours after we had departed Maui for the long trip back to Nashville.

I would not get the chance to take the measure of Williams either—he was sidelined due to academic ineligibility. Craig Hawley, a fine shooter (and future U of L law school graduate) would start at guard alongside usual starters Smith at guard and the experienced, athletic frontline of Ellison, Kimbro, and Payne. The only health issue for the Cardinals was that of their coach—Denny Crum had been felled with the flu and had not made the trip down the night before the game; he only came down a few hours before tip-off. We started the same quintet that had started the games in Maui—Kornet, Reid, and Grant up front with Booker and me in the backcourt. Not only was the game our home opener but it was also against a ranked opponent. With students having just returned from Thanksgiving break, there were more than 15,000 crammed into Memorial for what would be a memorable game.

On the game's first possession, Smith turned the ball over—a sign of things to come. We led early, 7-6, when Booker stole an entry pass, then went coast to coast with a stop-and-pop from 15, the first points in what would be one of his greatest games. A couple of minutes later, I hit the game's first three, giving us 10 straight points and a 12-6 lead. Ellison broke the run with a basket inside, then hit two free throws the next time down to cut our lead to two. Providing a big boost for us off the bench, Todd Milholland scored seven quick points to keep us on front, and a Wilcox steal led to a Booker breakaway dunk and a 22-14 lead with about eight minutes remaining in the half, and Book's 15-footer gave us a 24-16 lead with six minutes remaining. An Ellison putback cut the lead to six, but a beautiful alley-oop from Wilcox to Kornet returned the lead to eight. Ellison scored again, but Charles

Mayes answered with a driving layup for a 28-20 lead. Then Ellison scored on a tip-in, giving him 14 of his team's 22 points. But Mayes answered again, this time with a trey, giving us a 31-22 lead with three minutes remaining. The Cardinals, however, scored the game's final six points to cut our halftime lead to 31-28.

While we were disappointed that we had let Louisville cut our nine-point lead to three in the closing minutes of the first half, we were pleased overall with our play. We had been blown out by Michigan and Ohio State in Maui and were essentially out of contention in those games by halftime, but now we had stayed right with Louisville for the entire first 20 minutes. Could we put two solid halves together and score a huge win?

We drew first blood in the second half with two Reid free throws. Kimbro's layup off a steal—his first points of the game—cut the lead back to three, but his slam dunk off a fast break was nullified when he charged into Booker. We then went cold for several minutes. I missed twice on one trip, including a putback from about five feet; Kornet missed twice the next time down, including a putback from the same distance. Book got us going again with a left-handed layup and a 35-30 lead. Smith hit two free throws—his first points of the game—and then drew a charge on the other end, negating a Milholland basket. After an Ellison turnover, I hit a pull-up jumper off Book's assist, but Hawley answered with Louisville's first three-pointer of the game to cut our lead to two, 37-35. Two Kornet free throws pushed the lead back to four.

At this point, Louisville's athleticism began to take control, slowly but surely, over the next several minutes. After a Louisville steal, Kimbro hit one of two free throws to tie the game at 41 with 13 minutes remaining. LaBradford Smith then hit two free throws to give Louisville its first lead since 6-5, and his jumper gave U of L eight straight points and a 45-41 lead. Booker stopped the bleeding for us with a 10-footer in the lane, but Spencer's putback pushed the lead back to four. Then came a big play—40 feet from the basket, Ellison reached around Book as Barry dribbled past him and, trying for the steal, was whistled for his fourth foul, sending him to the bench with over 10 minutes remaining. The Cardinals didn't fold, however; they pushed the lead to 47-41, thanks to a Spencer layup inside the 10:00 mark. Things were beginning to look bleak.

Book then hit a huge trey, our first of the half, to cut the lead in half. After U of L came up empty on the offensive end, Sullivan converted a steal into a Wilcox foul and a free throw, giving the Cardinals a four-point lead. Derrick answered with a free throw that made it 50-47, but the Cardinals spurted again: Evrick Sullivan's jumper made it 52-47 with eight minutes to play, and after a Wilcox miss, he scored again to give the Cardinals a seven-point lead with 7:26 to play. Coach Newton's timeout didn't have the desired effect; after a Kornet miss, Kimbro hit a jumper in the lane and drew the foul. He had a chance to push the lead to double digits—a psychologically important margin with barely seven minutes to play—but he missed the free throw. Still, the Cardinals led by nine, 56-47, and were on a 34-16 run.

Sullivan gave us a break with a silly reach-in foul on Wilcox, and Derrick canned both ends of the one-and-one to cut the deficit to seven at the 6:30 mark. Spencer blocked Milholland's shot and drew the foul on Todd, but he missed the front end of the one-and-one, making him 0-for-4 from the line. But we struggled at the line too—Wilcox missed a one-and-one, then I missed one as well. Louisville, however, squandered these chances to put the game away, and after another Louisville turnover, Book hit a trey to make it 56-52, Louisville. Five minutes remained.

After a Louisville timeout, the Cardinals had two chances to extend their lead—Payne grabbed an offensive rebound off a missed jumper, but Sullivan shot an air ball from the baseline, and Reid claimed the rebound. Off a beautiful pass from Booker, Kornet scored on a layup: 56-54 Cardinals, 3:42 to play. Payne then missed a three-point jumper and Kornet rebounded. Off a patient offensive set, Book hit a leaning jumper from about 14 feet to tie the game at 56. We had scored nine straight points, and U of L called timeout with three minutes remaining. Out of the timeout, Ellison's putback—his first points of the second half—broke our 9-0 run and gave the Cardinals a two-point lead. But Reid found a cutting Booker at the free-throw line, and Book fed Kornet for an easy two to tie the game at 58. Two minutes remained.

We then got the benefit of a controversial call. Off a Smith miss, Book led a two-on-one fast break with Wilcox. Book dropped the pass off to Derrick for the open layup as Book collided into Smith. Smith was called for the blocking foul on Book, and the officials also counted Derrick's basket to give us the lead back at 60-58. Book missed the chance to make it a four-point trip, however, when he missed the one-and-one, meaning that he, Wilcox, and I each had missed one-and-one opportunities in the second half, leaving six potential points on the table. Sullivan promptly punished us for those misses with a jumper to tie the game at 60. Just over one minute remained, and we called time.

Out of the timeout, Ellison stole Wilcox's attempted lob pass to Kornet, but Payne missed a jumper and I rebounded. We could essentially hold the ball for the final shot, as there was about a three-second difference in the game clock and the shot clock. But Louisville kept up its aggressive defense and, swarming over Book, Sullivan committed a foul. This time, Book nailed both ends of the one-and-one to give us a 62-60 lead. Fifteen seconds remained. Needing only two to tie, Payne launched a three-point attempt for the win, but missed. The ball was batted around under the basket for a couple of seconds, and Kimbro finally got control with a five-foot putback to tie the game at 62. We called timeout to stop the clock with three seconds left.

With three seconds and the length of the court to traverse, there wasn't much we could do. When Perdue was around, we used his 7'0" frame to our advantage by throwing the pass about two-thirds of the length of the floor; Book and I, starting the play by standing together in the middle of the court, would peel off to opposite sides of the floor and Will would look for one of us. But without Will, that play really couldn't be used. So, it was the more conventional "take the ball and do the best you can" approach.

We had one less second to work with than at the end of regulation in the Pitt game, and unlike the Panthers, Louisville at least put players in the backcourt and feigned some full-court pressure. But the Cards also made the same mistake Pitt had made by not putting any pressure on the inbounds passer (here, Kornet). So, just like with Pitt, I caught the ball with my momentum heading toward our end of the floor.

I received the pass at Louisville's free-throw line and didn't encounter any resistance until I met Kimbro about 10 feet from the half-court line. He shadowed me, but at a respectful distance and with Sullivan trailing him, until I reached the half-court line with a second showing on the clock. I was about eight feet left of the center circle when I planted my right foot and launched a shot somewhere between 40 and 42 feet from our basket.

I can't say "it was in all the way," but I knew it had a chance when I saw the shot's trajectory. The game film bears out that belief: I ducked my head as I followed the ball toward the basket, as if to suggest it might go in. The ball seemed to hang in the air forever; I was nearly at our own free-throw line, 25 feet from where I had launched the shot, by the time the ball landed...in the basket! Coach Newton felt that he had the best vantage point of anyone in the gym, because he was practically standing under our basket when the ball left my hands. "I thought it was dead center," he said, at least half-jokingly, I'm sure. In the aftermath of the game, I hadn't been as certain. "I thought it had the distance," I said, "but I thought it was left."

Memorial Gym exploded when the shot went in. The fans, assuming that the game was headed into overtime, were relatively quiet for those final three seconds and then BOOM! Coach Martin described it well: "It was like watching a bomb land in those war movies," he said. "It was real slow, but clean on target. When it hit, there was a hell of an explosion." Pandemonium reigned as players, students, adults, and seemingly everyone in the gym rushed onto the floor to take part in the celebration.

As I noted later, this buzzer-beater "was so special to me since I'm from Kentucky, and it was the only chance I'll ever have to play them." While I received most of the postgame attention because of the shot, the truth is that Barry Booker was the star of the game and the real hero. In fact, of all our big wins he, Kornet, and I enjoyed in our four years, this was probably his best big-game performance: 20 points, tying Ellison for game-high honors, on 8-for-12 shooting, along with a game-high five assists. And he was incredible down the stretch; in the last five minutes, he had a hand in every point we scored before my winning trey with three-pointers, assists, free throws—first keeping us within striking distance, then giving us a late lead and a chance to win it after Louisville tied it in the final seconds. Meanwhile, his opposite number, LaBradford Smith, went only 1-for-4 from the field, scored only six points, and committed seven turnovers.

Kornet, meanwhile, had 14 points and eight rebounds—a fine performance against All-American Ellison, who had 20 and nine. I was our other double-figure scorer with 11 points, and I contributed five rebounds, as did Wilcox, which helped us remain competitive against the athletic Cardinals; their final rebounding margin was only 42-37. Todd Milholland had a solid game off the bench with seven points and five boards.

The win was an enormous boost for our confidence after our dreary play in Maui. Any win over a ranked team is a good one; a win over one of the real college basketball powers of the '80s was a tremendous statement. And, of course, there was the extra satisfaction for me, as a Kentuckian, of beating the Cardinals. But I grew up three hours from Louisville; what about the person on the team who grew up in Louisville? That was Wilcox, and he summarized the win nicely: "Like having two birthdays."

I jauntily walked into one of my Communication Studies classes the next day feeling good. Again, the course was taught by Professor Kassian Kovalcheck, who had good-naturedly needled me that my life "would go straight downhill" the day after the Pitt game. I waited until everyone was seated and Kass was about to begin the class. I then looked at him, flashed a big smile, and said, in a voice loud enough so that the entire class could hear, "Well, I guess you were wrong!"

20

DECEMBER CHILL

I

"Been beaten up, battered 'round"
—Traveling Wilburys, "Handle with Care" ('88)

The glow from the Louisville win and the electricity in Memorial Gym would have to last for a couple of weeks, because we were about to hit the road with a vengeance. And the road would hit back.

First up was the University of Alabama-Birmingham, coached by Gene Bartow, the man probably best known as John Wooden's successor at UCLA. After only two years in Westwood, Bartow resigned and moved to Birmingham, where he literally built that school's athletic program, serving as both athletic director and head basketball coach. UAB had only been playing basketball since the 1978–79 season, but by 1988, UAB was a solid program, and at one point Bartow took the Blazers to seven consecutive NCAA tournaments. As was seemingly every other coach in America, Bartow was friends with Coach Newton, and he had a favor to ask in spring 1988: UAB was opening a brand new on-campus arena; would Coach Newton do UAB the honor of bringing his Vanderbilt Commodores to Birmingham to christen the new arena against the Blazers? Coach Newton agreed. There was the usual pomp and circumstance associated with such a celebratory occasion as opening a new arena (which would be renamed the Bartow Arena upon the coach's retirement in 1996), including a speech by Birmingham's mayor. Plus, Coach Newton was given a key to the city.

Whether from nerves about their new digs, unfamiliarity with them, or whatever, the Blazers started out cold, and we took full advantage, roaring to a 9-0 lead. That set off a first half of spurts by both teams. UAB found its sea legs after the slow start and used a 16-2 run to forge a lead of 18-13. We responded with a 12-2 run for a 25-20 lead, which the Blazers answered with three consecutive three-pointers to claim a 29-25 lead. We then outscored UAB 10-4 for the remainder of the half to take a two-point lead into the locker room, 35-33.

Even though we had the lead at halftime, we had blown our chance at winning the game. The lead should have been much larger than two, and we would pay the price in the second half. In fact, UAB was white-hot from the field in the second half, hitting a scorching 72.7% from the field (16-for-22) and five of eight three-point attempts. We faded to 38.7% (12-for-31) from the field in the second half, including an abysmal 3-for-16 from behind the arc. Still, the game was tied at 40 at the 15:40 mark and knotted at 51 with 9:25 to play, and when I hit a trey with around seven-and-a-half minutes remaining, we led 55-53. But that was our last lead, and UAB went on a backbreaking 18-6 run to lead 72-61 with just over a minute to play. The final score was 76-69, Blazers.

The UAB player who wreaked the most havoc on us was Andy Kennedy (who later coached Ole Miss from 2006 to 2018). After a chilly first half, Kennedy found the mark in the second half, making three of his four three-point attempts and, for the game, going 6-for-7 from inside the arc. He led all scorers with 26 points. Our three seniors led the way in scoring (Booker 18, Kornet 15, me 13), but we also led the way in turnovers as well, combining for 12 of the team's 16 turnovers (Kornet six, Book and me three each). Our ballhandling continued to be an issue; until we corrected it, we were in for some difficult games.

II

"I was lyin' in my room and the news came on TV"
—Brian Wilson, "Love and Mercy" ('88)

A few days after the UAB loss, we arrived in Chapel Hill, North Carolina, for a rematch with the Tar Heels. Carolina, of course, was out for revenge after our thrilling 78-76 win in Memorial the previous December. The 'Heels would not be top-ranked this time around, but, with a 6-1 record, were still safely in the top 10 at #8.

The game would be played at what Dean Smith called the "Student Activities Center" but what everyone else called the "Smith Center" (Smith protested the facility being named in his honor), or, even more informally, the "Dean Dome," which seated over 21,000. That venue was only a couple of years old in fall 1988, and it had that too-large, Rupp Arena-like feel. For our rematch with UNC, the Tar Heels would be without J.R. Reid, who had been sidelined since October with a stress fracture in his foot. But they still had a slew of great players: Jeff Lebo, Scott Williams, Steve Bucknall, Kevin Madden, Rick Fox, Pete Chillicut, and King Rice made for a formidable seven-man rotation. The Tar Heels would compensate with quickness and the full-court pressure, predicted Bucknall: "The defensive scheme we are using this season is full-court pressure. We're going to get after you 90 feet." Boy, did he ever nail that one.

Before an ESPN national television audience, we went out and embarrassed ourselves. In our first 10 possessions, we turned the ball over eight times, many of those turnovers coming off the Heels' full-court press. By then, the Tar Heels led 15-0. It was like a layup drill for them. It seems unbelievable that a team could dig itself a 23-point hole less than nine minutes into a game, but it happened here: the Heels led 32-9 with 11:26 left in the first half.

It's in games like this that a team can show its character, or lack thereof. Just as against Duke in Cameron two years earlier, when we fell behind by 30, we had a choice either to pack it in and lose by 40 or try to make a game of it. And, just as occurred in Cameron, we made a spirited effort. In fact, after bottoming out at 32-9, we reversed the teams' fortunes, scoring 11 straight points and eventually cutting the deficit to seven, 46-39, at halftime. The Heels came out hot in the second half and built the lead back to 14, 68-54, midway through the second half. Still, we wouldn't go quietly; we reduced the lead to eight, 72-64, but we could not get any closer. The final score was 89-77.

Lebo flashed his All-America form with 25 points, including 5-for-8 three-point shooting, while Madden added 20. Scott Williams notched a double-double with 13 points and 10 boards. Rice, the future Kevin Stallings assistant at Vandy and current Monmouth coach, had seven assists in only 23 minutes.

Meanwhile, our backcourt play was awful. Collectively, this was probably the worst game Book and I combined to play all year: 6-for-21 from the field, including 1-for-9 from beyond the arc (he missed six of his seven attempts and I missed all three of mine), and eight turnovers (four each). My offensive game was particularly bad. Recalling the game in Memorial the previous December, Carolina Coach Dean Smith had observed before the rematch, "Barry Goheen's a great shooter. He had a field day against us." He must have been thinking of some other game and some other player. I had scored 13 points in the '87 game—not bad but by no means a "field day." But apparently the Heels were determined to prevent another "field day," because I missed my first eight shots and scored exactly one point in the first 37 minutes. I made three shots in garbage time to finish 3-for-11 from the field for eight points. Booker scored nine; it would be one of only two times all season that both of us failed to score in double figures in the same game. I was able to make myself useful in other ways by pulling down seven rebounds and passing out eight assists, tying my career high set in the NCAA win against Utah State in Lincoln. But that was little consolation.

The inside players led the way for us, as Reid and Kornet each went 8-for-14 from the field, with Eric adding a free throw for a team-high 17 points, with Frank's 16 close behind. But the real bright spot in this game was center, Fred Benjamin, who scored 13 points and a pulled down six rebounds in only 23 minutes. Coach Newton was so impressed that he announced after the game that "I plan on starting him Saturday night" when we next took the floor.

III
"Where do we go now?"
—Guns 'N Roses, *"Sweet Child O' Mine"* ('88)

One of my favorite "small world" stories occurred in 2009. Our next-door neighbors' son attended a boarding school in the Northeast. One Monday in the fall, the father called. He said that he and his wife had just returned from visiting their son at parents' weekend, and he had a question for me: "Do you know someone named Fred Benjamin?" I almost dropped the phone and instinctively laughed at the mere mention of Fred's name.

Fred was a New York City guy, having played his high school ball in Manhattan. He was an impressive two-sport athlete at Vanderbilt and led the Commodores to the SEC lacrosse championship in 1989, scoring the game-winning goal in the championship game. I'm not sure how Coach Newton wooed him to Nashville, but the hope was that the 6'11" "Freddie," as we called him, would back up Will Perdue in '87–'88 and gain enough seasoning to challenge for a starting spot in '88–'89.

Unfortunately, Fred was dealt a tremendous personal blow just as he started school in fall 1987: his father died suddenly. That tragedy set him back from a developmental standpoint, and he played only 39 minutes for the entire season. Off the court, though, Freddie was a riot, possibly the funniest person I've ever met. I'll never forget his story from spring 1988, upon returning from a visit home to New York. Freddie, who as a Manhattanite had not yet learned to drive, was a passenger in a car driven by a friend, and the two had gone through the drive-through at Burger King for a snack. They were driving along when suddenly they saw flames come up from under the car's hood. Fred's friend, the driver, panicked and fled. So, as Fred described it, he was sitting in the passenger side of a car, holding a sack full of Burger King hamburgers, with a car engine aflame, no one in the driver's seat, and the car rolling down some hill. The mere vision of Freddie, a seven-footer, in that situation, was hysterical.

Through a series of disparate, serendipitous events, Freddie, Charles Mayes, and I formed close relationships with the female students who led the Alpha Delta Pi sorority on campus. Fred practically became their little (maybe I should say younger) brother, and he would break up the group with his performance of the Guns N' Roses hit "Sweet Child O' Mine," especially the "where do we go now" refrain. Then, when one of our close-knit group, our friend Cheryl, asked Fred and me to be ushers for her wedding in 1990, it led to another memorable (for this group) event when Fred and I had trouble, to a hilariously embarrassing degree, unrolling the bridal carpet. Simply put, Freddie was a whole lot of fun.

Unfortunately, I lost touch with Fred not long after Cheryl's wedding. He transferred from Vandy and finished up at Norfolk State, played some pro ball, and then did some acting, playing, among other roles, Wilt Chamberlain in the 2007 box office hit *American Gangster*. Fred found his calling as a coach and teacher, and he was a good one, sending numerous players to Division I schools on basketball scholarships, including Georgia Tech. He also coached lacrosse, which was how my next-door neighbors met him on that parents' weekend, as their son played lacrosse at school. So, I briefly reconnected with Fred, and was pleased to learn that, like his teammates, he's done very well since he left Vanderbilt.

≈

Our brutal road stretch continued in Manhattan—not Fred Benjamin's hometown, but the town in Kansas, home of Kansas State University. We shared some similarities with the Wildcats, as one writer pointed out before the game. In fact, each school (1) "had its best season of the decade" in '87–'88; (2) "pulled off a stunning upset in the NCAA tournament before losing to the eventual champion Kansas Jayhawks"; and (3) lost its best player, "who was selected in the first round" of the NBA draft. Indeed, the Wildcats were coming off an Elite Eight appearance— right after Kansas ended our season in the Sweet Sixteen in Pontiac, K-State took the Silverdome floor and shocked #1-seeded Purdue, setting up an all-Kansas, all-Big Eight regional final. KU won, but K-State was again an NCAA-caliber team in 1988–89 despite the loss of its best player, Mitch Richmond, to the NBA. Guard Steve Henson was a high-quality player and the team's unquestioned leader post-Richmond.

At the pregame meal, as usual, Coach Newton went over some specifics for the game, focusing both on the opponent and us. For this game, C.M. talked about stepping up and making shots, whether from the field or from the line. Toward the end of this monologue, he said, "our best free-throw shooter is hitting only 60%." He turned to me. "Barry, you just need to step up there and make them." He was right, but that was easier said than done. For the first and only time in my career, I was in a mind-game struggle with performing a certain aspect of the game, in this case making free throws.

≈

I've always been fascinated with the mental aspects of sports. It seems that psychological problems crop up more often in baseball than in other sports. Star second basemen Steve Sax and Chuck Knoblauch famously entered the twilight zone of not being able to make routine throws to first base. Steve Blass, Rick Ankiel, Mark Wohlers, and other pitchers completely lost the ability not only to throw strikes, but even to throw the ball anywhere near home plate. The most notable mind-bender of the late '80s involved Mets backup catcher Mackey Sasser, who was unable to make the return throw to the mound. How is that possible?

Then again, how does a career 81.3% free-throw shooter—my three-year percentage based on exactly 300 free throws attempted coming into the season—fall to barely 50%? In fact, my free-throw percentage went south each of my four years at Vanderbilt. As a freshman, I shot 84.6% from the line (44-52). As a full–time starter as a sophomore, I didn't drop much—still a solid 83.8% (114-136). As a junior in 1987–88, though, there was greater decline, to 76.8% (86-112). Still, as in my first two years, that 76.8% was good enough to lead the team.

Things had hit crisis mode by the time the K-State game rolled around. I had missed two of three free throws against Louisville, two of four against North Carolina, and three of eight against Ohio State. My poor performance at the line had not yet affected the outcome of a game, but it surely would if it didn't improve. Coach Newton's pregame callout wasn't to criticize or belittle me. To the contrary, it was a vote of confidence. He wanted the team to see that he knew I could make them. And I remained the go-to player to shoot technical fouls; in fact, I had shot them in Maui when Ohio State coach Gary Williams was T'd up in that game. But it's a helpless feeling to shoot and *hope* the ball drops into the basket instead of *knowing* it will go in—even if they don't all go in, you have to know that they will; that's what prompts you to shoot the next one, and the next one, and so on.

Happily, Coach Newton's vote of confidence, coupled with a change in stance and positioning at the line, turned the tide. I would shoot nearly 80% from the line for the remainder of the season and experience only two more hiccups at the line, only one of which arguably affected the outcome of the game. But the experience proved that the games present mental as much as physical challenges.

❧

I didn't shoot any free throws against K-State, but no one shot many—each team shot only nine and made only five. Yet again, we played a poor first half though we started out a lot better than we had against UNC, leading 11-8 and 13-10 in the early going. But the Wildcats went on a 14-1 run to take a 24-14 lead, and they never looked back. The Wildcats led 43-32 at the half behind 62% shooting from the field. As happened in the Ohio State game, K-State extended the lead in the second half and turned the game into a rout, pushing the lead to 23 points, 67-44, with around seven minutes to play. But we rallied for 11 straight points to cut the lead almost in half. K-State, however, spurted back to a more comfortable margin, and we could not make a serious run after that. A Booker three at the buzzer brought the final margin under double digits to 71-62.

Steve Henson proved that he was more than capable of picking up the slack for the departed Richmond, scoring 27 points on 11-for-18 shooting, and, even more impressively, nailing five of his six three-point attempts. For the second and final time in my Vandy career, I led the team in the three major statistical categories, but they were awfully modest totals—12 points, seven rebounds, and seven assists. I attempted 15 shots from the field, the most I would ever take in one game at Vandy.

~

The K-State game was our final non-conference road game, and our final road game of any kind for four weeks. Our 2-5 record was disappointing, but the schedule had been brutal—four games against ranked teams, and only one game at home. "It's been a March-type run, like tournament games," Coach Newton observed. "All of these teams"—except for the NAIA's Chaminade—"will be an NCAA team. I don't think there's any question about that."

C.M. wasn't far off on that prediction. Of the six Division I teams we had played through the K-State game, four (Michigan, Louisville, North Carolina, Kansas State) would make the NCAA tourney, and Ohio State no doubt would have if Jay Burson had not been lost to injury in February. Still, the Buckeyes made the quarterfinals of the NIT, and our other opponent, UAB, made the semifinals of NIT, ultimately finishing third.

It would be good to return home and finally play some games in the friendly confines of Memorial Gym. But there would be no breaks, at least at first, as we would be returning home to begin SEC play.

21

RIGHTING THE SHIP

I

"Heading for the nineties, living in the eighties"
—Escape Club, "Wild Wild West" ('88)

We returned home not only to try and right the ship on the court but also to concentrate on the upcoming final exams that led into the holiday break. The three straight road games resulted in several full or partial days out of town, which required us to hit the books for the next seven to 10 days leading to the holiday break. It was comforting that there would be no more road trips for a while, but that didn't mean the games would be any easier; in fact, we would be jumping right into SEC play for our return home, even though it was only the middle of December.

Typically, we would play our first SEC game right around the first of the year—the previous season it was the New Years' Eve date in Rupp Arena against Kentucky. But in 1988–89, the SEC decreed that each team must play an SEC game in December to attract television. So it was that we would play Auburn on December 14, and the TV ploy worked—ESPN would be televising the game nationally.

Ironically, Auburn had been our last SEC home game in '87–'88, and that one had not gone well—the Tigers ruined Will Perdue's last home game by beating us soundly. The Tigers, however, had lost four starters, including stars Chris Morris and Jeff Moore. Still, Auburn had a couple of weapons, including center Matt Geiger and forward John Caylor, a Tennessean who had a fine outside shot. The Tigers also had a freshman point guard, Johnny Benjamin, who had averaged an incredible 52 points a game as a high school senior. On our side, Coach Newton made a surprising lineup adjustment, starting Wilcox instead of Booker. Fred Benjamin started his second consecutive game at center as Kornet, Reid, and I completed the starting lineup. The first half, however, was an unmitigated disaster. From a 14-13 deficit, Auburn scored 13 straight points to lead by a dozen, 26-14. We scored nine straight to close the gap, and eventually tied the game at 31 on my jumper with 5:36 left in the half. But we collapsed from that point, allowing the Tigers to outscore us 17-4 and take a 48-35 lead into the locker room at the half.

This season, as do all seasons, had several critical moments, but perhaps none more significant than what we faced at halftime of this first SEC game. We again had handled the ball terribly, committing 15 turnovers, which would be too many in the full 40 minutes, and is atrocious for only 20. Kornet was shut out. Absent a second half comeback, we would fall to 2-6 overall, 0-1 in the league, and the season really could get away from us if we weren't careful. "It wasn't panic," I said after the game, "but it was close.…There was a lot of soul-searching at halftime."

During the intermission, Coach Newton and his staff made the personnel decision that would save the season. Freddie had not played poorly—he hit two of his three shots and claimed a couple of boards in ten minutes of action—but the five best players on the team were Kornet, Booker, Reid, Wilcox, and Goheen. Why not just put the five best players out there and see what happens? That's what the coaches did in the second half, and positive results were immediate.

Auburn's first possession of the second half resulted in a turnover—a sign of things to come for the Tigers. Booker's layup began our comeback. A three-point play by Reid and a jumper by Wilcox cut the deficit to six, 48-42. A Keenan Carpenter trey pushed Auburn's lead back to nine, but a Reid dunk, a Booker trey, and a Kornet three-point play cut the Auburn lead to 51-50. Another Auburn turnover led to one of the highlight reel plays of the season: I led a two-on-one fast break with Mayes, with Kornet trailing. I flipped a behind-the-back bounce pass to Chuck, but I led him too far; Chuck, though, reached out on the dead run with his right hand and, in one motion, flipped the ball behind *his* back to the trailing Kornet for a thunderous dunk that brought the house down. All told, in the first 11 minutes of the second half, we outscored Auburn 32-5 to flip the margin: we went from a deficit of 48-35 to a lead of 67-53. We maintained that margin the rest of the way and won easily, 93-77.

After the goose egg in the first half, Kornet exploded for 21 second-half points, a game-high, and he also led all players with nine rebounds. Booker regained his form with 19 points, and I added 18 points, five rebounds, and a game-high seven assists. Reid was solid with 16 points and four boards, while Wilcox added eight points, seven rebounds, and five assists. Thus, the five best players scored 82 of our 93 points, a percentage that would hold for most of the rest of the season.

While Coach Newton hedged his bets post-game on whether those five would be the permanent starting lineup ("whether we are able to stick with it defensively depends on who we're playing"), it was clear that this was an elixir worth bottling. Indeed, in the second half, Benjamin did not play, while Alberto Ballestra, who had played eight minutes in the first half, played only 11 seconds in the second half. The ESPN national telecast enabled people all over the country to watch us play one of our finest halves of the season. In fact, a certain interested viewer in Chicago had seen the game and called me later that night to offer his congratulations. Will Perdue, rookie center for the Bulls, saluted our comeback and wished us continued good luck.

II

"This is the place I used to know"
—Smithereens, "House We Sued to Live in" ('88)

After the SEC opener, we returned to non-conference play for the remainder of the calendar year. First up was Murray State, alma mater of my parents and many of my friends from the western Kentucky area. This would be an emotional game for me. Murray State had its fair share of western Kentuckians—one of my high school teammates, in fact—and, more importantly, it had most of the players back from the team that had upset #3-seeded North Carolina State in Lincoln and had Kansas on the ropes in the second round before the Jayhawks prevailed on their way to beating us and three other teams for the NCAA title. But we caught a huge break when the Racers' best player, Jeff Martin, sat out our game with a leg injury. Still, one future NBA player subbed for another when freshman Popeye Jones garnered many of the injured Martin's minutes. The Murray game also fell right in the middle of semester exams; I had taken four exams in five days leading up to the game. "We had six guys in exams today," Coach Newton said, "who weren't even able to join us for the pre-game meal and meeting. That's tough."

I never got nervous before games, at least not in the "I'm afraid I won't play well" sense of nervousness—except for this game against Murray State. With the "home school" connection and the fact that it was my parents' alma mater, I was shaky before the game—a post-game note reported that "C.M. Newton said he had never seen Goheen so nervous before a game." In fact, replicating Kornet's first-half performance against Auburn, I was blanked in the first half against the Racers—0-for-3 from the field and 0-for-2 from the line. The first half against Murray wasn't as disastrous as the Auburn first half; we just shot it poorly—42.3% from the field and a terrible 1-for-9 from three-point range. Murray led by as many as 12 points in the first half, but we trimmed the deficit to two, 32-30 by halftime. As with Auburn, though, we caught fire in the second half. I scored 14 points, while Booker added 12 after being held to five in the first half. Still, the game remained close for the first 10 minutes of the second half. Wilcox's only three of the game tied the game at 49 with 11:26 remaining, and his free throw the next time down gave us a lead that we would not relinquish. We pulled away to win by 17, 74-57.

Booker had his second consecutive strong effort, leading the team with 17 points and adding six rebounds. My 14 points were second to Book, and I added five assists. Reid had one of his best all-around games with 12 points and game-high totals of 11 rebounds and six assists. We also received a big boost from freshmen Morgan Wheat and Todd Milholland, who combined for 14 points on collective 5-for-6 shooting from the field and 4-for-5 shooting from the line. For the first time all season, we had notched back-to-back wins.

&

While I survived the jitters of the Murray game, our next game, against Ivy League preseason favorite Dartmouth, would be a "Back to the Future" experience for my backcourt mate Barry Booker. While, as a high school senior, I was grappling with the likes of Tony Kimbro, Rex Chapman, and Keith Williams, I was blissfully ignorant of the recruiting machinations in 1984–85 that would affect our game against the Big Green in December 1988. Dartmouth's best player was senior Jim Barton, a 6'4" sharpshooter who came to Nashville averaging 28.2 points per game. Barton had been a star in high school at Memphis University School, and he had a strong Vanderbilt pedigree—his father had earned a law degree at Vandy, and an uncle had attended VU as an undergraduate. Barton, it seems, wanted to attend Vanderbilt, but he recalled that "Vanderbilt showed no interest." Why? As Barton explained, "Vanderbilt had signed Barry Booker and then later they signed Barry Goheen." So, Barton opted for Dartmouth.

But the story didn't end there. Booker led his high school, Battle Ground Academy, to the Tennessee state tournament in 1984–85, and who do you think he and his BGA mates faced in the tourney's first round? Memphis University High, led by Jim Barton—and in Memorial Gym no less. U-High beat BGA, 60-50. Like my lengthy wait to settle scores against high school rivals in the Louisville game, Book had to wait over three years for the chance at redemption against Barton, who, two nights before our game, went home and torched a ranked Memphis State team for 36 points in a narrow 79-75 loss.

Apart from the Louisville game, for the first time all season we answered the call from the opening tip and played with the type of intensity we would need when the SEC schedule began in earnest. Dartmouth led 13-11 about five minutes into the game, but my three-pointer triggered an eruption of 16 straight points and a 27-13 lead. Booker sparked the run with assists to Kornet and Wilcox for layups as well as a three-pointer, demonstrating that he was locked and loaded for this one. The Big Green never got the margin under double digits, and we were in total command by 15, 48-33, at the half. Dartmouth committed turnovers on its first two possessions of the second half, which we converted into baskets by Kornet and then Booker to push the lead to nearly 20 points. We stretched the lead to nearly 30, 90-61, before Coach Newton cleared the bench. The final score was a surprising 92-67 romp. "We had been looking for a full 40 minutes of basketball and tonight we finally got it," enthused Coach Newton after the game.

Barton never got on track, finishing 5-for-21 from the field and missing 11 of his 14 shots from three-point range, finishing with 13 points, less than half his average. Meanwhile, Booker enjoyed the sweetest type of revenge—he set career highs with 25 points and six steals, and tied a career high with 11 assists. He added five rebounds for good measure and hit three of his four attempts from three-point range (overall, he was 10-for-17 from the field). Characteristically, Book downplayed the "revenge" theme after the game, but even he reveled in his performance. "I wouldn't say revenge was my key motivation tonight," he said, "but yes, it was in the back of my mind. I consider us even now"—which does sound a lot like the definition of "revenge."

Knowing how much this game meant to Book, Coach Newton was rightly effusive: "Barry was outstanding," Coach Newton said. "He was so active, both with and without the ball." I was decidedly a mere supporting player in this melodrama, but, seemingly anticipating my future career, I delivered this closing argument to anyone who was still doubting who was better, complete with the requisite rhetorical question: "Barton is a great shooter, but is he the best all-around player? This game was irrefutable proof that Booker is the better player. This was Booker's best game ever."

Book, moreover, wasn't the only Commodore with a double-double against Dartmouth. I notched my first and only double-double as a Commodore, and with the thinnest of stats: 11 points and a career-high 10 rebounds, with five assists. Kornet went 9-for-12 from the field and scored 19 points, adding six boards, while Reid notched another solid all-around game with 13 points, six boards, and six assists. Wilcox rounded out an excellent game by all five starters with 6-for-8 shooting, 12 points, seven rebounds, and four assists. If there were any remaining doubts as to the wisdom of starting the quintet of Kornet-Booker-Goheen-Reid-Wilcox, the Dartmouth game settled those questions. For the first time all season, all five starters scored in double figures. Collectively, we went 35-for-54 from the field (65%), 4-for-7 from three-point range, scored 80 points, claimed 34 rebounds (everyone had at least five), and passed out 27 assists. The Dartmouth game would be one of our three or four most complete performances of the season, and it sent us to our Christmas break on a positive note at 5-5.

III

"Should I go north? Should I go south? Should I go west? Should I go east?"—Lone
Justice, "East of Eden" ('85)

We returned from a few days of Christmas break to close out 1988 with the Music City Invitational Tournament. The honorary chairman for the '88 event was Vince Gill, who was on the cusp of country music superstardom in fall 1988. Vince had been the lead singer of the country-rock band Pure Prairie League in the early 1980s; that's him singing lead on the band's hit "Let Me Love You Tonight," which he sang as part of his pre-tourney banquet performance for the teams aboard the General Jackson showboat. The seniors got the photo op with the MCIT chairman, and Kornet, Booker, and I enjoyed hamming it up with Vince for the cover shot of the program, which featured Vince's spinning a basketball on his index finger while the three of us looked on in mock amazement. Vince is also a big basketball fan, and he's married to one-time Vanderbilt student Amy Grant, a famous singer in her own right.

The three teams joining us in the '88 MCIT were Stanford, Furman, and Colgate, and we drew Colgate in the first game. In the context of our rugged non-conference schedule, this was the only game (Chaminade excepted) that looked like an easy win going in. And, in fact, it was a cakewalk; we closed the half on a 33-13 run to take a 49-26 lead into the locker room. At one point in the second half we led by 43 points, and the final score was 91-55.

Colgate was easy, but the championship game would be a much sterner challenge—the Pac-10's Stanford Cardinal, a senior-heavy team that was favored to win its conference. I had been recruited by Stanford in high school, and it was interesting how the Cardinal's fortunes had paralleled those of Vanderbilt over the past few years. Tom Davis was Stanford's head coach when I was in high school, so it was his staff that recruited me. But Stanford wasn't all that good back then—14-14 in 1982–83 and eighth in the 10-team Pac-10, and 19-12 in 1983–84 but only 8-10 in the conference, exactly Vanderbilt's SEC record. Of course, Stanford and Vanderbilt are strong academic schools, and Vandy was considerably closer to my hometown than Stanford, lovely as Northern California is. Plus, Vandy played in a stronger conference for athletics. Thus, I cast my lot with Vandy.

In 1984–85, my senior year in high school, Stanford finished with an overall record of 11-17—the same record as Vandy—and finished dead last in its conference, also like Vandy. Both schools began the long climb back to respectability in fall 1985, and both teams brought in strong recruiting classes. The Cardinal went 14-16 in 1985–86 (like our 13-15 record), then got over .500 in 1986–87 with a 15-13 record under new coach Mike Montgomery, just as we did, with our 18-16, NIT quarterfinalist performance. Both teams broke through in '87–'88—Stanford went 21-12 and fourth in the Pac-10, while we went 20-11 (fourth in the SEC) and went to the Sweet Sixteen. The Cardinal, however, had to settle for the NIT.

The 1988–89 Cardinal team was loaded, led by stellar seniors Todd Lichti, Howard Wright, Eric Raveno, and Terry Taylor. Taylor and Lichti were a potent backcourt, one of the best we would face all season. Lichti was the real deal—he would become the only the third player to make the All Pac-10 team four times—and in the Cardinal's opening round MCIT game against Furman, he set a Memorial Gym record by hitting all 12 of his field-goal attempts, finishing with 29 points in only 23 minutes. Wright and Raveno, both 6'8", were just as potent up front.

Our game was played in spurts, and Stanford had most of them. We scored 12 of the game's first 20 points, but Stanford used a 14-2 run to forge a 26-15 lead. The Cardinal's lead was 10, 32-22, with around four minutes remaining in the first half, when we suddenly caught fire with 13 consecutive points, built on three-point shooting (two by me and one by Booker). A Raveno deuce ended our run, but Booker's 12-footer beat the halftime buzzer and sent us to the locker room with a 37-34 lead.

The final four minutes of the first half were great; the game's other 36 minutes generally were awful, and the final 20 against Stanford was surely our worst second half of the season. We didn't score for the first five minutes of the half, until a Kornet layup broke the cold spell; we wouldn't score again until my free throw with about 12 minutes remaining. By then, Stanford had scored 20 points in the half and had built a comfortable lead that only kept growing. The Cardinal outscored us 55-31 in the second half and won in a rout, 89-68.

Wright and Lichti were as effective an inside/outside combination as we would encounter all year—Wright had 28 points and seven rebounds, while Lichti went for 20 and six and was, not surprisingly, named the tourney's most valuable player. Stanford shot an almost-unbelievable 78.6% from the field in the second half (22-28) and 62.3% for the game. Wright predicted after the game that "Vanderbilt will be one of the top three teams in the Southeastern Conference," but we didn't look or feel like one then. "Our players are really down," said Coach Newton. And we were. Kornet led the team with 21 points, and Booker was fine as well, scoring 17 and passing the 1,000-point career mark in the process. I was the other double-figure scorer with 10 but shot only 3-for-9 from the field and was practically embarrassed to be named to the all-tournament team, scoring a total of only 20 points on 6-for-19 shooting in the two games. (Kornet joined me on the all-tourney team.)

Stanford went on to win the Pac-10 regular season title. But the season wouldn't end well for the Cardinal—seeded third in the East Regional, they were upset by 14th-seeded Siena, 80-78, in the first round.

Thus, we ended the otherwise great year of 1988 on a sour note. There would be little time to mope about Stanford, though. We not only were about to turn the calendar to 1989, but were about to commence SEC play in earnest. "The pennant race," as Coach Newton liked to call it, was about to begin.

22

LAST CHANCE AT RUPP

I

"Working all day and the sun don't shine"
—*Roy Orbison, "California Blue" ('89)*

Coach Newton gave us New Year's Eve off, but he welcomed in 1989 with the season's hardest practices beginning on January 1—"two good, tough practices" according to the coach, having rightly called our performance against Stanford "an embarrassment." The message was that there could be no more half-game performances like the second half against Stanford. We had the potential to be one of the best teams in the SEC, but only if we played a full 40 minutes without any extended lapses. The tough practices after the Stanford debacle gave us a chance to wash those terrible halves out of our system once and for all. And, for the most part, we did.

We ended the November/December schedule with a 6-6 record, which wasn't all that bad considering that we had started by losing five of our first seven, and each of the six teams that beat us would be playing in a postseason tournament, four of them in the NCAAs (Michigan, North Carolina, Kansas State, Stanford). As for the SEC itself, the pundits had predicted that the league would be down. In their preconference tune-ups, the 10 teams turned in "a December of mediocrity." As the calendar turned to 1989, only two SEC teams were ranked, and they were at the low end of the top 20: Tennessee (#17) and Georgia (#20).

We welcomed Alabama to Memorial to begin the new year. The Tide had won eight of its first 10 games but had lost its first SEC contest in December by five points to SEC favorite Georgia. It was hard to fathom why the "experts" had picked 'Bama to finish in the bottom half of the SEC. 'Bama was a deep, talented team, led by terrific senior forward Michael Ansley, who came into the game averaging 21.6 points and 8.8 rebounds. Also, as we had discovered the previous season (and would learn again in '89), sharpshooter Alvin Lee could score points in bunches, especially from behind the arc. An athletic 6'8" center, David Benoit would cause us (and many other teams) problems in the post. And the Tide's roster included two players who enjoyed long and productive NBA careers—6'6" junior guard Keith Askins, and especially 6'9" freshman Robert Horry, who would make a career out of hitting big shots in the postseason.

In fact, we always had trouble with Alabama because of the Tide's combination of size, speed, and shooting. That may explain why we had a worse record against 'Bama than any other SEC team in my four years at Vandy. But, for this first game of '89, we managed to solve the Tide—with ease, surprisingly. After an early 10-10 tie, Booker—who always played well against 'Bama—nailed back-to-back treys, triggering an 18-4 run that gave us a 28-14 lead. A modest Tide rally cut the lead to 10, 32-22, at the half. Alabama opened the second half with a basket to cut our lead to single digits, but we quickly extended the margin back to 13, and we eventually built the lead to 28 points, 69-41, before Coach Newton cleared the bench. We won by 20, 73-53.

Booker's 18 points (4-for-5 from downtown) and five rebounds capped a great two-week run that resulted in his being named the SEC Player of the Week for the two-week holiday stretch that ended with the Alabama game. I chipped in with 13 points, five assists, and a team-high eight rebounds. The true star of the game, however, was Derrick Wilcox. It was Derrick's 21st birthday, and he celebrated by dishing out a school-record 13 assists—exactly one more than the entire Alabama team. (Billy McCaffrey and Atiba Prater currently share the assists record at 14.) The Memorial Gym announcer informed the crowd of the record after Derrick recorded assist number 13—but he didn't hear it. "I heard the crowd roar, but I thought they had announced another Southeastern Conference score," he said. "I didn't know what it was." Not until Book informed him of his feat in the locker room did Derrick realize he had set the school record. Even more remarkably, he had only one turnover against the quick Tide backcourt. "It probably was all-around our best game," I remarked, rather disjointedly, after the game. We would have several chances to improve my opinion over the next several weeks.

II

"Now cheaters have their way"
—Jane's Addiction, "Idiots rule" ('88)

The first chance to play a better "all-around" game would be three days later, at Kentucky. The game would represent one final opportunity to take down at the Wildcats in Rupp Arena. It would be the sixth consecutive season I had played a game in Rupp, and I had endured four losses in the previous five games there, beginning with that painful loss in the state tournament in March 1984. Since then, I had played in Rupp four more times, with the lone victory coming in summer 1985 when I (and Kornet, Tony Kimbro, Keith Williams, and others) helped the Kentucky All-Stars beat the Indiana All-Stars in the Kentucky "home game" of the two-game series. But my previous three trips to Rupp as a Commodore had been fruitless. In '86, we played Kentucky (17-1 in the SEC) tough the entire game, losing to the

12th-ranked Wildcats 73-65 in a game where we held UK All-American forward Kenny Walker to 2-for-6 shooting from the field, yet the officials sent him to the line 16 times, fouling out both of our power forwards (Steve Reece and Kornet) in the process.

The '87 trip was even uglier: we fell behind 36-21 at the half and lost 65-54. I am sure it was the only game in the two seasons that Perdue, Booker, and I started together that none of us reached double figures — Will scored eight while Book and I scored nine each, the only time in the seven games I played against the 'Cats in my last three years that I would fall short of double figures; and as a team we were a horrendous 12-for-27 from the free-throw line. In the locker room after that loss, Coach Newton delivered one of the all-time great post-game speeches, one we still talk about today. It went like this: "We just have to be tough. So tough. Damn tough. Tougher than the toughest of the tough. Tough." Do you think C.M. wanted us to be tough?

ʠ

In January 1989, however, there was more than just a game to play in Lexington. Kentucky was embroiled in an emerging scandal that not only threatened its season, but also found its way to C.M. Newton. There were multiple alleged NCAA violations swirling around, and they involved two primary events. First, in March 1988, UK assistant coach Dwayne Casey sent a videotape and $1,000 in cash in an Emery Worldwide package to the father of UK's prize freshman signee for 1988–89, Chris Mills; however, the package had accidentally been opened in transit and the $1,000 had fallen out. UK, of course, denied all of that and claimed that Emery, the package company, had been tipped off to the package and intentionally opened it, leading to Emery's immortal response: "If you believe that, then you believe in Santa Claus and the Easter Bunny."

The second scandal involved the previous season's star freshman, Eric Manuel, who was accused of cheating on his standardized college entrance exam. Already there had been fallout: UK Athletic Director (and all-time Wildcat hoops great) Cliff Hagan had been forced to resign in November, and Manuel, who would've been UK's best returning player in 1988–89, left UK, ultimately finishing his career at an NAIA school, Oklahoma City College. Infuriating UK fans, Dick Vitale publicly called for UK head coach Eddie Sutton and his staff, including Casey, to step down.

Popular opinion was that Kentucky was going to get hammered by the NCAA. The school somehow had avoided any serious repercussions from a 1985 Pulitzer Prize-winning series in the *Lexington Herald-Leader* exposing widespread cheating in the program, leading to one of the greatest lines in college basketball history, uttered by perennial NCAA thorn Jerry Tarkanian of UNLV: "The NCAA is so mad at Kentucky, it will probably slap another two years' probation on Cleveland State."

UK was obviously cheating, but the powers that be weren't stupid. They knew that the university had to replace Hagan with someone of unimpeachable integrity and a spotless record. Not surprisingly, the name of UK alum C.M. Newton was promptly and widely circulated as Hagan's potential successor. In fact, as early as December 10, *The Tennessean* had reported that "Vanderbilt basketball coach C.M. Newton has been mentioned by University of Kentucky President David Roselle as the man he would most like to have as UK's athletics director." Now, nearly a month later, with Coach Newton arriving in Lexington for the January 7 game with the 'Cats, the rumor mill really heated up. Just that week, *Sports Illustrated*, in its college basketball column written by *Herald-Leader* writer Billy Reed, reported on the "growing speculation that Vandy coach C.M. Newton would resign at season's end to become athletic director at Kentucky," adding that, after rejecting Roselle's initial overtures, "Newton is apparently reconsidering and has already had at least one conversation with Kentucky President David Roselle." Challenged by a reporter on the *SI* article before our game, C.M. cringed. "I'm here to coach a basketball game. I don't want any distractions." He added, "There's nothing to discuss. I am not interested in the job."

With all that white noise present, it was something of a challenge to weed out those distractions and play what, at that moment, appeared to be a talented but perplexing Kentucky team. These Wildcats were almost unrecognizable from the 1987–88 edition. Seniors Ed Davender, Winston Bennett, Rob Lock, Cedric Jenkins, and Richard Madison had graduated, and super soph Rex Chapman, who reportedly clashed often with Coach Eddie Sutton, had departed for the NBA. All told, those five departures had accounted for 80% of UK's offense in 1987–88. The 'Cats, as always, still had some talent on hand—enough for *Sports Illustrated* to rank Kentucky at the tail end of its preseason top 40—but not a lot of experience. Freshman Mills was their most talented player, sophomore center LeRon Ellis had potential, and guard Derrick Miller was the walking definition of "streak shooter," as we would find out in '89. Sean Sutton, son of the UK coach, was an adequate point guard, and small forward Reggie Hanson added some athleticism. The bench was populated by a bunch of Kentuckians—senior Mike Scott (my and Kornet's teammate on the 1985 Kentucky-Indiana All-Star team) and three freshmen, redshirt forwards John Pelphrey and Deron Feldhaus and guard Richie Farmer, a true freshman who had been Kentucky's Mr. Basketball in 1987–88 (a title Pelphrey had won the previous season).

Kentucky had staggered through its non-conference schedule, as some of its quality opponents settled some old scores. The 'Cats lost by over 20 to Duke (80-55), Indiana (75-52), and Louisville (97-75), while Notre Dame pounded them by 16 (81-65). They also were shocked in Rupp by Northwestern State and Bowling Green. They entered SEC play with a 5-7 record. But the Wildcats appeared to wake up when the SEC schedule kicked in. Three days before our game, UK spanked preseason favorite Georgia 76-65 in Rupp, suggesting that all of those non-conference thrashings had toughened the 'Cats for the conference grind. Maybe the 'Cats were rounding into shape.

It certainly looked that way in the first half. After a sluggish start by both teams, UK, especially Derrick Miller, caught fire. Miller keyed an 18-2 run with three treys they gave UK a 22-10 lead, and the Cats kept the lead in double digits for most of the rest of the first half. We scored only two baskets in a 10-minute span, and Miller hit another three just inside the final minute to get UK its biggest lead, 36-20. Two Todd Milholland free throws before the end of the half closed another dismal opening-half performance, and we trudged to the locker room staring at a 36-22 deficit.

I could not find any rhythm on offense. I hit my first shot attempt early in the game, but missed my other three attempts and just seemed out of sorts, along with the rest of the team. The locker room for this intermission was not a pleasant place to be, and Coach Newton directed his harshest words at me. This was one of the few times he really yelled at me in a halftime tirade, and he let it be known that I was far too passive on offense. He dryly noted later, "I spent most of the time at the half encouraging Goheen to get more shots. We try to stress team play. He must believe it." "I don't want him to get selfish," he added. "But I want to know who the hell to get the ball to."

Well, with carte blanche to start hoisting up some shots, and with the game nearly out of hand anyway with UK's 14-point bulge, there was little to lose by heeding Coach Newton's "advice" to take more shots. So, early in the second half, when I had a fairly open look behind the three-point line from the right side of the floor, I took it—and watched the ball hit the front rim, carom off the backboard, hit another part of the rim, and finally fall through the net, an unlikely result from 20 feet and the basketball equivalent of a 52-hopper finding a hole in the infield for a single to break a batting slump. But that's all it took to turn my shooting luck around. After that opening three, I hit another one. And another. And still another. "When you hit two or three shots in a row," I later said, "you feel like you can hit from anyplace." And I did, at least on this occasion: I hit five consecutive threes in the first 10 minutes of the second half, and the fifth cut UK's lead to 47-44 with 10:13 remaining. At some point during this run a fan yelled, "Goheen, ease up on the three-pointers"; I acknowledged the fan with a frown and sank another triple from the top of the key.

Unfortunately, Miller kept up his hot shooting, this time from inside the arc: he hit three 10-footers in the next four minutes to rebuild UK's lead to seven, 58-51. I responded with my fifth trey of the half to cut the Cats' lead to 58-54, and we launched one final run at the Wildcats, closing within two, 58-56, on Reid's basket with 4:41 remaining. Two Reggie Hanson free throws pushed UK's lead back to four, and then the 'Cats received the benefit of game-changing officiating: we went to "winner" mode, and I spun at the free-throw line and approached the basket, drawing three Wildcats, including Mills and center Ellis, to me, and dished to Kornet on the block for what appeared to be an easy dunk that would trim the lead back to two. But Ellis recovered and went up behind Frank for the attempted block on the dunk attempt, clearly fouling him in the process, and then hanging on the rim after that…except that no personal or technical foul was called. Coach Newton rightly blasted that non-call after the game: "That's inexcusable, with three officials. Kornet got knocked to the floor, and their guy [Ellis] should have got a technical for hanging on the rim after the play."

But that's why opposing players and coaches long have nicknamed the venue "Corrupt Arena"—every late-game call goes the home team's way, and this one became a killer when, after the teams exchanged turnovers, Miller hit a three-pointer to push the lead to seven, 63-56. The 'Cats wound up winning, 70-61.

Once again, we had dug ourselves too deep a hole in the first half, but at least we showed the character to come back and make a game of it in front of the 23,338 fans in attendance. Our 53 shots from the field were split almost evenly between two-pointers (27) and three-pointers (26), and that would be the most treys we would attempt in any game all season. Book and I combined for 22 of those attempts and all 10 of our makes—he was 4-for-12 and I was 6-for-10, and my 20 and his 14 led the team. Derrick Miller scored 27 points to lead all scorers, and LeRon Ellis notched a strong double-double with 17 points and 10 boards. Freshman Mills wasn't the spectacular performer that had been advertised, but he produced a solid line of 13 points and nine rebounds.

Nevertheless, the loss meant that I would go winless as a Commodore in Rupp Arena, which, as I remarked after the game, made the loss "especially painful." I added that UK "played a great game" and "[t]hey made the plays." UK, having beaten us and Georgia to open its SEC campaign ("Two wonderful games," remarked UK Coach Sutton), certainly seemed capable of making a run at another SEC title, and in fact the 'Cats were one of only two unbeaten teams in the conference at this early stage:

Tennessee	3-0
Kentucky	2-0
LSU	2-1
Vandy	2-1
Mississippi State	1-1
Alabama	1-2
Georgia	1-2
Ole Miss	1-2
Florida	1-2
Auburn	0-3

As things would transpire, this loss to Kentucky would be our worst of the year. Indeed, we would lose 14 games in 1988–89, and only one of those losses was to a team that would fail to make either the NIT or NCAA tournaments—the Kentucky Wildcats.

23

ZENITH

I

"It's time to take a stand"
—Lenny Kravitz, "Let Love rule" ('89)

In a scheduling coincidence, our fourth SEC game of 1988–89 would be at Ole Miss, just as our fourth SEC game of 1987–88 had been. Thus, we would tip it off in Oxford on January 11, 1989, exactly 52 weeks since our '88 visit to Oxford. What a difference a year had made between the two trips. In '88, we had lost our first three SEC games and were at our lowest point in my four years. But it's no exaggeration to say that everything changed that night in Oxford—the favorable whistle on the five-second call in the final minute, Book's go-ahead three and game-icing free throws after that, and a couple of defensive stops launched our seven-game winning streak that, about two months later, saw us crash the Sweet Sixteen. Beginning with that game, we had played an 18-game SEC schedule—the final 15 of 1987–88 and the first three of 1988–89. Our record in that 18-game span had been 12-6, near the top of the league. So, the challenge for this final trip to Oxford was not to reverse our fortunes but to maintain our standing as one of the league's top teams.

It would not be easy, of course. Despite the loss of the excellent guard Rod Barnes, this was the most talented Ole Miss team we would face in my four years. Newcomer Gerald Glass, a junior transfer from Division II Delta State (where Ole Miss coach Ed Murphy had come from), had raised some eyebrows by being selected to the preseason All-SEC team without having played a D-I game yet, but he had proven he belonged by averaging 26.7 points and 7.7 rebounds a game in the Rebels' first 11 games. (He also played bass for the Archie Singers, a gospel group that included his parents and several other relatives.) Glass's main offensive support would come from Tim Jumper, an athletic guard who had been hampered by a knee injury (missing six weeks earlier in the season) but who was expected to play in our game, and the fine post player Sean Murphy, the coach's son.

The game would be a nail-biter, just like the one 52 weeks previous. We led 31-25 at the half, but the second half was close all the way. Jumper's three-pointer tied the game at 56 with about 90 seconds remaining. We worked the shot clock down to its final seconds before attempting, and missing, the go-ahead shot. Now

Ole Miss would have a chance at winning, and everyone knew who would take that shot—Glass. The Rebels called time with about 20 seconds left to set up the final play. Glass got off a makeable jumper, but missed, and Mike Paul's desperation tip didn't fall, sending the teams to overtime.

The overtime frame began inauspiciously for us when Glass authored a spectacular dunk for a 58-56 Rebels lead, but from there the overtime period would be dominated by Derrick Wilcox. Derrick hit a three to give us a one-point lead with 3:58 remaining. Ole Miss reclaimed the lead with a Paul field goal, but Derrick nailed a 16-footer to put us back in front 61-60 with 2:46 left. He and I then sandwiched three-pointers around an Ole Miss field goal to give us a 67-62 lead with 38 seconds left. We weren't quite out of the woods yet, and, with the score 68-65, Jumper attempted a game-tying three with 12 seconds left but missed. Kornet rebounded and was fouled, and his free throws iced the game. Two more Wilcox free throws ended the scoring at 72-65, and, for the second consecutive year, we escaped Oxford with a huge, thrilling victory.

Clearly, the hero was Derrick Wilcox. In our previous three games (Stanford, Alabama, Kentucky), Derrick had gone 4-for-18 from the field (0-for-5 at UK) and had missed all seven of his three-point attempts. But a shooting tip from Coach Martin ("One thing he told me was to spread my fingers out on my shooting hand to give myself a better base and more control on my shots.") made all the difference: 8-for-11 from the field, including 3-for-4 from behind the arc, and 3-for-4 from the line for a team-high 22 points. Kornet was right behind him, posting an excellent double-double of 21 points and a game-high 10 boards. With Derrick scoring (he had just one assist), he and I essentially switched roles—I scored 11 as our other double-figure score and contributed a game-high six assists.

The win nudged us back over the .500 mark at 8-7 and, more importantly, allowed us to keep pace with Tennessee (4-0 in the league) and Kentucky (3-0 after a 69-56 whipping of Florida in Gainesville). And it kicked off perhaps the most bizarre two-week stretch in the annals of Vanderbilt basketball—incredible, even historic games on the court, earthshaking occurrences off it.

II

"We'd rather risk it all, roll the dice, let them fall"
—Jerry Harrison, "Man with a Gun" ('88)

The Ole Miss win was our first road win of the season, and it put us in good position in the league. Now we had to hold serve at home against Georgia. The Bulldogs, the league's preseason favorite, had not lived up to expectations thus far. While we were beating Ole Miss, the Dawgs were getting manhandled at Alabama, 80-62, their third straight loss, to fall to 1-3 in SEC play. And that wasn't the worst of it—Georgia's center, Elmore Spencer, averaging 12.6 points a game, had fractured his foot in the 'Bama game and would miss the rest of the season. Moreover, the team had to spend the night in the Atlanta airport due to rain and fog. So, Georgia might well be playing for its season in Memorial.

There was a reason the Dawgs had been picked to win the SEC: they had a lot of talent. Willie Anderson had taken his considerable skills to the NBA, but one of the country's top recruits, Litterial Green, essentially replaced Anderson in the backcourt and was averaging 14 points a game. Alec Kessler was one of the best big men in the league, averaging 10.5 rebounds a game; the other guard, Pat Hamilton, was one of the best defensive guards in the league, and the Dawgs had quality athleticism at other spots in 6'4" swingman Rod Cole and 6'8" forward Marshall Wilson.

We felt good after the win in Oxford. Plus, the Georgia game was the SEC Game of the Week and, therefore, would be televised regionally, which was a big deal in 1989. The 15,000+ in Memorial and the regional television audience would see one of the most memorable games in recent Memorial Gym history.

Atypically, I scored the first two points of the game, on a driving layup. From there, the first half was a back-and-forth affair of mini-spurts by both teams. Near the end of the half, Kornet's tip-in, his first field goal of the game, tied the game at 33. Georgia held for the final shot of the half, and on an inbounds play, Steve Grant was whistled for a foul. I had come out of the game before the inbounds play so that we could install a taller lineup, but with the dead ball before the free throws, I returned to the floor. There were three seconds left, and Georgia's Orlando Bennett made both free throws to give Georgia a 35-33 lead, which would seem to end the half.

Still, a lot can happen in three seconds, and there's no need just to take the inbounds pass and dribble out the clock. So I received the inbounds pass and spun around the Dawgs' Wilson, who had smartly come up to apply some pressure, and made my way up court for a couple of seconds before launching a shot from about 48-50 feet, just behind the half-court line, a split-second before the clock expired—and it banked cleanly off the backboard and into the net for a half-ending three-pointer to give us a 36-35 lead at intermission. Tongue firmly in cheek, Coach Newton upbraided me in the locker room for the shot: "I really hate that you wasted that at halftime because nothing is less important in life than the score at halftime." I "apologized" and said that I would try to save such dramatics only for the end of the game next time. But "next time" would come a lot sooner than anyone could have predicted.

We used the momentum from that shot to build a slight lead of 44-39 in the opening minutes of the second half. Then it was Georgia's turn for a spurt—six straight points to reclaim the lead. Wilcox's three-point play off a driving layup gave us a 47-45 lead, but Pat Hamilton nailed a three to make it 48-47, Dawgs. Kornet's basket was answered by a Wilson deuce, but Frank scored again, and we led, 51-50, with 12 minutes to play. Hamilton's two free throws made it 52-51, and a Lem Howard basket extended the Georgia lead to three. I scored underneath, then was fouled by Cole, and made one free throw to tie the game at 54, but not for long: Booker intercepted a lazy Georgia pass, and his breakaway dunk brought the crowd back to life and gave us a two-point lead with 10 minutes left.

Georgia refused to fold, though, and five straight points, capped by Jody Patton's trey, gave the Dawgs a 59-56 lead. We cut the lead to one with a deuce, but Cole's jumper made it 61-58 with 6:52 remaining, and Patton's jumper stretched Georgia's lead to five. Kornet's 15-footer cut the lead to three, then Booker stole Georgia's rebound off Frank's missed one-and-one for a goal to trim Georgia's lead to 63-62 with five minutes left. But Patton nailed another trey to give the Dawgs a four-point lead. Patton fouled Book on the other end; Book hit the first free throw and missed the second, but we claimed the rebound, which led to a Booker three— a four-point trip for Barry—to tie the game at 66 with 4:10 to play. We had a great defensive possession on the other end, forcing an air ball with the shot clock running down, but the ball fell right into Kessler's hands for the putback and a 68-66 Georgia lead. Kessler then blocked Book's driving shot, and when Wilson nailed a three on the other end, Georgia led 71-66 with 2:18 to play. Things didn't look good, and we called timeout.

Out of the timeout, I missed a three-point attempt and Wilson rebounded; I tied him up, but the possession arrow favored Georgia, so the Dawgs had the ball and a five-point lead with two minutes to play. Green then made a freshman mistake—instead of killing time off the shot clock, he got a step on Wilcox and went for a layup, but Derrick recovered in time to slap the ball away from behind; it landed in Green's hands as he was standing out of bounds, giving us the ball back. Then Hamilton made a rare defensive mistake, fouling Booker 35 feet from the basket as Book and I exchanged the ball. Book was clutch, hitting both ends of the bonus to cut the lead to 71-68 with 1:46 to play.

Again, Georgia was aggressive on offense, and this time it paid off—Hamilton drove on me and hit a jumper in the lane to make it 73-68, Georgia, with 1:25 to play. I then took the inbounds pass and headed straight down the floor, spun around Cole and went right at Wilson, drawing the contact and foul as I laid the ball in the basket. I hit the free throw to complete the three-point trip to slice Georgia's lead to 73-71. With a minute left, Green again got a step on Wilcox and had a makeable, but contested, layup; he missed it and Kornet rebounded. Then came what appeared to be a game-killing turnover: Wilcox and I got mixed up on his attempted pass to me out front, 30 feet from the basket; the ball flew out of bounds with 35 seconds remaining. On the ensuing inbounds play, Hamilton broke free, but Booker caught and fouled him with 32 seconds left. We called timeout, and when we broke the huddle, I told Wilcox, "If we get the ball back down two, I'm going for a three."

That didn't seem likely when Hamilton drained both free throws to push Georgia's lead to 75-71. But Green committed another freshman error when he fouled me on the dribble about 20 feet from the basket with 21 seconds left. I hit both ends of the one-and-one, making the score 75-73 and setting the stage for one of the most frenetic, fantastic finishes in Memorial Gym history, which unfolded like some sort of fever dream.

We did not call timeout after my second free throw; instead, we picked up Georgia full-court, man-to-man. I was supposed to be guarding Hamilton. Cole inbounded the ball to Kessler deep in the backcourt; he passed back to Cole, and I rushed up to guard him, trying for the steal or to foul him, but before I could do any of that, he threw about a 60-foot pass to Hamilton, who was wide open under the Georgia basket...where I should have been. All he had to do was lay the ball in the basket and the game likely was over. But he may have heard Eric Reid's footsteps as Eric hustled to try for the block from behind. Eric didn't get there, but Hamilton blew the layup with 14 seconds left. Georgia had another chance to put it away when Wilson came out of nowhere for a one-handed slam-dunk putback, but it clanged off the back of the rim. Booker claimed the rebound about 15 feet from the basket and steamed down the right side of the court. Eleven seconds remained.

Cole, who had made the pass to Hamilton from our end of the court, had stayed on that end and met Book while Kessler also harassed Barry as he crossed the midcourt line. I also had stayed on our end and was on the left side of the court, the opposite side from where Book was heading. I was wide open about 12 feet from the basket and frantically waved my arms, yelling for Book to pass me the ball. With eight seconds showing, Book, still moving forward on the dribble, left his feet about 12 feet from the basket on the right side of the floor, with Cole right in front of him. Book crashed into Cole as he passed the ball to me. I caught the ball about 10 feet from the basket, and by then I wasn't as open because Hamilton had raced downcourt to pick me up. I declined the 10-footer and, to the dismay of the 15,000-plus I'm sure, turned and dribbled for the three-point line. I got there, with Hamilton now in front of me, with six seconds left.

For reasons I have never figured out, Hamilton decided to try for the steal instead of just playing straight-up defense. He almost succeeded, as he poked the ball as I tried to spin on him. I nearly double-dribbled as I used both hands to reclaim control of the ball, with my back to Hamilton and the basket. Here's where all those game clocks in Memorial Gym came in handy: wherever you are in the gym, whether on the court or in the stands, you can easily spot one, and at this instant I looked for one to make sure there was still time. There was: the clock changed from five seconds to four as I checked the time. And that was when Hamilton made the fatal error of running around my right side to steal the ball or at least poke it away. But I was already turning to my left, away from him, while he was doing that; the result was that when I turned back to face the basket, Hamilton wasn't there; he was behind me, out of bounds. Now I had a wide-open shot, which I launched from just behind the three-point line with three seconds showing. It found nothing but net as the buzzer sounded—a game-winning three-pointer to give us a thrilling 76-75 victory.

III

"I'd have Al Jolson sing, 'I'm sitting on top of the world'"
—The Proclaimers, "I'm on My Way" ('88–'89)

For the third and final time in my Vandy career, I received a free ride off the floor from jubilant fans, students, and teammates, this time to the chants of "Goheen! Goheen! Goheen!" It was an amazing finish—the most thrilling end-of-game sequence (out of several candidates) I was ever a part of. In fact, of all the great finishes and buzzer-beaters, this Georgia game was the only one where I look back and think, "Did I actually do that?" This one game managed to combine the half-court heave of the Louisville game with the last-second three-pointer of the Pitt game into a single affair. "It's downright spooky to see two shots like that in one game," said Coach Newton. Even my mother was brought to tears by the drama: "I cried when he made the shot against Georgia," she said a few weeks later. "I've been excited before, but that's the first time I've cried."

Why would any sane person pass up an open 12-footer for a tie, dribble out to the three-point line, allow one or more defenders to converge and potentially disrupt the attempt, and possibly miss the shot and lose the game? Well, that's hard to say. "Most any rational person would have taken the 10-foot shot," I said a few days later. "[But] I've never been accused of being rational." I hadn't been joking when I told Wilcox that I was going for the three should the opportunity present itself. I guess the opportunity didn't exactly "present itself" as much as I created it, but I felt like we needed to win it or lose it right then and there. Perhaps, "a higher power takes over," as I said after the game.

The prevailing, but incorrect, answer to the question of "Why?" was put forth by Coach Newton in the on-court, post-buzzer pandemonium. The television cameras did a good job of conveying the chaos in Memorial after the shot fell, with fans rushing the floor, hoisting me on their shoulders for a ride, and so forth. One camera showed Coach Newton, arms folded and slowly breaking into a big grin while shaking his head (one writer opined that "Coach Newton's grin and shake of the head got almost as much air time as the two shots" at the half and at the end), asking me to return to terra firma from the post-game ride for a question, which any lip-leader could easily make out: "Did you know what the score was?" My response: "Yes. I just didn't think you could handle another overtime!" I said the same thing to the print media: "I didn't think Coach Newton could stand another overtime. We'd already put him through one at Ole Miss on Wednesday, so I figured I'd better go ahead and win this one in regulation." That was fairly cheeky in tone, but in a separate interview I phrased it differently. "I had a three-pointer in mind," I said. "I wanted to either win or lose the game with a three-pointer. So many things can happen in overtime....Did I know the score? Absolutely. But when I got the ball with five or six seconds left, I wasn't going for a two-pointer. I decided I was going to work for the three and win it or lose it with one shot."

In fact, in my Vandy career, the "things" that happened to us in overtime were mostly bad; in my four years, we won only two games that went into overtime, one of which had been at Ole Miss three days earlier. (The other one was notable: Pitt, NCAA tournament, 1988.) Because we had such a good record in close-game situations relative to our overall winning percentage, it's hard to explain why we didn't win more overtime games. Of course, I didn't have any of that going through my head in the frantic final seconds. "It seems like I shoot these things in a vacuum," I said, post-game. "I'm not aware of the crowd, the noise, the pressure or anything. I shoot, then I come out of the vacuum. I see the score, hear the crowd, then it sinks in." So, I guess the answer to the question of "Why" is a combination of hubris, stupidity, and confidence.

One thing's for sure: this easily was Coach Newton's favorite Goheen game, and he wound up turning my name into a verb: "We Goheened 'em at the end of each half." One reporter took the liberty of providing his own definition, Webster's style:

> "Goheen (goHEEN) vt. –heened, -heening [sportsese < Vanderbilt basketball player Barry Goheen] 1. *to defeat by making a last-second shot, preferably a three-pointer.*"

In an interview two decades later on the occasion of the 20th anniversary reunion of the '88–'89 team, Coach Newton was asked about the "shot against Louisville that Goheen hit," and C.M. professed not to "remember that one," and then volunteered: "The one that sticks out to me was the three-pointer he took against Georgia when he passed [on] a sure two pointer and dribbled it out to the line. I thought he didn't know the score, but he did. He just wanted to shoot the three." And in his book, Georgia is the only buzzer-beater he detailed, though he added a little poetic license with his post-game description: "I went directly to Barry, and before I could ask him if he knew the score he said, 'I knew the score, but I didn't think your heart could take an overtime.'"

Over the ensuing years, whenever he and I were at an event and he wanted to introduce me to a friend of his, C.M. would immediately launch into the Georgia game: "Let me tell you what this guy did one time against Georgia...." And I, of course, loved it—it's great to have carved out my own little place in the astoundingly accomplished and diverse legacy of C.M. Newton. And if the Georgia game is the one for which he best remembered me, then I couldn't be prouder.

✍

At some point after the game, Coach Newton interrupted his interviews when Georgia coach Hugh Durham came into view. C.M. offered his condolences. "We've all been there, Coach," he said, "but there can't be a much tougher loss than this one." Those were heartfelt sentiments, but I doubt that they did much to soothe Coach Durham. Indeed, Durham and his players were livid that Booker was not called for a foul when he crashed into Rod Cole as he delivered the pass to me that set up the final shot. "I think it was a gutless call," fumed Durham. "It was gutless because there was no call. I don't know if it was a charge or a block, but there was definitely contact. Hell, call something." He knew that he would receive a reprimand from the SEC for the post-game criticism, but he didn't care. "If I am [repri-manded]," he said, "then I'll have a reprimand and the officials will still have a blown call."

For his part, Book knew he got away with one. "I know that I got in the air without knowing where to pass and that was a mistake," he said after the game. "But I got away with it, finding Barry." He's held onto that view ever since. "I remember being down on the floor praying that a whistle didn't blow on this," he recently recalled. "I got rid of the ball a second before the contact. I think that's what saved me. It was just a total scramble situation. The refs were focused on the basketball and Goheen did the rest." I think he's right on the point that he had passed the ball a split-second before he, in his words, "slammed into Rod Cole." While that didn't necessarily eliminate the possibility of a foul, the fact that Book didn't have the ball made it easier, I think, for the refs to swallow their whistles.

Meanwhile, Pat Hamilton struggled to explain his end-of-game gaffes—miss-ing the game-icing layup and then losing me before the final shot. "I didn't know whether to pull out and not shoot, or put it up," he said of the layup. "Of all the things, I didn't think about missing the layup." That makes sense; I'm sure the last thing he expected was to find himself wide open under the basket with the ball and a possible layup that could ice the game; most players are taught to run the clock and play "keep away" from the defense. Hamilton had just made two free throws; he likely would've made two more if he had waited for Reid to catch him and foul him. But those are a lot of strategic options to process in about a half-second, and Pat lost his concentration and blew the layup.

His defensive lapse after the miss is harder to explain, though. "I look up and no one is on Goheen," he said. "I was just trying to scramble over to him…and went by." That's not really what happened; he tried to pick my pocket while I turned my back to the basket to reach the three-point line by reaching around, and when he missed, "I was wide-open," I said later. "I was surprised and a little off-balance, but I felt like I got a pretty good shot off." Years later, Book was still perplexed: "Goheen has his back to the basket. All Hamilton needs to do is keep guarding him, and for some reason Hamilton goes for the steal, leaving Goheen open for the winning shot. That was amazing." My own view is that Pat felt like he had to compensate for the blown layup by doing something to prevent me from tying or winning the game, so he went for the steal instead of just planting himself in front of me and forcing me to shoot over him, which would have significantly increased the degree of difficulty on the shot. But, as so often happens, one mistake (blown layup) begets another (ill-advised steal attempt), and we were able to snatch victory out of the jaws of defeat.

శ

Statistically, this was the strangest game of my career. I made the first and last shots of the first half, the latter of which was from about 45 feet. "That's six points he scores in two seconds," Coach Durham said, "—the last second of both halves." I then scored our final eight points of the game on a field goal, three free throws, and the buzzer-beating trey, making every one of those shots from the field and line. For the other 37 minutes of the game I scored three points on 1-for-9 shooting, which is crazy. "Those same shots he takes during the course of the game he won't hit," Litterial Green suggested later. "Then at the end of the game he puts one up and you know it's going in. Maybe he walks around with a Leprechaun in his pocket." Regardless, my 16 points tied Book for game-high honors.

Kornet was right behind Book and me with 15 points, nearly all in the second half, when he totally outplayed Kessler. The Dawgs played well, but the cold fact was that they now were near the bottom of the league five games in, while we were near the top, with the best Vandy start to an SEC season in a decade (the 1978–79 team started SEC play 5-0):

Tennessee	4-0
Vandy	4-1
Kentucky	3-1
Alabama	3-2
LSU	3-2
Mississippi State	2-2
Florida	2-3
Ole Miss	1-3
Georgia	1-4
Auburn	0-5

శ

The next afternoon (Sunday), Charles Mayes and I went to a restaurant near campus for dinner. Previous customers had left the Sunday *Tennessean* strewn across a couple of tables, and we read about all the hullabaloo surrounding the fantastic finish from the day before. At one point, Chuck laid down the paper and looked at me. "Did you ever think about what would have happened if you had missed it?" he asked. It was the first time I had even pondered the question, which I answered in one word: "No." In fact, the truth is that it never crossed my mind that I would miss it. "At the time, you never have time to think about the consequences," I said, "You never think; 'What if I miss it?' You just put it up." As a result, "I'm prepared to take the criticism if I don't make the shot." And that, I believe, is the key to success in a pressure situation—you have to *know* that you're going to make it, not *hope* you're going to make it, and be willing to live with the consequences. Or, as clutch marksman (and NBA champion coach) Steve Kerr once explained, "Fear of missing gets in the way of a lot of players," so "[y]ou have to be willing to live with the result. You have to be tough enough to live with the result."

It's also important to block out the situation and just treat the shot as if it were any other shot taken at any other point in the game. "In my experience, I guess it was easier to block out the situation and not think that we were behind one point with 10 seconds to go and this shot I'm about to put up will or will not mean the game whether it goes in or not," I said later. "I never thought about that." "I don't think a player should think about that, it should be like the first shot of the game or the first shot of practice. That's how I tried to view it." I also remarked, "I try to block everything out and concentrate on making the shot. I know that sounds simple, but you have to realize how many other things are going on."

And that mindset certainly paid off against Georgia.

CHAPTER 24

500

I

"Life gets mighty precious when there's less of it to waste"
—Bonnie Raitt, "Nick of Time" ('88–'89)

Temporarily lost in the furor over the Georgia win was the fact that it was victory number 499 in C.M. Newton's head coaching career. I didn't even know that Coach Newton was close to such a milestone as 500 victories until a reporter mentioned it to me as part of an article on the coming landmark win. "We haven't heard anything about it from Coach Newton," I said. "Personal goals don't mean that much to him. The team is the most important thing."

Coach Newton's 500th win would make him the 11th active coach in Division I to reach the 500-win plateau; the tenth, Indiana's Bob Knight, had notched win number 500 the same day we beat Georgia. North Carolina's Dean Smith led all active coaches with 652 wins, while two other '88–'89 opposing coaches were on the list: Florida's Norm Sloan (614) and UAB's Gene Bartow (503). C.M.'s 500th victory would make him the second coach on our staff with that many; Coach Martin had won 501 games as the head coach at South Carolina State and Tennessee State before joining C.M.'s staff.

Coach Newton's first, and hopefully only, try at 500 would be a challenging one: LSU, in Baton Rouge. More than any other team in the league, the Tigers were a two-man show. Back to torment us again was Ricky Blanton, whom we last had seen the previous March willing the Tigers to victory over us in the SEC tournament the day after burying his friend and former teammate, Don Redden. Now a fifth-year senior, Ricky had upped his game still further, carrying a 23.4 scoring average into our game.

The second member of the LSU two-headed monster was a 19-year-old freshman from Gulfport, Mississippi, named Chris Jackson, who made what was surely the most spectacular debut in SEC history: in the Tigers' first SEC game, in early December at Florida, he torched the Gators for 53 points in a 111-101 LSU victory. Jackson had a medical condition known as Tourette's Syndrome, a neurochemical disorder that frequently "manifests itself in uncontrollable means, arm- and hand-flapping, and spasmodic twitching and blinking." Blanton, Jackson's next-door neighbor in the Tigers' locker room, endured involuntary slaps from Jackson because of Tourette's. There is no known cure for the condition, though Jackson took medication to control it to some degree. Shaquille O'Neal, Jackson's LSU teammate in 1989–90, recalled that Jackson "was All World on our campus" who was treated "like a god." Shaq also termed Jackson "one of the greatest shooters I had ever seen," and I would have been the first to agree in 1989.

Even with Jackson's greatness, though, the Tigers had been highly inconsistent, losing at home to Oral Roberts, barely beating McNeese State, and losing their first SEC home game to cellar-dweller Mississippi State. But, in danger of falling to 2-3 in the conference, the Tigers rallied to beat Kentucky in Rupp Arena with Jackson scoring his team's final 16 points. Jackson came into our game averaging nearly 28 points a game, meaning that he and Blanton were combining for over 50 points a game. The rest of the team wasn't quite as formidable, though. Wayne Sims, a serviceable power forward, was back, along with Lyle Mouton, a 6'4" two-guard who would wind up playing major league baseball from 1995–2001, just like another former Tiger hoopster, Ben McDonald (a 6'7" backup power forward in '87 who became "the best college pitcher ever" and the top draft pick in the '89 amateur draft, by the Orioles). Rounding out the starting five was freshman Vernel Singleton. Beyond the starters, the Tigers did not have much depth.

The game began exactly as we had feared—Jackson and Blanton were unstoppable and the other three Tigers did nothing other than pass the ball to one of them. We weren't playing that poorly, but with a couple of minutes left in the first half, LSU had stretched its lead to eight, 41-33. We couldn't afford to trail by double digits at intermission; the way Jackson and Blanton were playing, that might be an insurmountable deficit.

In fact, those last two minutes were incredible for us. Charles Mayes hit a three-pointer. I made two free throws. After a Tiger miss, we worked for the last shot and missed it, but Kornet tipped in the miss with four seconds left. Rather than just hold the ball out of bounds and let the clock run out, Singleton flipped a lazy inbounds pass toward half-court, and I turned around and the ball almost hit me in the face ("He just made a dumb pass," I matter-of-factly said later). I caught it and launched about a 22-footer in nearly one motion, just beating the buzzer. The shot found nothing but net, and just like that, we had scored 10 straight points in the final two minutes to turn and eight-point deficit into a 43-41 halftime lead—my third straight buzzer-beater at a half after the halftime half-courter and end-of-game trey against Georgia. In the Tigers' locker room, Coach Dale Brown blistered his team for allowing our late spurt—he apparently "was so angry his veins were showing in the side of his face."

With that 10-point streak to end of the half, we were in a great position to come out of the locker room for the second half and maintain that momentum. And we did. I began the second half the way I had ended the first half—with a three-pointer, giving us 13 consecutive points and a 46-41 lead. Jackson answered with a basket, but Eric Reid's three free throws on consecutive possessions pushed our lead to six, 49-43. We then received an assist from LSU Coach Brown: after Eric's last free throw fell and LSU inbounded the ball, Brown, yelling at the officials, was slapped with a technical foul. Thus, LSU lost possession and we received two technical free throws, which I made. On our ensuing possession, I hit another three-pointer to stretch our lead to 54-43 with 18:35 to play. In less than four minutes, we had outscored LSU 21-2, and I don't think I ever had a better streak in such a short span (excepting, maybe, the recent three-point jag at UK), scoring 13 of those 21 points on three treys (the only ones I made in the game) and four free throws.

At that point, LSU woke up—specifically, Chris Jackson and Ricky Blanton, especially the latter. Jackson hit a jumper, and Blanton followed with two three-pointers and a dunk off a turnover, and LSU quickly made up the deficit. All told, Blanton matched my 13-point spurt by scoring 12 points in a 17-5 LSU run that erased our lead and put LSU back on top. From that point on, it was a tense, back-and-forth affair, with both teams proving that good offense can triumph over good defense. This was one of the best games of the year, as Coach Newton acknowledged after the game: "This was just a heckuva basketball game, with a jillion big plays." It seemed as if the team that had the last possession would win it.

We led 82-81 when LSU's Sims scored with 1:10 to play to give LSU a one-point lead. We came right back with a patient offensive set and worked the ball down low to Kornet on the post. Frank made the shot with just over 40 seconds remaining to put us back in front, 84-83. That meant LSU could work for the final shot if it so chose. And it did, dribbling around out front for nearly 30 seconds, making it clear that a win-or-lose shot was coming. We had played our zone for most of the game, and all the second half. One side effect to that defensive strategy was that we had not committed hardly any team fouls in the second half—in fact, only two, which meant that we could commit four non-shooting fouls before LSU would even be entitled to shoot free throws. Accordingly, Coach Newton instructed us to foul whatever LSU player had the ball before he could attempt a shot.

Not surprisingly, the LSU player with the ball was Chris Jackson, and Derrick Wilcox was guarding him. With about 11 seconds left, after 30 seconds of holding the ball, Jackson, about 35 feet from the basket, began to make his move; Derrick reached in and committed the foul, forcing LSU to inbound the ball near half court and start all over. Jackson took the inbounds pass about 30 feet from the basket and began his move again. This time, he got around Derrick before Derrick could commit the foul deep in the backcourt; by the time Derrick caught him and committed the foul, Jackson was at the free-throw line. The good news is that he was unable to take the shot before Derrick's foul; the bad news was that the foul was committed so deep in the frontcourt that LSU now would inbound the ball on the baseline underneath its basket, not on the sideline 30 or 35 feet from the basket. Four seconds remained.

Now it was Jackson that inbounded the ball. Blanton was stationed on the block right in front of him. Jackson lobbed the inbounds pass to Blanton, then stepped inbounds while Blanton, still with the ball, set a pick on Derrick, which gave Jackson just enough space to receive a pass from Blanton about 18 feet from the basket and launch a shot with about two seconds remaining. It found nothing but net as time expired, giving LSU a thrilling 85-84 victory, a stunning reversal of fortune for us after our similarly remarkable victory over Georgia four days earlier.

Jackson's buzzer-beater was clutch, but I wished Coach Newton had called timeout once it became apparent that LSU would receive the ball under the basket. There was no way anyone other than Blanton or Jackson would take the final shot. We could have, and probably should have, double-teamed Blanton so that Jackson could not have inbounded the ball to him; Ricky, a smart player, played it perfectly once he got the ball, as he simultaneously "made himself big," as Wilcox said, to set the screen and deliver the ball back to Jackson, who said, "I just got the ball and let it go." And I immediately regretted not doing something to prevent the winning shot. On the inbounds play, the Tiger I was nearest to was Dennis Tracey, a walk-on who had contributed some key plays in the second half, including a three-pointer. There was absolutely no way, however, that Tracey would have been an option to take the shot. I should have just abandoned Tracey and tackled Blanton after Ricky received the inbounds pass, thus forcing one more out-of-bounds play, this time with only two or three seconds to play, which likely would have prevented an additional pass after the inbounds pass, meaning that LSU's options would have been more limited.

Nevertheless, you had to hand it to Jackson. "He's a pressure player who made a pressure shot," I said after the game. Indeed, my post-game assessment of Jackson—"He's as good as advertised"—was, if anything, an understatement. Jackson went 15-for-25 from the field, including 4-for-7 from behind the arc, for 34 points. He added seven assists to boot. He had the quickest release I had ever seen—and I still haven't seen a quicker one in the last three decades. He needed hardly any space between himself and the defender to launch a shot, and he elevated well, making him seem taller than his listed height of 6'1".

That said, the most valuable player for the Tigers was Ricky Blanton. In addition to spearheading the Tigers' second-half comeback, he hit big shot after big shot in the final 10 minutes of the game. "This is one of the best games Ricky has played in his career," Coach Brown said after the game, and that wasn't puffery—Blanton went 12-for-17 from the field and, like Jackson, hit four of his seven three-point attempts and dished out seven assists, finishing with 28 points. In the end, as Coach Newton said, "Jackson and Blanton were outstanding. They hit big basket after big basket." The duo combined for 62 of LSU's 85 points, going 27-for-42 from the field; the rest of the team hit only eight field goals in 25 attempts.

We were much more balanced, and I led the way with 24 points, a season high at that point, including a perfect 9-for-9 from the line; my free-throw issues were behind me. Eric Reid had a great game with 16 points, seven rebounds, and three blocks, while Kornet added 14 points and seven boards. Booker scored 13, and while it was a tough loss, it really wasn't one that would bring us down. We had played well in a hostile atmosphere, and a great player had made a tough shot to beat us; those things happen. "We did everything we could have done and should have done to win the game," Coach Newton commented. "I congratulate LSU, but at the same time I'm very proud of our team." Kornet probably expressed it best from the players' perspective: "This is a really tough loss. It's disappointing to get so close to a big SEC win but I still think the race is wide open." He was exactly right. Still, the last-second win enabled LSU to tie us in the standings with a 4-2 record.

II

"Racing thru my brain, and I just can't contain this feelin' that remains"
—The La's, "There She Goes" ('88–'89)

Coach Newton's second try for win number 500 would take place in Memorial Gym three days after the LSU game. But it wouldn't be an SEC game; we would step outside the conference for our final non-conference game of the regular season. And, like the Notre Dame games of the previous two seasons, this conference play interruption was no gimme; our opponent was the Texas Longhorns, a power in the (now defunct) Southwest Conference. The Longhorns entered the game with a 13-3 record, and they were nicknamed the "Runnin' Horns" for a reason—they averaged 95.9 points a game, sixth in the nation. Impressively, four 'Horns combined to average 75 points a game—6'2" guard Travis Mays, 6'4" guard Lance Blanks, 6'8" frontcourter Alvin Heggs, and supersub guard Joey Wright. "They've got four Chris Jacksons," I observed, referencing our most recent foe. The Longhorns' coach, Tom Penders, was in his first season in Austin, having come to Texas from the University of Rhode Island, where he had coached the Rams to the Sweet Sixteen in '88.

The quest for 500 aside, this was going to be exciting: CBS would be televising the game nationally, which was a big deal in 1989. The usual 15,000+ would be cheering us on in what promised to be a high-scoring, up-tempo contest. We did not get off to a promising start, however. We spent the first five minutes "fumbling passes and blowing easy shots" to dig ourselves an early hole. In fact, the Texas lead ballooned to 13, 34-21, with around five minutes left in the first half. Then, as with the LSU game, we caught fire. I nailed a three-pointer and, after a Texas miss, Kornet carded a conventional three-point play to cut the Texas lead to 34-27. Joey Wright hit a jumper, but Morgan Wheat, substituting for a foul-plagued Eric Reid, answered with a three-pointer to make it 36-30. Morgan then rebounded a Texas miss, which led to a Kornet layup, and we tied the game at 36 on baskets by Booker and Wilcox. Wheat then made another big play, coming up with a steal that we cashed into two Kornet free throws and a 38-36 lead. The teams traded baskets before the half and we entered the locker room with a 40-38 lead, closing the half on a 19-4 run.

Just like our previous game against LSU, we sustained the momentum of our end-of-half spurt to begin the second half. Booker led the way this time, hitting a trey and adding a layup as we stormed to a 58-45 lead in the first five minutes of the second half. Over the 10-minute period spanning the last five minutes of the first half and the first five minutes of the second half, we had outscored the Longhorns 37-11. Then, I encountered uncharacteristic foul trouble, picking up two quick fouls early in the second half and heading to the bench with 14:27 left with four fouls. Charles Mayes replaced me for a more conventional lineup of two guards and three frontcourters. Charles played well, but the Longhorns slowly chipped away at our lead. By the 8:27 mark, our lead had been shaved to five, 69-64. But we were equal to the challenge this time. Mayes hit a twisting layup, then Booker struck again with a three-pointer and a steal-and-layup sequence that give us some breathing room. From that point, the countdown to C.M. victory number 500 was on. I finally re-entered the game with 1:33 remaining so that I could be on the floor for the final seconds. We closed it out with a 94-79 victory as most of the Memorial Gym patrons chanted "C.M.! C.M.!"

The chant was just the beginning of the celebration. Gold and black balloons fell from the rafters. Athletic director Roy Kramer presented Coach Newton with the game ball and made a brief but heartfelt speech to the crowd. "To win 500 games is a great accomplishment," he said. "To win it on national television is a great thing. To do it at home is a great thing. But to win 500 games with class, that's something extra special for this 15,000 here today." Chancellor Joe Wyatt—ironically, a graduate of the University of Texas—echoed those remarks: "There is not a classier person in the game, nor one with more integrity." For his part, C.M. gave credit to several people, including his wife, Evelyn (who, indeed, was one of the greats), Adolph Rupp (his college coach at UK), Bear Bryant (his athletic director at Alabama), and Coach Bostick. In fact, of C.M.'s 500 victories, Coach Bostick had been with him for 331 of them. "I share this with him," Coach Newton said. "I can't thank John enough, or repay him in any way for his loyalty."

The 500th victory reflected a true team effort. We blitzed Texas 54-41 in the second half, shooting a blistering 69.2% from the field. All five starters scored in double figures. Booker had 16 points, four rebounds, and four assists. Despite foul trouble, Reid (27 minutes) and I (22 minutes, my fewest all season other than the Chaminade game) scored 14 each. Wilcox scored 10 and nearly matched his three-week-old assists record by dishing out 12. The bench was stellar, led by Charles

Mayes; playing most of the second half in my place, Chuck hit all three of his shots from the field for six points, and he added five boards.

The real star of the game, however, was Frank Kornet. In fact, the Texas game was the crowning moment in a comeback from two years' worth of pain and inconsistent play. Frank began the 1988–89 season in positive condition, both physically and mentally. Plus, as his health and conditioning improved, Frank simply outworked most opposing big men. He hustled on every play and expected the same from his teammates, and he led by example. At least one SEC coach, Mississippi State's Richard Williams, thought Frank was as hard—or harder—to defend than his predecessor at center. "At times," he said, "I felt Frank gives you more problems in the post than Will Perdue....Will didn't turn and score as well as Frank does. Frank really presents different problems." It all came together for Frank against Texas. He scored 25 points (11-for-13 from the foul line) and pulled down 16 rebounds, both of which were, and would remain, career highs.

In a private moment after the game, Roy Kramer reflected further on his head basketball coach and his achievements at Vanderbilt. "You know," he said, "C.M. has set a standard of coaching ethics that puts our program on a high plateau. And in the process, he has won games, crucial games, raising the stature of our program nationally." He concluded, "I can go to sleep at night, not worrying about what's going on in our basketball program." Within 48 hours, though, Roy would be worrying, as the most spectacular twist in a season full of them was about to unfold.

25

RESIGNATION

We returned to the practice floor on Monday, January 23, to begin the preparation for our next opponent, Florida. With the pressure of delivering Coach Newton's 500th win behind us, we were loose, though the flu bug was beginning to infiltrate the team. Still, we had a crisp practice of the usual two hours. To my surprise, C.M. called a post-practice meeting in the locker room—not unheard of, but not that common either during the season. What could he possibly want to talk about?

Resigning his post at Vanderbilt to become the athletic director at the University of Kentucky, that's what.

I

"A strange dust lands on your hands and on your face"
—Morrissey, "Every Day Is Like Sunday" ('88)

Charles Martin Newton was born in Rockwood, Tennessee, in 1930. When C.M. was nine months old, the family—father, mother, and the three kids, of whom C.M. was the youngest—moved to Fort Lauderdale, Florida. With equal love, and, apparently, facility for both basketball and baseball (and football too), C.M.'s teams won state championships in both sports at Fort Lauderdale High. He was offered scholarships in several sports and to several schools, and chose the University of Kentucky because UK promised him that he would play both basketball (for the legendary Adolph Rupp) and baseball.

C.M. arrived in Lexington in fall 1948, playing on the freshman hoops team—freshmen were ineligible to play on the "varsity" in those days—and on the baseball team. In his junior season, the Wildcats won the 1951 NCAA basketball championship, beating Kansas State for the title. C.M., though, didn't play that much and was never a starter. Meanwhile, his baseball prospects were on the rise. After that junior season, the aspiring pitcher gave up his final season of basketball eligibility to sign with the New York Yankees, receiving a $10,000 bonus.

Then, a series of events triggered by the famous point-shaving scandal that engulfed UK's program (among others) in the early '50s led to C.M.'s becoming "Coach Newton" at Transylvania University, a small college in Lexington, where he coached the basketball team part-time while completing his degree at UK. In 1955,

C.M. left the Yankees organization and signed on as Transy's full-time basketball coach. C.M.'s 500th head-coaching victory was on January 20, 1989; his first official head-coaching victory had been way back in fall 1955 at Transy. Just a few years later, in 1959, Coach Newton had his first encounter with a member of my family, when my father, a sophomore on his high school basketball team that was participating in the state tournament in Lexington, practiced with his teammates in the Transylvania gym, courtesy of C.M. Newton.

After compiling a 169-137 record at Transylvania, C.M. was hired by Alabama athletic director/football coach Bear Bryant in 1968. Bryant had been UK's football coach when C.M. was a student there, forming with Adolph Rupp what was easily the greatest basketball/football coaching tandem in NCAA history. (Perhaps the runner-up tandem was coaching at Duke during the 1988–89 season—Steve Spurrier in football and Coach K in basketball.) Coach Newton did great things at Alabama. He integrated the program ("a pioneer in race relations in the Deep South," according to Dick Vitale), improved from a 4-20 record (1-17 in the SEC) in his first season of 1968–69 to a 13-5 record in the SEC by his fourth season, and would lead 'Bama basketball to at least 11 SEC victories in his last nine seasons. He coached the Tide to the SEC co-championship in 1973–74, though co-champ Vanderbilt would represent the SEC in the NCAA tournament by virtue of the Commodores' season sweep of the Tide, and he took the Tide to its first NCAA tournament in 1974–75. His 1975–76 team won the SEC title and gave Bob Knight's unbeaten Indiana Hoosiers their toughest test in the NCAA tournament on their way to being the last undefeated NCAA champion.

Coach Newton left Alabama in 1980, having won 211 games in 12 seasons. He accepted a job as an associate commissioner of the SEC, overseeing basketball operations, in 1980. At the 1981 SEC tournament—the same one I attended as an eighth grader and saw Vanderbilt upset Kentucky—C.M. ran into Roy Kramer, who began the process of recruiting C.M. to be the Commodores' next basketball coach. Coach Kramer's recruiting efforts were successful, and after only a year out of coaching, C.M. took the reins of the Commodores' program in fall 1981.

His first Vanderbilt team went 15-13, and the second, the 1982–83 squad, went 19-14 and made the school's first-ever NIT appearance, winning one game before losing in the second round. Things went south after that, though, as the Commodores went 14-15 in 1983–84 and bottomed out with the 11-17, last-place SEC finish in 1984–85, occasioned by what C.M. called his "recruiting mistakes." It had taken a lot of hard work, but Coach Newton had returned the Vanderbilt program to the position it had occupied for most of Roy Skinner's tenure, which meant that the program was consistently competitive in the SEC and on a national level. So why leave now?

II

"Everybody's talkin' all this stuff about me"
—*Bobby Brown, "My Prerogative"* ('89)

On December 31, 1988, the day after Stanford routed us in the MCIT final, Coach Newton drove to Elizabethtown, Kentucky—about two hours north of Nashville on Interstate 65—to meet with University of Kentucky President David Roselle. Roselle had forced UK's athletic director, Wildcat hoops great Cliff Hagan, to resign a couple of months earlier because of the storm clouds gathering over the UK hoops program, including the $1,000 Emery Worldwide package that Assistant Coach Dwayne Casey had sent to Chris Mills's father and the cheating allegations that surrounded Eric Manuel's standardized entrance test. Now, he wanted C.M. Newton to become the school's new director of athletics.

C.M. was, by his account, cold to the idea at first—"almost rude," he recalled. After all, he and Hagan had been teammates on UK's 1951 national championship team. So, he "turned it down," telling Roselle that "I wanted to coach Vanderbilt, that I was going to retire there." After that initial contact, C.M. told *The Tennessean*'s John Bibb that "I had no interest in going to Kentucky and that my only goal was coaching the Vanderbilt basketball team." This was probably an error in judgment on C.M.'s part—Bibb clearly remembered that statement.

At the New Year's Eve meeting in Elizabethtown, when Roselle had the chance to make a face-to-face pitch, he clearly made the most of his opportunity. What evidently turned the tide for C.M. was the difference between being "wanted" and "needed," with the latter a more powerful pull. "I was convinced by people I respect that I was not only wanted as the AD at Kentucky, I was needed," the coach said. "The needed part was more significant to me than the wanted part.... Things were in total disarray," he recalled. "It was my school and pretty screwed up.... To me it was important to come to my school and see if we couldn't get the thing straightened out." C.M. had one more meeting in Bowling Green, Kentucky, in January, with the chairman of the search committee, and after that meeting he was offered the job. None of the other 60 applicants was even considered.

And so it was that, in the early evening of January 23, 1989, C.M. Newton stood before us in our locker room to announce that he had accepted the position of athletic director at the University of Kentucky. (That he had insisted that he be called UK's "vice president in charge of athletics" and not "athletic director" was not exactly important to us.)

The words to describe my reaction, then and later, were "shock" (the day of the announcement: "It was a big surprise; it was a shock.") and "earth-shaking" (nearly 25 years later: "That was an earth-shaking event for us."). Another player compared it to "a death in the family."

It is true that Coach Newton had stood before us around the time of the Kentucky game in Lexington and said that he didn't intend to go anywhere, whether it was UK or anywhere else. I believed him then. Everyone did. "I think he was honest with us three weeks ago," I said at the time. "I think he was honest with us now. I think it was a difficult decision for him." And I am certain he believed it too: Circumstances change, and they can change quickly; no doubt, the UK events moved at warp speed because of the dire situation UK was facing.

As players, we were focused on the season, meaning the next game, and then the next game, and so on, not to mention keeping up with the academic side of things as we moved into the high-stress part of the season. But that necessarily myopic approach didn't mean that we were living in some bubble and hadn't heard all the rumors swirling around that this might happen; we had chosen not to believe them, I guess. "It came as a surprise to me," Kornet said, "although everybody had been hearing the talk." Perhaps if we had been less naïve, the announcement wouldn't have come as such a shock. Maybe this was just a collective case of cognitive dissonance. In any event, Coach Newton told us that he intended to finish out the season as our head coach; he would assume his new post at UK on April 1, 1989. That led to whispers—or louder—that C.M. was a "lame duck" coach, but he was having none of that: "I may be a duck and I may be lame, but I'm not a lame duck."

But that wasn't how some people, especially those at *The Tennessean*, saw matters. The paper's sports editor, John Bibb, felt that he had been lied to a few weeks earlier when C.M. told him that he wasn't interested in the UK position. Bibb's headline made it clear where he stood: "Newton should exit Vandy now." Bibb opined that "it is unwise for Newton to continue in his role as Vanderbilt coach" and that continuing as coach while having accepted the job at UK "drips with potential conflict-of-interest charges." I never bought into that "potential," and such a conflict never materialized anyway. C.M. would continue to be Vanderbilt's head basketball coach through March; he wouldn't be on UK's payroll until April 1. Any person of integrity—and C.M. was a person of the highest integrity—would focus his energies on making the last four to six weeks of his coaching career as successful as possible. And C.M. did just that.

The bottom line is that coaches change jobs all the time. I had undergone a head-coaching change in high school, and Vanderbilt's football players had experienced a change in head coaches between my freshman and sophomore seasons. College basketball coaches are a transient group; they resign, retire, or get fired with great regularity.

None of that, though, necessarily made Coach Newton's announcement easy to digest, especially at first. One issue was the fact that Coach Newton had pledged to me that he would be my coach for all four years. Of course, he had honored that pledge to me as well as to Kornet and Booker because we were seniors, but what about the rest of the team? "He told me he would be here all four years," I said. "I'm sure he told our freshmen and sophomores the same thing. I hope they'll understand, but I really can't blame them if they don't." Consider, for example, Scott Draud, who arguably was the player most adversely affected. Scott had lobbied for and was granted redshirt status for the 1988–89 season, no doubt on the assumption that C.M. Newton would be his coach for his final two seasons. Absent exceptional circumstances, players are given five years (if needed) to play four; now Scott had used his one redshirt season only to see the head coach resign in the middle of it. The new coach, Draud said, "will be a guy who didn't recruit me," but, he diplomatically added, "I'm looking forward to working under someone else's system"—which may or may not have been a comment on how C.M. had deployed Scott in his first two seasons of eligibility.

Still, I have always had a problem with the fact that C.M. announced his resignation right in the middle of the season. "The timing could have been better," I said then. "I wish he had been able to wait till after the season." On this point, I think C.M. sacrificed the best interests of Vanderbilt for the best interests of Kentucky. Indeed, I've never understood why it was important that C.M. announce what in effect was his future resignation. Technically, he wasn't resigning now, but rather resigning effective April 1—right after his 500th win and right in the middle of a heated SEC race, in which we were very much a factor. Draud echoed my thoughts on the timing: "I don't guess there was a good time to announce it, but if there is anything bad it's that it came at this time in the season." Booker agreed: "Right in the middle of the SEC race is a tough time to deal with it."

To me, the inescapable conclusion is that C.M.—perhaps pressured by UK's brass, perhaps not—made the announcement in January so that the NCAA, which was licking its chops to lower the boom on UK's basketball program, might immediately start considering some semblance of leniency toward the program. Had the announcement been made two months later, after the season had concluded, the NCAA might have been further down the road toward levying the harsh penalties everyone assumed were coming. But that was a problem, or set of problems, that UK had brought on itself. Whatever the penalties would be, presumably they would be deserved; announcing in January that C.M. Newton would take the helm of the athletic department in April was nothing more than the first step in a public relations charm offensive that UK hoped would eventually help its case with the NCAA—or, as one writer said, "a ploy by UK to buy itself some 11th-hour respectability." And, sure enough, just a couple of weeks later, UK delivered its written response to the NCAA's allegations of wrongdoing, and one of the things the school touted was its hiring of C.M. Newton as athletic director. Obviously, the school couldn't have publicized that "corrective action" if C.M. had insisted that the hire be kept under wraps until after the season.

Accordingly, we, the Vanderbilt players, were caught in the middle. I feel that C.M. used the timing of his announcement to put the interests of his future employer ahead of those of his soon-to-be former employer, so he exposed himself to the "conflict of interest" and other charges. Kornet saw C.M.'s side of things, saying, "I think he had to make the announcement now, because if he had tried to keep it quiet it would've leaked out. It was better that we heard it from him." I suppose that's one way to view it, but more important decisions than this one have been kept under wraps for a lot longer than two months. And, as C.M. said, he told only a few people. Plus, a simple "no comment" may have done the trick for a while. Clearly, reasonable minds could differ, but I still feel that the timing of the announcement could have been handled better under the circumstances.

C.M. defended his decision. "There's been so much speculation," he said. "I just felt that to end all the speculations, the distractions and so on that this was the appropriate time." If he was suggesting that he would end "the distractions" by announcing his resignation with two months remaining in the season, surely he was misquoted—it created an enormous distraction for us for the remainder of the season. It may have alleviated, or even eliminated, distractions on the UK side, but the distractions were just beginning for us, the Vandy players. I think C.M. knew there would be distractions either way, and he chose to lessen the distractions for UK while creating them for us.

III

"You can't erase a memory"
—*Living Colour, "Open Letter (To a Landlord)"* ('88–'89)

The basic issue of coaches leaving schools—and the players they recruited to those schools—is a complicated one. It's disappointing to read stories of coaches who ink long-term contracts with schools only to leave a year or two later for some job that didn't seem to be a good fit anyway, other than financially, for the coach. You have to question the integrity of those coaches. The situation with Coach Newton was different because UK was his alma mater. Vanderbilt had been the beneficiary of that same emotional pull just a couple of years earlier when 1960s Commodore football star Watson Brown, a fine man whom I always liked and respected, left a promising rebuilding job at Cincinnati to return to Vandy as the head coach and an even more challenging rebuilding job—and in a much tougher conference. "It gets in your blood," Watson commented on C.M.'s announcement. "You can't say no."

Moreover, C.M. didn't make the switch for money; by his account, he took a serious pay cut to return to UK. He was making $400,000 a year at Vanderbilt, and his base salary upon becoming UK's athletic director was only $110,000, though UK sweetened the pot with some sort of annuity. So, the common criticisms leveled at coaches simply didn't apply to Coach Newton's situation.

Still, the issue of the players left behind is a troubling one. While coaches can leave their school for another school without, for example, sitting out a year, players do not have the same privilege. If they want to follow a coach to his new school, they must sit out a year. Is that fair? Coach Newton articulated the prevailing view, no doubt consistent with the NCAA's: "No one person is the Vanderbilt program. The program and the school override the individual." Technically, that sentiment is, or at least should be, true; recruits shouldn't fixate on just the basketball program but should assess the entire university and try to project the college experience at that campus. On my first visit to Vandy in spring 1984, I visited the law school because I had expressed an interest in perhaps obtaining a law degree after college.

The reality, though, is that most recruits choose a school because of the program and its coaches. After all, it is the head coach and his assistants who do the recruiting, whether it is writing letters, meeting parents, or attending games at various high schools in metropolitan or rural areas all over the place. In fact, Coach Bostick attended a couple of my high school *baseball* games even after I had committed to Vandy. You don't see an economics or chemistry professor doing that!

What of the freshmen? Morgan Wheat explained that "Coach Newton and Coach Martin were 90% of the reasons I came here," and he warned that "I might have to leave if I'm not happy with the next coach." In fact, he did, though not immediately. And then there was Draud, who was in the middle of his redshirt season, thus leaving him with two years to play his final two seasons; transferring was no longer an option for Scott, and you could sense his frustration. "I came to Vanderbilt because of Coach Newton. Not only that, but I redshirted this season because of him," he said. "I've run out of options."

The second issue is the fact that Coach Newton was leaving the school that was renowned for "doing things the right way" for a school that was clearly cheating and that only reached out to him in the first place because (finally) its hand had been caught in the cookie jar (or at least the Emery Worldwide package). "Honesty appears to be lacking in that program," I said, "and Coach Newton is an honest person." "I know Coach Newton will go into Kentucky and clean it up," Kornet predicted. "He'll make it like Vanderbilt. There won't be any cheating going on."

Whatever the reasons and however pure Coach Newton's motives, it was difficult to accept that your coach had found a more attractive position and felt compelled not only to accept it but also to announce his acceptance in the middle of the season. Even though he was running to an opportunity and not running away from Vanderbilt, that distinction is just an exercise in semantics. So, it was hard to come to terms with the fact that, whatever his reasons, Coach Newton found, in effect, a prettier date for the prom. The feeling of rejection was inevitable. I guess, in the end, the tug of the alma mater was stronger than we players thought. "Obviously," Draud observed, "his loyalty to the University of Kentucky runs deeper than I thought." Me too.

Coach Newton's announcement meant that the last couple of months of the 1988–1989 season wouldn't just mark the final games of the Booker/Kornet/Goheen trio. Those final games would also mark the end of the C.M. Newton era at Vanderbilt. And many of them would be memorable.

26

THE TENNIS BALL GAME

Despite Coach Newton's resignation, the schedule did not come to a halt. The games still had to be played when and where the schedule told us. And that meant that about 48 hours after Coach Newton's resignation announcement, we were to take the Memorial Gym floor against Florida.

I

"I know life is hard…where to turn?"
—*R.E.M., "Get Up" ('88–'89)*

If ever a game were set up for a loss, it was this one, even though it was at home. How would we react to our coach's resignation? Plus, all five starters were in various stages of fighting the flu. Booker, Wilcox, and Reid were in bad shape, and Kornet and I were getting there. As a team that relied heavily on its starting five, a flu-ridden starting quintet was a definite disadvantage. An additional, though flattering, distraction was that ABC News was reporting a story on me and had set up the interviews for the couple of days preceding the Florida game, unwittingly walking right into the Newton-UK maelstrom.

Certainly, "maelstrom" was the proper word to describe the situation because when we took the practice floor on Tuesday for the first time since the resignation announcement, we encountered what was accurately described as a "media siege that completely disrupted" our practice session. It seemed that every credentialed media person in the Commonwealth of Kentucky—whether print, radio, or television—had descended on Memorial Gym. There were enough people in there to qualify as a decent-sized crowd for a school like, say, Mississippi State. Obviously, Coach Newton was the object of most of the media's interview requests, but Kornet and I, as Kentuckians and seniors, had to endure the onslaught as well. It was draining, even more so given that we were both fighting off the flu (unsuccessfully as it turned out). There are only so many times I could say "it was a shock" and "the timing could have been better," while wanting to say what was most important and immediate at the moment—"we've got to get ready for Florida."

꙳

Florida was one of the preseason SEC favorites, but had not played to those expectations through 18 games. The Gators came to Nashville with a 9-9 record, 3-4 in the SEC. They had lost four of their first six conference games but showed signs of rounding into form with an 81-57 thumping of Mississippi State the previous Saturday.

The Florida game meant another visit from the Gators' 7'2" mullet-topped center, Dwayne Schintzius, who was "known in basketball circles as the most hated center in college basketball" and "one of the bad boys in college basketball." Dwayne had burnished those credentials with an off-season incident that was the first in a daisy chain of events that would come to a head in our game. He had gotten into an altercation with a couple of Florida students outside a Gainesville nightclub at 2 a.m. Apparently, looking to even his odds because he was outnumbered, Schintzius brandished a tennis racket against his would-be assailants. That semi-comical event resulted in Dwayne's being suspended for Florida's opening games of the season. Further, the headline-making contretemps gave the fans of Florida's opponents plenty of ammunition for Schintzius, who was an easy target anyway because of his stature and well-known attitude problems. But he claimed to be a new man on the eve of our game: "I was known as a crier and a whiner…I was cocky, arrogant, and self-centered," he said, speaking as if those character flaws were a thing of the past. He asserted that his summer experience as part of the Olympic trials had turned him around. "I grew up a lot over the summer."

This new-found maturity was sorely tested by Gator opponents in the wake of the tennis racket incident. Opposing student sections came to games armed with tennis balls, with which they would remind him of his off-season misstep. It happened at both Georgia and Tennessee, and on each occasion technical fouls were called on the home team. In the Tennessee game, the UT students hurled their tennis balls onto the floor at the start of the game, "and covered the floor with literally hundreds of tennis balls." In the Gators' other SEC road tilt prior to our game, a tennis ball fired from the Ole Miss student section hit Schintzius in the ankle.

The tennis ball shenanigans overshadowed the reality that Schintzius had, in fact, become a better player. The previous season, he'd been embarrassed by Pittsburgh's Charles Smith, who outscored him 30-2 in a Pitt romp; then, in the SEC tournament, Schintzius inexplicably refused to report back into the game with one second remaining in a 72-70 loss to Georgia. So far in 1988–89, however, he was averaging a solid double-double of 19.9 points and 10.4 rebounds a game.

Schintzius was one-third of what was easily the best frontline in the SEC, and one of the best in the entire country. Dwayne Davis was a 6'8" bruiser with practically no shooting touch outside five feet but who was a terrific rebounder. Livingston Chatman was a 6'7" forward with a soft and accurate shooting touch out to 16–18 feet. Those three frontcourters had to carry the team because the Gators had lost their fine backcourt of the year before with the departures of Vernon Maxwell and

Ronnie Montgomery. Senior Clifford Lett proved to be a capable starter, with Renaldo Garcia and long-range marksman Kelly McKinnon also manning the backcourt. And that was it; the Gators only played six men.

Florida's coach, Norm Sloan, suddenly shared something in common with Coach Newton: both had decided to leave one coaching job for another before the season was over. In Sloan's case, in 1980 he decided to resign from his head-coaching position at North Carolina State, which he had led to the 1974 NCAA championship, to take the head-coaching job in Florida. Unlike C.M., Sloan decided not to announce his decision until after the season, but he firmly supported C.M.'s decision to announce his resignation now: "I admire his courage for taking the honest way out."

II

"People say I'm obsessed"
—Fine Young Cannibals, "She Drives Me Crazy" ('89)

As usual for an SEC game, Memorial was practically full: 15,498 were in attendance. The fans were warned before the opening tip that "throwing objects onto the court" would result in a technical foul being assessed on the home team. Those fans would see what, even 25 years later, was termed "the most bizarre ending to a game that Vanderbilt fans would ever witness." The game started out benignly enough; in fact, a bit of drama concerned what reception the fans would give Coach Newton as his name was announced after the player introductions. In fact, C.M. received a standing ovation. After that, though, we played like a team that had just lost its coach and whose five starters were under the weather—in other words, like zombies. Florida, though, didn't play much better. The two teams combined to shoot an abysmal 31% in the first half, and the visitors led by the unimpressive score of 25-24 at the half.

Both teams found their offensive rhythm in the second half, which made for an exciting half of basketball. We found our sea legs first, scoring the first eight points of the half to claim a seven-point lead. But Schintzius began to assert himself inside while guards Garcia and McKinnon each hit two three-pointers in the second half. That inside/outside combo enabled the Gators to erase our early second-half lead and forge a five-point advantage of their own. We countered with our own inside-outside duo to keep it close. Kornet worked effectively against the taller Schintzius while Booker heated up from beyond the arc, draining five threes in the second half, which prevented the Gators from pulling away. Eventually, we caught the Gators and tied the game twice in the closing minutes, at 63 and 67. But we couldn't get over the hump. Each time we knotted the game the Gators would untie it. So it was that Florida broke in front again, 70-67, in the final minute.

That's when the real craziness began. Florida had a chance to extend the lead at the free-throw line, but Lett missed; we came down with a chance to tie with a three. We tried one but came up empty; Kornet, however, claimed the rebound. I was stationed behind the three-point line around the area of the top of the key, and Frank delivered the ball to me. Lett, who had been in the paint area as part of the scrum for the rebound, came flying at me as I attempted the three-pointer. He didn't clip my shooting hand, but he knocked my legs out from under me as the ball left my hand, knocking me to the floor for a foul...right as the ball went in the basket for a game-tying three. Suddenly, the game was tied at 70 with 27 seconds to go, and I had a free throw that would give us the lead.

I was as shocked as everyone else at this turn of events. This was only the third season of the three-point line, and I had never seen a four-point play before, but one here might give us the victory. I hit the free throw for the four-point play and a 71-70 lead. If we could hold the lead, this might be my favorite game-winning shot of them all.

We retreated downcourt to our familiar 2-3 zone, looking for the defensive stop that might secure the victory. We didn't need one: Florida got lazy on the entry pass once it crossed into the frontcourt, and I stepped right into the passing lane and intercepted. Now we had the ball and a one-point lead, and with only about 20 seconds remaining, Florida had to foul us, or we would run out the clock. I then did something that I've regretted ever since—I passed the ball. Players generally are taught, or even instinctually are aware, when they know that the opposing team needs to foul, that they should try to get rid of the ball to a teammate before an opposing player can commit the foul; I guess this is some heightened form of "keep away," with the idea that finding an open teammate, who will then do the same, and so on, until the final seconds melt away, is the preferred course of action.

So, I got rid of the ball to the first teammate I saw, who was Barry Booker. Before Book could make a pass, though, he was fouled and went to the line for the one-and-one. Book had been quite hot from three-point range in the second half, but he had not shot a free throw in the entire game; on the other hand, I had just hit a free throw a few seconds earlier, and I would not have missed these. But Book would be the shooter, not me, and he missed the front end of the one-and-one. Florida rebounded and had another chance for victory, still trailing us by a single point. Inside 10 seconds to play, the Gators attempted their shot and missed. Again, there was a heated scramble for the rebound, and again it was Kornet who outhustled and outmuscled everyone to grab it. Desperate now, the Gators fouled Frank to force another one-and-one opportunity. Six seconds remained. Frank hit the first free throw to give us a 72-70 lead, but he missed the second. The Gators rebounded and had a final chance to tie the game with a field goal or win it with a trey.

Without any timeouts, the Gators were a little flustered, even though six seconds is plenty of time to work some late-game magic, as we had proven many times in the past few seasons. Lett rushed the ball down the floor and looked for Schintzius, who had hustled the length of the floor after Frank's miss. With just a couple of seconds left, Lett cut loose a pass toward the basket from 35–40 feet away, aiming for Schintzius, but he airmailed it, and the ball sailed over Schintzius's head out of bounds. That was the ballgame, or so it seemed.

The fans thought it was over, too, or at least some of them did, because some of them tossed tennis balls on the floor in Schintzius's direction. Dwayne picked one up and menacingly faked throwing a fastball back into the stands. Typical post-game hijinks, I thought. Except that this wasn't "post-game." In fact, the scoreboard clock still showed 00:01; the game was not over. And because it wasn't, the referees still were in charge, and one of them, John Clougherty, dramatically made the "T" sign with his hands, signaling that he had called a technical foul on the Vanderbilt crowd, which meant that Florida would receive two free throws.

The whole thing happened so quickly that I couldn't really process what had just transpired. I clearly remember what I was thinking, though, when I saw none other than Dwayne Schintzius step to the line: "Huh? There's no way he'll make both under the circumstances." When a technical foul is assessed, the opposing team can choose any of the five players then on the floor to shoot the free throws. That player is almost always a guard or sweet-shooting forward. Whoever heard of a 7'2" center shooting technical foul shots when the team needs to make both to extend the game? Unfortunately, my confidence in Schintzius's abilities at the line was seriously misplaced. With the crowd roaring, he calmly made both, and I don't think either one even touched the rim. And, just like that, the game was tied at 72. The technical also meant that Florida regained possession, but it couldn't do much in one second from half court, where it received the ball. Thus, we headed to overtime.

Just as Pitt had experienced in our NCAA battle the year before, we had lost what seemed like a sure victory and found ourselves playing an extra five minutes we never expected to play. Coupled with the fact that the five starters were run down by illness anyway, asking for another five minutes was too much. Still in shock, we had little chance of recovering from the stunning technical foul. We didn't even score until 20 seconds remained in overtime, and by then Schintzius had scored seven unanswered points, fouled out Kornet, and put the game away. The final score was 81-78, Gators.

III

"What a wicked thing to do"
—Chris Isaak, "Wicked Game" ('89)

The shock of the tennis ball incident had not worn off by the time we entered the locker room. It was like a morgue. Everyone was devastated. Not surprisingly, anger was the prevailing emotion. Coach Newton termed the ball-tossers "damn yokels who got carried away." I blustered that whoever threw the balls "better run. They've got about 12 guys after them." Most of us would've agreed with Coach Newton's summation that this was "the toughest loss I've ever been associated with." Of the players, no one was more upset than Frank Kornet; I never saw anyone more affected by single loss in a game than Frank was in this one. He was in tears, and defiant: "We didn't lose this game. Our basketball team did not lose this game." Until the tennis balls came flying onto the court, Frank had played Schintzius to a draw, with 14 points and 11 rebounds, which was about what Schintzius had submitted to that point. But Dwayne's tying free throws and productive overtime elevated his stats to a game-high 24 points and 12 boards.

Dwayne also proved that reports of his maturation were grossly exaggerated, evidenced by a series of snarky post-game remarks. "Tell whoever it was threw the balls that Dwayne Schintzius thanks them very much." On the other hand, one could hardly blame him for gloating after he was targeted by flying objects, then exacting the sweetest type of revenge by tying the game at the end of regulation and winning it in overtime: "I can't believe anyone was stupid enough to do that just so they could say they hit the Dwayne Schintzius with the tennis ball. Isn't that a really big thrill? Well, it cost Vanderbilt the game."

The burning question, of course, was whether a technical foul should have been called in the first place. Coach Newton maintained that Clougherty exercised "poor judgment" in making the call, and he filed a complaint with the SEC's director of officials. "Our basketball players had done nothing wrong," Coach Newton said, "and the ball-throwing incident—while unfortunate and uncalled for—had absolutely no bearing on the game at that point." Predictably, Florida coach Norm Sloan took exactly the opposite view: "The only thing that surprised me was that there was not a second technical called, as more tennis balls came after the first." He also referenced the improbable ending to our most recent SEC home game: "I feel sorry for C.M. and the Vanderbilt team, but they got one against Georgia where they got a break. These things happen."

Indeed, the Georgia and Florida games had more in common than just spectacular, improbable finishes. They also had an official in common: John Clougherty. That's right: when Booker crashed into Rod Cole as he delivered the pass to me that resulted in the buzzer-beating three, it was none other than John Clougherty who swallowed his whistle and did not call a foul. Plus, he was part of the crew in the Louisville game where we benefited from another controversial late-game call—the charge by Booker as he dropped off a pass to Wilcox for a layup, where the officials counted Derrick's basket even though it occurred after Book had committed the foul. So maybe these things do even out.

None of that, however, should excuse Clougherty. I agree with C.M. that he did use poor judgment and that there was no reason to make that call with one second remaining in the game. Moreover, the fact that Clougherty didn't share his side of the story with the media after the game represents one of the great frustrations players and coaches in all sports have with officials—they seem unwilling to explain or defend controversial calls. When a coach announces his resignation in the middle of the season to take a job at a rival conference school, he needs to explain himself Likewise, when a player goes 1-for-7 from the field in the Sweet Sixteen against Kansas and his team loses, he likewise has to face the media and explain himself; it's not pleasant but it has to be done. Apparently, though, officials don't have to do that. They can make game-changing (or, in this case, season-changing) calls but not be answerable to the media either immediately after the game or at any later time, choosing to hide behind bland statements from the conference's director of officials, who uniformly delivers unsatisfactory responses. It would have been interesting to hear Clougherty's view of things; he may have had a good explanation. But because he chose to remain silent on the call, one can easily conclude that he lacked the moral fiber to explain the call.

In fact, Clougherty did not officiate another game in Memorial that season, which can hardly be explained away as a coincidence. Moreover, we only encountered him one other time, late in the year in a game that didn't figure to require controversial, late-game calls (at Auburn). Until the day he left the SEC, Clougherty was justifiably booed every time he refereed a game in Memorial; the Memorial fans would never forget the '89 game against Florida. Nor should they.

I have looked at it from another angle ever since the game ended: why was there one second on the clock anyway? The ball flew out of bounds, so I have always assessed some blame on the clock operator for not letting the clock run to all zeroes, thus ending the game. If the tennis balls came out at that point, I doubt that even Clougherty would have T'd up the crowd then—there was no game because it was over. It seems that the worst that could have happened at that point is that the officials would have put a second back on the clock, cleaned up whatever tennis balls were on the floor, and restarted the game where it left off—our ball, one second left, and a two-point lead. So, I think the clock operator deserves some blame for facilitating the terrible events. So much for home cooking.

Of course, one can't place 100% of this incredible defeat on the fans, officials, and a scorekeeper. C.M. believed that we put ourselves in a position to win ("Our players ground it out, made the plays down the stretch and did everything in their power to win the game."). But it exaggerates matters to say that we had done "everything in [our] power to win the game." For the only time all season, none of the five starters hit half his shots from the field: Kornet and Reid were 5-for-11, I was 5-for-13, Wilcox was 1-for-5, and Booker was 8-for-19. And we hit only half our free throws (8-for-16). Had we made even one of the missed free throws in the last 20 seconds (the missed one-and-one, the second of a one-and-one), we would have triumphed anyway, and the tennis ball call would have been nothing more than an amusing footnote to an exciting game.

Booker, in fact, had a great game—he led the team with 23 points, five assists, and two steals, and his eight rebounds trailed only Kornet's team-high 11. I added 15 points, but was totally spent in the overtime, getting blanked. Florida's frontline lived up to expectations—Davis supported Schintzius's 24/12 with 16 points and 15 rebounds. All in all, it was an even game—statistically, the kind of game that can be decided on an unfortunate set of events. And was.

We could protest and complain all we wanted, but the harsh truth was that the loss was not going to be reversed and would remain on the books. That made for two spectacular SEC losses in a row—the Chris Jackson buzzer-beater at LSU and the Florida tennis ball defeat. The loss dropped us into a tie for fifth in the SEC, while Florida improved to seventh:

LSU	6-2
Tennessee	5-2
Kentucky	5-2
Alabama	5-3
Ole Miss	4-3
Vandy	4-3
Florida	4-4
Mississippi State	2-5
Georgia	2-6
Auburn	0-7

As the *Nashville Banner*'s Joe Biddle wrote the day after the game, "Put this one in the books. It will be talked about for years. The Tennis Ball Game." He was right. The devastating Florida loss became known as the Tennis Ball Game—initial capitalization required.

27

CHARACTER

I

"You've got to learn to live with what you can't rise above"
—Bruce Springsteen, "Tunnel of Love" ('88)

The Florida game ended the most remarkable two weeks of my Vanderbilt career. In the span of just 15 days, we (1) won an overtime game, (2) won a game on a buzzer-beater, (3) lost a game on a buzzer-beater, (4) won a game for our head coach's 500th career victory, (5) had that coach resign 48 hours later, and (6) lost an overtime game thanks to tennis balls thrown from the crowd. Many players don't experience such scintillating highs and crushing lows in an entire season, maybe an entire four years; we experienced them in five consecutive games spread over a mere 15 days. Still, when the roller coaster ended after the Florida game, we were only 4-3 in the SEC and 10-9 for the entire season, records that wouldn't even merit an NIT bid, much less a repeat invite to the NCAAs. With 11 games remaining on the schedule, and coming off the 48-hour double-whammy of Coach Newton's resignation and the Tennis Ball Game ("one of the most tumultuous weeks in the history of Vanderbilt basketball," one writer observed), we were at a lower point even than in mid-December, when we were 2-5 but had three-quarters of the season still in front of us. Approaching the end of January, time was becoming a factor.

Book, Frank, and I are proud of several things we helped the program accomplish in our four seasons, and at or near the top of that list is the aftermath of the Florida game. The easy way out would have been to pack it in after Florida—after all, Coach Newton had resigned, we were counting down our final games as seniors, and we could have been excused for letting down. We had helped elevate the program to a level of prominence it had not enjoyed in over a decade, with a Sweet Sixteen appearance, wins over nationally ranked powers, and a seven-game SEC winning streak in 1987–88. Those were accomplishments we could savor, and whoever the new coach would be, he would take over a program that was in much better shape than it had been in fall 1985 when the three of us arrived on campus.

But the easy way out simply wasn't an option. We had (and have) more character than that. The last memorable game for the Booker/Kornet/Goheen trio could not be a crushing loss on a fluke call. Besides, our 4-3 SEC record was only a game in the loss column behind the three league leaders (LSU, Tennessee, Kentucky), all three of whom still had to visit Memorial before the end of the season. So, it was time to man up and play on.

~

The turnaround for the 1987–88 team occurred in Mississippi when, staring at an 0-4 start to the SEC schedule, we rallied for a late-game win over Ole Miss, the first of seven wins in a row. The turnaround for the 1988–89 team, if there were to be one, would have to begin in Mississippi as well, this time in Starkville against Mississippi State. "We can't afford to stay down," I said before that game. "We can't just sit around feeling sorry for ourselves. Mississippi State drilled us down here last year and they'll do it again if we aren't ready to play."

The Bulldogs were on a four-game losing streak, but they had done something we had not done—beaten LSU, one of only two SEC losses the Tigers had sustained to that point in the season. Under normal circumstances, it was a game we should win—but these weren't normal circumstances, and the last-place Bulldogs had thrashed us in Starkville in the final regular-season game of 1987–88. That game was frustrating because we started the game hot, but the Bulldogs blitzed us in the first half and we never regained the momentum. Now, in '89, we started well again, with two Kornet dunks, igniting a strong start as we sprinted to a 14-point lead and took a 44-34 lead to the locker room. We couldn't sustain our level of play to begin the second half, however, and the Bulldogs came out firing. They outscored us 16-4 in the first five minutes of the half to take a 50-48 lead. It was beginning to look like déjà vu in Starkville as the Bulldogs stretched the lead to five, 61-56, with eight minutes to play. We were staring into the abyss of a lost season.

A year earlier, in Oxford, it was Barry Booker who hit the big shot that gave us the win that turned our season around. And it would be Book who came up big again to turn things around. With State holding a 66-63 lead, Book hit a trey to tie the game. State scored to reclaim the lead, but Book answered with a conventional three-point play to put us up 69-68 with 3:53 left. Book's back-to-back three-point excursions broke the Bulldogs' spirit. State would score only two points in the final three minutes, while we took (and mostly made) good shots and nailed our free throws. We ended the game on a 15-2 run to win going away, 81-70.

Normally, a win over an also-ran like Mississippi State wouldn't be cause for celebration, but everyone knew this was a huge win. Coach Newton wasn't overstating things where he said, "This wasn't just a good win, it was a great win." He also used that word "character": "To have been through what they went through Wednesday, and to have several guys struggling with the flu…I think this just goes to show the character of our basketball team." I agreed: "This shows we have the character to come back from such a heartbreaking loss."

Kornet celebrated his 22nd birthday with a team-high 20 points, and his seven boards tied Reid for team honors. Eric posted a solid 14 points on 5-for-7 shooting from the field and a perfect 4-for-4 from the line. Wilcox was superlative as well with 14 points (6-for-8 from the field) and eight assists. It was a tale of two halves for Booker and me. I had an uncharacteristically hot first half, scoring 14 points. But, still fighting the flu, I completely ran out of gas in the second half, missing several open shots and scoring only two points to finish with 16. Conversely, Book scored only two points in the first half, then heated up in the second half, scoring 15 points to finish with 17. In fact, for what surely was the only time in my four years at Vanderbilt, the starters scored every point in the game—all 81, with no starter scoring fewer than 14. All in all, it was a terrific win to improve our SEC record to 5-3.

II

"This ain't a dream, I can't escape"
—The Ramones, "Pet Sematary" ('89)

After the Mississippi State trip, we returned to Memorial for the first time since the Tennis Ball Game. Crowd control would be tighter, and it was sure to be loud—the Tennessee Volunteers were coming to call.

Just a couple of weeks before our game, the Vols had a stranglehold on the SEC. They won their first five conference games to seize early control of the race and rise to a #16 national ranking. But they came to Memorial on a three-game losing streak, and all three were agonizing: Kentucky stole a win in Knoxville when Vol buzzer-beating specialist Greg Bell missed a three-pointer at the buzzer; they lost another at home to Georgia when Alec Kessler hit a 10-footer with four seconds left; and, most dispiritingly, a Michael Ansley tip-in at the buzzer gave Alabama an overtime victory over the Vols, even though replays showed that the tip-in came after the buzzer. Now 5-3 in the league, the Volunteers easily could have been 8-0.

This was the first time in my Vandy career that a Vandy-UT game had ramifications for first place in the SEC. Both teams were 5-3 in the league, as were Kentucky and Ole Miss. Those four teams were even on the loss side with 6-3 Alabama, and a game back of first-place LSU (6-2). The winner of our game could find itself tied for first place at the halfway point in the conference schedule, and at a minimum would break up some of the logjam in the three-loss group of teams. The two teams were the most experienced in the SEC. We started three seniors and two juniors, while UT started five seniors—Dyron Nix and Mark Griffin at forward, Doug Roth at center, and Travis Henry and Clarence Swearingen at guard.

Nix, as always, was a matchup problem for us, just as he was for practically every other team in the league. He came into the game averaging 22.5 points and 9.3 rebounds. Swearingen and Roth averaged in double figures as well, but Nix was the centerpiece—only LSU's Ricky Blanton had that type of offensive versatility in the SEC, but Dyron was a little quicker than Ricky and more explosive.

Because of the Nix matchup problem, Coach Newton made what was, for him, an historic decision: he decided to play a zone defense for the entire game—"only the second time in his 32-year coaching career," it was later reported. We always began every game in a man-to-man defense—bar none. We might switch to a zone after just a few possessions and stay in the zone for most of the rest of the game, but we always began the game in a man-to-man defense. Not this time, though—we had to keep an eye on Nix and make sure that, if the Vols were to beat us, it would be by someone other than him. Unfortunately, the all-zone strategy didn't fool the Vols or Nix in the first half, and we put ourselves behind the eight ball with another slow start. Nix scored 11 points in the first half, and Griffin—Book's and my pal from our recruiting visit to Vandy in September 1984—took advantage of the zone by draining several three-pointers (he would hit four in the game). Meanwhile, after several games of quality ball control, we committed 12 turnovers in the first 20 minutes. All in all, it was a miserable first half, which ended with the Vols leading, 31-23.

Once again, we faced a crucial crossroads to the season. Another half like that and we would be 5-4 at the turn, with two home losses while staring at a trip to the hottest team in the league (Alabama). In the locker room, though, the coaches decided to stay with the zone, but with a couple of adjustments: Book would be stationed on Nix's side of the floor, and he would slide down to front Nix when Dyron stayed on the block as the ball was entered to his side of the floor. It was, in fact, close to a matchup zone because we (mostly Book) would stick with Nix for the entire possession.

Even that adjustment did not pay immediate dividends in the second half, however. Griffin began the second half with a bucket and a free throw to push Tennessee's lead to double digits. We cut into the lead slightly over the next few minutes, and a Kornet jumper cut our deficit to six, 41-35. But Griffin answered that with another trey to make it 44-35 Tennessee with 13:29 remaining. Then came the most incredible run of the season, and maybe in all four of my seasons in Nashville. Kornet hit a field goal and added a free throw. Reid tipped in a miss. Wilcox hit a jumper. Off a Reid rebound and outlet pass, I took it the rest of the way for a layup; suddenly the game was tied. Tennessee called timeout, but we weren't finished: Kornet scored again, then turned in a three-point play. Wilcox hit a free throw, and Kornet hit a turnaround jumper. In the span of six minutes, we scored 17 straight points to turn a 44-35 deficit into a 52-44 advantage. The Memorial Gym crowd was deafening (but respectful—no tennis balls or oranges were tossed on the floor at any point in the game), the Vols were stunned, and we were in control. The final score was 68-56, as we outscored the Vols 33-12 over the final 13:29.

Kornet had a great game—21 points and seven rebounds—and he was especially remarkable in the second half, scoring 18 points as the Vols tried three different players on him, none of whom succeeded. Eric Reid was excellent as well, putting up the game's only double-double with 13 points and a game-high 10 rebounds. We won this game with great second-half defense, and strong, aggressive play at the basket (we shot 29 free throws to the Vols' six).

All told, as Coach Newton said, we "played about as well as a team could play for that final 20 minutes." It was especially gratifying to win our first game in Memorial since the Tennis Ball Game, giving us two in a row since the Florida disaster. "This team has been through so much, but we won two games since then and I can't think of any situation from which we can't come back," Booker said. Plus, Kornet's great second-half led to his being named in the SEC Player of the Week: in the wins over Mississippi State and Tennessee, Frank totaled 41 points on 14-for-21 shooting from the field, and 14 rebounds. Frank's tears after the Florida game were, at least temporarily, forgotten.

The UT win gave us a 6-3 SEC record at the halfway point in league play. And we did, in fact, break out of the three-loss logjam: suddenly-hot Florida beat Alabama, and LSU drilled Ole Miss. Meanwhile, Kentucky beat Mississippi State, meaning that we were tied for second with the Wildcats after nine games:

LSU	7-2
Vandy	6-3
Kentucky	6-3
Alabama	6-4
Tennessee	5-4
Ole Miss	5-4
Florida	5-4
Georgia	3-6
Mississippi State	2-7
Auburn	0-8

In fact, if not for a last-second Chris Jackson jumper and a couple of ill-timed tennis balls, we would have been 8-1. On the other hand, if Gerald Glass had hit a makeable jumper at Ole Miss and if Patrick Hamilton had made a wide-open layup in the waning seconds of the Georgia game, we would have been 4-5 and in serious trouble. So, the 6-3 record was about right given the extreme highs and lows we had experienced over the first nine SEC games.

I felt confident we could at least match that 6-3 record in the final nine games. "If we can get 7-2 or 6-3 in the last half of the race, we'll have a shot [at the title]," I predicted. Realistically, though, six other teams could say the same thing—each of the seven teams with records of at least 5-4 had the potential to win it.

III

"We're gonna take a look inside…it's time to search our souls"
—Glenn Frey, "Soul Searchin'" ('89)

While we were trying to right the ship after the Tennis Ball Game, the rumor mill had quickly gone into overdrive as to who Vanderbilt's next head basketball coach would be after Coach Newton officially took over as Kentucky's AD on April 1. Some of the rumors made sense. David Lipscomb's Don Meyer seemed an obvious candidate; he had established the Nashville-based Bisons as a national power at the NAIA level, and at the time of C.M.'s resignation, Lipscomb was 27-0 and ranked number one in the NAIA on its way to a 38-win season. While allowing that "Vanderbilt is interesting from the standpoint [of] it's in town, it's a program I've been around for 14 years [and I] wouldn't have to uproot my family," Coach Meyer said. "I've got one of the best jobs in the country." (In fact, Coach Meyer would stay at Lipscomb until 1999, when he moved on to Northern State, where he would break the all-time men's coaching victories record.)

Other names seemed to make sense as well, though the chances of those coaches coming to Vanderbilt were remote. Those names included Stanford's Mike Montgomery, Kansas State's Lon Kruger, and Duke's Mike Krzyzewski. Meanwhile, experienced hands such as Auburn's Sonny Smith and Purdue's Gene Keady made no sense at all—unless Smith's annual pilgrimage to The Nashville Network on Auburn's trip to Nashville counted as a local tie. And then there was C.M.'s chief lieutenant, Assistant Head Coach John Bostick, who declared, "I consider myself a candidate. I would very much like to have the job." At the time of C.M.'s resignation, Coach Bostick had been a part of 331 of Coach Newton's 500 head coaching victories. Those 331 wins (now 333 after Mississippi State and UT) were the culmination of a 20-year climb up the college coaching ladder for John Bostick.

When Coach Newton took the Alabama job in 1968, he retained the only holdover assistant from the previous coach's staff: Wimp Sanderson. It was Sanderson who connected coaches Newton and Bostick. Coach Bostick was a native Alabaman, born in Winfield, and he graduated from Florence State in 1957 (now the University of North Alabama). An outstanding athlete, he earned an amazing 11 varsity letters—four each in basketball and baseball and three in football. After a stint in the U.S. Army (he coached the Army's hoops team), he coached two different Alabama high schools to nearly 180 wins in 10 seasons. At that point, C.M. Newton came calling.

C.M. was looking for someone from the high school ranks, and, as he recalled, he hired Coach Bostick "because everybody said he was the best high school coach in Alabama." The catch was that the position was not a full-time assistant's position—it was a graduate assistant position, meaning, as Coach Bostick recalled, "he could give me a scholarship, but he couldn't pay me anything." To take (and then maintain) the job, Coach Bostick cashed in some of his retirement funds and used the G.I. Bill—which speaks volumes about Coach Bostick's character and explains Coach Newton's longstanding loyalty to him.

Enduring some rough seasons at Alabama before he, C.M., and Wimp got the program rolling in the right direction, Coach Bostick was elevated to a full-time (and fully paid) assistant coach in the early '70s. Coach Bostick was a trusted aide to Coach Newton from that time forward. When Coach Newton left Alabama in 1980, Coach Bostick stayed, working as an assistant for the new head coach, Sanderson. When Coach Newton was offered the Vandy job a year later, he asked Coach Bostick to come along, telling him, "I am not sure I'll go if you don't go with me." According to C.M., Coach Bostick's response was enthusiastic: "Let's go!" And with that, Coach Bostick and his vivacious wife, Betty, relocated to Nashville, with his official title being "assistant head coach."

Coach Bostick worked with the forwards and centers during his time at Vanderbilt. It's a testament to his coaching skills that, under his tutelage, such players as Jeff Turner and Will Perdue went from little-used freshmen to all-SEC players and, from there, to long and productive NBA careers. Also, he was basically in charge of managing full-team defensive drills, especially the defensive conditioning drills and sprints that concluded most practices. In fact, Coach Newton rarely ended a practice until he received an approving nod from Coach Bostick, which was the latter's stamp of approval that we had worked enough for the day.

Coach Bostick was (and is) extremely soft-spoken in everyday conversation, but he could be fiery on the bench, both with the players and the officials. He was especially vigilant about pointing out any illegal screens to the officials, usually with one shouted word: "ILLEGAL!" Meanwhile, he also monitored each player's academic performance, checking in periodically (or more frequently than that, depending on the player) with professors to make sure the players were attending class, keeping up with their schoolwork, and so forth. In almost every way, he was the perfect assistant—someone who could be trusted with the on-court preparatory and off-court details while the head coach provided the overall vision and in-game decision-making for the program.

Alas, even though the longtime assistant replacing the retiring head coach isn't unheard of—in 1997, North Carolina replaced the retiring Dean Smith with his longtime assistant Bill Guthridge—it wasn't to be for John Bostick and Vanderbilt. However our season would end, whether it be the NCAA or NIT (or neither), it was clear that the Vanderbilt basketball program would be in much better shape in spring 1989 than when Coach Newton accepted the head coaching position eight years earlier. As a result, Athletic Director Roy Kramer would have some attractive choices for the job, likely a younger coach who was leading a program from a smaller conference looking to move to one of the power conferences. The two Vandy head coaches prior to C.M. Newton—Wayne Dobbs (three seasons) and Richard Schmidt (two seasons)—had no head coaching experience at the Division I level prior to taking the reins of the Commodore program, and the program fell significantly from the levels it had enjoyed under Roy Skinner. It was likely that Kramer, who had hired Schmidt, didn't want to hire anyone that lacked collegiate head coaching experience, even one as trusted and seasoned as John Bostick.

Even though Coach Newton believed that "Roy Kramer made a mistake in not naming John Bostick to replace me"—which, in its own strange way, meant that C.M. did not consider Coach Bostick a candidate for the Kentucky head-coaching job, which surely would come open after the season—I doubt that Roy ever gave serious consideration to Coach Bostick, who would once again follow C.M. to a new job, in this case becoming director of compliance at UK ("the first full-time compliance administrator anywhere") with C.M. as athletic director. And, like Coach Newton, Coach Bostick would try his hardest to exit his successful coaching career with an NCAA bid—and perhaps even an SEC title. That effort would continue in Coach Newton's and Coach Bostick's former stomping grounds, Tuscaloosa, with the game against Alabama.

ȣ

This would be Coach Newton's final trip to Tuscaloosa as a head coach. And 'Bama, where C.M. had literally built a program in the 1970s, had great memories of his days as the Tide's coach, and his replacement as Tide head coach, Wimp Sanderson, made a thoughtful presentation to his predecessor right before our game: a photograph of Coach Newton and his college coach at Kentucky, Adolph Rupp, which Wimp had blown up and framed. Wimp already had gotten off the best line about the 48-hour period where C.M. won his 500th game and then resigned: "I sent him a telegram for his 500th victory; I guess I'll have to send him another one. That SOB is really costing me some money."

Despite the touching gift, I never quite figured out the relationship between coaches Newton and Sanderson. Wimp didn't just maintain what C.M. (and Coach Bostick) had built at 'Bama; he took it to another level in many ways, winning several SEC tournament titles and sending several players to the NBA, many of whom had extremely productive careers, including Derrick McKey, Latrell Sprewell, Robert Horry, Buck Johnson, and Keith Askins, to name a few. Several of those stars played during Coach Newton's 1982–89 tenure at Vanderbilt, when, as Wimp tactfully wrote, "I was fortunate to have some super players and some outstanding teams." Translation: C.M. rarely got the better of Wimp while he was coaching Vanderbilt. Did that bother our coaches? I don't know, but it probably would have bothered me if I'd been in that situation.

I think it would be only natural for Coach Newton to feel a twinge of something—regret? jealousy?—at his former assistant's success. In fact, the toughest in-season practice we ever had in my four years at Vanderbilt occurred after a loss to Alabama: in my freshman year, the Tide beat us soundly by double digits in Memorial Gym—we played poorly before the home folks, and the next day Coach Newton put us through a nearly three-hour practice that featured several sessions of wind sprints and "suicides." I doubt that practice would have been that severe if we had lost to any team other than Alabama.

Certainly Wimp had made basketball something more than an afterthought at the University of Alabama. C.M. related the story of how he came to the decision to leave Alabama—the Tide beat LSU and Kentucky on the road, only to return home to see barely 6,000 fans (in a gym with a capacity of 15,000) turn out for a game against Georgia, which the Tide lost. After some injudicious remarks in his post-game radio show, C.M. made the decision to quit. Sanderson, though, had begun filling those 15,000 seats in Coleman Coliseum regularly. Between his eye-catching plaid sport coats and scowling histrionics on the sidelines, Wimp had made Alabama basketball an event. Our game would be the third consecutive sellout at Coleman—a record to that point in the program's history, and the school "could have sold another 2000 tickets for the game" according to the Tide's ticket manager.

The 15,000+ in attendance would not go home disappointed. We spurted to an early 12-7 lead, three of those points coming on my trey. But I shot blanks from then on. Alvin Lee, the sharpshooter who had scorched us for 36 points in Tuscaloosa the previous season, hit a three to cap a 7-0 run for the Tide, giving them a 14-12 lead. A Steve Grant dunk gave us an 18-17 lead about midway through the first half, and it would be our last lead of the game, even though the halftime score was a manageable 34-31 in favor of the Tide. We needed a quick start to the second half, and we didn't deliver: David Benoit scored four quick points on a basket and two free throws to push the Alabama lead to seven, and we had to battle uphill for the rest of the night. Great shooting by Booker kept us in range, but Lee, who played all 40 minutes, always seemed ready with a three-point dagger of his own. We never got closer than five after Benoit's opening flurry in the second half, and the final score was 77-67.

Lee and Book staged an impressive three-point shooting contest, combining for an incredible 13-for-16 beyond the arc. Lee went 6-for-7 and finished with a game-high 24 points, while Book went 7-for-9 and scored a team-high 23, adding five steals to boot. In contrast to the Tide's four players in double figures, only Kornet (17 points) joined Book in double figures on our side, while I submitted a dud of Shakespearean proportions. Claudius said, "My offence is rank." And my "offense" was truly rank against Alabama—my worst game of the year, 1-for-11 from the field

(1-for-7 from behind the arc) for only three points. Coupled with my 1-for-8 showing in our '88 trip to Tuscaloosa, I was an awful 2-for-19 in my final two games at Alabama.

≈

In the 10 days following the Tennis Ball Game, we had shown great character in refusing to let that game and Coach Newton's resignation derail our season. As I said late in the season: "The tennis ball game and the announcement [that C.M. was resigning] all happened in the same week. We could have fallen apart and rolled over for the rest of the season. Or, we could have done what we did—pull together and play through the adversity. We have." We bounced back with two big wins, and the loss to Alabama was not a crusher; they were literally unbeatable at home (14-0 for the season after our game). "We played well but they played better," Coach Newton remarked. Still, we were at 6-4 in the league—and 'Bama passed us at 7-4 while Mississippi State did the rest of the league a favor by beating LSU for the second time in the season to drop the Tigers to 7-3—and only 12-10 overall. Anything worse than 6-2 in our final eight games would keep us at home in March.

28

SO MUCH FOR CONFLICT OF INTEREST

On Wednesday, February 8, 1989, exactly sixteen days after Coach Newton announced that he was resigning as Vanderbilt's head basketball coach as of April 1 and accepting the position of athletic director at the University of Kentucky, the basketball teams of his current and future employers would collide. And, with the arrival of the Wildcats in Nashville, calls for Coach Newton to "recuse" himself from coaching in the game grew louder and more persistent.

I

"Finally the tables are starting to turn"
—Tracy Chapman, "Talkin' 'bout a Revolution" ('88–'89)

Under the law, a "conflict of interest" is defined as "a clash between public interest and the private pecuniary interest of the individual concerned." More broadly, it means "[a] situation in which regard for one duty tends to lead to disregard of another." Thus, to use a common example, a judge should not preside over a case where one of the parties is a corporation in which (s)he might own stock; that situation illustrates the "clash" between "public interest" (the impartial administration of justice and, equally important, the public's perception of impartiality of the judiciary) and the judge's "private pecuniary interest" (the partial ownership of a party to a lawsuit, whose financial health might be affected depending on how the judge decides the case). When a conflict of interest is present, the result should be a "recusal"—"[t]he process by which a judge is disqualified on objection of either party (or disqualifies himself or herself) from hearing a lawsuit because of self-interest, bias or prejudice." When a judge recuses, another judge comes in to adjudicate the case.

What do any of these legal concepts have to do with basketball? Well, some in the media—especially those writing for *The Tennessean*—suggested that "there is some feeling that [Newton] is leaving himself open to perceptions of divided loyalties when he plays his school-to-be." C.M. was offended by that suggestion, asserting that Chancellor Wyatt and Athletic Director Kramer "certainly don't perceive any conflict of interest." For his part, Kramer added that the possibility of the head coach sitting out the Kentucky game "has never been discussed."

I never quite understood the logic behind the "conflict of interest," because I figured Coach Newton's motivation would be exactly the opposite from what the media was asserting. If anything, Coach Newton would want to thump UK, especially because it would be one more nail in the coffin of Kentucky coach Eddie Sutton; a bad finish to the season by UK would make it much easier for Coach Newton to include Eddie in the anticipated housecleaning C.M. would undertake beginning on April 1. Plus, C.M.'s gentlemanly demeanor masked a fierce desire to win; opponents that mistook his placid exterior as a lack of competitive desire did so at their own peril. As longtime friend and opposing coach (and Kentucky native) Hugh Durham said, "Conflict of interest? Who're you kidding? Nobody's going to lay down for anybody. C.M.'s a competitor and there's nobody he'd rather beat than Kentucky. Guys write that stuff because they don't have anything else to write."

Coach Newton had some fun with it at a luncheon on the day of the game. Maybe he should have "recused" himself from coaching against Florida, he mused, because he had grown up in Fort Lauderdale; or not coached against Tennessee because he was born in Rockwood and had a sister who dated the Volunteers' former basketball coach; or not coached against any SEC school because he served in the commissioner's office the one year between leaving Alabama and becoming Vanderbilt's head coach. Suffice it to say there would be no "recusal," and all coaches and players would report for duty on February 8 at 7 p.m. Central Time.

꙳

The coaching angle was interesting, and maybe unprecedented: how many games have ever matched two head coaches whose relationship just a couple of months later would change from opponents to boss-employee? That imminent new world order in Lexington required some tact on the part of both coaches, Newton and Sutton, for the rest of the season, especially the latter, who was likely to be looking for work come April 1. Thus, Sutton would need to avoid doing things like needlessly bashing the end-of-game no-call in our Georgia contest that preceded my game-winning trey. "I thought it was tragic," he said, "what happened to the University of Georgia." That was a poor choice of words, but Sutton continued to engage in the exercise of "open mouth, insert foot" by claiming that "I happened to see the game" and that "Pat Hamilton was fouled on the layup" while "Booker drove right over one of Georgia's players." If Sutton rerally had watched the game, he would have known that Hamilton was untouched on his blown layup, and no one from Georgia ever claimed otherwise. Those imprudent remarks were made about a week before C.M. announced his acceptance of the UK athletic director's job, and C.M. surely knew by that point that he was taking that position, but he took the high road—sort of. "[I]f I responded, I'd just be adding to Eddie's problems," he said. Our task now was to add to those "problems."

If Coach Sutton thought that his rousing defense of Georgia would lull the Bulldogs to sleep for their next game with Kentucky, he was wrong. The 'Cats and

Dawgs played in Athens on Sunday afternoon, and Georgia avenged its early-season loss in Lexington by beating the 'Cats 84-72. Worse, the UK team was stranded in Georgia by an ice storm and wound up having to travel directly to Nashville from Athens. In any event, both we and the Wildcats entered the game with identical 6-4 SEC records—the third consecutive game where we and our opponent had the same number of conference victories entering the game. UT and Florida also were 6-4, while 'Bama was 7-4, all trailing 7-3 LSU. That meant that six teams were within a game of the league lead, and ours was the only game matching two of those six teams—the four teams with the same or better records than us and UK were matched against the bottom four teams, so one would assume victories for the other four top teams in the league. Thus, it was imperative that we keep pace at home.

The teams would start the same five players they started in Lexington—Reggie Hanson, Chris Mills, LeRon Ellis, Derrick Miller, and Sean Sutton for Kentucky, and the Kornet/Booker/Goheen/Reid/Wilcox quintet for the Commodores. Neither team used its bench much—ours had scored zero, four, and six points in the last three games while UK's primary reserves were four Kentuckians: Mike Scott (team-mate of mine and Kornet's in the Kentucky-Indiana games in summer 1985 after our high school graduation) and three not-yet-ready-for-prime-time freshmen—red-shirt frosh Deron Feldhaus and John Pelphrey and true freshman Richie Farmer, all three of whom had been heavily recruited by Coach Newton to come to Vanderbilt, and who, ironically, would in fact have the opportunity to "play" for Coach Newton once C.M. officially assumed the athletic director duties in Lexington.

II

"People think you're down and out, you can show them what it's all about"
—*Steve Winwood, "Roll with It"* ('88)

The coaches had combined to win 932 games prior to this one—502 for Coach Newton and 430 for Coach Sutton. Obviously, that number would be 933 after our game, and we wanted the win to go on the Newton side of that ledger. UK had a distinct scheduling advantage, too—after our game, the 'Cats would have only three road games remaining, and two of them were against the worst teams in the league, Auburn and Mississippi State. Having already won at Florida and at UT, the Wild-cats were well positioned to catch LSU if they could beat us in Memorial.

The game started unremarkably enough. After a couple of possessions, Mills drew a foul and hit one of two free throws. That 1-0 advantage would be the only lead UK would enjoy the entire game. We promptly scored six straight, five by Book, for a 6-1 lead. After an Ellis basket, I turned it over but stole it right back for a feed to Reid for a dunk and an 8-3 lead, then went coast-to-coast after UK missed three shots on offense for a driving layup and a 10-3 bulge. After an Ellis basket, my first three of the game widened our lead to eight, and we traded baskets to lead 15-7 eight minutes in.

Out of a media timeout, energized by Mayes and Grant off the bench, we trapped off UK's inbounds pass at half-court, resulting in a Wilcox steal and layup to push our lead to double digits. That same trapping defense the next time down forced another turnover, which we again cashed in, this time in spectacular fashion as Kornet authored a one-handed slam dunk putback of Wilcox's missed three. The lead went to 13, 22-9, when Mayes hit a three after two Mills free throws, and it was 25-13 with seven minutes left. A Miller free throw made it 25-14, but Booker's offensive rebound off my missed three led to a Grant dunk and a 27-14 lead. Hanson's three-point play cut our lead to 10 and tagged Kornet with his second foul, creating an opportunity for the 'Cats to close the gap before the half, especially when Mills had a makeable three after an empty trip on our end. But he missed it, and Booker hit a trey on our end for a 30-17 lead, and from that point the rout was on. About 10 seconds later I picked off Deron Feldhaus's lazy pass for the easy dunk and a 15-point lead. After a Richie Farmer miss, I hit another trey and the lead ballooned to 18, 35-17, and it was 36-18 with about 50 seconds remaining.

The half closed with one of those "I had a feeling" moments. We worked the clock down for the final shot until about 14 seconds remained and I found myself in front of Miller about 23 or 24 feet from the basket. I launched it right then—why not? We were ahead by 18—and it found nothing but the net. The "three-pointer of epic proportions" sent us to the locker room with an unexpected 21-point lead, 39-18. That was my fifth field goal of the first half, just one less than the entire UK team had made in the first 20 minutes.

We didn't let the Wildcats get back into the game in the second half. I hit two free throws to stretch the lead to 23. Then, after a UK turnover Wilcox led a beautiful fast break with a lob pass to Kornet, who simply outhustled his UK frontcourt counterparts down the floor and laid it in with his left hand for a 25-point lead. After a Mills bucket came another beautiful play—a classic "give and go" where Booker fed Kornet in the post and cut to the basket; Mills, guarding Book, turned his head for a split second to Frank, and that was all the opening Frank needed to hand the ball to Book, who rose over everyone for a slam dunk, igniting the crowd yet again. Then a UK turnover resulted in another Wilcox-to-Kornet fast-break feed, and Frank's layup made it 47-20 with 17:22 remaining, forcing (finally) a UK timeout. But that pause did not interrupt our momentum in the least; yet another open-court opportunity, this one started by Kornet, resulted in my three-pointer and an almost-unimaginable 30-point lead, 50-20. The next time down was proof positive that UK had given up: Wilcox drove the lane and missed an off-balance eight-footer, but four UK players stood around and made no effort for the rebound, and Derrick claimed it himself and laid the ball in, unmolested, for a 52-20 bulge. With 15 minutes to play, it unexpectedly became garbage time.

A few minutes later, with the score 64-32, came a play that showed how locked in we were. Against UK's man-to-man defense, we employed a 1-2-2 offensive set with Wilcox at the point, Book and me on the wings, and Kornet and Reid on each block. Derrick entered the ball to Book, with Frank on the strong side block; that meant Eric had to cut from the offside block to the top of the key, which he did, and Book passed him the ball. I was alone on the other side to receive the swing pass, but Miller, a poor defender, tried to anticipate Eric's pass and lunged to steal an imaginary pass; when he did, I cut to the basket, received a perfect bounce pass from Eric, and laid it in for an easy basket. The only time the ball hit the floor after Derrick's entry pass to Book was the single bounce of Eric's pass to me. Four people touched the ball, and perfect execution made for an easy basket. Reid's three-point trip moments later stretched the lead to 35 points, 72-37.

Frankly, we engaged in a bit—maybe more than a bit—of hot-dogging in the second half, to keep the crowd (and ourselves) interested, I guess. I flipped a behind-the-back pass to Wilcox on a fast break, and a couple of minutes later Reid did the same to Kornet. We also tried a couple of ill-advised alley-oop lob passes that were probably better reserved for a Brooklyn playground. All in good fun, I guess—at least for us. "It is easier to pass behind the back and do all those other things when you are 30 points ahead," I later said.

It was inside three minutes before Coach Newton removed Booker and Kornet from the game with a 30-point lead. I added a free throw and finally came out of the game with just over two minutes left. The score at that point was 79-46. Frank came half the way to the scorers' table to greet me, with Book just a couple of steps behind. It was a sweet, memorable—and loud—moment. The final score was 81-51.

By any measure, it was an historic evening. It was UK's third-worst defeat in the previous 40 years, exceeded only by a 39-point loss in 1950 and a 35-point rout the 'Cats suffered at the hands of LSU in 1987. The 30-point margin blew away the Vanderbilt program's previous largest victory margin against Kentucky, a series that was 131 games strong at the time, which was 18 points in a 97-79 win in 1965—and, nearly three decades later, the 30-point margin has been topped only once, in the memorable 41-point shellacking the Shan Foster-led 'Dores put on the 'Cats in February 2008.

There's nothing more satisfying than playing a great game in a must-win situation to lead your team to victory. After my abysmal three-point, two-rebound line in 37 minutes against Alabama, I led all players in the Kentucky game with 23 points and nine rebounds—probably the only time I ever led all players in scoring and rebounding. Kornet added 18 points and seven rebounds, while Book went for 15 and six, along with a game-high four steals; thus, the three seniors alone outscored the entire Kentucky team. "I don't think that we could play any better," Coach Newton summarized, as "our guys responded with the best 40 minutes of the season."

All of that added up to a nightmare for UK, especially for Derrick Miller, who had torched us for 27 points in Lexington. In this game, though, we blanked him from the field—he missed all eight of his field goal attempts, and only a single free throw kept him from a complete shutout. He had the type of game I had just experienced in Tuscaloosa—decent shots, but they didn't fall, and in his case his aim worsened as the game progressed, as he completely missed the rim a couple of times. Chris Mills, whose recruitment had started the mess in which UK currently found itself, wasn't much better, going only 3-for-12 from the field and, like Miller, missing all four of his three-point attempts.

The one Wildcat that showed some real guts was Sean Sutton, the point guard and son of Coach Eddie Sutton, whose job security, already tenuous before the game, likely had suffered a mortal blow with this embarrassment delivered by his future boss, Coach Newton. Sean, fighting the flu, led Kentucky with 14 points, including the only three treys the team hit; the rest of the team went 0-for-11 from behind the arc. Coach Newton was sufficiently impressed by that performance that he sought out Sean after the game and complimented him on his effort. "I just told him I really admired him, and I wanted him to know it," said the coach. Sean returned the compliment, saying, "Maybe this is the way it's supposed to be—Coach Newton's last game against Kentucky becoming a huge win for Vanderbilt. He deserves it. He's a great man."

There wasn't much Sean's father, Coach Sutton, could say, so he chose his words carefully. "It would have to be very meaningful for C.M.," he said. "The fact that this may be the last chance he had to beat his alma mater, and to beat them so badly, must have been very special for him." "We deserved to get beat by 30," he said later, and "they [Vandy] deserved to win by 30 by the way they played."

In a supreme irony, Coach Newton, having defended accusations that he shouldn't coach against UK because he might not try hard enough to win, now found himself addressing questions that made exactly the opposite charge—that he had run up the score. He reacted just as angrily as he had to the "conflict of interest" charges, responding, "I wasn't trying to run up the score, I was trying to win the basketball game." True enough, but several writers from both schools noted that C.M. left his starting five on the floor until about roughly four minutes remained in the game—at a time when the score was 72-37.

My own view is that C.M. wasn't running up the score. First, he probably felt like he needed to err on the side of keeping the pedal to the metal for as long as he could so that he could, once and for all, silence the "conflict of interest" critics. Second, Coach Newton let the players enjoy the rout, especially the two senior Kentuckians—Kornet and me. "Coach Newton didn't do that so we could put a thrashing on them," Frank said. "Coach Newton wanted us to enjoy every minute of it." I agreed: "I wanted to stay in the whole way. It was sweet, and I think he [Newton] may have sensed that and left us in to enjoy it."

Those who look for signs of "rubbing it in" normally search, as was done here, for signs that the winning team's best players were on the floor longer than they needed to be at the end of the game, given the margin. But that's just one way to look at it. Another is how much those players were on the floor, period. For example, before Coach Newton finally pulled me with two minutes left in the game, I had played the entire second half—18 straight minutes—even though our lead was never less than 20 at any point in the half, and it was over 30 most of that time. Likewise, Booker and Kornet played straight through the second half before they were pulled a minute or so before I was. So, while I doubt that C.M. had any inclination of running up the score, I do think he was sending some sort of message by playing the three seniors nearly the entire second half.

Kornet, the Lexington native, was grinning from ear to ear after the game, a 180-degree turnaround from his and the team's devastation of the Tennis Ball Game exactly two weeks earlier. "It's hard to express," he said, then proceeded to express it perfectly: "I'm really overjoyed. This is a very special win for everybody from Kentucky, especially Coach Newton."

Despite the emotion of the game and the margin, the most important accomplishment was simply winning the game over a team with whom we were tied in the SEC standings going in. As expected, the four other teams in the SEC race beat the four also-rans, meaning that we merely kept pace with everyone else, moving to 7-4, still a game behind LSU:

LSU	8-3
Alabama	8-4
Tennessee	7-4
Florida	7-4
Vandy	7-4
Kentucky	6-5
Ole Miss	5-6
Georgia	5-7
Mississippi State	3-8
Auburn	0-11

༇

One thing was for sure: no one would ever raise the "conflict of interest" issue again after this 30-point beatdown. "I hope that's a dead issue," Coach Newton said, and he would be right—the "conflict of interest" stuff never reared its head after this game. John Bibb, *The Tennessean*'s sports editor who had been the ringleader of the "conflict of interest" brigade in the media, cried "Uncle" after the game. As C.M. returned to the court for his postgame radio show, Bibb called down from the press box, and waved a white handkerchief, shouting, "I surrender." C.M. waved back, and that was the end of that. Perhaps the title of *Nashville Banner* sports editor Joe Biddle's column the next day said it best: "So much for conflict of interest."

IN THE ZONE

I

Ole Miss, our next opponent, continued to hang on the fringes of the SEC race, but a three-game losing streak essentially had dropped the Rebels from serious contention. Their coach, Ed Murphy, admitted before our game that the NIT was their "realistic goal now." Moreover, the Rebels had received a double dose of pain while we were thrashing Kentucky: they not only lost a heartbreaking 55-54 decision to Alabama in Oxford, but also lost starting forward Mike Paul for the season with a fractured thumb.

For our part, we had to avoid a letdown after the emotional victory over Kentucky. Again, this is where veteran leadership would come into play. The presence of three seniors and two juniors was important to overcome the double whammy of Coach Newton's resignation and the Florida heartbreaker, but it would be just as important to put the euphoria of the UK game in the rearview mirror quickly and focus on Ole Miss. "Anybody who thinks we're in for an easy game is crazy," Kornet said. I added that "I think we'll play well, but we don't expect another 30-point game." Frank and I were both right on the money with those statements.

Indeed, the game was hard fought all the way. The Rebels served early notice that they were in it for the full 40 minutes by jumping to a 14-8 lead. We answered with a 14-2 run to take the lead, which we held for most of the rest of the first half. Glass hit a three-pointer at the buzzer to trim our lead to one, 37-36, at intermission. Ole Miss nudged in front a couple of times early in the second half, but then we scored eight straight points to resume control. We eventually stretched the lead to 11 points, and we were still in charge by eight, 66-58, with around five minutes left when disaster struck in the form of turnovers on offense and poor work on defense, aided by some highly questionable officiating. Ole Miss came all the way back to tie the game at 67 with two minutes remaining. Then we turned it over again, and Tim Jumper's deuce with 1:23 left gave the Rebels a 69-67 lead. Now we had to play catch-up, but that didn't work either: Kornet's shot was blocked, and the Rebels recovered inside the final minute. Now the Rebs could practically ice the game with a basket, and Jumper had a makeable eight-footer inside 30 seconds, but he missed. We rebounded. Needing two points to tie, Wilcox drove to the basket and was fouled; the pressure tremendous, Derrick sank both ends of the one-and-one with 11 seconds remaining to tie the game at 69, setting the stage for one final, frenetic, fantastic Memorial Gym finish.

We had not yet committed enough fouls in the second half for Ole Miss to be awarded free throws on a nonshooting foul (i.e., Ole Miss was not "in the bonus"). Accordingly, we could afford to be aggressive on defense and go for a steal, and that was the instruction from Coach Newton. If we were called for a foul, no big deal; Ole Miss simply would inbound the ball and start all over, only with fewer seconds remaining on the clock in its effort to take and make a game-winning shot. The situation was similar to the final seconds of the LSU game in Baton Rouge.

Naturally, Ole Miss sought out Glass for the final sequence, and he received the ball in the backcourt, clearly with the intention of dribbling as far as we would let him and then taking the shot—not unlike the game in Oxford when he had a shot for victory at the buzzer in regulation. This time, though, Eric Reid was guarding him closely, and Eric stepped in front of Glass to impede his progress, with Wilcox assisting. "Eric cut Glass off and wanted to draw the charge," Derrick described after the game. "Glass was trying to make a move to go around Eric. When he put the ball down, I tipped it away and Booker picked it up." When I saw the ball come loose, I started streaking toward our basket, and had a step on the Ole Miss defender as Book led me with a perfect pass. I left the floor for a right-handed layup and the defender, John Matthews, caught me and fouled me as I laid the ball in for the apparent game-winning layup and potential three-point play with two seconds showing on the clock.

Except that the officials didn't count the basket.

That's right—even though Matthews didn't even make contact with me until I had left the ground for the layup, so that I was obviously in the act of shooting when he fouled me, the official, Gerald Boudreaux, who was staring right at the sequence about eight feet from where it transpired, waved off the basket, which I didn't see because I was facing the crowd and celebrating the layup. But I still remember Booker telling me, with the "waving off" signal (which is the same as a "safe" call in baseball), "They waved it off!"

I was incredulous, as were the 15,646 people in the sold-out gym. This was a worse call, viewed in isolation, than the tennis ball call; how can a basket not count, i.e., be deemed "not in the act of shooting," when the foul wasn't committed until the ball was practically in the basket? Maybe Boudreaux felt remorseful for not calling a foul on us when we stole the ball from Glass; maybe he intended to call a two-shot foul and didn't think I would make the layup, and when I did, he changed his mind and nullified the basket; or maybe he was just incompetent at that moment.

Regardless, the call was even more absurd in light of a call earlier in the game when Glass had the ball at the free-throw line, drove around our player, who hacked him across the wrist for the foul, then took a dribble and laid the ball in, and the officials counted the basket (leading Kornet to quip after the game, referencing the professional league's then-hot promotional slogan, "The NBA…It's fan-tastic").

Whatever the reason, it was a terrible call, and now, instead of shooting one free throw for a three-point lead, I needed to make both ends of the one-and-one simply to give us a two-point lead. Ole Miss called timeout, ostensibly to let me think about the free throws, but which was fortunate because it allowed me to gather my thoughts and calm down after the terrible call. "I really wasn't all that nervous," I said after the game. Indeed, the Rebels' "icing" tactic didn't work; I swished both free throws to give us a 71-69 lead. Still, the game wasn't over; two seconds remained and Ole Miss would attempt a long pass to Glass and hope that he could produce some buzzer-beating magic. Our strategy remained the same—we still had a foul to give, so we could be overly aggressive in not allowing a long pass or uncontested shot. Once again, our strategy worked perfectly, as Reid knocked the ball away from Glass, no foul was called, and at last the buzzer sounded. We pulled a victory out of the fire, 71-69.

The game may have been over, but the excitement wasn't. Ole Miss coach Ed Murphy was irate at the end-of-game no-calls, and he intended to give the officials a piece of his mind. The problem was that the officials' locker room was accessible only through the tunnel next to our bench; Murphy and the Rebels were 94 feet away underneath the opposite basket. So, Ed took off on a walk/run to chase down the officials before they reached the safety of their locker room; of course, he was unsuccessful, leaving him to vent his considerable frustrations to the media in a series of scathing remarks. "They just tackled Glass," he said, "Hell, they were trying to tackle him, and the officials wouldn't call it." That rant led to his ridiculous assertion that "When we play down in Oxford next, we're going to break a kid's arm at the buzzer and they better not call a foul." After reading that, I was glad I didn't have to play in Oxford anymore! Murphy did, however, echo the complaint I've always had about officials: "I mean, the officials are so arrogant you can't even talk to them, which makes it worse."

You had to feel somewhat sympathetic for Murphy. We had won all four games against his team in the last two seasons, but the Rebels easily could have won three of them: a too-quick five-second call inside a minute to play facilitated our comeback win in Oxford in '88, Glass's missed jumper in Oxford in '89 allowed the game to go into overtime, where we won, and now controversial end-of-game officiating affected our second win against Ole Miss in '89. Murphy may have had a legitimate gripe, especially on the Glass turnover that preceded my layup/free throws, but he was off the mark to the extent he was suggesting that the officiating was one-sided in our favor. It was, quite simply, a poorly officiated game. As C.M. said, "I don't know what he's got to complain about. I thought there were a lot of no-calls in the game, but I thought most of them went against us." He was right, and that didn't even take into account the horrendous wave-off of my should-have-been game-winning layup. "How they couldn't count that basket was incredible," he said. "That's incredible!" Naturally, I agreed that the basket "absolutely should have counted" and that "I was in shock like the rest of the players and the rest of the fans" that the layup didn't count. Still, all's well that ends well, I concluded: "I suppose everything turned out okay." That was an understatement.

It was unusual for us to win a game with only two players in double figures, but we managed to do that against Ole Miss, which was a Kornet/Goheen-led affair. I scored 23 and Frank scored 21; no one else scored more than seven. He and I combined for 18 of the team's 27 field goals (nine each); no one else made more than two field goals. But that was just enough to give us the victory. In fact, I kept up the hot streak after Kentucky, marking the first time I had ever scored over 20 points in consecutive games. The nine field goals were the most I ever made in a game at Vanderbilt, and the 9-for-13 performance from the field was one of my best. Clearly, I had entered "the zone," that rarefied air where the goal seems bigger, the game slows down, and things just seem a little easier. The SEC took notice, too: with 46 points in the Kentucky and Ole Miss games (16-for-24 from the field, 6-for-9 from behind the arc, 8-for-10 from the line, 14 rebounds, seven assists), I was named the SEC Player of the Week. That meant that all three seniors received POW honors at some point during the season—a fitting tribute to all three of us that demonstrated that each of us took a leading role at various points in the season.

II

"I'm heading down the Atlanta highway"
—B-52's, "Love Shack" ('88–'89)

We moved from Ole Miss to Georgia, and from one angry opposing coach to another—Bulldogs coach Hugh Durham was still seething from the no-call on the Booker/Rod Cole collision that preceded my buzzer-beating three in Nashville. In fact, Georgia—most prognosticators' preseason favorite to claim the SEC title—had not quite recovered from that game. While the teams entered the game in Athens with similar overall records (we were 14-10 and Georgia was 13-10), we were 8-4 in the league, tied for second, while the Bulldogs were 5-7 and tied for seventh, pretty much out of the race with a third of the league slate left to play. They were also coming off a non-conference thumping two days earlier, an 80-66 drubbing dealt them by New Mexico.

In this second game, it would take a near-historic conclusion to match, let alone surpass, the craziness of the final seconds in Nashville. But, as events would transpire,

Hugh Durham was up to the challenge. The second game was much like the first—nip-and-tuck most of the way with Georgia maintaining a slight edge much of that time. Still, our defensive plan, which was to keep the Dawgs' All-SEC center, Alec Kessler, from getting many touches, was working well; we used a zone defense, with Kornet staying stationary near Kessler and one of the guards, primarily Booker, helping. That of course meant that we were vulnerable to long-range shots, and the Dawgs would hoist 18 three-pointers in the game. But they made only six (three by sixth man Jody Patton, who had burned us from the outside in Nashville). They made enough in the first half to build a nine-point lead, but we cut the Bulldogs' lead to four, 37-33, at the half.

The game stayed tight in the second half, and we received a critical boost from backup center Alberto Ballestra, who scored five points in a one-minute span to keep us within a basket of the Bulldogs. We caught the Dawgs twice, 46-46 and 48-48, before taking the lead at 50-49 on a Kornet 15-footer. From there, we slowly pulled away. The Dawgs' Marshall Wilson, who had played well in Nashville, fouled out with around six minutes remaining; as the only other Bulldog with any real size, his departure enabled us to gang up on Kessler even more. Two Rod Cole free throws brought the Dawgs within two, 59-57, with 5:23 to play. But we took command with eight straight points, scored by the three seniors—two Kornet free throws, my three-pointer, and Book's conventional three-point play—to lead 67-57 with 2:16 left. Georgia hung around, though, and Litterial Green's three-pointer drew the Dawgs within six with about a minute remaining. The score was 73-67 after we made two free throws with 33 seconds left. And that's when things got crazy and Hugh Durham came unglued.

We retreated downcourt and set up our zone defense, with Kornet firmly positioned on one of the blocks under the basket. Green took the inbounds pass and steamed down the floor as fast as he could. It was obvious from the first or second dribble what Green's plan was—he would eschew a three-point shot (he missed seven of nine attempts for the game), but instead would drive to the basket, try to draw contact from one of our players as he was shooting a layup or similarly close-range shot, and with luck would score a conventional three-point basket to cut our lead to three and make it a one-possession game.

The problem for Green, though, was that Kornet stood stationary on the block from the moment Green received the ball 75 feet away. So, when Green plowed into Frank while attempting the shot, there was only one call the officials could make—charge on Green, our ball, and the game pretty much in our back pocket. "It was an obvious charge," Frank observed after the game.

At that point, no doubt realizing the game was over, the frustrations of what had become a lost season boiled over in Coach Durham, and he vented those frustrations right then and there by storming onto the court. He confronted one of the three officials—loudly—and received a technical foul. He then raced to a second official, yelled something similarly impertinent, and was slapped with a second technical. It took three technical fouls for a coach to be ejected from a game in 1989 (the rule was soon thereafter changed to the current two techs), so Durham found the third official, screamed more invective, and was assessed a third technical foul, finally ending his night on the floor. He hurriedly shook hands with Coach Newton and walked to the Dawgs' locker room.

We received two free throws for each technical, plus the one-and-one Kornet would shoot for Green's foul. Frank made both for a 75-67 lead. I then stepped to the line for *six* free throws and made them all, then added two more after I was fouled on the ensuing inbounds play. The final score was a highly misleading 85-72.

Unsurprisingly, the Durham meltdown was the hot topic of postgame conversation. And the man himself found the humor in it: "I've already been reprimanded by the conference and can't talk about the officiating anymore," he said, referencing his highly critical comments about the officiating in the final seconds of our win in Nashville. "But I did hear a guy behind me tonight say this game was the worst-called game he had ever seen. I didn't say that, but I heard someone say that." In a moment of greater seriousness, he confirmed what had been obvious to us on the court: the outburst was entirely premeditated. "It was a planned thing, though. Once I got a tech, it was over. I didn't lose my composure. I knew what I was doing."

Durham's late-game histrionics overshadowed what was a great win for us—our fourth in a row against Georgia over the last two seasons. And I kept my hot streak going, staying in the zone. During his TV show recapping the game, Coach Newton voiced over a clip where I nailed a 15-footer, saying, "That's like a layup for him right now." I hit seven of 10 shots from the field, meaning that in the past three games I was 23-for-34 from the field, a blistering 67.6%, the best sustained hot streak I ever enjoyed at Vanderbilt. That hot streak extended to the free-throw line, where I had been bedeviled early in the season. The last-minute flurry of free throws, most occasioned by the Durham ejection, resulted in my shooting 13 free throws—and I made all 13, which, at least at the time, was my one and only Vanderbilt record: "Best Free-Throw Percentage, Road Game." Everyone else picked it up at the line as well; we came into the game shooting a lackluster 67.9% from the line as a team, but against Georgia we went 32-for-37, for 86.5%; the makes, attempts, and percentage would remain our season best. (Amazingly, we hit 18 straight free throws in the final 1:07 of the game.)

For the third straight game, Kornet and I dominated the scoring. We had combined for 41 points against Kentucky and 44 against Ole Miss, and we topped ourselves against Georgia, combining for 52 points behind my career-high 28 and his 24. And we combined to shoot 80% from the field—he bettered my 7-for-10 by going 9-for-10 from the field, and 95% from the line (Frank hit six of seven free throws to go with my 13 straight). And for the second year in a row, Eric Reid had a great game in his home state, posting a double-double of 11 points and 12 re-bounds. Moreover, for the second straight season, we made only a single three-pointer in a game, and, like that prior game (at Notre Dame), I made it. We missed our eight three-point attempts other than my late-game trey, so for the second consecutive season we came within a whisker of ending Vandy's famous streak of never being shut out from behind the arc before the streak ever had the chance to garner much attention.

Most importantly, our third win in a row, and fifth in six contests since the Tennis Ball Game, moved us to 9-4 in the SEC. It also set up the next biggest game of the season—and maybe the biggest game in my four years at Vanderbilt with LSU coming to town.

<h1 style="text-align:center">III</h1>

"When I was a boy, I thought it just came to ya"
—John Hiatt, "Slow Turning" ('88–'89)

Our three wins in a row and five of six had enabled us only to keep pace with LSU, not gain ground. The Tigers had won nine of 10, including a headline-making non-conference win over Georgetown, then the #2 team in the country. In that game, played in late January before over 54,000 fans in the New Orleans Superdome (at the time, the largest crowd ever to see a regular-season college basketball game), the Tigers struck a blow for SEC pride by upsetting the Hoyas, 82-80, on Ricky Blanton's putback at the buzzer. That game moved LSU into the Top 20 at #19. Other than a hiccup at Mississippi State on the same night we lost at Alabama, the Tigers were on a roll, and freshman Chris Jackson was leading them.

Indeed, Jackson not only hadn't cooled off since his buzzer-beater defeated us in Baton Rouge, he somehow had upped his game. He scored 26 in the Georgetown win, 34 in a 99-80 romp over Kentucky, and an incredible 50 in a 122-106 demolition of Tennessee. Those feats led *Sports Illustrated* to put Jackson on the cover of the magazine's February 20, 1989, issue, referencing LSU's greatest hoopster: "He's a Pistol." That issue would be on newsstands when the Tigers arrived in Nashville.

We couldn't let Jackson explode for 50 like Tennessee did, but we knew he would get his points. The real challenge was trying to control Ricky Blanton, who was the straw that stirred the Tigers' drink. As I said before the game, "Blanton, without question, is their team leader." We had to keep him from matching Jackson's assumed 30-point game with one of his own, and we had not been able to control him in recent games. In fact, Blanton had never lost to Vanderbilt—the season we swept LSU, 1986–87, Ricky had redshirted with a knee injury. The three years Ricky had been active—'84–'85, '85–'86, and '87–'88—were Tiger sweeps of the Commodores, with the one-point decision in Baton Rouge earlier in 1988–89 giving Blanton a perfect 8-0 mark against Vanderbilt. No one else on the LSU team bothered us too much or threatened to explode for 20-25 points; this was a two-man show, and we at least had to hold Jackson and Blanton to a combined 50 points, which was exactly their average (Jackson 28.3, Blanton 22.2), and they had scored 62 of LSU's 85 in Baton Rouge.

The players and coaches went out of their way to avoid antagonizing each other before such a big game. Assessing our team, Blanton said, "they don't have the best athletes, but they have good athletes and are well-coached," and that "[t]hey really have so many good shooters that you can't concentrate on just Goheen. Both Barry Booker and Derrick Wilcox can also hurt you." Meanwhile, LSU coach Dale Brown discounted his team's recent success against us. "[W]e've been fortunate to have good personnel matchups," he said, adding that "I've always been impressed because they play hard, and unselfish, and they have extremely good shooters." What he said privately to his team, however, was a little more derogatory: "They aren't a super defensive team. They aren't super quick. They aren't a super rebounding team. You have done it three out of the last four years up here and beaten them. So, the same thing will apply tomorrow night, and you will beat them again." He picked "the key matchup" as "Blanton on Barry Goheen."

Without doubt, this was the toughest ticket in my four years at Vandy—much tougher than the Indiana, North Carolina, Louisville, and Kentucky games. It also was the most highly anticipated game of those four years—and longer back than that. Some even called it "the biggest game in Vanderbilt history," and at least "the most important game played here [in Memorial] since 1974." We were ready. ESPN's broadcast team of Tim Brando and Bill Raftery foresaw a close game. Pressed for a prediction before the game, Raftery—a fine man and announcer—said, "LSU, man to man, has more talent. But there is a great chemistry on the Vanderbilt team." For his part, as the ball went airborne for the opening tip, Brando observed, "Most people believe this will be a high-scoring affair." That seemed like a safe prediction; LSU was averaging 95 points per contest.

It's impossible to describe the noise and electricity in Memorial Gym for this game. It was deafening, and the crowd was on fire from the moment the starting lineups were announced. The post-game description of "a deafening partisan crowd of 15,646" was spot-on. Indeed, these are the games that justify all those off-season workouts, the preseason conditioning, the dreary October and November practices. This is why players want to play sports at a high level. If you can't get excited for this game, well, you should never have picked up a ball in the first place.

I had been playing so well lately that I decided to be more aggressive on offense early in the game. Booker seemed to start many of our biggest games in Memorial with a three-pointer; now it was my turn. We controlled the tip, and with Blanton guarding me, I faked rolling off a Kornet screen at the top of the key intended to send me to the block; instead, I popped out behind Frank, received the pass from

Book, and drained a triple to begin the evening. Mouton answered with an 18-footer, but a minute or so later we ran a double screen that broke me open at the top of the key; same spot, same result: 6-2, Commodores. But I shot blanks for the rest of the half and Kornet picked up two quick fouls, putting him on the bench for the rest of the half. Still, we led 19-12 about seven minutes in, and everyone made significant contributions to keep the Tigers at bay. A Steve Grant putback stretched our lead to nine, and after an LSU run cut our lead to two, 24-22, at the 10:00 mark, Steve's turnaround from the block made it 26-22, and a Wilcox jumper made it 28-22. But another LSU spurt—Jackson's fast-break layup, Singleton's put back, and a Jackson 15-footer—tied the game for the first time since the opening tip. Ballestra's tip-in off a Reid miss gave us the lead back, 30-28, and it was our turn for a spurt. Wilcox hit a three; Reid missed a 14-footer over Blanton, but Ricky failed to block him out, and the rebound caromed right back to Eric, who took a power dribble and delivered a two-handed slam that stretched our lead to seven, 35-28, and reignited the crowd.

LSU wouldn't go away, though—the Tigers scored five straight points to pull within two with two minutes remaining. LSU had a chance to tie when we misfired again, but Wilcox drew a charge from Singleton with 90 seconds remaining. Todd Millholland hit from eight feet off a nice pass from Ballestra, but Jackson's trey cut the lead to one, 37-36, with a minute left. Todd hit again to put us up by three. LSU held for the final shot, but Jackson made a tactical error and took the shot too early, an 18-footer with about 10 seconds left; it rimmed out, and we rebounded with a few seconds to do something. And we did; completing the role reversal where I started the game with the three, Booker played the role of buzzer-beater by nailing a 14-footer just as the horn sounded. The crowd exploded again, and we went to the locker room with a 41-36 lead, and with a ton of energy and momentum, knowing that Kornet would be rested and ready for the second half. But we could not have anticipated the incredible second half that was about to unfold.

Dale Brown was confident too, and why not? We had led the Tigers by two at the half in Baton Rouge, stretched it to double digits early in the second half, and watched the Tigers rally for the victory. Brown predicted that "[t]he key will be the first four minutes," and if his team could hang close, "we can knock them out then." We were determined not to let that happen. In fact, of the 252 halves of basketball I played at Vandy, the second half of this game would be the best.

LSU had played zone most of the first half, especially after Kornet went to the bench; as a result, we launched 14 three-pointers in the first half. In the second half, though, we became much more aggressive in attacking the basket, resulting in more points in the paint and more free throws. In fact, Kornet announced his return to the game by rebounding his own miss for a putback and a seven-point lead. I added two free throws—my first points since the two opening threes—and the lead was back to nine. Sims hit a three, but Wilcox beat Jackson off the dribble, drew help from Kornet's defender, and laid off a beautiful feed to Frank for the dunk and a 47-39 lead. Booker then intercepted a pass, and seconds later I fed him for a corner three that put our lead in double digits for the first time and forced a Dale Brown timeout less than two minutes into the second half. The crowd was absolutely deafening.

The timeout didn't work for the Tigers. Sims missed a jumper and Kornet beat his frontcourt counterpart down the floor, allowing me to feed him for another rim-rattling dunk and a 13-point lead. Sims scored underneath, but I answered with two more free throws. Jackson hit two free throws, but Kornet hit a nifty left-handed hook from eight feet. Jackson scored again, but once more we set the crowd afire with a great hustle play: I blew a layup underneath and LSU rebounded, but Kornet tipped LSU's outlet pass toward our bench, then made a spectacular save by flinging the ball blindly to half-court, where Wilcox retrieved it. Seconds later, Booker recovered, fed me underneath, and this time my layup in traffic was true, and we led 58-45. Seconds after that, Wilcox made the evening's greatest defensive play, blocking Jackson's shot from behind, which led to another drive-and-foul as I continued to press against LSU walk-on Dennis Tracey. My two free throws stretched the lead to 15. Mouton temporarily calmed the crowd with a layup, but Booker hit a 10-footer, and, after an LSU miss, I rebounded and went coast-to-coast for a layup over Tracey and a 64-47 lead. After I hit two more free throws—I made eight in a row in the first six minutes of the second half—a Booker jumper and a Kornet free throw pushed our lead to 70-54 with 13 minutes to play, and it looked a blowout was at hand. But not yet.

Reminiscent of their early second-half spurt in Baton Rouge that erased our double-digit lead, the Tigers mounted a quick run of nine straight points on two threes by Jackson and one by Blanton, quickly cutting our lead to seven, 70-63. After a Kornet miss, Jackson, who already had 33 points, launched a three that would have cut our lead to four. The LSU bench rose as one anticipating another trey; for the only time all night, the crowd was relatively quiet. But this time Jackson missed, and on the other end, Booker scored a layup off a backdoor cut to stretch the lead to nine with 11 minutes to play. Jackson reduced the lead back to seven with a jumper, but Reid tipped in his own miss to return the lead to nine. We converted a Blanton miss into a four-point play when Reid was fouled while making a layup; he missed the free-throw, but Booker rebounded and, seconds later, hit another layup off a back cut, returning our lead to 13. LSU was clearly fatigued. Jackson hit a three to make it 78-68, but he was running on fumes and would not score again. I answered his three with my final three of the evening for an 81-68 lead. Singleton's two free throws made it 81-70 with eight minutes left. If the Tigers could mount one last charge, they might be able to steal the victory.

Instead, the opposite happened, and it was all Commodores for the rest of the evening. We buried LSU with an alley-oop to Kornet, a three-point play by Wilcox off the fast break, a baseline jumper by Reid, my final two free throws of the night, and a Reid five-footer off a back screen. Suddenly we enjoyed a 92-70 bulge with five minutes remaining, and, as one writer put it, every time we scored, "Memorial Gymnasium sounded like a powder keg exploding." Brown called timeout, but it was futile. Kornet scored again, and Booker's 12-footer made it 15 straight points and a 26-point lead with three-and-a-half minutes remaining. At that point, Brown raised the white flag, emptying his bench. C.M. kept the five starters in for another sequence, then replaced three of them at the next dead ball, while Wilcox and I stayed on. Our run reached 20 consecutive points before Wilcox and I exited to sweet, thunderous applause. The reserves kept the heat on as well: Mayes hit a three with 30 seconds left and Wheat attacked the goal for a layup with two seconds left, which did not make Dale Brown very happy. The final score was, as reported by LSU, "a 108-74 massacre," and the crowd chanted the familiar "We're number 1" in the closing seconds as we tied LSU for the league lead.

The joy in our locker room was unrestrained, as were our post-game comments. There's nothing like playing your best game in a sold-out gym before a national television audience. "I can't think of a bigger game, I can't imagine a bigger win," I enthused. "We accepted the challenge of playing the first-place team with a chance to tie. We came out fired up; it was the best crowd of the year and it was our night." Coach Newton made similar remarks: "They [the players] were presented with the challenges all intercollegiate athletes long for. They were playing for the Southeastern Conference lead, before the hometown fans and before a national television audience. They couldn't ask for anything more, and they responded by playing their finest game of the season."

Dale Brown had to agree: "We didn't give up. Vanderbilt just played so brilliantly. It was an old-fashioned whipping." He added that "Vanderbilt tonight looked like a professional team." Still, the two coaches chatted for several seconds at midcourt in the post-game handshake, and it was Brown who was doing most of the talking. I don't think he was very happy about the final few minutes when C.M. didn't remove any of the starters until about three minutes remained and after Brown already had removed his starters. Plus, the reserves kept pouring it on, hoisting three-pointers and aggressively seeking to score rather than simply dribbling out the clock. In other words, I may not have figured out the relationship between C.M. Newton and Wimp Sanderson, but I think I had a better handle on the Newton-Brown relationship—C.M. didn't like Dale very much, and for this last game he would coach against Brown, maybe C.M. wanted to make sure he went out with a bang. And if that meant a slight running-up of the score, so be it.

Coaches Newton and Brown did not see eye to eye on several things, most notably Proposition 48, the then-controversial initiative, enacted by the NCAA in 1986, designed to improve the academics of incoming freshmen that required at least a 2.0 GPA in high school and minimum scores on the SAT and/or ACT exams. Failure to qualify under Prop 48 meant that the player would lose a year of eligibility.

Brown, along with other high-profile coaches such as Georgetown's John Thompson and Temple's John Chaney, charged that Prop 48 was racist because it prevented a disproportionate number of African-American athletes from participating fully in college athletics. Coach Newton, on the other hand, believed strongly in the "student" part of "student-athlete," and always supported measures that would portray college athletics as more than the training-for-the-pros breeding ground it increasingly was becoming.

Brown also had a long-running feud with Indiana head coach (and close C.M. Newton friend) Bob Knight, whose IU team had beaten Brown's LSU team in the 1981 Final Four, then did it again in the 1987 Elite Eight, both times propelling the Hoosiers to the NCAA title.

But the incident that really drove a wedge between the two men went back exactly a decade, to 1979. LSU was hosting Alabama, coached by C.M., with a chance to clinch the Tigers' first outright SEC title in school history. The Tigers thrashed the Tide, 86-66, and with just 38 seconds remaining and the crowd going wild, Brown pulled one of the all-time bush-league moves: he called timeout and used the timeout to order that an "LSU: SEC Champions" banner be dropped out of the rafters. C.M., understandably, was incensed; he confronted one of the officials and said, "If you don't get this game started before I get back to the bench, we're leaving the floor and you'll have to finish the game without us. We're not going to participate in their damn celebration." Then-Tide assistant coach Wimp Sanderson recalled, "C.M. was...as mad as I had ever seen him." Years later, Brown said (lamely) that "it wasn't really planned" and, anyway, "[i]t really didn't have an impact on the game." According to Sanderson, Brown showed up in the lobby of Alabama's hotel the next morning and tried to apologize, but, as Wimp said, "he didn't get far in that regard."

The bottom line was that, in C.M.'s words, "Dale and I were natural antagonists because we had such different personalities and probably because we were both competing for SEC championships." And they were both competing for the 1989 SEC championship. So maybe C.M., who had not enjoyed much success against LSU since the 1979 fiasco, felt like a modest twisting of the knife in the last few minutes of the last game he would ever coach against Dale Brown was a way to even the score a decade later.

Predictably for a 34-point blowout against a strong opponent, every starter was superlative. I led the team in scoring for the fourth straight game with 23 points, adding five assists and five rebounds and hitting all 10 free-throw attempts, giving me a 23-for-23 week at the line. Book scored 21 and claimed eight rebounds, while Kornet went for 17 and seven. Reid scored 12 with a game-high nine boards, while Wilcox added 13 points and a game-high seven assists. The bench play was great as well, especially Todd Milholland, who hit all four shots from the field (most in the first half in relief of Kornet).

Meanwhile, Jackson did get his points—38 on 14-of-25 shooting from the field—along with a healthy number of "oohs" and "ahhs" from the crowd. But he got tired midway through the second half thanks to Wilcox's relentless pressure. As Kornet commented, Wilcox's defense "won't show up in the stats" because Jackson scored 38 points, "but he earned every one of them." Critically, we held Blanton to a mere seven points on just 3-of-10 shooting, which was a tribute to Booker's persistent shadowing of Ricky wherever he was on the floor. The seven points broke a streak of 29 consecutive double-figure scoring games for Blanton. As expected, no one else hurt us much, and we dominated LSU on the boards, 43-23, which I found shocking: "Forty-three to 23. That's almost unheard of to almost double a team's rebounds."

The LSU blowout, coupled with Florida's 99-81 spanking of Tennessee, created a three-way tie at the top of the conference:

Vandy	10-4
LSU	10-4
Florida	10-4
Alabama	9-5
Tennessee	8-6
Ole Miss	6-8
Kentucky	6-8
Georgia	5-9
Mississippi State	5-9
Auburn	1-13

We did more than beat LSU—we "shattered their confidence," according to an LSU writer. The Tigers would win only one more SEC game. Now, with LSU out of the way, we could look ahead to the next biggest game of the year, just seven days out—the rematch with Florida.

30

REMATCH

I

"Step by step...higher and higher"
—Bruce Hornsby & the Range, "Jacob's Ladder" ('88–'89)

As we returned to the practice floor to begin the week, we knew that Florida loomed at the end of the week. But first we had to take care of business at Auburn. These days, the Auburn game would be called a "trap game," meaning a game against a lesser opponent for a team coming off a big win and possibly looking past the lesser opponent toward another huge game with a better team.

Trap game or not, Auburn should not have posed that much of a challenge. In fact, the Tigers were terrible. They were 2-13 in the SEC, having beaten Kentucky two nights before our game. It's amazing how perceptions can change in 10 weeks; we first saw the Tigers in Nashville in mid-December for our SEC debut when we were 2-5 and they were unbeaten, and we rallied from a 13-point halftime deficit to win 93-77. That seemed like a good win at the time, but subsequent events proved otherwise: beset by injuries and other problems, the Tigers lost their first 11 SEC games.

The Tigers of December weren't very good, but the Tigers of February were even worse: forward John Caylor was injured, and hotshot freshman Johnny Benjamin had been dismissed from the team, leading coach Sonny Smith to declare, "it's been a simply disastrous season"—so disastrous that he would resign at the end of the season and take the head coaching job at VCU. Still, those absences opened the way for senior Keenan Carpenter to give his best Chris Jackson impersonation—in fact, he scored 44 points in a 104-91 loss to Jackson-led LSU, had scored at least 30 points in five games, and was averaging 23.8 points per game in league play. Plus, our tilt was his final home game in an Auburn uniform, the first of four consecutive games in which we were part of a team's final home game (including our own), a scheduling oddity.

Coach Newton, who was presented with a plaque prior to the game to honor his final appearance at Auburn as a head coach, asserted that "I think Auburn is going to be very difficult. It will probably be the most difficult game we've had." I can't imagine he believed that, though. We were playing with a ton of confidence, and

Auburn simply didn't have the horses to keep up. If we played it even half as well as we had played against LSU, we would win.

We played a whole lot better than that in the first 10 minutes. In fact, we picked up right where we had left off against LSU. Booker hit a three-pointer to open the game, and the first 12 minutes were like a layup and shooting drill, highlighted by a two-on-one fast break where I flipped a behind-the-back bounce pass to Grant, who threw down a monster tomahawk jam as if we were running a practice drill. Auburn had no enthusiasm, and Sonny Smith tried to inject some into his team by drawing a technical foul a mere eight minutes into the game. That didn't work either (though I missed one of the two technical foul shots, ending my streak of over 25 made free throws), and at the 7:49 mark of the first half, we led by an incredible 24 points, 32-8. That meant that (1) in our last 21 minutes of play, we had outscored our opponent 62-14 (coupling the 30-6 run that closed the LSU game) and (2) we had outscored Auburn 90-37 in the last 32 minutes of play against the Tigers that began with the second half in Nashville when we blitzed the Tigers 58-29 in the final 20 minutes. Things leveled from there and we were in control by 20 at the half, 44-24, and coasted to a 77-62 victory. Booker led a balanced scoring attack with 18 points, while Kornet and I added 15 and 14, respectively. It was a solid, workmanlike victory.

Meanwhile, Florida beat another SEC bottom-dweller, Mississippi State, for its ninth SEC win in a row. LSU had played twice since the demolition in Nashville, beating Georgia on Monday to temporarily reclaim the league lead, but then losing to Alabama to fall behind the two leaders (permanently, as it would turn out):

Vandy	11-4
Florida	11-4
LSU	11-5
Alabama	10-5
Tennessee	8-7
Ole Miss	7-8
Kentucky	7-9
Mississippi State	5-10
Georgia	5-11
Auburn	2-14

Thus, we would head to Gainesville for the rematch with Florida with both teams tied for first.

II

"Sometime from now you'll bow to pressure"
—*Michael Penn, "No Myth"* ('89)

Florida still had not lost since before the Tennis Ball Game. The Gators were riding a nine-game SEC winning streak that brought them to the top of the conference with us with an 11-4 record. The teams also had identical overall records of 17-10.

Florida coach Norm Sloan termed the contest "the biggest game we've been in since I returned here in 1980," and it would be hard to argue with that statement given that Florida had never won an SEC title coming into the season. The notoriously rowdy Gator fans—accurately described as "[l]oud, biting, knowledgeable and above all obnoxious"—would be ready. Kornet opined that the O'Connell Center is "the hardest place we play in the SEC." And they somehow knew every tidbit about each opposing player. "They must get a media guide," I said. "They know everything about you."

Still, I wasn't that worried about the crowd, noting that "Florida and LSU are supposed to be the two toughest places to play, and at LSU they had to hit a shot at the buzzer to beat us. I didn't think we let the crowd intimidate us and LSU and I don't think we'll let the crowd intimidate us here, either." It's probably not much of a stretch to say that the phenomenal success of Florida basketball in the last 30 years—several SEC championships, multiple Final Fours, and two NCAA titles—can be traced to the 1988–89 season in general and to this game in particular. The O'Connell Center was packed to capacity (12,042).

Unsurprisingly, the media felt compelled to revisit the Tennis Ball Game and debate what effect, if any, that heartbreaker would have on the rematch. Sloan thought that "Vandy will come in here with a 'let's-get-even' thinking." Coach Newton disagreed and predicted that "I don't think that will be part of this game." He then grew uncharacteristically testy when he was asked more questions on the subject: "Hell, that has nothing to do with this game. Let's talk about the damn game, not tennis balls."

Okay, so about that "damn game." Florida had displayed little depth in Nashville, and since that game that minimal depth had been compromised further when Kelly Mackinnon, who hit three treys off the bench in Nashville, was absent for the rematch. The Gators would rely on only five players—the outstanding quintet of guards Clifford Lett and Renaldo Garcia, bruising forwards Livingston Chatman and Dwayne Davis (incredible 72.5% field-goal shooting), and old friend Dwayne Schintzius.

In the late 1980s, before every SEC game was televised somewhere, the fact that a game was televised as the regional game of the week was a big deal. By sheer luck, this game had been chosen as the game of the week before the season even started.

Who could have predicted that these two teams would be tied and playing for the SEC lead on the regular season's penultimate weekend when the television schedule had been announced in October? But that's how it worked out, and the knowledge that SEC hoops fans would be able to view this critical game added yet more excitement to the contest. As we were warming up, the excellent play-by-play man Tom Hammond asked me about my knee, which I had tweaked during the Auburn game, forcing me to wear a protective sleeve over it. I gave him a thumbs-up. It was "go time."

We came out ready to play. We were simply playing with loads of confidence. We didn't let the crowd bother us, and we were sharp on both ends of the floor. I was hot from behind the arc, making my first two three-point attempts, and scored 15 points in the first half. Plus, Kornet was out-maneuvering Schintzius inside; Frank scored eight straight points in one stretch that gave us a 28-20 lead, our largest margin of the half. Our lead was a respectable 38-34 at intermission. The Gators adopted a different strategy in the second half and began keying on me while taking their chances that Booker would not heat up from three-point range. Nevertheless, we came out of the locker room on fire and built the lead to double digits. With just over 13 minutes remaining, we stretched the lead to 14, 57-43. And, after a scrum on Florida's end of the floor, we recovered a loose ball and directed it to a wide-open Eric Reid, who went for the uncontested dunk that would extend our lead to 16, and maybe the rout would be on; the crowd was muffled, and the Gator players lacked the enthusiasm and energy with which they had started the game.

Except that Reid missed the dunk.

Yep, Eric clanged the dunk off the back of the rim, and it landed in the hands of the Gators, who converted the miss into a basket to make it 57-45. If this were a hackneyed novel, the Gators would turn that missed dunk into the momentum and they needed to get back in the game and ultimately prevail. Well…

Our offensive sharpness deteriorated; we became tentative on defense. Florida went on a 12-3 run in the next four minutes and, crucially, drew the fourth fouls on Reid and Kornet, putting both of our inside starters on the bench. Still, we did just enough to keep the Gators at bay. We still led by four, 69-65, with two minutes to play, and Reid had a chance to extend it at the free-throw line. But Eric, whose missed dunk was part of a nightmarish game (0-for-7 from the field), missed the front end of the one-and-one—one of four free-throw attempts we missed in the final four minutes. Lett converted that miss into a three-pointer to cut our lead to a single point, 69-68, with just over a minute to play. Again, we worked the 45-second shot clock down to the final seconds, and again we were fouled; this time it was Kornet who drew the foul, and he did so in the act of shooting, giving him two shots. Eerily recalling the first game, when he made one of two at the line immediately preceding the tennis ball theatrics, Frank missed the first and made the second. We led 70-68 with 19 seconds to play.

Needing only a deuce to tie, Florida pounded the ball inside and Davis made a six-footer in the lane to complete Florida's comeback, tie the game at 70, and send us into overtime. Florida, as in the first game, had all the momentum. We scored the first point in overtime to take a 71-70 lead, but the Gators scored the next eight points, and we never caught up. Kornet's field goal with 58 seconds left was our first field goal since Book's trey with seven minutes remaining in regulation—an 11-minute dry spell from the field. My three-pointer at the buzzer brought the final margin closer, but that was all. The Gators prevailed, 83-80.

I've long believed that this second overtime loss to Florida was more heartbreaking than the first. In the second game, we couldn't blame a bunch of "damned yokels" (to use Coach Newton's term), poor judgment by an official, or questionable timekeeping by the scoreboard operator, all of which combined (along with Schintzius) to snatch defeat from the jaws of victory in Nashville. No, we simply played poorly for the final 15 minutes (the final 10 minutes of regulation and the five-minute overtime period) and failed to step on Florida's throat when we had the chance. This one was on us. "This was a very tough loss" was my post-game understatement.

I had given it my all, playing an exhausting 44 minutes—the most of my career—and led the team with 25 points, seven assists, and four steals. I hit a career-best percentage of 5-for-6 from behind the arc and 8-for-11 overall. Plus, Kornet thoroughly dominated Dwayne Schintzius. Limited to 32 minutes because of foul trouble (he would foul out in overtime, as he had in the first game), Frank scored 23 points and led all players with 14 rebounds, while holding Schintzius, who played in the entire game before fouling out in the final seconds of overtime, to 12 and six.

Behind Frank and me, though, the stats weren't pretty. He and I combined to shoot 17-for-28 from the field (him 9-for-17, me 8-for-11), but the rest of the team went only 10-for-42 from the field. Book had 18 points and nine boards but struggled from the field—6-for-20 overall, 5-for-14 from behind the arc. Our bench produced only one field goal and four points.

As with the first game, shaky free-throw shooting played a big role in our loss. We made only 14 of 23 shots from the charity stripe, barely 60%, with crucial end-of-regulation misses by Reid and Kornet; I added to the misery by missing two free throws late in overtime after having hit all four of my previous attempts. Florida wasn't that much better, hitting 21 of 31 (67.7%), but it was enough, and they made theirs when it counted, unlike us. "Give Florida the credit," Coach Newton observed after the game. "They got to the line and made free throws and when we got to the line, we missed ours. That was the difference in the game."

It was inevitable that tennis balls would litter the court when the game ended, regardless of the outcome. I knew it and expected it, as did everyone on the team. And we would not be disappointed. Not only were tennis balls thrown at us, so were paper cups, ice, and other assorted debris as we tried to leave the floor as quickly as possible after the final horn sounded. I wasn't surprised. "We kinda expected some classless act like that," I said. Kornet was livid. "I've never seen fans like these at Florida," he said. "They're very immature. We've played before fans at Duke, which is supposed to be one of the toughest places to play. But their fans aren't like these— they are not rude and crude."

The most serious post-game incident occurred when our assistant coach, Ed Martin, was struck in the face by a tennis ball on his way off the floor. Coach Martin exploded and charged back toward the floor, only to be held back by Coach Newton. That encounter was benignly reported as the two coaches "exchanged words," but "heated words" is closer to the truth, and the fact is that the two men almost came to blows. I've rarely seen someone angrier than Ed Martin was at that moment, and I've always suspected that it wasn't solely because of tennis balls.

III

"I'm telling you the day will come when this man gets what he merits"
—Elvis Costello, "Stalin Malone" ('89)

In 1989, few, and probably no, assistant coaches in NCAA Division I had achieved what Ed Martin had achieved as a head coach. He hailed from Allentown, Pennsylvania, becoming the first African-American to graduate from Allentown High School. After a stint in the Navy, he enrolled at North Carolina A&T University, graduating in 1951. Just like Coach Newton, Coach Martin played baseball and basketball in college, and, like C.M., Coach Martin played professional baseball— in his case, in the Cincinnati Reds organization. That was impressive enough, but in fact Coach Martin had been orphaned at an early age (his mother died when he was six, his father when he was 16), and he not only put himself through college, but his younger sister as well. In the mid-1950s, he embarked on a highly successful basketball coaching career, beginning with a high school in South Carolina where, in just three seasons, he posted a 66-6 record with two state championships and one state runner-up.

Coach Martin's high school success led him to the college ranks, and from 1955 to 1968 he was the head coach at South Carolina State University in Orangeburg. His teams won seven Southern Intercollegiate Athletic Conference championships, going to three NAIA and five NCAA playoffs. From South Carolina State, Coach Martin moved to Nashville and Tennessee State University. His work at TSU was remarkable: in 17 seasons (1968–84), he compiled a record of 287-148, coaching 12 future NBA players (including Lloyd Neal, Ted McLain, and NBA rebounding champ Leonard "Truck" Robinson). His teams were named College Division Champions in 1970, 1972, 1973, and 1975. He was selected national coach of the year in 1972. After amassing 501 wins as a college head coach, Coach Martin resigned from

TSU in 1984 and joined C.M. Newton's Vanderbilt staff as an assistant in July 1985—thus entering the program with Booker, Kornet, and me.

Coach Martin did a little bit of everything as an assistant—he worked with the centers and forwards; he scouted numerous opponents; he was active in recruiting. He also was a first-class wit, always ready with a quip, or so it seemed. Someone who took unnecessary risks might "walk through Hell in kerosene underwear." Someone who was old (and he often referred to himself) had "been through three wars and two uprisings." All in all, Ed Martin was invaluable to the Commodore program in my four years. Coach Martin thought so, too, and felt that he should be given a chance to succeed C.M. Newton as the Commodore head coach, announcing his intent to put his hat in the ring just days after C.M. resigned: "It would be an opportunity I've always wanted." As weeks passed, he became more vocal and passionate, declaring near the end of the season that "I've never wanted anything more than I want his job."

But he had at least three things working against him. One, to put it bluntly, was race. Race shouldn't factor into any hiring decision, let alone SEC head-coaching hiring decisions. Though two African-Americans have since piloted their SEC basketball teams to NCAA titles—Nolan Richardson of Arkansas in 1994 and Tubby Smith of Kentucky in 1998—as of the end of the 1988–89 season, no SEC school had yet hired an African-American head coach in either football or basketball. (It would be after the '88–'89 season when Tennessee hired Wade Houston as the SEC's first African-American men's basketball coach; Jerry Stackhouse became Vandy's first African American men's hoops coach 30 years later in 2019.)

Coach Martin had interviewed at Indiana before the Hoosiers hired Bob Knight and at Louisville before U of L hired Denny Crum. He knew the interviews had been "tokenism" and was uninterested in going through that again. He felt that his record spoke for itself, and that any colorblind administrator would see that. Coach Martin felt that Vanderbilt's relatively progressive record on athletic race relations, particularly the fact that Perry Wallace had broken the color line for SEC basketball over two decades earlier, might give him a chance.

His second obstacle was age. Coach Martin would turn 62 a couple of months after the season—he was nearly seven years older than Coach Bostick and three years older than Coach Newton. All signs seemed to point toward Athletic Director Roy Kramer hiring a younger, up-and-coming head coach to take Vanderbilt basketball into the 1990s. The age factor would work against both Coach Martin and Coach Bostick.

Third, Coach Newton was publicly lobbying for Coach Bostick to succeed him, and he made no effort to put in a good word (at least publicly) for Coach Martin. I think that wounded Coach Martin; it must have stung to read the glowing recommendations Coach Newton made on Coach Bostick's behalf in the newspapers and elsewhere while not receiving any such recommendations on his own behalf. While

Coach Martin may not have been surprised, given the close, long-term friendship between coaches Newton and Bostick, Coach Newton's failure to support Coach Martin likely would have hurt just the same.

So, it seemed to me that an errant tennis ball to the head in Gainesville triggered an eruption of emotions that went beyond that incident. Coach Newton wasn't supporting him in his head-coaching quest, and now C.M. was directing him off the floor to the locker room and, therefore, not supporting him now, either. Hence this unfortunate internal row that took place after a bitter loss. It all added up to an especially funereal mood in the locker room.

The Gators' day got even better when a resurgent Tennessee thumped third-place Alabama in Knoxville, 84-69, to keep the Tide two games behind Florida. Thus, going into the final week, the standings looked like this:

Florida	12-4
Vandy	11-5
LSU	11-5
Alabama	10-6
Tennessee	9-7
Ole Miss	7-9
Kentucky	7-9
Mississippi State	6-10
Georgia	5-11
Auburn	2-14

Again proving that his self-proclaimed assertions of maturity were wildly overstated, Schintzius autographed tennis balls for young Gator fans in their locker room after the game. He also found time between autographs to utter some bulletin-board material for the Gators' final two opponents, LSU and Alabama: "We'll find a weakness in Chris Jackson and go right at it and beat LSU. Then we'll beat Alabama. Going down the home stretch all we have to do is keep playing strong."

Alas, these final weeks of the 1988–89 season were the apex of Dwayne Schintzius's collegiate career. He would earn first team all-SEC honors, finishing the season with impressive averages of 18 points and 9.7 rebounds per game. But his senior year of 1989–90 was a disaster: with the program mired in scandal, Norm Sloan was fired in October 1989 for, among other things, using university funds to send starting guard Vernon Maxwell to a Boston Celtics' camp in 1987, and Don DeVoe took over as interim head coach. He and Schintzius clashed repeatedly, and

Schintzius ultimately quit the team in January 1990. He then embarked on a checkered NBA career that lasted eight seasons, but he played for six different teams and never played more than 43 games in a single season.

In 2009, Dwayne was diagnosed with myelomonocytic leukemia. He received a bone marrow transplant from his brother in early 2010 and was declared cancer-free, but further issues required a second bone marrow transplant, which failed. He died at the age of 43 in April 2012. Dwayne Schintzius is the only player in SEC history with more than 1,000 points, 800 rebounds, 250 assists, and 250 blocked shots, and unless and until the rules change dramatically that will require or encourage college basketball players to stay in school longer than just a year or two, Schintzius likely will forever be the only member of that particular club.

R.I.P., Dwayne.

31

GOODBYE, MEMORIAL

I

"Let me take a long last look before we say goodbye"
—*Don Henley, "The End of the Innocence"* ('89)

The Florida loss was a crusher, but I thought we could still win the SEC, or at least tie the Gators for the title. Florida was playing great basketball, but the schedule maker had done the Gators no favors: our game was their final home game, and their final two games would be stern tests—first at LSU, then at Alabama, the two teams (other than us) that the Gators were trying to fend off. "Florida had to have this game," I said afterward. "They have to play two contenders [LSU and Alabama] this week. LSU beat them here and Alabama has not lost at home yet this season. I can't see them winning both of them." In fact, I believed Florida had no better than a 50/50 chance of winning even one of those two, and it was inconceivable to me that the Gators would win both. For that reason, I predicted that "if we win our last two games, we'll be wearing a ring" designating that we were the conference champions.

Of course, our task wasn't an easy one either. We had Mississippi State at home, which we felt good about, but we then had to travel to Knoxville for a tough game with Tennessee. And that first game, against State, carried not only huge implications for the SEC race but also the added emotion of being the last home game for Kornet, Booker, and me in our Vanderbilt careers. It was going to be an emotional night in every way imaginable.

I first set foot in Memorial Gym as a high school junior in February 1984—that was when I first glimpsed future teammate Will Perdue in the pregame shootaround. By then, the gym was over three decades old, and it has since celebrated its 65th birthday. The gym was named as a dedication to all Vanderbilt men and women who served in World War II. The first game there was played on December 6, 1952, a 90-83 victory by the Commodores over Virginia. The original capacity for Memorial was 6,583, but when the Clyde Lee-led Commodores became a national power in the 1960s, the gym was expanded in 1967 to a capacity exceeding 11,000 with "The Balconies That Clyde Lee Built." Another expansion in 1969 added over 4,000 to the capacity, bringing its capacity to 15,646.

We defended the home court well in my four years, posting a 47-15 record in those seasons. And we lost only to quality teams—no slip-up losses to inferior opponents. For example, in my freshman season of 1985–86, we lost six games at Memorial, but all six teams made the Sweet Sixteen (Duke, Iowa State, Alabama, Kentucky, LSU, Auburn), four of them made the Elite Eight (all but Iowa State and Alabama), and two made the Final Four (Duke and LSU). And we would post an impressive 27-4 home mark in my final two seasons, again losing only to NCAA-bound teams (LSU and Auburn in 1987–88 and Florida and Stanford in 1988–89). In fact, of the 14 regular season losses in those four years (one was in the postseason NIT), only one was to a team that didn't make the NCAAs that year—Tennessee in 1986–87, and that one deserved an asterisk because Coach Newton did not coach that game due to illness. For my part, I felt that "I play better in Memorial because the crowd is behind you from the time we go through the warmup to the end of the game. The fans can really intimidate an opponent."

Of course, I didn't know any of that in February 1984; I was being recruited by Vanderbilt and made the 120-mile trip from my hometown with my father, high school coach, and a family friend to get a taste of what the home team's fans and gym were like. The opponent that day was Kentucky, the best team in the SEC and a Final Four participant that March. While Vandy wasn't without talent—Phil Cox and 1984 Olympian/future NBA player Jeff Turner could play anywhere—there was no question that UK had more talent. But the game was close all the way, and I was mightily impressed by the energy of the home crowd on this Sunday afternoon. And it was *loud*. Everything about Memorial was, and is, unique: the odd configuration, which required multiple scoreboards and also contributed to the awful acoustics (terrible place for a concert, great place for a basketball game) that, perhaps counterintuitively, made everything louder; the raised floor, which means that the scorer's table and some front-row seats are *below* floor level; and, of course, the bane of all visiting coaches, the placement of the teams' benches in the end zones instead of on the sidelines. It was immediately clear that Memorial was a special place; and, coming from a high school program where the gym seated over 5,000 and was routinely full for our games, it was important to me to attend a school with equally rabid and passionate fans. Who would want to attend a school where the gym is only full half the time (or half-full all the time)?

Despite a game effort by the Commodores, UK prevailed, 58-54. For sure, that game was instrumental in my decision to attend Vanderbilt, and I am sure that I was neither the first nor last Commodore recruit to be enchanted by his first visit to Memorial Gym.

Still, filling the gym is one thing; winning the games played there is another. The 1985–86 season had one memorable win, the remarkable comeback against Tennessee where we turned an eight-point deficit with 50 seconds remaining into a one-point win. That was great, but Tennessee wasn't that good that season, and we didn't follow it up with anything dramatic for the rest of the season with the minor exception of a one-point win over Florida, where I hit a shot in the lane over Vernon Maxwell with about 30 seconds to go to give us the lead and eventual victory.

The "Memorial Magic" aura began to build in 1986–87. The Indiana victory, in early December, was the real headline-grabber, but it also overshadowed some other solid wins at Memorial that year, including a 91-75 drubbing of a ranked Auburn team, a victory over Sweet Sixteen-bound Notre Dame, and a Perdue buzzer-beating victory over Elite Eight entrant LSU. In that season, we began to establish the reputation that memorable games, and Vanderbilt wins, could happen against any opponent at Memorial. And, as we proved over the next two seasons, no opponent was immune to "Memorial Magic"—not even the #1 team in the country, as we had proven against North Carolina in December. We had nearly averaged a sellout for SEC home games the last two seasons—15,377 in 1987–88 and 15,246 in 1988–89—so the gym was full, and the fans were treated to some thrilling basketball.

II

"We might even win this time, guys—you never know"
—*The Replacements, "Talent Show" ('89)*

I was touched—as I'm sure Frank and Barry were—by the outpouring of accolades and compliments as we closed our Vanderbilt (and Memorial Gym) careers. One writer noted that we were "[t]hree special people" and that "[i]t's difficult to place a price on the contributions made to the Commodore program by Barry Booker, Barry Goheen and Frank Kornet." This same columnist must have been reading my mind when he wrote that "it doesn't seem like four years have passed since they came on campus." Another writer asserted that we were "genuine student athletes" who were "living proof it's possible for athletes to exist in a big-time sports environment for four years and come out with their heads high and their noses clean."

The three of us anticipated a heart-tugging night. "I could get a little emotional," I predicted, adding that "[w]hat we need to do is channel that emotion." Booker's words were particularly well-chosen: "[T]he years have really blown by. This final home game will be special because it's ending a period in your life. It's hard to believe it's over."

A privilege afforded the seniors in the C.M. Newton era at Vanderbilt was that each senior received some space in the program for the final home game to write whatever he felt like writing to express his emotions before his final appearance at Memorial. I took the opportunity to reference David Letterman's popular "Top 10 List" shtick from his late-night show to count down my top 10 Vanderbilt wins from the (nearly) four years. Delivered "from the home office in Calvert City, Kentucky," I listed the following games:

10. 108-74 blowout of LSU (1988–89)
9. 60-59 comeback win over Tennessee (1985–86)
8. 78-76 win over #1 North Carolina (1987–88)
7. 65-62 win over Louisville on half-court shot (1988–89)
6. 74-57 win over Murray St., my parents' alma mater (1988–89)
5. 81-51 blowout of Kentucky (1988–89)
4. 79-75 upset over #2 Indiana (1986–87)
3. 80-74 (OT) win over Pitt in NCAA tourney (1987–88)
2. 83-66 win over Kentucky (1987–88)
1. left blank because "I hope the biggest win is yet to come!"

The pregame ceremonies were indeed emotional. In response to a post-game question that there "were a few misty eyes when the foursome [Book, Frank, C.M., and me] and their families were introduced," I said, "I know there were two. It got to me a little bit. I didn't think it would, but my parents and grandparents and brother were out there with me, and the crowd was standing and cheering. It was a very special moment."

With all the hubbub surrounding the game, it was easy to forget about the game itself. We couldn't afford to let up against eighth-place Mississippi State, the team against whom we had begun our road to improved emotional and on-the-floor health after the double-whammy of C.M.'s resignation and the Tennis Ball Game. Now, after a second devastating loss to Florida, we would need to get well against State again. The Bulldogs were hard to figure—they had only six SEC wins, but three of them were LSU (twice) and Alabama.

The previous season, we played a poor final home game—Will Perdue's Memorial Gym finale—and lost to Auburn. State in 1989 was not as good as that '88 Auburn team, but we couldn't afford to let the Bulldogs hang around. A fast start was imperative; otherwise, this might not be our final Memorial Gym appearance after all because we would be back for an NIT game. With 17 wins on the season, I felt good about our NCAA chances, but every additional win would help.

We got the pregame emotions out of the way with the presentations of the three seniors and their families (in my case, my parents, grandparents, and, most surprisingly and touchingly, my brother, who drove down from the University of Kentucky, where he was attending college, to take part in the ceremonies). Our extra home jerseys hung from the gym's ceiling and we and our families were showered with warm applause from the crowd. And it was also the last home game for another important person in the Vanderbilt program—head coach C.M. Newton, who likewise was treated to a fine sendoff from the sellout crowd as he and his wife, Evelyn, walked to the center of the court, for more and louder cheers. It was touching and emotional, but all four of us were anxious to get the game going.

And we got going early. We displayed absolutely no hangover from the Florida game, blitzing State by scoring the game's first 15 points. We led 19-2 nine minutes into the game; State didn't register a basket from the field until less than 10 minutes remained in the first half. We led comfortably at halftime, 36-21.

The second half was a different story, however. The Bulldogs chipped away at our lead, reducing our lead to three, 49-46, with 9:08 left. Wilcox's 15-footer made it 51-46, but when Bulldogs reserve Chris Hall hit a three-pointer with 8:15 remaining, our lead was down to two, 51-49. We missed again on our end, and the Bulldogs rebounded with a chance to tie or take the lead. Then came two game-changing whistles. State missed a shot, and Kornet broke for our basket and received the outlet pass, but as he went for the rim, State's Greg Lockhart hammered him—and was called for an intentional foul. That not only gave us two free throws but also allowed us to retain possession. Frank hit the free throws to give us a four-point lead. Then, on our ensuing possession, Lockhart and I dove for a loose ball, and he was called for a foul, and when he jumped up to protest, he was assessed a technical foul. I hit the technical foul shot plus the two free throws off the personal foul and suddenly we had some breathing room, 56-49. State didn't go away entirely, cutting the lead to 59-55 with just inside five minutes to play, but four straight points by Eric Reid kept us in control, and we built a deceptively large lead at the end thanks to State misses, our free throws, and a technical foul called on State coach Richard Williams. The final score was 77-58.

Before the final buzzer sounded, though, Coach Newton gave us seniors one final, emotional moment by removing us from the game to soak up deafening cheers of the crowd. Between the pregame ceremonies and the late-game sendoff, it was an emotional evening, as all three seniors acknowledged after the game. "I didn't think I'd get too emotional, but I guess I did," I said. Kornet concurred: "It was definitely emotional out there. The way time has flown by is unbelievable. It seems like just yesterday we were freshmen and now there we were, being introduced for the last time." "There were memories here tonight that my family and I will always carry with us," Book added.

Appropriately, the seniors led the way—Kornet had 20 points and 11 rebounds, and I added 17 and four. Book scored 11 points and dished out a game-high seven assists. After the Florida disaster, Reid bounced back with the brilliant game of 12 points and a game-high 13 rebounds. Wilcox scored 11 and had five assists, and those five dimes gave him 151 for the season, breaking the program's single-season assists record, set by Jan van Breda Kolff in 1974. All in all, it was a great game and a memorable win. Every Commodore hoopster would surely agree with Kornet's post-game assessment of the Memorial Gym crowd: "These are the greatest fans in the world." And the last-home-game win would earn a place on my personal Top 10, wrapping up a seven-game stretch of my best basketball at Vanderbilt—we went 6-1 and came within a hair of winning all seven, and I averaged nearly 22 points a game for that stretch.

ȣ

While we were fighting our emotions and Mississippi State in Nashville, a titanic game was being played at about the same time in Baton Rouge between LSU and Florida. In those days before iPhones and real-time Internet access to scores in any sporting contest being played anywhere, there was limited knowledge as to what was happening in Louisiana. Periodically during timeouts in the first half of our game, we would hear a mighty roar from the crowd, which we assumed meant that LSU was beating Florida. But those roars ceased during the second half of our game. I guess that would qualify as "scoreboard listening." Unlike our game, where we never trailed, the LSU-Florida game was a roller coaster of sorts. Riding the momentum of the comeback win against us, the Gators shot to a 15-4 lead. But Chris Jackson went on an incredible roll from there, scoring 26 points in the final 15 minutes of the half as LSU rallied and took a halftime lead of 50-44.

Just as we had done the previous Saturday in Gainesville, LSU came out hot in the second half and built its lead to double digits, taking a 60-48 lead early in the half. And, just as they had done in Gainesville, the Gators fought their way back, eventually reclaiming the lead and building it to six points. LSU cut it to three and had the ball with a chance to tie in the final seconds, but Jackson missed a hurried three-pointer on which the LSU fans claimed he was fouled. Florida rebounded, was fouled, and went to the line for the game-icing free throws with a single second remaining. You can guess what happened next: tennis balls, along with ice, cups, and other assorted debris, rained down from the stands. A technical foul was called on the LSU crowd, and Coach Dale Brown received a couple more for protesting the first technical. By the time the smoke cleared, Florida was a 104-95 winner clinching a tie for the SEC championship, ahead of us by one game heading into the final weekend:

Florida	13-4
Vandy	12-5
LSU	11-6
Alabama	11-6
Tennessee	10-7
Kentucky	8-9
Ole Miss	7-10
Mississippi State	6-11
Georgia	5-12
Auburn	2-15

We would not leave Tennessee for a while—our final regular-season game would be in Knoxville against UT and we would be right back there the following week for the SEC tournament. And we were still fighting for the title with one game left.

32

THE KNOXVILLE FLOP

I
"This is out of our reach"
—*Nirvana, "Negative Creep"* ('89)

On the regular season's final Saturday, four of the league's top five teams would play each other as we visited Tennessee and Alabama hosted Florida. Our game was scheduled to tip-off one hour ahead of the Florida-Alabama game, so we had a chance to go out early and put some pressure on Florida if we could get an early lead.

Our opponent, the Volunteers, had been a bit of an enigma. They started the season very well and led the SEC in the opening couple of weeks, then hit a stagnant stretch for about a month that threatened to derail what looked like a surefire NCAA bid. But, heading into our game, the Vols had made a late-season correction with back-to-back wins over Georgia and Alabama to put them back into NCAA contention. The impetus for this recent charge was a personnel change—UT coach Don DeVoe had decided to move his best player, Dyron Nix, from the starting lineup and make him a super sixth man, an astute move that meant that the Vols would not have any offensive letdown when DeVoe went to his bench, and a far cry from what we could expect from our bench, which had scored a combined 10 points in our last two games.

Nevertheless, we expected Nix to start our game because it was his final regular-season home game (but not his final home game since UT would host the SEC Tournament the following week) along with four other seniors. This group—Nix, center Doug Roth, guards Travis Henry and Clarence Swearingen, and forward Mark Griffin—was talented but had been, overall, an underachieving bunch. They would make only two postseason tournaments in four years and would not win an NCAA or NIT game. Still, with a 17-9 overall and 10-7 SEC record, the quintet had led UT to its most victories since 1985 and most SEC wins since 1982.

We had played exceptionally well for seven consecutive games, winning six of them. Amazingly, in five of those games we had led for nearly the entire game—we never trailed, even for a second, in the wins over LSU, Auburn, and Mississippi State, and trailed for only the first 30 seconds against Kentucky. We led for nearly all of regulation against Florida. We had been jumping out early and maintaining a high level of play for nearly the entire 40 minutes—which made our performance in our 18th and final regular-season SEC game even more disappointing.

We started the game relatively well, scoring nine of the game's first 13 points. We still led 12-8 a little more than six minutes in when the wheels began to come off. Reminiscent of our 17-point streak in the teams' first game in which we blitzed the Vols in the second half to take control of the game, UT scored 13 straight points to take a 21-12 lead. We answered with seven of our own to cut the lead to two, but the last few minutes of the half were disastrous: turnovers, poor rebounding, and missed shots, along with hot shooting by the Volunteers, added up to a 21-7 run and put the Vols in command at the half, 42-26. "The last four or five minutes of the first half were as poor as we have played all year," I commented afterward. The second half was no better, as the UT lead eventually ballooned to 22 points, 56-34, and we made no real run from there. The final score was a disappointing 78-61.

It is amazing how two teams can play just four weeks apart and the games have such disparate outcomes. In the first game, we dominated UT on the boards, 39-29, and four players had at least seven; in the second game, they annihilated us 44-26 in the rebounding department, and I led us with only six. And this would be the only SEC game of the season where both Booker and I would fail to reach double figures: we only scored only eight apiece. Wilcox led the team with 15 points on solid 6-for-7 shooting; the rest of the team shot an abysmal 15-for-38.

The Vols received contributions from many players, but the clear star was Dyron Nix, who led all players with 22 points, 14 rebounds, and three steals. He clearly was the best player on the floor on this day, full of energy and enthusiasm, talking up a storm—not necessarily trash talking (though he certainly was not averse to that either); he just needed an outlet for his energy. In the game in Nashville, after a change of possession, he and I walked to the other end of the floor and chatted the entire 60 or so feet (which led to my friend Wendy chastising me after the game for "fraternizing with the enemy").

જે

Dyron and I had come a long way from our memorable first encounter as freshmen in January 1986, where he fouled me on the putback that led to the three-point play and capped our amazing last-minute rally to win the game. I won that one, and he won the finale.

Those memories, and others, came flooding back to me in December 2013 when I received the shocking news that Dyron Nix had passed away at the age of 46 in our shared, adopted hometown of Atlanta. That didn't seem possible. The cause of death was pneumonia; apparently Dyron had gone to an Atlanta hospital complaining of breathing difficulty and died a short time later.

I attended the visitation just prior to the funeral. It was jarring and emotional to see Dyron Nix in a casket. He had played only one season in the NBA but had played numerous seasons in France, Israel, Spain, and Greece. He was named to Tennessee Basketball's All-Century Team in 2009.

Several of Dyron's college teammates came to the service, and I caught up with old UT rivals such as Tony White and Elvin Brown, both shaken by the death of their teammate. Dyron's fellow 1989 senior Clarence Swearingen performed the service.

I would prefer to recall Dyron the way his college coach, Don DeVoe, put it upon learning of his passing: "Dyron was a very talented young man and an extremely confident player. He was just an absolutely strong and powerful inside player…. [H]e was just quick as a cat getting above the rim and slamming the ball." That, too, is how I will remember Dyron Nix.

Our loss meant that Florida would win the SEC title regardless of what occurred in the Gators' game at Alabama. As it turned out, that game was a blowout too—the Tide rolled 80-62 to complete an unbeaten season at home. And that win also meant that 'Bama caught us in the standings, and we wound up in a tie for second with the Tide.

With two blowouts providing little drama on the regular season's final day, it was left to the fifth team in the top half of the league, LSU, to enliven things. And the Tigers and their opponent, Ole Miss, delivered probably the best conference game of the year and certainly one of the greatest individual shootouts in conference history, as Chris Jackson and Gerald Glass combined to score over 100 points in a 113-112 Ole Miss overtime victory: Jackson scored 55 points to Glass's 53, but Glass hit the game-winning free throw in overtime to give the Rebels the victory. The loss knocked LSU, which had been leading the SEC only two weeks before, down to the fifth seed in the conference tournament. The final SEC standings looked like this:

Florida	13-5
Vandy	12-6
Alabama	12-6
Tennessee	11-7
LSU	11-7
Kentucky	8-10
Ole Miss	8-10
Mississippi State	7-11
Georgia	6-12
Auburn	2-16

Thus, the two overtime losses to Florida prevented us from delivering the first SEC championship to Vanderbilt since 1974. Still, Book, Frank and I completed a near worst-to-first journey for the program, which finished last in the SEC with a 4-14 league record in 1984–85. We joined the next season and improved to 7-11 the next two years, went 10-8 in 1987–88, and improved again to 12-6 in 1988–89—a net improvement of eight wins in four seasons, from SEC doormat to SEC contender. We were, and remain, immensely proud of our role in lifting the Vanderbilt program to a level of prominence that it has more consistently enjoyed in the last 30 years.

II

"I feel like I'm in the prime of my life"
—Billy Joel, "I Go to Extremes" ('89)

It was now time to turn our attention to the SEC tournament, which required a return trip to Knoxville and the unsightly Thompson-Boling Arena. While Book, Frank, and I had accomplished a lot in nearly four full seasons in Nashville, one significant gap in our collective resume remained: we had not won an SEC tournament game. The last Vanderbilt victory in the SEC tournament had been in Memorial Gym in 1984. And the last Vandy victory in a conference tournament game not played on its home floor? It was—wait for it—none other than that 1981 game against Kentucky in Birmingham, which I witnessed as a 13-year-old. "We don't need to be reminded," I snapped before the game. "We've won about everything else since we've been here but not a conference tournament game, and this is our last shot."

It was, therefore, ironic and appropriate that the 1989 SEC tournament brackets matched us against Kentucky for this final chance at a conference tournament win. We were the third seed (Alabama, also 12-6 in the league, was seeded second because it beat champion Florida and we didn't), which paired us with sixth-seeded UK, and that was a great break for us; had we been the second seed, we likely would play seventh-seeded Ole Miss (provided the Rebels beat 10-seed Auburn in a first round game), a team we barely beat on both occasions. The Wildcats, on the other hand, had let the distractions of the season get the best of them.

It seemed like months had passed since our 81-51 whipping of Kentucky in Memorial, with the "conflict of interest" nonsense and so forth, but in fact it had been only four weeks. That had been long enough for the teams to head in completely opposite directions. Both teams had entered that game with identical 6-4 league records; including that game, we went 6-2 the rest of the way while the 'Cats went 2-6 to finish with a losing SEC record of 8-10. And, with an overall record of 13-18, they were clearly marking time until the end of the season, when Coach Eddie

Sutton almost certainly would be fired, probably by C.M. Newton, who would assume the athletic director position on April 1, and there likely would be substantial player attrition as well. The new coach would have some significant challenges in front of him.

Still, even if UK was playing out the string, we couldn't afford to overlook the talent on hand. Chris Mills and LeRon Ellis could play with anyone in the SEC, and if Derrick Miller got the hot hand like he had against us in Lexington, anything could happen. The 'Cats had four wins over likely NCAA teams—one against us, an improbable sweep of Tennessee, and, in what looked like, in retrospect, the most surprising win of the entire SEC season, a 13-point win at Florida. They also had suffered some agonizingly close losses: two points to LSU, four points to Alabama, two points to Auburn (one of the Tigers' two SEC wins). They closed their regular season with a heartbreaking one-point loss at Mississippi State.

We weren't too worried, but we couldn't take the Cats too lightly. With 18 wins, I felt good about an NCAA bid—after all, that was the same number of wins we had posted in the 1987–88 regular season, which were deemed sufficient for an at-large bid: "We've played a tougher schedule this year than we did last year when we made it," I argued, conveniently omitting the significant fact that the conference was much better in 1987–88 than in 1988–89.

While there was always additional media attention when we played Kentucky, this third game didn't carry the emotion of the February game in Memorial. There was no "conflict of interest" silliness swirling around the game; it was just two teams playing basketball. The problem was that only one of those teams began the game playing good basketball, and it wasn't us. Clearly, UK was still smarting from the 30-point embarrassment in Nashville ("You don't forget things like that," said 'Cats point guard Sean Sutton. "That was the most embarrassing loss I've ever been associated with. We are glad to have another shot at Vanderbilt."), and we were on our heels. I had warned the day before the game that "[w]e can't fall behind early," but that's exactly what happened—eight minutes into the game, UK had stormed to a 13-point lead, 21-8, prompting a Coach Newton timeout where he let us have it. We picked up the intensity, but positive results were not immediate; UK still led by nine with 7:20 left in the half. From that point, though, we took charge and never looked back. We scored on 15 of 17 offensive possessions and turned the 13-point deficit into an eight-point halftime lead of 38-30—a 30-9 run in the last 12 minutes of the half.

To their credit, the Wildcats didn't quit in the second half as they had done in Nashville, but they didn't have the firepower to make up a double-digit deficit, which it faced early in the second half. We stretched the lead to 15 on a couple of occasions in the second half before the 'Cats made one more run at us, cutting the lead to seven, 64-57, with 6:39 to play. But Eric Reid scored eight straight points to restore order, and within moments we were savoring our first SEC tournament win,

77-63. The win pushed our record to 19-12 and, we all felt, assured us of an NCAA bid. "My gut feeling is that we deserve a bid," remarked Coach Newton. I agreed: "I think this win puts us over the top."

Meanwhile, Kentucky closed the books on the worst season in its modern hoops history (which almost everyone defines as beginning with the tenure of Adolph Rupp in 1930) with a 13-19 record. In fact, it was the worst record (in fact, the only losing record) for UK in 62 years, and the program hasn't come close to matching it since. Mills reportedly apologized to his teammates in the locker room after the game "for being the centerpiece of the season-long controversy and investigation." If this was to be his last game in a Wildcat uniform (and, in fact, it was), he went out in style: 17 points and 18 rebounds. LeRon Ellis went for 20 and six, but no one else hit double figures, and Derrick Miller scored only five points on 2-for-15 shooting—and those two makes were early in the game when UK raced to its 13-point lead. Combined with his 0-for-8 showing in Nashville, Miller was 2-for-23 in our final two contests against the 'Cats.

In contrast, we featured a balanced offensive attack where all five players scored in double figures, with Booker and Kornet each scoring 17 points and grabbing six rebounds. Reid added 14 and a team-high seven boards, while Wilcox chipped in with 13 points and a team-high four assists. I scored only 10 on woeful shooting of 3-for-10 from the field and 3-for-6 from the line, but the bottom line was that we finally had secured an SEC tournament win and, likely, an NCAA tourney berth. "I feel like we finally got a monkey off our backs," I said after the game. For the first time, we would be playing on the weekend of the SEC tournament. Meanwhile, we ended "the bleakest [period] in UK's long and illustrious basketball history"—the "11-month period between the discovery of the Emery package and the end of the 1988–89 season." And nine days after the end of that "bleak season," on March 19, 1989, Eddie Sutton resigned as the head coach of the University of Kentucky.

III

"Hey, look me over; tell me, do you like what you see?"
—Prince, "Baby I'm a Star" ('84)

After our January game in Lexington, the one where I hit five second-half threes in an effort to rally the team from a deep halftime hole, Eddie Sutton, in the post-game handshakes, offered the obligatory "good game" handshake and said something that wasn't obligatory at all: "If I had been the coach here when you were in high school, I would have recruited you." I was so flabbergasted by that statement I didn't know what to say, so I blurted out something like, "If you had been the coach, I probably would have come." Surely I didn't mean that, and I can't imagine that things would've turned out any better for me at UK than they did at Vanderbilt.

First, the SEC tourney win in my final game against Kentucky meant that I could finally and forever put to rest the fiction someone had invented early in my career that I had not been recruited by Kentucky. This persistent untruth had gained real currency in my final two years, where we had played well against the 'Cats and, except for the '89 SEC tourney game, I had played extremely well in all of them. In 1988–89 alone, that canard had been trotted out after the January game in Lexington, the February blowout in Nashville ("Goheen…was…ignored by Kentucky recruiters"), and even a week earlier on the occasion of our final home game in Memorial ("Goheen…had been shunned by his home state teams of Kentucky and Louisville"). I finally cleared the air following the SEC tourney win. "I wasn't snubbed by Kentucky," I said. "They showed a lot of interest in me, but I wanted to sign early, and Kentucky wanted to wait. Vanderbilt offered me a chance to sign early, and I took it. I think I made the right decision." The only questionable phrase in that statement was the "I think" part. It was *definitely* the right decision.

That was Kentucky's M.O. for in-state high school players in those days. The program, headed by Joe Hall when I was in high school and by Eddie Sutton during my four years at Vandy, never completely ignored a first team all-stater—especially if that player was white. Such players as a Richie Farmer and John Pelphrey, freshmen in 1988–89 and enduring the pain of the Wildcats' terrible season (the former was 0-for-4 in the tourney game, while the latter committed four turnovers in 13 minutes) but destined for much greater things in seasons ahead, received the same treatment from UK; unlike me, they had a burning desire to wear a Wildcat uniform—much more than I did. So, they waited, knowing that they had other quality opportunities (including, in both cases, Vanderbilt) if the Wildcats didn't come through—and their patience was rewarded. With no desire to have the issue hanging over my head for my senior year in high school, I committed to Vandy early in my senior year. It was a decision I've never regretted.

Plus, a comparison of Vanderbilt and Kentucky during the three years that I was a full-time starter (1986–87, 1987–88, 1988–89) reveals that the schools' on-court accomplishments weren't as different as one might think:

	Team W-L	Record vs. each other	SEC W-L	NCAA App.	NCAA W-L	NIT App.	NIT W-L
VANDY	57-41	3-4	29-25	2	2-2	1	2-1
KENTUCKY	56-35	4-3	31-23	2	2-2	0	0-0

On top of that, I was fortunate to have played well in those games, tallying 113 points for an average of over 16 points per game, about four more than my average in all other games. The bottom line is that I was glad I went to Vandy—things couldn't have worked out better for me. And I was also glad that we ended UK's season while we got to keep playing.

IV

"Time to eat all your words, swallow your pride"
—Tears for Fears, "Sowing the Seeds of Love" ('89)

Our SEC semifinal game would match us against Alabama, a 64-56 victor over Mississippi in the evening following our afternoon game. Like the Kentucky game, this third contest between the teams would act as a tiebreaker of sorts given that each team had beaten the other on its home floor. Unlike Kentucky, however, Alabama was playing its best ball of the season.

Beating the Tide was incentive enough, but we desperately wanted another shot at Florida, and there was absolutely no doubt in my mind that we would take down the Gators if we played them again. The Gators had persevered through injuries to subs and role players all season, eventually shrinking their bench to practically no one, but now the injury bug had hit one of their starters—Dwayne Davis, the star power forward, suffered a leg injury, and the Gators barely survived lowly Georgia, 62-61, in their first game. Somehow, they pulled it together and narrowly beat Tennessee on the Vols' home floor in the first semifinal game, thus clinching a spot in the final. To me, our game with 'Bama was the real SEC championship game, as the winner almost certainly would beat Florida the next day for the title.

This game would be much more tightly contested than the two regular-season games, which were decisive victories for the home team. We jumped out quickly, twice leading by five points in the opening minutes, but 'Bama took a 12-11 lead on an Alvin Lee triple nearly six minutes into the game and we would be playing catch-up for the rest of the contest, and a Tide spurt toward the end of the half gave them a 43-35 lead at intermission. The Tide built on that lead in the opening minutes of the second half, and led by 14, 75-61, with seven minutes to play. We got it together for one final run, as three straight baskets by Kornet and two free throws by Reid cut the Tide's lead to six, 75-69, with 4:37 left, but 'Bama kept us at bay, and we couldn't catch the Tide. My three-pointer with 1:10 left made it 81-75, but we got no closer until Wilcox's three at the buzzer, which made the final score 83-79, Crimson Tide.

All five players scored in double figures, led by Booker—who again lit up the Tide with 24 points powered by 6-for-10 shooting from behind the arc, earning him

a spot on the all-SEC Tournament Team. Yet again, Alvin Lee burned us from behind the three-point line, hitting four of five attempts and tying Book for game-high
honors with 24 points. "He couldn't throw it in the ocean in their game with Ole
Miss the first night," I remarked of Lee after the game, "then against us he hits everything he throws up." It was a very good basketball game by both teams, as C.M.
acknowledged: "It was just a heckuva game; I don't think we can play a whole lot
better than we played today."

And I was right that the winner of this game would win the SEC Tournament.
The next day, Alabama pounded Florida, 72-60, to win the first of three SEC titles
in a row. The Tide has not won another since the last of those three straight titles in
1991, and one year later Wimp Sanderson's otherwise-glorious reign in Tuscaloosa
ended in ignominy with his firing in the wake of a sexual harassment scandal. Meanwhile, we would have to be satisfied with a semifinal showing in the conference tournament. We took the bus back to Nashville to await our fate with the NCAA Selection Committee.

33

FINIS

I

"Some things are hard to give up, some things are hard to let go"
—Tom Petty, "Love Is a Long Road" ('89)

As angst-ridden as the NCAA selection process had been in 1988, I had no doubt that we were going to be selected for the 1989 tournament. We were 7-3 in our previous 10 games and, apart from the Tennessee game, had played well in all 10. A second-place showing in one of the country's best conferences would clinch the spot. While I said after the Alabama game that it "will be an anxious 24 hours," I was confident of a bid. The committee must have felt the same way. As much as it seemed that the committee had toyed with us in '88, when we were one of the last four teams announced in the brackets, there was no such drama in 1989. We were one of the first four teams announced when the brackets were unveiled; we were placed in the East Regional as an eight-seed, to be matched against ninth-seeded Notre Dame, in a first-round game in Providence, Rhode Island. We joined four other SEC teams in the tournament: Florida, Alabama, LSU, and Tennessee.

Of course, we were pleased to return to the Big Dance and became the first Vanderbilt team to register consecutive NCAA tournament appearances. It would be another 20 years before that feat was repeated (with Kevin Stallings' teams of 2006-07 and 2007-08).

We were familiar with Notre Dame, having played and beaten the Irish the previous two seasons. Those Irish squads were NCAA tourney teams too, but the 1988–89 edition of the Irish was quite a bit different because their great point guard, David Rivers, had graduated in 1988. His departure meant that Coach Digger Phelps had to restructure his team and mindset, and he did so around a talented freshman from East St. Louis, Illinois, named LaPhonso Ellis. The subject of an intense recruiting battle among Notre Dame, UCLA, and Illinois, Ellis was a dynamic 6'9" forward, averaging 13.2 points and 9.0 rebounds a game, helping Notre Dame to an astounding rebounding margin of +9 per game, second in the nation. We held a slight rebounding edge on our opponents for the season (+1.5) but had been badly beaten on the boards in our last three games (-18 Tennessee, -8 Kentucky, -9 Alabama), so that foretold trouble for us.

Notre Dame guard Joe Fredrick, who had considered transferring the previous Christmas, only to be talked out of it by Phelps, was the team's leading scorer at 16.6 points per game and is currently Notre Dame's all-time leader in three-point field goal percentage. Center Keith Robinson (12.7 points per game, 9.6 rebounds per game) was, like Fredrick, a junior and had started the '88 game, so they were familiar to us. Another junior, Jamere Jackson, who had come off the bench in the '87 and '88 games, was a starter in 1988–89 and averaged 13.5 points per game.

The 1988 game in South Band had been something of a coming-out party for Frank Kornet, who led the team with 17 points and, as it turned out, previewed his great play for the entire 1988–89 season. Notre Dame's coaches and players certainly remembered that game. "Kornet is the player who took control of the game," remarked Coach Phelps. "He just kinda exploded on us." I had played well in both prior games, scoring 29 points on 11-for-17 shooting from the field, the team's second-leading scorer in both games, and I was ready for a good game after escaping Knoxville. Book, on the other hand, mysteriously, and almost unbelievably, had not scored from the field in either game and had totaled exactly one point combined in the two games, a single free throw in the '88 win in South Bend. Reid and Wilcox had been superlative in the '88 game, combining to hit all seven shots from the field and scoring a collective 23 points—and we would need all five starters to play well: in the two SEC tournament games, the bench had scored a total of only seven points.

II

"Ciao, baby"
—The Cult, "Edie" ('89)

We would be playing the second game of the evening in Providence. As the "8/9 game," we and Notre Dame assumed that the winner of our game would play the #1 seed in the region—in this case, Georgetown—because a 1 seed had never lost a "1/16 game" (and didn't until 2018). But that first game on this night would turn out to be the most famous 1/16 game in tournament history: Princeton versus Georgetown.

It seemed like it should be a blowout on paper, and seeing the teams take the floor didn't change my mind—Ivy League champs Princeton, slow and methodical, locking horns with the Hoyas, the Big East champs led by star freshman Alonzo Mourning and 1988 Olympian Charles Smith, a fine point guard. But, amazingly, the Tigers stuck with the Hoyas from the opening tip, and it didn't take long for the entire crowd of 12,000 in the Providence Civic Center—minus the very few who came up from Washington, D.C., to root for Georgetown—to turn into Princeton fans. It became the most surreal atmosphere I ever witnessed in a basketball arena.

The Tigers were 25-point underdogs to the Hoyas, but they sure didn't play like it. They held leads of 15-10 and 24-16 in the first half, and, improbably, took a 29-21 lead to the locker room at halftime. We had to move to our own locker room at the half to prepare for our game, but we could tell how things were playing out on the floor: thunderous roars would mean good news for Princeton, while tepid applause or even boos would mean good news for the Hoyas. We were rooting hard for Princeton; as Georgetown was discovering, playing the Tigers was a difficult task. They spread the floor and ran a series of back cuts from off-the-ball screens that resulted in either layups or three-point shots (and seemingly nothing in between). In fact, Princeton is one of the other two teams, in addition to Vanderbilt, that has made a three-pointer in every game since the three-point line was introduced across all of college basketball in 1986–87. But we had played (and beaten) the Tigers when I was a freshman, and there was little doubt in my mind that we would beat them if they shocked Georgetown and we beat Notre Dame. And then we would be in the Sweet Sixteen again.

We were kept abreast of events as we continued our game preparation. Princeton maintained its cushion early in the second half and led 37-30 near the 10-minute mark. The Hoyas finally went on a run to take a 41-40 lead, but a Princeton three-pointer gave the Tigers the lead back, 43-41. It was close the rest of the way. The score was tied at 49 inside one minute to play when Mourning was fouled. He made the first free throw but missed the second; Princeton rebounded with a chance to win. In the locker room, we heard a tremendous roar, and then...nothing. That's when we knew Georgetown had escaped. Mourning had blocked two shots—the first a jump shot that left the Tigers with only a second left, and the second block on a shot attempt by the Princeton center that fans thought should have been called a foul (though replays suggested it was a clean block)—and the Hoyas prevailed, 50-49.

Those things shouldn't affect a player's warm-up and mindset, but it was human nature that we would feel a mental letdown after learning of the Georgetown victory. We wouldn't matchup well at all with Georgetown, especially with Mourning. And there was one other thing working against us: the date was March 17. Yes, the mischievous NCAA Selection Committee had assigned Notre Dame to a "Friday–Sunday" first weekend, meaning that we were to play the Fighting Irish on St. Patrick's Day. Who said the committee lacks a sense of humor? Predictably, Digger Phelps took full advantage of the situation to outfit his troops in green uniforms with a white shamrock on the shorts. As an added motivator, the Irish players didn't wear those unis in their initial warm-ups—they returned to their locker room for final pregame instructions and found the green jerseys waiting for them. So now we were grappling with Notre Dame and St. Paddy himself.

It would be a relatively one-sided affair. Not surprisingly, after the high drama of the Georgetown-Princeton game, practically all emotion (and thousands of fans) had been drained from the arena. There was no energy in the crowd, and we failed to generate much enthusiasm on our own. We scored the first points of the game on two Eric Reid free throws, then managed just three field goals over the next 11½ minutes. Notre Dame wasn't much better in the early going, but Joe Fredrick, who had not started the game because of a sprained ankle, provided a spark off the bench. His three-pointer with 5:21 left in the first half gave the Irish a 12-point lead, 28-16. We found some life, though, and made a run that cut the deficit to four, 30-26, with 2:25 left. The Irish maintained margin for the rest of the half, and my two free throws with two seconds left sent the teams to halftime with the Irish ahead, 34-30.

We came out for the second half seemingly ready to make a run at the lead. Wilcox buried a jumper to cut Notre Dame's lead to two. The Irish missed on the other end, and we rebounded. Wilcox launched a three that would have given us the lead…but it spun out, and with it our hopes to overtake the Irish, who scored on their end to lead again by four. Their lead was six when a Kornet deuce made it 38-34. But we could get no closer. Notre Dame—especially LaPhonso Ellis—dominated the boards and he and Fredrick formed an effective inside-outside tandem on offense.

With a couple of minutes remaining, Coach Newton removed the three seniors so we could receive a final round of applause from the Vanderbilt fans who had made the long trip to Providence. Our Vandy careers were over, ending in a disappointing 81-65 defeat. The Irish dominated the glass with a 38-22 rebounding edge—Ellis pulled down 18 all by himself to go with his 17 points.

I bounced back with a solid game in this lackluster swansong, leading the team with 18 points and five rebounds. Kornet scored 17, but he and I were the only players in double figures. The Irish, as they had done in the '87 and '88 games, proved very effective at defending the three-point shot—we had shot only six in the '87 game (all by Scott Draud) and a mere two in the '88 game—and they held us to six attempts in Providence, and only three makes (one each by Booker, Wilcox, and me). It was an unfortunate way to end four seasons filled with thrilling wins and great accomplishments.

The suddenness with which my Vanderbilt career ended was jarring. There always had been another game to look forward to; if not another game, then another season. Now what? Every player has a final game some time, but it's difficult to prepare for that certainty until it happens. "I'll remember this as my best year," I offered later. "It was the best year for Frank and Barry too. That's the way it should be. Your senior season should be your best season. It was really tough to go out by not playing our best game. As a team we can look back on this season with pride."

We weren't the only SEC team to lay an egg. In fact, the SEC turned in what was surely the worst performance by a power conference in the modern NCAA tournament era (i.e., post-expansion to 64 teams and beyond). All five teams lost, four of them by double-digit margins. West Virginia beat Tennessee 84-70. Florida was blown out by Colorado State, 68-46. LSU's Chris Jackson outscored Texas-El Paso's

Tim Hardaway 33-31, but UTEP bested the Tigers 85-74. And the most surprising result came in Atlanta, where the SEC team playing the best ball, Alabama, blew a 19-point lead to in-state rival South Alabama and fell to the Jaguars in the final seconds, 86-84.

III

"Put me in coach, I'm ready to play!"
—*John Fogerty, "Centerfield"* ('85)

The Notre Dame game had been my 126th in a Vanderbilt uniform, at the time a school record (since broken many times). It had been nearly 40 months since my first official game in a Commodore jersey, 125 games ago. Like the NCAA tournament game against Notre Dame, my first game was the second game of a double-header and was played on a neutral court on a Friday night. The twists of fate in that first game seemed to set the stage for the next 125.

The setting was Clemson, South Carolina, home of the Clemson University Tigers. Clemson hosted a Thanksgiving weekend tournament called IPTAY—which, I was told, stands for something like "I pay 30 a year," meaning dues for an athletics booster club. The IPTAY tourney was one of those four-team tournaments that many schools hosted in December and late November to play a couple of games before the conference season kicked in. Like nearly every other school-hosted in-season tournament, including Vanderbilt's own MCIT, the IPTAY has gone the way of the cassette tape and Walkman and is no more.

Only a few hundred fans—and that's probably being generous—would see the debut of the 1985–86 Vanderbilt Commodores, as the host team, Clemson, played (and won) the first game on this Friday night. We would take the floor against South Florida, a team coached by Lee Rose, who had played for C.M. Newton at Transylvania University and, moreover, succeeded C.M. as the Transy head coach when Coach Newton went to Alabama in 1968. Presumably, we would win and play in the final the following night against Clemson.

This was a new-look Commodore team—at least that was the hope given that the 1984–85 squad had finished in the SEC cellar. Six new players entered the program—the three (non-redshirting) freshmen of Kornet, Booker, and Goheen; a junior college transfer, Randy Neff; sophomore (in eligibility) Will Perdue, who was returning to the program after a redshirt season; and Bud Adams, a Georgia Tech transfer who would become eligible in a few weeks upon the conclusion of the fall semester. We joined six returning veterans (seniors Brett Burrow, Jeff Gary, and Darrell Delaney; juniors Steve Reece, Bobby Westbrooks, and Glen Clem), meaning there was robust competition for playing time. In this first game of the season, Coach

Newton played just about everybody, occasionally mixing and matching combinations of players and seeing which combos played well together.

South Florida held the lead late in the game. Then one of our senior guards fouled out with under a minute to play. I entered the game in his place. Inside 10 seconds to play and down by three (and with no three-point line in effect; that wouldn't come until the following season), we scored to cut the South Florida lead to one. We called timeout to stop the clock. On the ensuing inbounds play, I was guarding the Bulls' best player, Tommy Tonelli. A Bulls player moved over to set a pick on me that would allow Tonelli to receive the pass, but the screener was still moving as Tonelli made his break toward the ball. Such a "moving screen" is a foul, and when I made contact with the screener, the whistle blew and the foul was called. So now I went to the free-throw line for a one-and-one with five seconds left, our team down by a single point, in my first college game. I hit the first to tie the game, then swished the second to give us a one-point lead and an apparent victory. But not quite: I hounded Tonelli for three-quarters of the court and forced him to put up an off-balance 25-footer from the right wing with a couple of seconds left. It sailed over the rim...where a South Florida player was waiting under the basket, took the ball as it caromed off the backboard, and gently laid it in just as time expired to give South Florida a one-point victory.

It would be hard to concoct a more thrilling first college game than that one, and it eerily forecast the four seasons to come—close games decided in the final seconds that turned on good luck, bad luck, great plays, misplays, clutch plays, favorable calls, unfavorable calls, and every other factor that can decide a close game—and I was in the middle of all of them. The confluence of events in that first game in the nearly vacant Littlejohn Arena led to so many things: the improbable Tennessee comeback seven weeks later...a game-winning shot against Florida later that season...a buzzer-beating, game-winning shot against Penn in fall 1986...the Pitt shots in the '88 NCAA tournament...the half-court heave to beat Louisville in late November '88...the improbable last second shot to beat Georgia in January '89...and the game-winning free throws (just like against South Florida, both ends of the one-and-one) to beat Ole Miss in February '89.

"All-Americans have gone their whole careers and not had as many exciting moments as I've had," I said a few weeks after the end of the '89 season. The building blocks for those great wins and moments were put in place, at least in part, in my very first game in a Vanderbilt uniform. They combined to lead to that final weekend in Providence, Rhode Island, which had a disappointing conclusion, but was the culmination of a ton of thrills in the 40 months leading up to that final game.

What a ride.

EPILOGUE

I

"If I had the chance I'd do it all again"
—Prince, "Raspberry Beret" ('85)

With our early exit, we became spectators for the remainder of the tournament. In a remarkable run, Michigan—the team that routed us in Maui in the season's first game—won its regional to clinch one of the Final Four berths in Seattle, and their march to the title featured a couple of ironies not lost on us.

First, on March 15, after the NCAA brackets were announced but before the Wolverines were to start tournament play, their head coach, Bill Frieder, announced that he had accepted the head coaching job at Arizona State. He intended to coach the Wolverines through the NCAAs and then decamp to ASU, but Michigan's athletic director, head football coach Bo Schembecler, would have none of that: he replaced Frieder with assistant coach Steve Fisher, who, as interim head coach, led the Wolverines to the Final Four. I still recall watching an interview with Frieder in the aftermath of his resignation/firing in which Frieder invoked Coach Newton's situation as "precedent," i.e., announcing during the season that he had accepted another job effective after the season ended and yet remaining as head coach. But it was not to be. Meanwhile, Fisher coached Michigan into the championship game against Seton Hall with a semifinal win over fellow Big Ten school Illinois.

The championship game was a classic, as Seton Hall fought back from a 51-39 deficit in the second half to tie the game on Johnny Morton's late three-pointer, forcing overtime with the teams tied at 71. Seton Hall led 79-78 in the closing seconds of overtime when controversy arose: the Wolverines' Rumeal Robinson drove the lane and drew a controversial foul that put him at the line. Robinson hit both ends of the one-and-one and Michigan was the improbable NCAA champions for 1989. That official who called that last-second foul was none other than John Clougherty, Mr. Tennis Ball Game, and like in our game he felt compelled to inject himself into the spotlight and mar an otherwise excellent game.

I was in Seattle that weekend as well for the NABC (National Association of Basketball Coaches) All-Star Game, which featured some of the top seniors in the country in an East-West format. When UCLA's Pooh Richardson withdrew from the game at the last minute, I was summoned as his replacement for the West team, which meant that I played against a number of my SEC colleagues who were on the

East team, including Tennessee's Dyron Nix and LSU's Ricky Blanton. My West team was coached by Arizona's Lute Olson, a fine gentleman and one of the all-time coaching greats. We routed the East by over 20, and I had a great game—4-of-5 from the field, including 3-for-4 from three-point range. UTEP's Tim Hardaway, foreshadowing a long and productive NBA career, was named the game's MVP.

As had Perdue in 1987–88, Frank Kornet led the team in both scoring and rebounding, posting solid stats of 16.8 and 7.1. For the third consecutive season, I was the team's second-leading scorer, averaging 14.6 per game, a tad more than Book's 14.4. Reid's 10.2 points per game gave us four double-figure scorers. We also had three people exceed 100 assists, led by Wilcox's team-record 173 (since bested by Frank Seckar and, later, Atiba Prater), while I had 130 and Book 118. Not only was this the first time three Vandy players had dished out more than 100 assists, it was also the first time even *two* players had done so. The team's total of 562 assists was a school record at that time, and still is the fourth-highest in school history. Those assists translated into 2,548 points, also a school record at the time. Plus, Kornet and I were selected to the ten-man Coaches' All-SEC Team, a real thrill for both of us. I finished in the top 15 in four statistical categories—scoring (15th), three-point percentage (5th), assists (10th), and free throw percentage (9th). And I was honored to be named Vanderbilt's Male Athlete of the Year for 1988–89.

II
"I spent four years prostrate to the higher mind, got my paper and I was free"
—Indigo Girls, *"Closer to Fine"* ('89)

Meanwhile, the search for Coach Newton's replacement concluded in late March with the hiring of Eddie Fogler as Vanderbilt's new basketball coach. Eddie came to Nashville from Wichita State, where he had been the head coach for three seasons, compiling a 61-32 record with two NCAA appearances and one in the NIT. But his real calling card was his Tar Heel pedigree—he had played for Dean Smith at the University of North Carolina in the late '60s and then spent 15 years as an assistant coach on the Smith staff before taking the head coaching job in Wichita.

The formal, and ceremonial, passing of the torch occurred at the annual team banquet in early April. Speaking at that ceremony, Coach Newton reflected, "When I came here the program was not stable and I feel we've brought stability to it. We have also gained respect on a national level. It's time to let Eddie Fogler take over and take Vanderbilt to the next level." And with that, Eddie himself took the podium and added a few well-chosen words, then set about fulfilling C.M.'s wish of taking the program "to the next level." He did a good job of it, capping his four-year tenure in Nashville with an SEC regular-season title in 1992–93 and a Sweet Sixteen appearance.

Appropriately, Book, Frank, and I were selected tri-captains for the season and shared the team's MVP award. The Vanderbilt Rebounders gave me a wall clock with the inscription "Barry's Buzzer Beaters," which listed the seven games where my late-game scores either tied the game (Pitt '87–'88) or won it (Tennessee and Florida '85–'86, Penn '86–'87, Louisville, Georgia, and Ole Miss '88–'89). The clock still hangs on my office wall today.

On May 12, 1989, graduation day dawned warm and sunny. Frank and Book and I were honored to see Coach Newton at the ceremony, fulfilling his earlier promise to attend our graduation "to shake the hands of Barry Goheen, Barry Booker, and Frank Kornet as they walk across the stage." By then, C.M. had been at UK for over a month, and we were touched that he (and Coach Bostick) made the trip down from Lexington. We were the final three seniors in the esteemed coaching career of C.M. Newton, and we capped his perfect graduation record at Vandy: "In eight years, we graduated 21 of 21 senior players. That's very special and meaningful to me."

And just like that, we all went our separate ways. Coaches Newton and Bostick returned to Lexington, where C.M., as athletic director, pulled off one of the all-time great hiring coups in June 1989 by luring Rick Pitino from the NBA's New York Knicks to Lexington, where he rebuilt the decimated Wildcat program with astonishing speed. Only three years later, in 1991–92, after the inevitable house-cleaning (Eddie Sutton resigned, son Sean transferred to Purdue and then to Oklahoma State when Eddie was hired there in 1990, Chris Mills transferred to Arizona, LeRon Ellis transferred to Syracuse), and the first season the program was eligible for postseason play after the NCAA dropped the hammer in 1989, the Wildcats went all the way to the Elite Eight. Those same guys we had humiliated twice in a month's span in '89 by a total of 44 points—Deron Feldhaus, John Pelphrey, Richie Farmer, and Sean Woods (who was on the '88–'89 Wildcat squad but ineligible due to academic issues) were now seniors and joined Jamal Mashburn and others to play defending champ Duke in what is surely the greatest college basketball game of all time. Christian Laettner hit a buzzer-beating 16-footer to give Duke an amazing 104-103 win and a trip to the Final Four, where the Blue Devils repeated as NCAA champs. But the UK program was undoubtedly back—Pitino took the team to the Final Four the next season, and the 'Cats won it all in 1996. Then, under Pitino's successor, Tubby Smith, they won it again in 1998.

Meanwhile, C.M., who was on USA Basketball's selection committee, was instrumental in the process that brought NBA players to the United States Olympic Team in 1992—the original "Dream Team." Having restored both USA basketball and Kentucky hoops to their accustomed places at the head of their respective classes, Coach Newton retired in 2000 in a star-filled event held at Rupp Arena in Lexington and hosted by CBS's Jim Nantz. Kornet, Booker, Will Perdue, and I were among the attendees. Coach Newton and his wife, Nancy, whom he married after Evelyn's untimely death in the early 2000s, enjoyed a wonderful retirement in Tuscaloosa, Alabama. The Newtons spent many hours with their good friends John and Betty Bostick, who also returned to the Alabama town where the coaches integrated Alabama hoops and turned the Crimson Tide into an SEC (and even national) power.

Coach Martin, as he feared, was not given serious consideration for the head coaching job and was left without a job when Eddie Fogler took over. He was understandably frustrated at that, particularly because he was a tenured professor at Tennessee State when he left TSU to come to Vanderbilt. Assisted by some apparent lobbying by Coach Newton, Coach Martin was named associate professor of human development at Vanderbilt's Peabody College in 1989. He passed away at the age of 75 in 2005. Ed Martin was inducted into the Vanderbilt Athletics Hall of Fame in 2010—the first member of the 1988 or 1989 teams so honored. (The second—and to date only other—inductee from our teams was Will Perdue, honored in 2011. It is a mystery to me why Coach Newton has not yet been inducted.)

Mark Elliott remained an assistant coach under the Fogler regime. He did not follow Fogler to South Carolina when Eddie took the Gamecocks job in 1993, but instead went into private business in the Nashville area. In 2011, C.M. Newton performed an evaluation of the athletic department of Trevecca Nazarene University in Nashville and recommended that the school move from NAIA to Division II. C.M. also convinced the school's administration to hire the right athletic director to help the school with that transition, and he recommended Mark Elliott. That recommendation was enough for Trevecca, and since July 2011 Coach E has been the athletic director at Trevecca. When he arrived at Trevecca, Mark encountered a familiar face—Mike Petrone. Petro had been an assistant coach at Trevecca for roughly a decade when Mark arrived in 2011, and served in that capacity for several more seasons.

Barry Booker attended NBA camp with the San Antonio Spurs, coincidentally coached by Larry Brown, who took the Spurs job after leading Kansas to the '88 NCAA title, beating us in the Sweet Sixteen along the way. Despite some familiar SEC faces in San Antonio—Vernon Maxwell and Willie Anderson had finished their rookie seasons that spring—Book didn't make the cut. He graduated from Vanderbilt's Owen Business School in the mid-'90s and has worked mostly in the banking field since. Many hoops fans, however, see Barry in the winter as a color analyst for SEC games, a "hobby" in which he has been engaged for over 20 years. Barry does a fine job, as his effervescent personality and genuine love and knowledge of basketball shine through each broadcast to make the game a more rewarding experience for the viewer.

Frank Kornet was the 30th overall selection in the 1989 NBA draft, an early second-round selection of the Milwaukee Bucks. He played with the Bucks for two seasons, then played professionally in Italy for a couple of seasons before retiring from basketball. Like the Booker family, Frank and his wife, Tracy, live in Nashville, which not coincidentally is where their youngest child (of three), Luke, attended school—at Vanderbilt, playing for Kevin Stallings and then Bryce Drew, often demonstrating impressive three-point shooting for a seven-footer.

Like Frank and Barry, I also gave the NBA a whirl, attending summer camp with the Chicago Bulls, where Will Perdue was coming off his rookie season. My heart wasn't in it, and it showed—I was cut after the summer season by the Bulls' new head coach, Phil Jackson, who was (and is) one of the biggest jerks I've ever met, 11 championship rings and all. I left basketball for good at that point and, like Book, went to grad school—Vanderbilt Law School, where I graduated in 1994. After practicing for two years in Nashville, I moved to Atlanta and have practiced law there since 1996. And haven't missed basketball since.

∽

I have, however, missed my coaches and teammates. We've had formal and informal reunions from time to time, which are great occasions to get together and catch up on each other's lives. The 1987–88 team was honored by the school in 2000; the 1988–89 team was feted in 2009. Many of us congregated in Nashville on the 20th anniversary of the '88 team in winter 2008 for dinner and a Commodore game. We also informally celebrated the 25th anniversary of the Sweet Sixteen run in 2013, then did it again in January 2018 for the 30th anniversary. And, since 2011 I have hosted, for the Atlanta Tip Off Club's annual golf outing in Atlanta, some combination of Perdue, Booker, Kornet, Charlie Dahlem, Steve Reece, and Coach Newton for a weekend of golf and reminiscing. And those recollections almost always revolve around one (or all) of three things—Perdunks, the Sweet Sixteen, and Memorial Magic.

Those years were more than the experience of playing, and often winning, great games against big-name opponents. I learned, as we all did, about teamwork, performing under pressure, and leading (or being led, as the case may be). I wasn't perfect then, and I'm not perfect now, in any of those categories, but those learning experiences in college were invaluable in making me a better person and a better professional—certainly better than if I had never had those experiences. Those experiences are transferable—and that is why college athletics are so important. People from different backgrounds, upbringings, ethnicities, and all other manner of differences come together for a common purpose, bonding (not without conflict) along the way.

The best teams, like the best organizations, have a strong leader at the top (in our case, C.M. Newton), with a delegation of responsibility to others (for us, coaches Bostick and Martin). But there also should be empowerment and structure within the team, and the coaches placed significant trust and responsibility in each season's seniors, who would often liaise with the coaches to discuss problems, challenges, and other issues that invariably arise during the long season. Certainly, our 1987–88 and 1988–89 teams benefited from strong senior leadership, as each of those teams hit rough patches that could have sent those seasons into an irreversible downward spiral absent effective leadership at the top and with the seniors. One might not think that problem-solving is important to playing college basketball, but it is, just as it becomes important in the "real world."

In the end, my four years at Vanderbilt could not have worked out better for me. Great coaches, close and enduring friends, thrilling games, and a first-class education.

Everyone should be so lucky.

CODA

On June 4, 2018, C.M. Newton died at the age of 88. The previous three or four years had been tough on the coach; he had undergone cancer surgery a few years before and never quite fully recovered. Happily, his accomplishments were celebrated in 2017 in an excellent ESPN and *SEC Storied* documentary titled *Courage Matters: The C.M. Newton Story*. Because Coach Newton's health prevented him from being interviewed for the documentary, his older brother, Richard, whose voice uncannily resembled C.M.'s, provided the narration. I was honored to participate in the documentary.

The funeral service was held in Tuscaloosa on the warm and muggy morning of June 14, 2018. All four schools that C.M. led (Transylvania, Alabama, Vanderbilt, Kentucky), were represented—the then-head coaches of Alabama (Avery Johnson) and Kentucky (John Calipari) were present, as were title-winning coaches such as Tubby Smith and Billy Donovan (who was an assistant in the early '90s at UK under Rick Pitino). Alabama legends such as Wendell Hudson, Leon Douglas, and T.R. Dunn attended. On the Vandy side, it was disappointing that not a single member of the current Vanderbilt administration attended, but we former players more than made up for that whiff—in addition to me, former Commodores Barry Booker, Scott Draud, Charles Mayes, Will Perdue, Chip Rupp, Jeff Turner, and Doug Weikert arrived from such places as Atlanta, Orlando, Louisville, Nashville, and Lexington (among others) to mourn and, more importantly, celebrate the life of the man who had taught us so much more than being good basketball players. It was the end of an era.

ACKNOWLEDGMENTS

A METHOD TO THE MADNESS

This book is the culmination of eight years' worth of writing, researching, editing...and repeating those steps multiple times. Even though the events chronicled here occurred 30 or more years ago, I had some stellar assistance in my sources.

John Feinstein's *A Season Inside* is the best source to understand what college basketball was like in 1987–88. After the smashing success of *A Season on the Brink*, in which he followed a single team—the Indiana Hoosiers—for an entire season, Feinstein followed several teams over the course of the 1987–88 season for the book that became *A Season Inside*. Coincidentally, two of those teams were our last two opponents of the year—Pittsburgh and Kansas. (The only SEC team Feinstein followed was Tennessee.) For the Vanderbilt games, my parents' scrapbook of that season, which contained numerous game accounts from *The Tennessean* and *Nashville Banner*, filled out many details.

For the 1988–89 season, I was the beneficiary of a thoughtful yet mysterious gift. After the memorable 1987–88 season, an unidentified Vanderbilt fan resolved to prepare a scrapbook covering the beginning of the season through its conclusion. For whatever reason, the fan gave me the scrapbook and after the season I received a large, leather-bound book containing articles and accounts on all 33 games we played that season. I've held on to that memento ever since, a reminder of the generosity of one Vanderbilt fan—a proxy for all Vanderbilt fans.

Lest you think I have a photographic memory with the ability to recall nearly every play of some of our most critical games, particularly given their lengthy discussions in this book, I watched entire games for purposes of writing the book—the first time I had ever watched any of my Vanderbilt games. My parents converted old VHS tapes to DVD, and I viewed the following games from start to finish for purposes of this book:

1986–87:	Indiana
1987–88:	North Carolina, Kentucky, @ Notre Dame, Utah State (NCAA), Pitt (NCAA)
1988–89:	Louisville, Georgia, Kentucky, LSU

I also have the DVD of the 1984 regional semifinal game of Marshall County vs. Paducah Tilghman, probably the most tension-filled game I ever played in, high school or college.

Game statistics for the 1987–88 and 1988–89 seasons come from the official scoresheets for those games, which were compiled for and contained in the NCAA Media Guide produced by the Vanderbilt Athletic Department. Those guides contain all relevant individual and team statistics for all games except Utah State, Pitt, and Kansas (1987–88 guide) and Notre Dame (1988–89 guide).

Thank you to the individuals who reviewed early drafts of the book and provided invaluable comments—Richard A. Schneider, L. Joseph Loveland, and J. Kevin Buster. A heartfelt thanks to the wonderful individuals at Mercer University Press, especially Marc Jolley, who shepherded this book from its early stages to final publication.

Finally, thank you to my family—wife, Margie, and daughters, Aldyn and Katherine, who allowed me the time to work on this book (unknowingly in the case of Aldyn and Katherine). They provide me with more happiness and pleasure than a hundred buzzer-beaters ever could.

IN MEMORIAM

Bertie Goheen, 1903–2002
Tye Goheen, 1905–1993
Betty Goheen, 1943–2008
Brad Goheen, 1970–2010

"If you all get to heaven say a prayer for my mother, say a prayer for my father, say a prayer for my brother—but most of all please say a prayer for me"
—Terence Trent D'Arby, "If You All Get to Heaven" (1987–88)

ABBREVIATIONS

1988–89 SICBP	1988–89 Sports Illustrated College Basketball Preview
89 SEC Guide	1989 Southeastern Conference Men's Basketball Guide
AP	Associated Press
BT	*Basketball Times*
BW	*Basketball Weekly*
CHC	Commodore History Corner
CFP	*Chattanooga News Free Press*
GG	*Go Gold*
LCJ	*Louisville Courier-Journal*
MCS	*Marshall County Star*
NB	*Nashville Banner*
PS	*Paducah Sun*
SI	*Sports Illustrated*
TN	*The Tennessean*
TSN	*The Sporting News*
USAT	*USA Today*
VH	*Vanderbilt Hustler*
VMBFB	Vanderbilt Men's Basketball Fact Book
VMBMG	Vanderbilt Men's Basketball Media Guide

NOTES

Prologue: Oney, Steve, *A Man's World: Portraits* (Macon, GA: Mercer University Press, 2017) 93; Sheinin, "Last four seconds a blur to Goheen," *VH*, March 22, 1988; ESPN, Editors of, *ESPN College Basketball Encyclopedia: The Complete History of the Men's Game* (New York: Ballantine Books, 2009), 734, 743, 752.

Chapter 1: Huggins and Williams, "The Golden Past: Celebrate," *GG*, January 1987, 17–19; *2015–16 VMBFB*, 105; *The Cats' Pause Official Kentucky Basketball Yearbook 1987–88*, 92; 1987–88 VMBMG, 7, 9, 14; Fowler, "UK expects a dandy from Vandy, which is more than Perdue," *LCJ*, December 31, 1987; Traughber, "Mark Elliott was a fan favorite," CHC, February 21, 2013: www.vucommodores.com/sports/historycorner/spec-rel/022112aaa.html; Wilentz, Sean, *Bob Dylan in America* (New York: Doubleday, 2010) 238–40; www.calvertcity.com; Russell, "Basketballer Goheen's extraordinary body control is a floor show in itself," *NB*, February 1989 (undated); Derr, Andrew, *Life of Dreams: The Good Times of Sportswriter Fred Russell* (Macon, GA: Mercer University Press, 2012) 237; *SI*, August 2–9, 2010; Rice, Russell, *Adolph Rupp: Kentucky's Basketball Baron* (Champaign, IL: Sagamore Publishing, 1994) 204; Foust, "Barry Goheen is chosen to play in prestigious European tour," *Tribune-Courier*, March 7, 1984; "Uncertain over playing time, Rupp quits Vandy basketball," *NB*, November 1987 (undated).

Chapter 2: *SI*, November 18, 1987; Woody, "Perdue's 29 leads Vandy in 91-62 rout of Hawaii," *TN*, November 28, 1987; Traughber, "Perdue reflects on his basketball career," CHC, February 29, 2012: www.vucommodores.com/sports/m-baskbl/spec-rel/022912aai.html; Sakamoto, "Perdue Has Filled Big Shoes," *Chicago Tribune*, July 1, 1988; Walton, "A Tall Order," *GG*, January 1987, 12; Wilderman, "Ex-Gators Recruit Perdue Has Vandy's Engines Humming," *Florida Sun-Sentinel*, March 2, 1988; 1987–88 VMBMG, 9, 39; Newton, "Now Hear This," *GG*, April 1986, 3; Robinson, "Steve Reece: His Year to Cheer?," *GG*, December 1986, 19; Davy, "The Last Word," *GG*, December 1986, 30; Biddle, "21 1/2 AAAAAAA: If the Shoe Fits…," *TSN*, January 4, 1988.; Scarbinsky, "Vanderbilt making sweet music in Nashville," *BW*, February 1988 (undated); Vitale, Dick, and Dick Weiss, *Dick Vitale's Fabulous 50 Players & Moments in College Basketball* (Overland Park, KS: Ascend Media, 2008) 79–80; Woody, "Booker bombs Lehigh with long distance shots," *TN*, December 1, 1987; McCarter, "Sour with the Sweet," *GG*, April 1986, 23.

Chapter 3: Einhorn, Eddie, with Ron Rapoport, *How March Became Madness: How the NCAA Tournament Became the Greatest Sporting Event in America* (Chicago: Triumph Books, 2006) 149; Feinstein, John, *The Legends Club: Dean Smith, Mike Krzyzewski, Jim Valvano, and an Epic College Basketball Rivalry* (New York: Doubleday, 2016) 44, 96–97, 214–15, 284, 330–32; Roth, John, *The Encyclopedia of Duke Basketball* (Durham: Duke University Press, 2006) 15, 30–31, 125–29; Bilas, Jay, *Toughness: Developing True Strength On and Off the Court* (New York: New American Library, 2013) xiii, 108; Vitale, Dick, and Dick Weiss, *Dick Vitale Living a Dream: Reflections on 25 Years Sitting in the Best Seat in the House* (Champaign, IL: Sports Publishing, L.L.C., 2003) 100; Traughber, "Elder Kornet enjoyed successful All-SEC career for Commodores," CHC, January 21, 2015: http://www.vucommodores.com/sports/historycorner/spec-rel/012115aac.html; Lucas, Adam, *Carolina Basketball: A Century of Excellence* (Chapel Hill: University of North Carolina Press, 2010) 1–5, 81–82; Smith, Dean, with John Kilgo and Sally Jenkins, *A Coach's Life: My 40 Years in College Basketball* (New York: Random House, 1999) 27;

Traughber, "Vanderbilt Upsets No. 1 Tar Heels," CHC, February 21, 2007: www.vucommodo-res.com/genrel/022107aab.html; Feinstein, John, *A Season Inside: One Year in College Basketball* (New York: Simon & Schuster, 1988) 77–79, 157, 277; Williams, Roy, with Tim Crothers. *Hard Work: A Life on and off the Court* (Chapel Hill: Algonquin Books of Chapel Hill, 2009) 86; WZTV game telecast, December 5, 1987; Woody, "Commodores head over 'Heels," *TN*, December 6, 1987; *SI*, December 14, 1987; Woody, "Toppled!," *TN*, December 6, 1987; Richards, "Commodores look to upset Hoosiers again," *Indianapolis Star*, December 8, 1987; "Vanderbilt soaks in its shock of No. 1," *USAT*, December 7, 1987; *Los Angeles Times*, December 6, 1987.

Chapter 4: Knight, Bob, with Bob Hammel, *Knight: My Story* (New York: St. Martin's Press, 2002) 112–16, 120–21, 222, 239–41, 252; Feinstein, John. *A Season on the Brink: A Year with Bobby Knight and the Indiana Hoosiers* (New York: Simon & Schuster, 1987) 16–25, 118–23, 316; Alford, Steve, with John Garrity, *Playing for Knight: My Six Seasons with Coach Knight* (New York: Fireside, 1989) 63, 68–72, 203–10, 247; Vitale and Weiss, *Dick Vitale's Fabulous 50 Players & Moments*, 51–52, 113–14; Newton, C.M., *Newton's Laws: The C.M. Newton Story as Told to Billy Reed* (Lexington, KY: Host Communications, Inc., 2000) 108, 110, 137, 138; Hammel, Bob, *Beyond the Brink with Indiana* (Indianapolis and Bloomington, IN: The Bloomington Herald-Telephone and Indiana University Press, 1987) 25, 49–50, 73–76; Woody, "Knight's normal self at podium," *TN*, December 10, 1986; *SI*, December 22, 1986; Laise, "Goheen becomes Vandy's take-charge guy," *NB*, December 10, 1986; game telecast, December 9, 1986; Big Ten Elite, *1987 Indiana Basketball*, Big Ten Network, 2013; Traughber, "Elder Kornet enjoyed successful All-SEC career for Commodores," CHC, January 21, 2015; Woody, "Good Knight! VU Stuns Hoosiers," *TN*, December 10, 1986; Climer, "VU's Clem contains Alford," *TN*, December 10, 1986; Biddle, "Will history be kind to Bobby Knight?," *NB*, December 10, 1986; Vitale with Weiss, *Living a Dream*, 92; 1987–88 VMBMG, 9; Feinstein, *Season Inside*, 104–105, 108; "Smart comes off the bench, sparks 63-61 Indiana victory," *USAT*, December 9, 1987; *SI*, January 11, 1988.

Chapter 5: Freligh, "Vanderbilt Slips Past Penn, 71-70," *Philadelphia Inquirer*, December 14, 1986; UPI, December 14, 1986; Woody, "Vandy rips Cornell 95-79 to win MCIT," *TN*, December 30, 1987; 1987–88 VMBMG, 14; Neel, Roy M., *Dynamite! 75 Years of Vanderbilt Basketball* (Nashville, TN: Burr-Oak Publishers, 1975) 51; 89 SEC Guide, 13, 24; Rice, *Adolph Rupp*, 204; Woody, "Chapman leads late Kentucky surge past Commodores, 81–74," *TN*, January 1, 1988; Brown, Dale, with Don Yeager, *Tiger in a Lion's Den: Adventures in LSU Basketball* (New York: Hyperion Books, 1994) 49–52; Smith, "Hello Trouble, I'm Dale Brown," *SI*, November 18, 1985; Kriegel, Mark, *Pistol: The Life of Pete Maravich* (New York: Free Press, 2007) 289–92; Hunter, Bruce, *Don't Count Me Out: The Irrepressible Dale Brown and His LSU Fighting Tigers* (Chicago: Bonus Books, Inc., 1989) 73; Woody, "LSU puts freeze on Vandy, 51-39," *TN*, January 7, 1988.

Chapter 6: Dortch, Chris, *String Music: Inside the Rise of SEC Basketball* (Dulles, VA: Brassey's, Inc., 2002) 13, 64, 122, 226, 233–34; Smith, "Booker scores in final seconds as Vandy wins," *TN*, January 14, 1988; Smith, "Ole Miss remembers near miss," *TN*, February 13, 1988; Scout.com interview: Barry Booker, April 14, 2008: www.vanderbilt.scout.com/2/746176.html; Lopresti, "To a degree, precedent set for Vandy star," *USAT*, December 1987 (undated); Traughber, "Barry Booker recalls his career," CHC, January 4, 2012: www.vucommodores.com/sports/historycorner/spec-rel/010412.aai.html; McCarter, "Barry-Picking Produces Only Thorns for Tennessee," *CNFP*, February 11, 1988; Ward, "The Old Bomb Squad," VandySports.com, April 5, 2004: www.//vanderbilt.rivals.com/content.asp?CID=282935; Williams, "The Triumph of the Pencil-Necks," *GG*, February 1987, 11; Sanderson, Wimp, *Plaid and Parquet: An Autobiography of Wimp Sanderson* (Sterrett, AL: Five Pants South Productions, 2000)

191–93; Laise, "Vandy's hot shots cool off Alabama," *NB*, January 17, 1988; Scarbinsky, "Vanderbilt making sweet music in Nashville," *BW*, February 1988 (undated); Woody, "VU avenges past routs, rips 'Dawgs," *TN*, January 21, 1988; Hammel, *Beyond the Brink with Indiana*, 85–88; Laise, "Mayes' 3-pointers bury Auburn for VU," *NB*, January 24, 1988.

Chapter 7: Woody, "Perdue's final stuff for loyal Vandy fans," *TN*, January 28, 1988; Einhorn with Rapoport, *How March Became Madness*, 97, 104, 107; Kindred, Dave, *Basketball: The Dream Game in Kentucky* (Louisville: Data Courier, Inc., 1976); Schmidt, "Hot Seats," *PS*, January 27, 1988; WZTV game telecast, January 27, 1988; Fowler, "Vanderbilt turns back Kentucky, 83-68 [*sic*]," *LCJ*, January 28, 1988; Woody, "Vandy ends Kentucky jinx, 83-66," *TN*, January 28, 1988; Carey, "Vandy slays another giant," *USAT*, January 28, 1988; Davy, "Commodore gunners stun Cats' Chapman," *TN*, January 28, 1988; Schmidt, "Guards exploit 3-pointer," *PS*, January 28, 1988.

Chapter 8: Traughber, "Barry Booker recalls his career," CHC, January 4, 2012; Traughber, "C.M. Newton recalls career," CHC, January 28, 2009: www.vucommodores.com/sports/m-baskbl/spec-rel/102809.aai.html; Woody, "Vandy prepared early for 3-point goal," *TN*, December 23, 1987; Ward, "The Old Bomb Squad"; 1988–89 VMBMG, 31, 41, 51; Williams, "The Triumph of the Pencil-Necks," *GG*, February 1987, 11; *SI*, February 8, 1988, 83; Katz, "Committee extends men's 3-point line to 20-9," espn.com, May 3, 2007; Walton, "A Tall Order," *GG*, January 1987, 14; Biddle, "21 1/2 AAAAAAA: If the Shoe Fits . . .," *TSN*, January 4, 1988; O'Neil, "Ed Steitz's 3-point dream turns 25," espn.com, November 3, 2011: www.espn.go.com/mens-college-basketball/story/_/id/7178690; Canfield, "Vandy coach opposed new rule," *PS*, March 21,1988; "Vandy's Bombs Sink Pitt," *TSN*, March 28, 1988; Woody, "Newton offers apology to architect of 3-pointer," *TN*, March 21, 1988; Einhorn and Rapoport, *How March Became Madness*, 104; Dortch, *String Music*, 88, 188; Povtak, "Vandy Toys with Florida in 92-65 Rout," *Orlando Sentinel*, January 31, 1988; Shearer, "Sloan's concerns verified after Commodores' charge," AP, February 1, 1988; "VU sets NCAA record at free-throw line," 60 Moments in Memorial Gym, February 28, 2012: www.vucommodores.com/sports/m-baskbl/spec-rel/022812aac.html; Traughber, "Perdue reflects on his basketball career," CHC, February 29, 2012; Wilderman, "Ex-Gators Recruit Perdue Has Vandy's Engines Humming," *Florida Sun Sentinel*, March 2, 1988; Davy, "VU streak, roar of crowd rekindles memories of '67," *TN*, January 31, 1988; Maraniss, Andrew, *Strong Inside: Perry Wallace and the Collision of Race and Sports in the South* (Nashville: Vanderbilt University Press, 2014) 229–35; *ESPN College Basketball Encyclopedia*, 751; Huggins and Williams, "The Golden Past: Celebrate," *GG*, January 1987, 18; *TN*, February 1, 1988; *USAT*, February 1, 1988; Hunter, *Don't Count Me Out*, 220–21; Woody, "State 7th SEC victim for Vandy," *TN*, February 4, 1988.

Chapter 9: Kriegel, *Pistol*, 296; Dortch, *String Music*, 165, 258; Biddle, "Newton breaks out proven wardrobe to snap streak," *NB*, February 1988 (undated); McCarter, "Sour with the Sweet," *GG*, April 1986; Feinstein, *Season Inside*, 19–20, 99, 185, 270, 390; WSMV-TV report, January 16, 1986; "Goheen scores final five points to pull out improbable win over Tennessee," 60 Moments in Memorial Gym, March 1, 2012: www.vucommodores.com/sports/m-baskbl/spec-rel/030112aac.html; Smith, "Ole Miss remembers near miss," *TN*, February 13, 1988; Laise, "Vandy guards cross up Volunteers' playmakers," *NB*, February 12, 1988; Woody, "VU swamps struggling Tennessee," *TN*, February 11, 1988; ESPN telecast, February 11, 1988; McCarter, "Barry-Picking Produces Only Thorns for Tennessee," *CNFP*, February 11, 1988; Smith, "Vandy machine rolls over Rebs," *TN*, February 14, 1988; Traughber, "C.M. Newton recalls career," CHC, January 28, 2009.

Chapter 10: Laise, "Looking Back," *NB*, March 1988 (undated); Woody, "Moving to the Top," *TN*, February 21, 1988; Woody, "Auburn spoils Perdue's farewell party," *TN*, February 25, 1988; Phelps, Digger, with Tim Bourret, *Tales from the Notre Dame Hardwood* (Champaign, IL: Sports Publishing L.L.C., 2004) 10, 17, 65–67, 122–23, 145, 147; Wojnarowski, Adrian, *The Miracle of St. Anthony: A Season with Coach Bob Hurley and Basketball's Most Improbable Dynasty* (New York: Gotham Books, 2005) 302; Neely, Tim, *Hooping It Up: The Complete History of Notre Dame Basketball* (Notre Dame: Diamond Communications, 1985) 265; Pearlman, Jeff, *Showtime: Magic, Kareem, Riley, and the Los Angeles Lakers Dynasty of the 1980s* (New York: Gotham Books, 2014) 353; Heisler, John, ed., *Strong at Heart: Profiles of Notre Dame Athletics 2013* (South Bend: The University of Notre Dame Athletics Department, 2013) 81; Feinstein, *A Season on the Brink*, 314–15; WGN game telecast, February 6, 1987; Coffey, Michael, *Echoes of the Hardwood: 100 Seasons of Notre Dame Men's Basketball* (Lanham, MD: Taylor Trade Publishing, 2004) 203; ESPN game telecast, February 27, 1988; McGee, "Kornet out to end Irish luck again," *NB*, March 1989 (undated); 1988–89 VMBMG, 39; Woody, "Perdue's 29 leads Vandy in 91–62 rout of Hawaii," *TN*, November 28, 1987; Woody, "Phelps gives conquering Commodores good review," *TN*, February 28, 1988; Traughber, "Elder Kornet enjoyed successful All-SEC career for Commodores," *CHC*, January 21, 2015; McGee, "Kornet trying to make up for lost potential," *NB*, January 7, 1989; Biddle, "Kornet inflicting his own brand of pain on Vanderbilt opponents," *NB*, February 2, 1989; Woody, "Perdue-less Commodores find new road to victory," *TN*, February 28, 1988; "Vanderbilt basketball beats Austin Peay, extends 3-point streak to 1,000 games," *TN*, November 11, 2017; Dawson, "Good Things Come in Threes," *Commodore Nation*, February 2017, 8; Woody, "Vandy romps; NCAA hopes now soaring," *TN*, February 28, 1988.

Chapter 11: Winderman, "Schintzius the Big Difference as UF Rips Vandy," *Sun-Sentinel*, March 3, 1988; Woody, "Commodores hurt by Bulldogs' bite," *TN*, March 6, 1988; "Newton, VU face biggest task today," *TN*, March 18, 1988; Miller, "Quick fixes, 'freak defense' helped LSU make Final Four history," *USAT*, March 24, 2011; Wolff, "A Band of Renown at Last," *SI*, March 31, 1986; Miller, "Don Redden's death still hurts LSU teammate," *USAT*, March 24, 2011; Brown, Dale, *Dale Brown's Memoirs from LSU Basketball* (Champaign, IL: Sports Publishing L.L.C., 2004) 151, 154–55; Brown, *Adventures in LSU Basketball*, 152; Laise, "Late-season travel, injuries, books take heavy toll on Commodores," *NB*, March 1988 (undated); Hersch, "King Rex and His Top Cats," *SI*, March 21, 1988; Smith and Ourand, "Stories behind Selection Sunday," *Street & Smith's Sports Business Journal*, March 14–20, 2016, 20; Taaffe, "Airing Those Pairings," *SI*, March 21, 1988; Woody, "Newton says VU deserves NCAA berth," *TN*, March 14, 1988.

Chapter 12: *PS*, November 23, 1983; Stewart, "Tornado's breaks down Marshals," *PS*, January 1, 1984; Neel, *Dynamite!*, 121; Verducci, "Moveable Beast," *SI*, June 1, 2015, 51; Willingham, "Goheen outduels Shumpert, but Tilghman downs Marshall," *PS*, January 1984 (undated); Willingham, "Marshall withstands Charleston pressure; Smith leads Massac," *PS*, January 1984 (undated); "Patriots Win Three, but Marshalls Prevail in Classic," *Metropolis Planet*, January 26, 1984; "Powell leads Marshall past Reidland," *PS*, January 1984 (undated); *USAT*, February 25, 2004; www.mchoopfest.org/history/html; White, "'Tornado' no breeze in region," *LCJ*, February 14, 1984; Willingham, "Goheen leads Marshals past Tilghman," *PS*, February 12, 1984; Bland, "Goheen's 42 propel Marshals past Lakers," *MCS*, March 1984 (undated); Mackay, "Real Men Don't Eat Quiche? So Says Bruce Feirstein, a Writer with—Well—Crust," *People*, August 2, 1982; Russell, "Marshals capture thrilling win over Tilghman," *Tribune-Courier*, March 1984 (undated); Harrison, "Marshals: 1 down, 1 to go?," *PS*, March 1984 (undated); game video and simulcast, WCBL, March 8, 1984; Willingham, "Goheen plays lead, Miller finishes off Marshals overtime drama," *PS*, March 10, 1984; official game boxscore, March 9, 1984; play-by-plays reprinted in

MCS, March 1984 (undated); Stewart, "'Sweet' trip ahead," *PS*, March 10, 1984; photograph of billboard in *MCS*, March 20, 1984; Embry, Mike, *March Madness: The Kentucky High School Basketball Tournament* (South Bend, IN: Icarus Press, 1985), preface; O'Brien, Keith, *Outside Shot: Big Dreams, Hard Times, and One County's Quest for Basketball Greatness* (New York: St. Martin's Press, 2012) i, 2–3; Clay, "Bourbon wins in OT on goal by Royce," *Lexington Herald Leader*, March 17, 1984; Schmidt, "Marshall plagued by mistakes, too much 'Bourbon,'" *PS*, March 17, 1984; Farrell, "Bourbon County slips past Marshall as Royce rolls in OT," *LCJ*, March 17, 1984; Schmidt, "Player of the Year is 'icing on the cake' for Marshals' Goheen," *PS*, March 1984 (undated); *LCJ*, April 8, 1984.

Chapter 13: Woody, "Utah St. barring Vandy's new start," *TN*, March 18, 1988; game preview, *TN*, March 18, 1988; CBS-TV telecast, March 18, 1988; Laise, "Vandy back to basics in victory," *NB*, March 19, 1988; Strange, *NCAA Encyclopedia*, 226, 239–47; Goheen, Benny T., *With Shirttails Flying: The Story of the 1959 North Marshall Jets* (Mayfield, KY: King's Publishers, 2005), 147–54; Embry, *March Madness*, 91–93; Aubrey, Will, Sid Easley, Steve Parker, Kim Trevathan, and Jimmy Wilder, *Banner Years: Murray State Basketball 1925–2013* (Morley, MO: Acclaim Press, 2013) 150–53, 163–67, 234–35; Hager, Tom, *The Ultimate Book of March Madness: The Players, Games, and Cinderellas that Captivated a Nation* (Minneapolis, MN: MVP Books, 2012) 168–69; Feinstein, *Season Inside*, 391.

Chapter 14: Starkey, "Goheen reflects on beating Pitt in '88," *Pittsburgh Tribune*, March 24, 2007; Feinstein, *Season Inside*, 16, 61–64, 159–61, 287–88, 338, 384–85; Sciullo, Sam Jr., *Tales from the Pitt Panthers* (Champaign, IL: Sports Publishing L.L.C., 2004) 88–89; Lowenstein, Michael E., *We All We Got: Pitt Basketball in the Golden Era* (Tarentum, PA: Word Association Publishers, 2009) 8; *SI*, November 18, 1987; Hruby, "Jerome Lane dunks is way into history," espn.com, March 10, 2011: http://sports.espn.go.com/espn/page2/story?page=hruby/110310_jerome_lane_shattered_backboard&sportCat=ncb; Cosentino, "Jerome Lane's Backboard-Smashing Dunk Was 25 Years Ago Today," deadspin.com, January 25, 2013; Vitale with Weiss, *Living a Dream*, 309, 311–12; Musselman, "One bad night cost '88 team its legacy," *Pittsburgh Post-Gazette*, February 24, 2008; Calipari, John, with Dick Weiss, *Refuse to Lose* (New York: Ballantine Books, 1996) 52–53; "Arizona's Miller Still Living Down 'Tonight Show' Cameo," www.lostlettermen.com/tonight-show-sean-miller (May 9, 2011); Price, Why John Calipari Can't Catch a Break," *SI*, March 14, 2011, 40; Strange, *NCAA Encyclopedia*, 595, 606; Howard-Cooper, "A Winning Solution: The Pittsburgh Basketball Team Is Doing It with Mirrors—and a Whole Lot of Talent," *Los Angeles Times*, January 23, 1988; Woody, "Challenged by criticism, Reid really came through," *TN*, March 21, 1988; CBS telecast and postgame interview, March 20, 1988; Visser, "A Second-round Pitt Fall: Commodores Halt Panthers in OT," *Boston Globe*, March 21, 1988; Sheinin, "Oh my! Goheen miracle puts VU in Sweet 16," *VH*, March 22, 1988; Biddle, "Shot was Barry, Barry good," *NB*, March 21, 1988; "Barry Goheen Found!," si.com College Basketball Mailbag, March 13, 2002: http://sportsillustrated.cnn.com/inside_game/grant_wahl/news/2002/03/13/mailbag; http://www.jimtraber.net/forum/printer_friendly_posts.asp? (May 24, 2007); Ringel, "What's It Like to Hit a Buzzer-Beater in the NCAA Tournament? This Big Law Partner Knows," *Daily Report*, March 15, 2017; *Courage Matters: The C.M. Newton Story*, SEC Storied, ESPN, 2017; http://www.youtube.com/watch?v=ULuPi8ycQrA.

Chapter 15: *NB*, March 21, 1988; Biddle, "Shot was Barry, Barry good," *NB*, March 21, 1988; Traughber, "Barry Booker recalls his career," *CHC*, January 4, 2012; Stiles, T.J., *The First Tycoon: The Epic Life of Cornelius Vanderbilt* (New York: Alfred A. Knopf, 2009) 560–61; McGee, "Commodores seek repeat of NCAA thrill," *NB*, March 1989 (undated); Holmes, "Thousands greet victorious Dores," *VH*, March 22, 1988; Laise, "March Madness at Vandy," *NB*, March 22,

1988; Davy and Woody, "Fans rock when Vandy dunks Pitt," *TN*, March 21, 1988; www.hooph-all.com/hall-of-famers/tag/r-william-jones; McCallum, Jack, *Dream Team: How Michael, Magic, Larry, Charles, and the Greatest Team of All Time Conquered the World and Changed the Game of Basketball Forever* (New York: Ballantine Books, 2012) 7; Knight, *My Story*, 222; Feinstein, John, *One on One: Behind the Scenes with the Greats in the Game* (New York: Little, Brown and Company, 2012) 119–20; Feinstein, *Season Inside*, 385–86; Scullio, *Tales of the Pitt Panthers*, 87, 90; Cosentino, "Jerome Lane's Backboard-Smashing Dunk Was 25 Years Ago Today," deadspin.com, January 25, 2013; Nance, "Vanderbilt, Kansas win with late-game heroics," *USAT*, March 21, 1988; Laise, "Notes, quotes, anecdotes," *NB*, March 21, 1988; Feinstein, "Vanderbilt Topples Pitt," *Washington Post*, March 21, 1988; Hruby, "Jerome Lane dunks…"; "Pitt Players Blame Coach for NCAA Loss," AP account, *Los Angeles Times*, March 22, 1988; Visser, "A Second-round Pitt Fall: Commodores Halt Panthers in OT," *Boston Globe*, March 21, 1988; "Vandy's Bombs Sink Pitt," *TSN*, March 28, 1988; Sheinin, "Oh my! Goheen miracle puts VU in Sweet 16," *VH*, March 22, 1988; Woody, "Vanderbilt, Goheen and the Sweet 16," *TN*, March 21, 1988; Starkey, "Goheen reflects on beating Pitt in '88," *Pittsburgh Tribune*, March 24, 2007; Musselman, "One bad night cost '88 team its legacy," *Pittsburgh Post-Gazette*, February 24, 2008; Hagen, *Ultimate Book*, 346–47; Lowenstein, *We All We Got*, 10–11; Culpepper, "How it feels to lose one game short of the Final Four—over and over again," *Washington Post*, March 14, 2017; Conti, "10 most disappointing moments in Pitt sports," http://blog.triblive.com/trib-list/2014/03/24/10-most-disaapointing-moments-in-pitt-sports (March 24, 2014); Perdue, NCAA diary, *NB*, March 21, 1988; *USAT*, March 21, 1988; Laise, "In the end, Newton's right choice pays off," *NB*, March 22, 1988; Olney, "'The shot' lives in infamy for those who attempt it," *NB*, March 22, 1988; Cook, "Sean Miller calls Dixon an elite coach," *Pittsburgh Post-Gazette*, March 23, 2013; Laise, "Vandy's NCAA victories worth almost $500,000," *NB*, March 21, 1988; Bibb, "'Net' worth now priceless for Vandy," *TN*, March 21, 1988.

Chapter 16: Feinstein, *Season Inside*, 122–26, 380, 386–88; Woodling, Chuck, *Against All Odds: How Kansas Won the 1988 NCAA Championship* (Lawrence, KS: University Press of Kansas, 1988) 11–13, 30–31, 42, 46–47, 80, 86–88, 94–96, 105, 114–22, 131, 153; Fulks, Matt, ed., *Echoes of Kansas Basketball: The Greatest Stories Ever Told* (Chicago: Triumph Books, 2006) 2, 152; Rice, *Adolph Rupp*, 7–13; Winn, "The Freshman," *SI*, October 14, 2013; Foster, "Manning (38) vexes Vandy," *Detroit Free Press*, March 26, 1988; Laise, "Looking Back," *NB*, March 1988 (undated); Newton, *Newton's Laws*, 159–60; Vitale and Weiss, *Dick Vitale's Fabulous 50 Players and Moments*, 131; "NCAA bans SMU from 2016 postseason, Larry Brown for nine games," espn.com, September 30, 2015; 89 SEC Guide, 11, 126–28; 1988–89 VMBFB, 6, 7; www.hoopedia.nba.com/index-php?title=NBA_Draft_1988.

Chapter 17: Stewart, "Goheen's shots echo into 1989," *PS*, November 9, 1988; Woody, "There's life after Will for Vandy," *TN*, October 1988 (undated); Woody, "Vanderbilt needs help at center," *TN*, November 1988 (undated); *1988–89 SICBP*, 58–77; Laise, "Schedule rates as toughest," *NB*, October 1988 (undated); Vandy Blog, C.M. Newton Interview, February 18, 2009: www.vandypride.com/2009/02/18/cm-newton-interview; Fitzpatrick, Frank, *And the Walls Came Tumbling Down: Kentucky, Texas Western, and the Game That Changed American Sports* (New York: Simon & Schuster, 1999) 209–17 [*Author's note*: The '66 title game is often viewed as a watershed moment because an all-black five took down an all-white five, and many media and fans piled on to claim that the coach of the all-white UK losers, Adolph Rupp, was a racist for never having had a black player in a UK uniform. Those unsubstantiated claims quickly gained currency, were hurtful to the Rupp family, and have never been entirely erased, unfortunately. In fact, numerous luminaries have strongly pushed back on the "Rupp was racist" claims, including

Red Auerbach ("He got a bad rap for that") and C.M. Newton ("He may have been a lot of things, but he wasn't a racist. It really burns me when I read that stuff by some of today's writers.") (Auerbach, Red, and John Feinstein, *Let Me Tell You a Story: A Lifetime in the Game* [New York: Little, Brown and Company, 2004] 86; Newton, *Newton's Laws*, 57). Plus, the SEC's first African-American hoopster, Vandy's Perry Wallace, played for Rupp in a post-season college all-star game and recalled Rupp as "extremely welcoming and gracious" (Maraniss, *Strong Inside*, 362)]; Pearlman, *Showtime*, 114; Wolff, "Conference Call," *SI*, November 30, 1988, 79; Biddle, "Vanderbilt to redshirt Draud," *NB*, November 1988 (undated); 1988–89 VMBFB, 31.

Chapter 18: Woody, "Perdue-less Commodores show style," *TN*, November 18, 1988; McGee, "In Hawaii, VU meets No. 3 team," *NB*, November 25, 1988; Hoff, "Vanderbilt in Hawaii sends Perdue card: Wish you were here," *NB*, November 26, 1988; Vitale and Weiss, *Dick Vitale's Fabulous 50 Players and Moments*, 123; Feinstein, *Season Inside*, 127–28; "Kornet's 19 lifts Vandy for first win," *TN*, November 27, 1988; "'D,' turnovers haunt Vanderbilt," *NB*, November 28, 1988.

Chapter 19: Combs, ed., *The Cats' Pause 1984–85 Kentucky Basketball Yearbook*, 30, 84–85, 171, 187; "60 Moments at Memorial Gym": http://www.vucommodores.com/sports/m-baskbl/spec-rel/022712aam.html (Feb. 27, 2012); Einhorn and Rapaport, *How March Became Madness*, 91–94; Kindred, *Basketball: The Dream Game*, 143; Hager, *Ultimate Book*, 100–01; Vitale and Weiss, *Dick Vitale's Fabulous 50 Players and Moments*, 197–98; McGee, "Air LaBradford," *NB*, November 30, 1988; *Street and Smith's Official Yearbook 1984–85*, 22; Thurman, Tom, ed. *Hardwood Heaven: Basketball in Kentucky 1895–1966* (Louisville, KY: Butler Book Publishing Services, Inc., 2003) 142–43; Embry, *March Madness*, 102–109; Stewart, "Marshall fails to succumb to Seneca's early landslide," *PS*, December 21, 1984; White, "Williams' free throws save Seneca from Goheen and Marshall County," *LCJ*, December 21, 1984; Stewart, "Marshall's gains will have to offset Bluegrass losses," *PS*, December 22, 1984; Millizer, "Stock at Marshall increases," *PS*, December 1984 (undated); "Bluegrass losses provide LIT benefits," *PS*, January 16, 1985; "Fern Creek gets Goheen treatment," *PS*, January 1985 (undated); Branch, "Marshall Co. 'tried harder' but Kimbro scores 30 for relief," *Louisville Times*, January 1985 (undated); "Seneca gets past Marshall to title game," *PS*, January 1985 (undated); Bridgeman, Jeff, *Kentucky High School Basketball Encyclopedia 1916–2013* (Morley, MO: Acclaim Press, 2013) 413; *ESPN College Basketball Encyclopedia*, 959; *1988–89 SICBP*, 62, 70; game preview, *NB*, November 30, 1988; Bozich, "Sharp Shooters," *Southern Magazine*, January 1989, 35; game telecast, November 30, 1988; Biddle, "Trigger-happy Goheen does it once again," *NB*, December 1, 1988; Biddle, "Goheen's a man of miracles for Vanderbilt," *BT*, February 29, 1989; Brown, Goheen's 45-foot heave at buzzer leaves Cards agonizing 65-62 loss," *LCJ*, December 1, 1988.

Chapter 20: Davis, Seth, *Wooden: A Coach's Life* (New York: Times Books, Henry Holt & Company, 2014), 457–58; Woody, "UAB tests new gym, new Vandy," *TN*, December 3, 1988; Woody, "Vandy falls victim to UAB celebration," *TN*, December 4, 1988; McGee, "UAB's Kennedy uses 3s to gun Vanderbilt down," *NB*, December 5, 1988; "No. 8 Tar Heels tough test," *TN*, December 7, 1988; Lucas, *Carolina Basketball*, 173; McGee, "Tar Heels' players, fans remember loss to Vandy," *NB*, December 7, 1988; McGee, "VU Tar-Heeled and feathered," *NB*, December 8, 1988; Woody, "UNC whips Vandy 89-77," *TN*, December 8, 1988; Biddle, "Cameras roll, but Vandy a no-show," *NB*, December 8, 1988; Olney, "VU tries to take Manhattan—Kansas, that is," *NB*, December 10, 1988; Woody, "Kansas State hands Vandy third straight loss," *TN*, December 11, 1988; Olney, "Vandy road trip proves really no place like home," *NB*, December 12, 1988.

Chapter 21: Olney, "Tigers bringing unfamiliar faces to play Vanderbilt on national TV," *NB*, December 14, 1988; Olney, "Vitale living out everyone's dream," *NB*, December 14, 1988; Woody, "Kornet ignites Vandy to rally past Auburn, 93-77," *TN*, December 15, 1988; Climer, "Kornet assumes leadership post to key Commodore turnaround," *TN*, December 15, 1988; Woody, "Tough tests steeled VU for future foes," *TN*, December 1988 (undated); Woody, "Goheen revives to spark Vandy," *TN*, December 20, 1988; Olney, "Exam slate throws Vandy out of whack," NB, December 19, 1988; Olney, McGee, and Biddle, "Vanderbilt 74, Murray State 57," *NB*, December 20, 1988; McGee, "2nd-half magic saves VU again," *NB*, December 20, 1988; McGee, "Quick-shooting Barton back to haunt Vandy," *NB*, December 22, 1988; McGee, "VU goes by the Book," *NB*, December 23, 1988; Woody, "High-spirited VU whips Dartmouth," *TN*, December 23, 1988; Woody, "Booker gets sweet revenge," *TN*, December 23, 1988; McGee, "Music City Invitational hosts Colgate's blues," NB, December 29, 1988; Woody, "Smiling Vandy brushes off Colgate 91-55," *TN*, December 30, 1988; *1988–89 SICBP*, 74; Woody, "Mission Impossible: shut down Lichti," *TN*, December 30, 1988; McGee, Lichti shoots down Memorial Gym record," *NB*, December 30, 1988; McGee, "Stanford stuns Vanderbilt," *NB*, December 31, 1988; Woody, "Stanford brings end to VU's home magic," *TN*, December 31, 1988; "Stanford 89, VU 68," *NB*, December 31, 1988; Woody, "Vanderbilt mugging exposes inside woes," *TN*, December 31, 1988.

Chapter 22: Woody, "Vanderbilt rolls past Alabama, 73-53," *TN*, January 5, 1989; Woody, "Vanderbilt mugging exposes inside woes," *TN*, December 31, 1988; Climer, "After preliminaries, no clear favorite," *TN*, January 4, 1989; Woody, "Vulnerable VU hosts Alabama," *TN*, January 4, 1989; "Booker wins SEC award," *TN*, January 6, 1989; McGee, "Wilcox 'assists' VU win," *NB*, January 5, 1989; Davy, "Wilcox at head of class with record 13 assists," *TN*, January 5, 1989; Wojciechowski, Gene, *The Last Great Game: Duke vs. Kentucky and the 2.1 Seconds that Changed Basketball* (New York: ESPN Books/Blue Rider Press, 2012) 24–25, 77; Feinstein, *Season Inside*, 460; Vitale with Weiss, *Living a Dream*, 210; Dortch, *String Music*, 132–36; Kirkpatrick, "Dodging a bullet," *SI*, May 29, 1989; "C.M. Newton top choice of UK prez," AP account, *TN*, December 10, 1988; Reed, "Lexington Bound?," *SI*, January 9, 1989, 106; McGee, "Newton shrugs off magazine report," *NB*, January 7, 1989; *1988–89 SICBP*, 77; Bridgeman, *Kentucky High School Basketball Encyclopedia, 1916–2013*, 413; Embry, "Miller outguns Goheen's last shot at Rupp," AP report, *PS*, January 8, 1989; Woody, "Newton's ole Kentucky home bad news again," *TN*, January 8, 1989; Tipton, "Poised Wildcats Beat Vandy 70–61," *Lexington Herald-Leader*, January 8, 1989; McGee, "Goheen's scoring binge can't beat Cats' 9 lives," *NB*, January 9, 1989; Woody, "Distractions name of game for Vandy," *TN*, January 9, 1989.

Chapter 23: Davy, "Vandy faces glare of Ole Miss' Glass," *TN*, January 10, 1989; McGee, "VU poses triple threat for Ole Miss, Murphy," *NB*, January 10, 1989; *1988–89 SICBP*, 57; Davy, "Vanderbilt survive [*sic*] close encounters," *TN*, January 12, 1989; McGee, "Shooting star lifts Vandy," *NB*, January 11, 1989; Davy, "'Big-hearted' Wilcox fuels VU victory," *TN*, January 12, 1989; McGee, "Georgia looks to fill expectations," *NB*, January 13, 1989; Davy, "Run of bad fortune has Georgia baffled," *TN*, January 13, 1989; Jefferson-Pilot game telecast, January 14, 1989; Woody, "Goheen's shot lifts Vanderbilt over Georgia," *TN*, January 15, 1989; Stewart, "Marshals' pride winds down Vandy career," *PS*, February 7, 1989; Harris, "Mr. Clutch: Vanderbilt's Barry Goheen," *St. Petersburg Times*, January 19, 1989; "icewater in the veins, part two," vandymania.com, December 19, 2004: http://vanderbilt.scout.com/2/331616.html; Woody, "Give Vandy an inch and its shorts take games," *TN*, January 16, 1989; Biddle, "Grandpa Goheen will have quite a story to tell young 'uns," *NB*, January 16, 1989; Woody, "VU's Newton seeks 500th against LSU, *TN*, January 18, 1989. *Author's note*: "To be 'Goheened' meant being defeated at the buzzer, which Barry did seven times, including five at Memorial" (Sweetland, "Memorial Gym Provides Decades of Megical Moments," *Commodore Nation*, January 2006, 5); Tipton, "You can look it up—in the dictionary," *Lexington Herald-Leader*, February 8, 1989; www.vandypride.com/2009/02/18/cm-newton-interview; Newton, *Newton's Laws*,157; Bibb, "Clutch shot: save best for last," *TN*, January 15, 1989; Woody, "UK's Sutton enters Vandy-Georgia spat," *TN*, January 17, 1989; Davy, "'Collision' happened before 'shot,'" *TN*, January 15, 1989; Traughber, "Barry Booker recalls his career," CHC, January 4, 2012; Davy, "VU mates call Goheen miracle man," *TN*, January 15, 1989; Stone, "Georgia faces Goheen sting one more time," *Athens Daily News*, February 15, 1989; Baker, "Georgia Gunned Down by Goheen," *CNFP*, January 15, 1989; Woody, "Big Shot," *TN*, December 13, 1990; *Atlanta Journal and Constitution*, February 1989 (undated, untitled); Bilas, *Toughness*, 91; "Interview With Barry Goheen," Basketball Interview Challenge, September 9, 2008: http://interviewbasketball.wordpress.com/2008/09/08/Barry-Goheen/; Biddle, "Goheen's a man of miracles for Vanderbilt," *BT*, February 29, 1989.

Chapter 24: McGee, "Vandy coach has earned respect as well as wins," *NB*, January 18, 1989; Woody, "VU's Newton seeks 500th against LSU, *TN*, January 18, 1989; Climer, "After preliminaries, no clear favorite," *TN*, January 4, 1989; Hunter, *Don't Count Me Out*, 129, 182–85, 190–91, 202–203, 221–23, 233–34; Kirkpatrick, "Can't Hold That Tiger," *SI*, February 20, 1989; O'Neal, Shaquille, with Jackie MacMullan, *Shaq Uncut: My Story* (New York: Grand Central Publishing, 2011) 52; *USAT*, January 16, 1989; Nightengale, "There's nothing guaranteed in this game, 'only the money,'" *USAT*, June 3, 2009; Woody, "Tables turned, VU stunned," *TN*, January 19, 1989; Olney, "Blanton, LSU continue hex on Vandy," *NB*, January 19, 1989; McGee, "Jackson's action clips VU," *NB*, January 19, 1989; Woody, "Miracle Man tabs Jackson new member of fraternity," *TN*, January 19, 1989; McGee, "LSU 85, Vanderbilt 84," *NB*, January 19, 1989; Woody, "High-scoring Texas motors into VU today," *TN*, January 21, 1989; McGee, "Texas presents BIG (naturally) problems for Vanderbilt," *NB*, January 20, 1989; Feinstein, *Season Inside*, 390; McGee, "VU borrows from 'Dores old, new to give visiting Longhorns the blues," *NB*, January 23, 1989; Woody, "No substitute for VU reserves," *TN*, January 22, 1989; Woody, "Vanderbilt rolls, gives Newton 500th win," *TN*, January 22, 1989; McGee, "Friends share in Newton's joyous 500th," *NB*, January 23, 1989; Gates, "Goheen proud of Vandy," *Knoxville News-Sentinel*, March 1989 (undated); Davy, "Newton winning his way with class," *TN*, January 22, 1989.

Chapter 25: Newton, *Newton's Laws*, 34, 39–40, 43–44, 52, 55, 57–58, 59–66, 68–69, 76–78, 99–104, 107–10, 122, 125, 131, 161–65; Kindred, *Basketball: The Dream Game*, 97–113; Goheen, *With Shirttails Flying*, 131–32; Jacobs, Barry, *Across the Line: Profiles in Basketball Courage: Tales of the First Black Players in the ACC and SEC* (Guilford, CT: The Lyons Press, 2008) 123–46; *Vitale with Weiss, Living a Dream*, 38; Maraniss, *Strong Inside*, 385, 392–96; Neel, *Dynamite!*, 190; Knight, *My Story*, 165; 1988–89 VMBMG, 10–11; Wojciechowski, *The Last Great Game*, 24–27; Traughber, Bill, *Vanderbilt Basketball: Tales of Commodore Hardwood History* (Charleston, SC: The History Press, 2012) 134; *Dortch, String Music*, 135; Hampton, "Newton's decision surprises players," *NB*, January 24, 1989; Traughber, "Barry Goheen: Mr. Memorial Magic," CHC, March 20. 2013: www.vucommodores.com/sports/historycorner/specrel/032013aaa.html; McGee, "Vandy fights shock," *NB*, January 25, 1989; McGee, "Newton accepts Kentucky AD job," *NB*, January 24, 1989; Read, "Vandy students express surprise," *NB*, January 24, 1989; Bibb, "Newton should exit Vandy now," TN, January 25, 1989; "Who Says You Can't Go Home Again?," *Oscar Combs' Big Blue Basketball*, February 1989, 17; Woody, "Stunned VU braces for Gators," *TN*, January 25, 1989; Woody, "UK preys on Newton, his naivete," *TN*, January 25, 1989; "Newton appointment cited by Kentucky," *TN*, February 1989 (undated); Biddle, "VU's Newton felt needed by Kentucky," *NB*, January 25, 1989; Davy, "Younger Commodores anxious over next coach," *TN*, January 24, 1989; Bozich, "He'll do it right," *BT*, February 29, 1989.

Chapter 26: *ABC World News Tonight*, January 28, 1989; Woody, "Stunned VU braces for Gators," *TN*, January 25, 1989; McGee, "'Monster' Gator tries to bite Vandy," *NB*, January 25, 1989; McGee, "Gators enjoy FAN-tastic finish," *NB*, January 26, 1989; Hunter, *Don't Count Me Out*, 201; Woody, "Newton questions official's judgment on call," *TN*, January 27, 1989; Climer, "Only fans, not fanatics, need apply," *TN*, January 27, 1989; McGee, "Florida 81, Vanderbilt 78," *NB*, January 26, 1989; Climer, "Sloan turns wrath on Newton critics," *TN*, January 25, 1989; Woody, "Week's surprise 'volleys' shell Commodores on court and off," *TN*, January 26, 1989; Traughber, "Barry Goheen: Mr. Memorial Magic," CHC, March 20, 2013; Voigt, "Florida escapes with backhanded win in OT," *VH*, January 27, 1989; Woody, "Thrown tennis balls cost VU overtime loss to Gators 81-78," *TN*, January 26, 1989; Woody, "Kornet still bothered by loss," *TN*, January 27, 1989; McGee, "VU crowd becomes Florida's 6th man," *NB*, January 26, 1989; Biddle, "Blame a few thoughtless Vandy fans," *NB*, January 26, 1989.

Chapter 27: Woody, "Vandy seeking group therapy," *TN*, January 28, 1989; Hunter, *Don't Count Me Out*, 221–23; Woody, "Taunts ignite Vandy in win," *TN*, January 29, 1989; Woody, "There's no place like road for harried Vandy players," *TN*, January 29, 1989; McGee, "Barry bookends help Vandy bash Bulldogs," *NB*, January 30, 1989; Woody, "Vandy, UT collide tonight in crucial match," *TN*, February 1, 1989; Segrest, "Wanted: the buzzer-beaters," *NB*, February 1, 1989; McGee, "Patience pays off for Commodores," *NB*, February 2, 1989; Woody, "Quick strike: VU gold rush humbles Vols," *TN*, February 2, 1989; Woody, "Vandy makes Alabama trip at high Tide," *TN*, February 4, 1989; Davy, "Fatal attraction dooms Vols," *TN*, February 2, 1989; Woody, "VU's Kornet nets SEC player award," *TN*, February 4, 1989; Olney, "Meyer best man for Vandy," *NB*, January 24, 1989; Olney, Buster, *How Lucky You Can Be: The Story of Coach Don Meyer* (New York: Ballantine Books, 2010) 135, 162–64; Olney, "Bostick top candidate for Commodore post," *NB*, January 24, 1989; Woody, "VU aides Martin, Bostick among many candidates," *TN*, January 25, 1989; McGee, "Friends share in Newton's joyous 500th," *NB*, January 23, 1989; Newton, *Newton's Laws*, 101, 105, 113, 126–27, 164, 169; 1988–89 VMBMG, 13; Lucas, *Carolina Basketball*, 176–79; Biddle, "Wimp's gift to C.M. a fine gesture," *NB*, February 6, 1989; Sanderson, *Plaid and Parquet*, 85, 177; McGee, "Alabama 77, Vanderbilt 67," *NB*, February 6, 1989; Woody, "Vandy can't stay afloat in Crimson Tide," *TN*, February 5, 1989; Gates, "Goheen proud of Vandy," *Knoxville News-Sentinel*, March 1989 (undated).

Chapter 28: *Black's Law Dictionary* (6th ed.), 277, 299; Woody, "Newton resents conflict of interest suggestions," *TN*, January 31, 1989; Woody, "Sloan turns wrath on Newton critics," *TN*, January 23, 1989; Woody, "Questions about loyalty to Vanderbilt concern Newton as key game nears," *TN*, February 7, 1989; Biddle, "So much for conflict of interest," *NB*, February 9, 1989; Woody, "UK's Sutton enters Vandy-Georgia spat," *TN*, January 17, 1989; *NB*, February 6, 1989; "UK tickets hot item on cold VU campus as student-campers pull 'all-nighter,'" *TN*, February 5, 1989; Jefferson-Pilot game telecast, February 8, 1989; Tipton, "Vandy creams Cats 81-51," *Lexington Herald-Leader*, February 9, 1989; Davy, "VU seniors win one for 'Old Kentucky Home,'" *TN*, February 9, 1989; "'Cat skinnings," *TN*, February 9, 1989; Davy, "Wildcats wondering: what went wrong?," *TN*, February 9, 1989; McGee, "Vandy 81, Kentucky 51," *NB*, February 9, 1989; Fowler, "Newton's troops bomb UK 81-51," *LCJ*, February 9, 1989; Woody, "Vandy shows napping 'Cats who's boss," *TN*, February 9, 1989; Reed, "Rout shows where Newton loyalty lies," *Lexington Herald-Leader*, February 9, 1989; Wiedmer, "Vandy Pounds UK by 81-51," *CNFP*, February 9, 1989; Embry, "Kentucky delegation blocks Wildcats' path," *PS*,

March 10, 1989; McGee, "VU's happy feet, stifling defense turn back 'Cats," *NB*, February 9, 1989.

Chapter 29: Woody, "Vandy back to earth for Ole Miss clash," *TN*, February 11, 1989; Woody, "Goheen cool in another hot finish," *TN*, February 12, 1989; McGee, "Wilcox foul shots big in Vandy win," *NB*, February 13, 1989; *VH*, February 14, 1989; Woody, "Ole Miss' Glass cries foul after refs' critical no-call," *TN*, February 12, 1989; Walker, "Goheen tosses break Rebel cause," *VH*, February 14, 1989; 1988–89 postseason VMBMG, 12; McGee, "VU paints Dawgs into a corner," *NB*, February 16, 1989; Woody, "Vandy wins as mad Dawg howls," *TN*, February 16, 1989; Biddle, "Durham latest to lose his Dawg-gone mind?," *NB*, February 16, 1989; Kirkpatrick, "Can't hold this Tiger," *SI*, February 20, 1989; Brown, *Tiger in a Lion's Den*, 152–53; Hunter, *Don't Count Me Out*, 19, 78, 88, 90, 251–54, 263, 266, 268–69; McGee, "VU, LSU battle in 1st-place fracas," *NB*, February 18, 1989; Bibb, "Blanton, Kornet: real heroes," *TN*, February 18, 1989; Davy, "Vandy shoots at LSU's lead," *TN*, February 18, 1989; ESPN telecast, February 18, 1989; Davy, "Vanderbilt gains share of SEC lead," *TN*, February 19, 1989; Bibb, "Vandy saves its best for rout of LSU," *TN*, February 19, 1989; Maraniss, "Hot shooting lifts Dores over Tigers," *VH*, February 21, 1989; Newton, *Newton's Laws*, 111; Sanderson, *Plaid & Parquet*, 165; Brown, *Dale Brown's Memoirs from LSU Basketball*, 24.

Chapter 30: Dortch, *String Music*, 65, 89, 259; McGee, "Tough road blocks VU's title hopes," *NB*, February 21, 1989; Hunter, *Don't Count Me Out*, 259; McGee, "Heat at top," *NB*, February 22, 1989; Woody, "VU rips Auburn to set up battle for first," *TN*, February 23, 1989; McGee, "With help, Vandy grabs SEC lead," *NB*, February 23, 1989; Woody, "Vandy, Florida face second set," *TN*, February 24, 1989; McGee, "Can Vandy overcome O'Connell?," *NB*, February 24, 1989; Woody, "VU serves in Florida's court," *TN*, February 25, 1989; Woody, "Florida beans Vandy in OT for SEC lead," *TN*, February 26, 1989; Fraley, "Gators Close in on First SEC Title, Beat Vandy," *Atlanta Constitution*, February 26, 1989; Woody, "Newton blames misguided media for SEC image," *TN*, February 27, 1989; Woody, "Vandy players rip Gator fans," *TN*, February 26, 1989; McGee, "Florida 83, Vandy 80," *NB*, February 27, 1989; Woody, "Fighting the Odds," *TN*, February 1989 (undated); Biddle, "Martin just wants a shot at Vandy job," *NB*, January 1989 (undated); Woody, "VU aides Martin, Bostick among many candidates," *TN*, January 24, 1989; Biddle, "Gators finally at top of SEC class; now if they could only find some," *NB*, March 1989 (undated); McGee, "A 'Lett' ball for Vanderbilt, *NB*, February 27, 1989; *SI*, April 23, 2012.

Chapter 31: Woody, "Goheen says Vandy will wear ring," *TN*, February 26, 1989; McGee, "A 'Lett' ball for Vanderbilt, *NB*, February 27, 1989; 1988–89 VMBMG, 96–97; Neel, *Dynamite!*, 94; Traughber, "Barry Goheen: Mr. Memorial Magic," CHC, March 20, 2013; 1989–90 VMBMG, 94; Biddle, "Vandy seniors leave special legacy," *NB*, March 1, 1989; Woody, "VU seniors spell relief: C-L-A-S-S," *TN*, March 1, 1989; Woody, "Newton's Farewell," *TN*, March 1, 1989; Vanderbilt v. Mississippi State game program, March 1, 1989, 2; Biddle, "VU trio leaves something to remember," *NB*, March 2, 1989; Woody, "Disputed calls lead to Vandy win," *TN*, March 2, 1989; McGee, "Vandy embraces 2nd place in SEC," *NB*, March 2, 1989; Davy, "Goheen, fellow seniors go out in style," *TN*, March 2, 1989; Hunter, *Don't Count Me Out*, 281–83.

Chapter 32: Climer, "Stakes high in UT-Vandy clash," *TN*, March 4, 1989; Climer, "Vols ruin Vandy's shot at crown," *TN*, March 5, 1989; McGee, "UT's defense Nixed Vandy's title hopes," *NB*, March 6, 1989; www.exnba.com/articles-news/ex-nba-forward-dyron-nix-dead-at-46 (Dec. 17, 2013); www.local8.com/home/headlines/former-Vol-Dyron-Nix—235951331.html (Dec. 16, 2013); Hunter, *Don't Count Me Out*, 289–90; Woody, "VU, Kentucky in tense, pivotal clash," *TN*, March 10, 1989; McGee, "Vanderbilt vs. Kentucky," *NB*, March 9, 1989; Davy, "Goheen, fellow seniors go out in style," *TN*, March 2, 1989; McGee, "VU aims to keep 'Cats out of 1st-half spurts," *NB*, March 9, 1989; Woody, "VU's rare tourney win well done," *TN*, March 11, 1989; McGee, "What a relief! Vanderbilt win gets SEC tourney monkey off its back," *NB*, March 11, 1989; Woody, "VU players: couldn't lose to a 'team like Kentucky,'" *TN*, March 11, 1989; Wojciechowski, *The Last Great Game*, 28–29; Dortch, *String Music*, 15, 135 [*Author's note*: "If I had been the coach": to his credit, Eddie Sutton was always very complimentary toward me and the other Kentuckians. He offered these flattering words before the SEC tourney game: "I think Goheen is a player in our league who is not given enough credit. He's got those intangible qualities you always want in a player. He's a winner. He's a great competitor" (Embry, "Kentucky delegation blocks Wildcats' path," *PS*, March 10, 1989)]; Davy, "VU seniors win one for 'Old Kentucky Home,'" *TN*, February 9, 1989; Biddle, "Vandy seniors leave special legacy," *NB*, March 1, 1989; Woody, "Ansley ails, but manages to lift Bama," *TN*, March 12, 1989.

Chapter 33: Evans, "Finals chance," *PS*, March 12, 1989; Davis, *Wooden*, 487; Phelps, *Tales from the Notre Dame Hardwood*, 127–28; McGee, "Commodores to face tough rebounders in Notre Dame," *NB*, March 16, 1989; Coffey, *Echoes of the Hardwood*, 205–06; Woody, "Irish game trumpeted Kornet's play," *TN*, March 16, 1989; Woody, "VU fights Irish," *TN*, March 17, 1989; Hager, *Ultimate Book*, 258–59, 268–69; McGee, East Regional Notebook, *NB*, March 18, 1989; Woody, "Irish kiss VU goodbye," *TN*, March 18, 1989; Biddle, "SEC ya later," *NB*, March 18, 1989; Hunter, *Don't Count Me Out*, 319–22; 1989 Vanderbilt NCAA Tournament Media Guide, 18; Newton, *Newton's Laws*, 70; Biddle, "Goheen's a man of miracles for Vanderbilt," *BT*, February 29, 1989.

Epilogue: Beckett, John, *Mission Accomplished! Michigan's Basketball Miracle, 1989* (South Bend, IN: Diamond Communications, 1989) 61–62, 64, 131–37; Hager, *Ultimate Book*, 294–95; McGee, "Vandy honors Goheen," *NB*, May 1989 (undated); Woody, "Books, basketball hook new VU coach," *TN*, March 1989 (undated); Woody, "Fogler still packs punch at Carolina," *TN*, March 1989 (undated); Woody, "Newton's farewell fond one," *TN*, April 1989 (undated); Dortch, *String Music*, 137: Wojciechowski, *The Last Great Game*, 244–47 [*Author's note*: The quartet of Feldhaus, Pelphrey, Woods, and Farmer was nicknamed "The Unforgettables," and, as a tribute to their sticking with the program, C.M. retired their jerseys in 1992 (*ibid.*, 282–83). I never understood that—three of the four (all but Farmer) already had used a redshirt or academic penalty year and couldn't transfer anywhere without giving away one of their final three years; regardless, given how at least two of those four have fared post-UK, it was a hasty decision on C.M.'s part. Farmer, who was Kentucky's agricultural commissioner from 2004 to 2011, was convicted of misappropriating public funds while in that position and sent to federal prison in March 2014; he was released in December 2015 (Gerth, "Richie Farmer to be released from prison," *LCJ*, December 15, 2015). Woods, always a pugnacious sort, was in his fifth season as head coach at Morehead State when, in December 2016, he was charged with misdemeanor battery on two of his own players; he resigned a few days later (AP, "Sean Woods resigns as Morehead State men's basketball coach," December 15, 2016). Those misadventures are part of a troubling string of problems among several Wildcats of the late '80s. Winston Bennett was fired as the head coach at Kentucky State after striking one of his players in 2003. Ed Davender, the only UK player in history with at least 1,500 points and 400 assists, was convicted in 2010 of a ticket scam that had defrauded thousands of UK hoops season-ticket holders; he served part of his eight-year sentence and died in April 2016 at age 49, days after suffering a heart attack (AP, "Former Kentucky guard Ed Davender dies," April 30, 2016). Most (in)famously, in September 2014, Rex Chapman, who made over $22 million in a lengthy NBA career, was arrested in Scottsdale, Arizona, on nine counts of organized retail theft and five counts of trafficking in stolen property (Davis, "The Demons of Rex Chapman," *SI*, July 27, 2015, 46–51). He avoided jail time with a plea deal.]; McCallum, *Dream Team*, 52, 71, 75; Woody, "VU assistant Martin left without options," *TN*, March 30, 1989; Traughber, "Mark Elliott was a fan favorite," CHC, February 21, 2013; Traughber, "Barry Booker recalls his career," CHC, January 4, 2012; Traughber, "Elder Kornet enjoyed successful All-SEC career for Commodores," CHC, January 21, 2015.